SOVIET FICTION SINCE STALIN:
SCIENCE, POLITICS, AND LITERATURE

SOVIET FICTION SINCE STALIN:
Science, Politics and Literature

Rosalind J. Marsh

BARNES & NOBLE BOOKS
Totowa, New Jersey

©1986 Rosalind J. Marsh
First published in the USA 1986 by
Barnes & Noble Books
81 Adams Drive
Totowa, New Jersey, 07512
Printed in Great Britain

Library of Congress Cataloging in Publication Data

Marsh, Rosalind J.
    Soviet fiction since Stalin.

    Bibliography: p.
    1. Russian fiction—20th century—history and
criticism.   2. Science in literature.   3. Science and
state—Soviet Union.   4. Literature and science.
5. Literature and state—Soviet Union.   I. Title.
PG3098.4.M28   1986   891.73'0876'09   85-30610
ISBN 0-389-20609-1

CONTENTS

To my mother and father

ACKNOWLEDGEMENTS

I should like to record my gratitude to Dr Zhores A. Medvedev for according me an interview, to Mark Popovsky, Leonid Finkelstein and Efim Etkind for their helpful letters, and to the late Mr Max Hayward and Dr T. J. Binyon for supervising some of the research on which this work was based. Special thanks are due to Neil Cornwell, Robert Porter, Julian Graffy, Michael Berry, Ronald Hill and my colleagues in the Twentieth-century Russian Literature Study Group. My parents Ernest and Joyce Marsh offered invaluable research assistance, and Líam Kennedy, with his unfailing tolerance and humour, provided the encouragement necessary for me to complete this book.

Note

Translations are my own, unless otherwise stated. The transliteration system is a modified version of that used in the *Cambridge Companion to Russian Literature*. Proper names have been rendered in a simplified fashion, and the surnames of well-known figures such as Khrushchev, Beria, Ehrenburg, Mandelstam and Yevtushenko are given in their more familiar, rather than their more strictly transliterated forms. The titles of literary works will be given in English translation, and accompanied, wherever possible, by the original date of publication in Russian, although reference in the notes may be to subsequent, more accessible editions. References to literary works will only be given on the first occasion that they are mentioned; more detailed notes can be found in my unpublished D. Phil thesis, R.J. Wells, 'The Theme of Science and Technology in Soviet Literature of the Post-Stalin Period 1953–64', Oxford, 1981. The bibliography contains a list of those works of Russian fiction mentioned in the book which have been translated into English.

LIST OF ABBREVIATIONS

Bulletin	*Bulletin of the Institute for the Study of the USSR*
CDSP	*Current Digest of the Soviet Press*
DN	*Druzhba Narodov*
EG	*Ekonomicheskaya Gazeta*
FLPH	Foreign Languages Publishing House
FN	*Filosofskie Nauki*
ISS	*Irish Slavonic Studies*
KGB	Committee of State Security
KP	*Komsomolskaya Pravda*
L	Leningrad
LG	*Literaturnaya Gazeta*
LM	*Literaturnaya Moskva*
LO	*Literaturnoe Obozrenie*
LR	*Literaturnaya Rossiya*
M	Moscow
MG	*Molodaya Gvardiya*
MLR	*Modern Languages Review*
MVD	Ministry of Internal Affairs
NM	*Novy Mir*
NR	*Nauka i Religiya*
NS	*Nash Sovremennik*
NTR	'Scientific and technological revolution'
NY	New York
NZ	*Nauka i Zhizn*
PC	*Problems of Communism*
PZ	*Partiinaya Zhizn*
RSFSR	*Russian Soviet Federated Socialist Republic*
RM	*Russkaya Mysl*
Sob. soch.	*Sobranie sochinenii*
SS	*Soviet Studies*
SSU	*Studies on the Soviet Union*
UG	*Uchitelskaya Gazeta*
VAN	*Vestnik Akademii Nauk*
VF	*Voprosy Filosofii*
VL	*Voprosy Literatury*

INTRODUCTION

Most Western studies of Soviet literature have either concentrated on traditional literary criticism, or have analysed Soviet literary policy from the point of view of a political scientist. This book, while making use of insights obtained from both these approaches, has a different purpose: it is a political and historical study of the way in which one important subject — the theme of science and technology — has been treated in Soviet fiction in one period of Soviet history. Its principal aim is to explore the relationship between literature, science and politics in the post-Stalin era, and thus to make a contribution to the study of Soviet political, social, intellectual and cultural history.

Different aspects of the literary treatment of science and technology are considered in the three parts of the book. The first part examines the presentation in Soviet fiction of some of the socio-political problems associated with science and technology in the Stalin, Khrushchev and post-Khrushchev periods. An attempt is made to ascertain to what extent fiction on scientific themes conforms to or deviates from the propaganda line of the party; and to what extent literature can be used as a significant source of evidence about the history of Soviet science. The second part discusses general attitudes to science held by a variety of Soviet writers whose sentiments reflected views prevalent in Soviet society as a whole; and investigates authors' use of the theme of science as a vehicle for the exploration of deeper moral, political and philosophical ideas. The third part explores the interaction between science, literature and public policy in the USSR. An attempt is made to define the creative individuality of writers by analysing how and why they select, emphasise and treat certain subjects against a background of adaptation to the party's dictates; and the way in which they respond to literary controls. This is followed by an evaluation of the reception of literature dealing with scientific themes in the USSR and its impact on scientists, writers and policy-makers. A consideration of such issues enables us to draw conclusions about Soviet political and scientific thought in the post-Stalin era, the structure of Soviet society, the development of Soviet fiction, and even about the history of Soviet science itself.

1

The literary treatment of science and technology merits attention, because science is a major theme in Soviet fiction which touches on many other significant political, social and philosophical questions. It is a subject which links many different authors and approaches, and includes both hack writers and some of the best writers in the country. The post-Stalin period is of particular interest for the study of fiction on scientific themes, because it has been characterised by a variety of literary tendencies and a profound change in the writer's relationship with the political authorities. Khrushchev's 'Secret Speech' at the Twentieth Party Congress of February 1956 marked an epochal break with the past, initiating a general reappraisal of the effect of the Stalin era on both art and science; and the party's more flexible cultural policy ensured that literature on the theme of science no longer invariably repeated official platitudes, but was able to treat scientific and social problems with greater frankness than before.

Review of Previous Literature

The only detailed study by a Western scholar of the relationship between science and literature in the post-Stalin era is by Anton Hiersche, who summarises Soviet cultural debates about scientific development up to 1974 and analyses the impact of science on the themes and form of Soviet literature, especially poetry.[1] Other more limited studies by Western scholars include surveys of the portrayal of scientists and academics in different periods of post-Stalin fiction;[2] the discussion of the treatment of the theme of science by individual writers such as Granin and Solzhenitsyn;[3] and my own investigation of the way in which the genetics dispute is treated in Soviet literature.[4] The most comprehensive work by a Soviet critic is V. G. Lartsev's survey of Russian poetry on scientific themes from the time of the scholar and poet Lomonosov (1711–65) to 1970.[5] Other Soviet commentators either concentrate on relatively uncontroversial topics such as the depiction of the scientist as a 'positive hero' and the psychology of scientific research, or discuss, from a rigidly party-line standpoint, the social problems illustrated by the portrayal of the honest scholar's conflict with careerists and bureaucrats.[6]

No previous literary studies — Soviet or Western — have

sought to use fiction as a major source of information about science and intellectual life in the USSR; to relate fiction dealing with the theme of science to political events and developments in the scientific world; to highlight the contrast between the reality of Soviet science and its representation in literature; or to study the different attitudes towards science expressed in Soviet fiction.

Fiction as a Documentary Source

Since the official press and most non-fiction works on science and technology published in the USSR are primarily concerned with publicising Soviet scientific achievements, fiction possesses some limited value as an alternative source of information about the real history and sociology of Soviet science. General investigations of the sociology of science by Western scholars often limit themselves to evidence drawn from the USA and Western Europe, largely ignoring the variety of other modes of behaviour and organisation in other parts of the world. Previous Western studies of Soviet science have been restricted to the statistics and generalities of an OECD survey[7] and scholarly works by political scientists based mainly on published factual sources.[8] Although two books by the Soviet *émigrés* Zhores Medvedev and Mark Popovsky containing valuable 'inside information' about the workings of Soviet science[9] have somewhat diminished the value of fiction as a repository of factual information, literature can still be regarded, in the absence of a systematic sociological survey, as a primary source of evidence about the views held by Soviet scientists, engineers and policy-makers. Western critics and historians have, with increasing frequency, used literature in this way as a source of information about other aspects of life in the Soviet Union.[10]

Naturally, the use of fiction as documentary evidence about society is not without its dangers, since literature presents imaginary plots and characters, establishes its own narrative conventions and traditions and is not necessarily a faithful picture of reality. Allowance must also be made for incomplete knowledge or prejudice on the part of the author. Above all, the elements of reality in literature published in the Soviet Union have been stringently selected by the party and moulded by writers themselves according to ideological demands and self-censorship. A formidable apparatus of literary controls has ensured that literature is placed directly at the service of the economic and political policies of the Soviet government.

Nevertheless, with these important qualifications, fiction provides a medium through which we can detect or elicit independent information on various facets of Soviet life. As Soviet writers are expected to select a 'typical' problem — technical, social or moral — and to provide detailed instructions on how to overcome it, it can be assumed that a recurrent theme in Soviet literature reflects a topical and widespread problem in Soviet society. Moreover, the government's direction of literature cannot be as strict as its control over the press and other factual sources. In spite of the orthodoxy imposed on them, writers of fiction have enjoyed one advantage which has rendered their regimentation troublesome: their work demands the use of their imagination and thus affords the opportunity of displaying some individuality. Through the mouth of a character or by implication, writers are often able to suggest ideas which they could not express openly in their own names. Obscure allusions or intriguing clues concealed beneath the obligatòry main theme of a novel may provide brief glimpses of the reality of Soviet life. If a work of fiction describes certain events and problems later discussed in the press or mentioned in Soviet government decrees, we are inclined to trust the writer.

Literature, moreover, provides certain types of information which can only rarely be found in the stringently controlled official press. It is not principally a source of new factual information (although it can sometimes be), but rather affords insights into social attitudes. *Feuilletons* in the Soviet press can also provide interesting anecdotal evidence about the reality of Soviet science, but fiction is able to paint a more intimate portrait of life in scientific institutes, explore the psychological effect of official policies on the scientific community in greater depth, and portray the lives of recognisable individual scientists. Fiction is significant because it offers two types of information simultaneously, on the one hand illuminating the values which the party attempts to inculcate in the Soviet population, and on the other hand revealing, if indirectly, the real values, thoughts and feelings of Soviet people.

Science, Literature and Soviet Society

Science and technology have always figured prominently in Soviet literature as a direct consequence of the dominant position which they occupy in Soviet society. In the first place, they have played a vital practical role in the economic and political transformation of Russia by the Communist Party from an underdeveloped country into an industrial superpower. Secondly, science has been accorded great ideological significance in the USSR. Since the Soviet leaders claim that Marxism-Leninism is a 'science', they regard all other sciences as their allies in the task of building a communist society. They have elevated science to the level of an ideal in itself, almost a substitute for religion. Science has been eulogised as a means of achieving happiness and prosperity for the peoples of the USSR and the whole world.

The promotion of scientific progress became even more important in the USSR after Stalin's death, when the party leaders recognised the political importance of a highly developed science in the modern world. They devoted enormous resources to science and technology in order to ensure national security, create a higher standard of living and raise their country's prestige in the eyes of the world. At the Central Committee Plenum of July 1955 Bulganin declared that 'We stand on the threshold of a new scientific and technological revolution.'[11] The phrase 'scientific and technological revolution' (*nauchno-tekhnicheskaya revolyutsiya*, hereafter NTR) was enshrined in the new Party Programme of 1961,[12] and has ever since been constantly used by Soviet theorists to denote a fundamental qualitative transformation of science and technology associated with the transition from capitalism to socialism and communism. At the Twenty-Fourth Party Congress of 1971 Brezhnev emphasised that the implementation of the NTR was an indispensable element in the building of a communist society, and the congress report spoke of the need 'to unite organically the achievements of the scientific and technological revolution with the advantages of the socialist economic system'.[13] Similarly, Suslov asserted in 1976: 'The contemporary scientific and technological revolution opens up before society unseen possibilities in using science for mastering and protecting the forces of nature and solving social problems . . . and at the same time acts as material preparation for communist civilisation.'[14] This statement exemplifies the

Soviet authorities' view of science both as a semi-magical force and as a provider of legitimacy for the party.

Since the 1930s the Soviet authorities have exploited all the means of communication, including literature, in their extensive propaganda campaign for science and technology which aims at creating an increased supply of scientific personnel and at spreading a knowledge of science among the population. Fiction is more effective than the standard means of mass persuasion (schools, political agitators and the daily press) because it can appeal to the emotions and create vivid images with which the reader can identify. Since 1932 it has been incumbent on Soviet writers to contribute to the party's science campaign, for the official doctrine of socialist realism has enjoined them to select subjects from contemporary life and particularly themes which the party considers topical and important at any given time. The importance of scientific and technical themes became paramount in the 1930s, when Stalin was determined to industrialise the country at breakneck speed. At the First Writers' Congress in 1934 Andrei Zhdanov, Stalin's spokesman on cultural matters, gave the 'production' theme a special blessing: 'In our country the principal heroes of literature are the active builders of the new life — workers . . . collective farmers, party members, managers, engineers . . . '[15] Similarly, Gorky recommended to Soviet writers in the 1930s that 'Science, its discoveries and achievements, its workers and heroes — all this should become the domain of poetry.'[16] In 1946 Zhdanov officially instructed writers to handle topics directly relevant to current problems of post-war reconstruction and economic development, including the achievements of Soviet science and technology.[17]

As Katerina Clark has shown, political control over literature did not merely reflect the Soviet authorities' need to direct every aspect of Soviet life, but also their desire to preserve literature's vital function as a generator and repository of myth. Soviet fiction has frequently provided myths affirming and maintaining the values of the Soviet regime: thus during the years of the First Five Year Plan (1928–33) it celebrated technological change and the mass effort of the working class; and later in the 1930s upheld the hierarchical structure of Stalin's Russia by its emphasis on leaders and managers.[18] These themes represent different facets of the major officially-sponsored myth propagated in Soviet fiction — the depiction of man in the closest association with work performed for the good of party and state. In the post-Stalin period, writers' choice of scientists and engineers as heroes could be interpreted as an extension of the old theme of 'man and his work' in a world increasingly affected by the advances of science and technology. As one Soviet critic stated in 1960: 'The new age is knocking at the door of literature, demanding to be portrayed. The new hero is the scientist with his sophisticated thought processes, the new subject matter is the world of science.'[19] Post-Stalin fiction helped to sustain the fundamental myth sponsored by the Soviet authorities: the belief that the NTR would transform society and create communism.

However, as Geoffrey Hosking has argued, a political line cannot determine the actual content of fiction; it can only establish the limits within which writers operate.[20] It was natural that Soviet writers, nurtured by the long-standing Russian tradition of using literature as a major vehicle for the scrutiny of topical social issues, would choose to discuss science and technology, since they exert such a vital influence on the Soviet Union and modern society in general. Even before the doctrine of socialist realism had been formulated, some Soviet writers had treated the theme of science. Mayakovsky's poetry, with its boundless faith in man's power to refashion himself and his society through the triumph of science over nature, represents a highly personal reaction to the promise of the Revolution. In the mid-1920s literature was often concerned with the struggle between the old and the new, sometimes presented, as in Olesha's *Envy* (1927), as the confrontation between man and machine. During the period of the First Five Year Plan such works as Leonov's *Soviet River* (1931) and Kataev's *Time, Forward!* (1933) expressed genuine enthusiasm for technological progress and rapid social change.

The selection and treatment of scientific themes by Soviet authors cannot therefore be ascribed solely to the didactic purposes of the party. Undoubtedly the inherent interest and importance of the subject for writers themselves also played a part. Some had a personal interest in science because they had previously had a scientific training: for example D. Granin had worked as an electrical engineer; A. Solzhenitsyn and V. Grossman had taken degrees in physics and mathematics. Others, such as V. Dudintsev, E. Dorosh and V. Tendryakov, had begun their careers as journalists, and had been sent on research trips to factories, institutes and collective farms. Many writers, including V. Kaverin, L. Leonov, I. Ehrenburg, A. Voznesensky and Yu. Daniel, were closely associated with the world of science, possessing friends and allies among the scientific intelligentsia, a class from which they also drew their readership.

In the post-Stalin era many Soviet writers have publicly referred to the influence of science and technology on their work. In answer to a questionnaire of 1962 Gennady Gor stated that modern man 'wants scientific knowledge to permeate the story, the novel and the novella with the same inevitability with which it has permeated all the pores of society', while Vasily Aksyonov, a doctor by training, maintained that 'the relationship between science and life' and 'the spiritual life of the new technical intelligentsia' were among the most important themes of contemporary Soviet literature.[21] In 1977 the 'village prose' writer Valentin Rasputin said that 'in a century of great speeds, huge social transformations . . . man must understand the general meaning of scientific and technological progress'.[22]

The post-Stalin period was an age of rapid scientific advance, exemplified by such dramatic events as the explosion of the first Soviet hydrogen bomb, the launching of the first satellite and first manned spaceship; such successes were accompanied by a great expansion of the scientific workforce and a further growth of popular interest in science. At the same time the Soviet authorities were concerned with technological innovation and the reorganisation of science and industry. All these developments widened the subject matter of literature about science, ensuring that it was an attractive theme for Soviet writers and a topical, interesting subject for Soviet readers.

In 1959 C. P. Snow commented on the fact that science and the scientist play a significant part in Soviet literature, whereas they are rarely encountered in Western literature:

> If one reads contemporary Soviet novels, for example, one finds that their novelists can assume in their audience — as we cannot — at least a rudimentary acquaintance with what industry is all about . . . An engineer in a Soviet novel is as acceptable, so it seems, as a psychiatrist in an American one.[23]

Apart from the genre of science fiction, science has, indeed, rarely been a prominent subject in modern Western literature except in the works of Snow himself and the American writer Mitchell Wilson, which are more highly regarded in the Soviet Union than in their own countries. In general, technology has little appeal for

Western authors; the work of the engineer is not thought to fire the imagination or to raise profound human problems. To the Soviet writer, however, the design of an aeroplane engine, a leak-locator or a centrifugal pipe-casting machine — the subjects of three well-known Soviet novels of the 1950s, Bek's *The Life of Berezhkov* (1956), Granin's *The Seekers* (1954) and Dudintsev's *Not by Bread Alone* (1956) — does not appear tedious or insignificant, as it would in the West, but an important, dignified task capable of enlisting a man's entire dedication and creative energies.

Science plays a far larger part in Soviet than Western fiction both because of the obsession with science in society and because literature is harnessed to social purposes. As Abram Tertz (Andrei Sinyavsky) suggests, Soviet literature is teleological — every minor technical improvement is seen in the wider context of the movement of the whole of Soviet society towards the ideal communist state.[24] Moreover, in Western literature scientists and engineers are often depicted as a race apart; the type of the amiable eccentric or the mad inventor has frequently been a figure of fun or an object of fear. In Soviet fiction, however, talented inventors are not viewed as cranks, but as normal, highly respected and vitally necessary members of the population.

Soviet writers regard scientists and engineers as suitable literary heroes because of their social and psychological importance in the USSR. In the first place, since scientists belong to a privileged elite which enjoys great prestige and material benefits, a portrait of a scientist can offer the ordinary reader a rare glimpse of the life of someone far above him in the social hierarchy, and can provide ambitious young people with a goal to which they can aspire. In the second place, progressive writers of the immediate post-Stalin period considered the portrayal of the original scientist or inventor to be an especially suitable means of highlighting one of their major preoccupations — the conflict between the creative forces of society and the rigidity of the bureaucratic system. The intervention of ignorant careerists and indifferent bureaucrats acquires a particular dramatic force when it obstructs an invention or scientific project which may have the power to improve the quality of life and alleviate human suffering.

Another reason why the nature and consequences of scientific progress have continued to feature so prominently in Soviet fiction is that, since the 1950s, the NTR has remained one of the most popular subjects of public cultural debate in the Soviet Union.

After the Twentieth Congress of 1956, science was awarded uncritical admiration until the 'physicists and lyricists' debate of 1959 raised the question of the relationship between science and art in the modern world.[25] In further debates on the subject of 'literature and the NTR' it was generally agreed that science and technology could not replace the aesthetic and ethical function of literature, but instead created new social and moral problems which constituted a legitimate subject for literature.[26] The limitations and possible negative aspects of scientific progress were increasingly recognised, and the NTR was no longer regarded as a major determining factor, but as just one aspect of historical progress.[27] In the 1970s and 1980s Soviet fiction has not only fulfilled the function of extolling the NTR, but has frequently acted as a counterweight to the increasing emphasis on science in Soviet society, stressing the value of morality and the life of the individual.

Soviet Literary Politics since Stalin

Literature on scientific themes should be viewed against a background composed of the broad political issues, the changes in scientific policy and the condition of Soviet literature. The political and scientific aspects will be discussed later in connection with specific themes. At this point, however, it will be useful to give a brief survey of Soviet literary politics of the post-Stalin era, in order to understand the fluctuating attitudes of Soviet authors dealing with science and technology, and to set works on scientific themes into a wider context.

There was no rigid dichotomy in literary politics between the Stalin and post-Stalin periods. Although the 'Zhdanov era' of the late 1940s was an extremely repressive period for Soviet writers, some interesting works, such as Nekrasov's *In the Trenches of Stalingrad* (1946), Kazakevich's *Star* (1947) and Panova's *The Factory Kruzhilikha* (1948) nevertheless appeared. In 1952 Alexander Tvardovsky, the editor of the journal *Novy Mir*, published two controversial works: Grossman's novel *For the Just Cause* and Ovechkin's sketch *Weekdays of a District*. The limited experimentation permitted in 1952 demonstrates that even a totalitarian regime cannot impose complete uniformity on writers.

The period 1953–64, from the death of Stalin to the fall of Khrushchev, was by no means a monolithic one: it can be divided into a number of shorter intervals in which the party's policy towards Soviet writers varied considerably. It is clear now that these alternating periods of 'thaw' and 'freeze', as they were called in the Western press, were created primarily by non-literary, political factors, such as the conflicts between opposing factions in the highest councils of the party and the changes in the international situation, particularly the Hungarian revolt of 1956 and the Cuban crisis of 1962. But within the larger political framework there is a fairly regular pattern produced by purely literary factors: the authorities' efforts to preserve an equilibrium between opposing forces; and the conduct of the writers themselves who reacted to political events, endeavouring to probe the boundaries of their freedom, but whose every attempt at liberalisation appeared to threaten the stability of the regime and was met with official measures designed to restrict and suppress them.

Stalin's death on 5 March 1953 created a sense of liberation, but the first six months of 1953 represented a continuation of the previous pattern, not a new departure. The first sign of 'thaw' was the publication in June of Tvardovsky's poem *Horizon beyond Horizon*,[28] but it was not until the winter of 1953–4 that the whole of orthodox Soviet literary theory and practice was called into question by Vladimir Pomerantsev's famous essay 'On Sincerity in Literature'[29] and other outspoken critical articles in *Novy Mir*. Although the appearance of such works was partly a genuine attempt by writers and critics to challenge Stalinist literary dogmatism, fiction and literary criticism published at this time closely reflected the economic debate being conducted by the party leaders, and in retrospect there is enough evidence to suggest that the cultural liberalisation may have been sanctioned by Malenkov or Beria in order to gain the support of the intelligentsia prior to an exposure of Stalin's misdeeds. In 1954 the contrast between the hard-line views propounded on such liberal literary works as Part One of Ehrenburg's *Thaw* in the party newspaper *Pravda* and the more sympathetic attitudes expressed in the government organ *Izvestiya* indicates that culture was being used as a political weapon in the power struggle between Khrushchev and Malenkov.[30] The dismissal of Tvardovsky from the editorial board of *Novy Mir* in August 1954 coincided with Khrushchev's reassertion of power. The Second Writers' Congress in December 1954 showed that, while the conservatives in the Writers' Union were still overwhelmingly strong and could rely on the support of the party leaders, two camps, which became known as 'liberals' and 'dogmatists', now existed in Soviet literature.

The uneasy truce between the two camps was ended by the Twentieth Party Congress of February 1956, when Khrushchev's encouraging message to the cultural intelligentsia[31] and his 'Secret Speech' with its denunciation of the 'cult of personality' in Stalin's time shifted the balance towards the liberals.[32] The dramatic effect of Khrushchev's speech is evident from a *samizdat* account of a remarkable meeting of party members of the Writers' Union in March 1956 which raised the subject of the guilt and responsibility of various prominent literary officials for the persecution of writers in the Stalin era.[33] The dethronement of Stalin stimulated writers to depict what they considered to be the deficiencies in Soviet society and lessened the fear that frankness would lead to arrest or repression. The summer and autumn of 1956 were marked by the publication of a number of controversial works, such as Granin's story *Personal Opinion* and Dudintsev's *Not by Bread Alone*. The most significant literary event of 1956, however, was the publication of the two volumes of the anthology *Literaturnaya Moskva* by a group of authors who attempted to establish an independent organisation of Moscow writers outside the party-controlled Union of Soviet Writers.

After the abortive Hungarian revolt of November 1956, Khrushchev, alarmed at the role that writers of the Petöfi Circle had played in precipitating social unrest in Hungary, attempted to stop the process of liberalisation within the USSR, and gave political support to the hard-line dogmatists. On 13 May 1957 Khrushchev himself met writers at a dacha near Moscow and warned them to adhere to the principles of socialist realism and to remember that they were servants of the party.[34] The conventional interpretation of literary politics in the years 1956–7 is that Shepilov sanctioned the cultural 'thaw', and that after Khrushchev's defeat of his political opponents in the 'Anti-Party Group', including Shepilov, in July 1957, he turned his attention to literature and dismissed Simonov, the current editor of *Novy Mir*, for his liberal publishing policy. Frankel, however, has convincingly argued that a hard-line cultural policy had been re-established by February 1957, that Shepilov merely followed Khrushchev's line, and that Khrushchev subsequently evaded responsibility for the events of 1956 by incriminating him. Tvardovsky's reappointment as editor of *Novy Mir* in July

1958 reflected Khrushchev's desire to conciliate Soviet writers by revitalising the content of *Novy Mir*.[35]

The evidence certainly suggests that after the 'Anti-Party Group Affair' Khrushchev felt secure enough to attempt to establish an equilibrium between the two camps of writers. The return of the liberal Tvardovsky was balanced, in the wake of the scandal caused by the publication of Pasternak's *Doctor Zhivago* and the award of the Nobel Prize to its author in October 1958, by the establishment in December of the reactionary Union of Writers of the RSFSR, designed to counteract the influence of the rebellious Moscow writers. At the Third Congress of Soviet Writers in May 1959 Khrushchev struck a moderate, conciliatory note, suggesting that literary matters could be left to the corporate judgement of the writers themselves, provided that they achieved 'consolidation' — that is, if the rival factions could learn to coexist peacefully.[36]

The new Secretary-General of the Writers' Union, Konstantin Fedin, pursued the policy of 'consolidation', and the two groups coexisted until the Twenty-Second Congress of October 1961 speeded up the process of de-Stalinisation and created another literary 'thaw'. The climax of this liberal phase was reached with Khrushchev's personal authorisation of the publication of Solzhenitsyn's short novel *One Day in the Life of Ivan Denisovich* in November 1962.[37] Only a few days later, however, Khrushchev initiated an extremely repressive policy towards the arts after his notorious visit to an exhibition of paintings by unofficial artists at the Manège Gallery in Moscow.

Khrushchev's creation in 1962 of a special Ideological Commission of the Central Committee under Leonid Ilyichov, a member of the Party Secretariat from 1961 to 1965, has generally been interpreted as evidence of Khrushchev's intention to give higher priority to literature and the arts, and to demonstrate his ability, after the Cuban crisis, to take severe measures against the intelligentsia without being dominated by his more conservative colleagues. The dissident historian Roy Medvedev, however, suggests that Khrushchev and Ilyichov were antagonists rather than allies, and that the visit to the exhibition was probably arranged as a 'provocation' at the highest level by Ilyichov and his collaborator Dmitry Polikarpov, head of the Cultural Department of the Central Committee, rather than, as Priscilla Johnson implies, merely by 'the painter-bureaucrats' V. Serov and A. Gerasimov.[38] The militant campaign against liberal artists and writers waged by Khrushchev and Ilyichov until April 1963 has also been associated with two of Khrushchev's hard-line opponents in the Presidium, F. Kozlov and M. Suslov, although Khrushchev himself in retirement allegedly attributed it to Ilyichov's ambition to become a member of the Presidium.[39]

There was a certain irresolution in cultural policy until another shift occurred in August 1963, when Khrushchev made the extraordinary gesture of asking Tvardovsky to read his unpublished poem *Tyorkin in the Other World*, a powerful satire on the Stalinist bureaucracy, before an audience of Soviet and foreign writers. This decision may have been prompted by Khrushchev's belief that his internal position had become more secure, and by a desire to launch a new anti-Stalin and anti-Chinese offensive, while at the same time placating the West. An unstable equilibrium between liberals and dogmatists persisted throughout 1963–4, although the party continued to sanction cautious de-Stalinisation.

After Khrushchev's fall from power in October 1964 and his replacement by Brezhnev and Kosygin there were some immediate changes. The Commission for Ideology was disbanded and the Central Committee's Department of Culture returned to supervise literature. New instructions were issued to publishers which prevented the publication of Lydia Chukovskaya's previously approved work *Sofiya Petrovna*. However, there was a confused interval of transition lasting from late 1964 into 1966, during which some interesting literary works and articles by historians and military experts were allowed to appear. This brief period of relaxation can, perhaps, be attributed to the natural caution of the new leadership, a temporary neglect of cultural policy because of continuing power struggles in the Kremlin, and possibly also to the pacification of the literary bureaucracy by the award of the Nobel Prize to Sholokhov in 1965.

By September 1965 the increasing influence of the neo-Stalinist Politburo member Shelepin and his ally, the KGB chief Semichastny, led to the imposition of a repressive policy against literary dissidents: three copies of Solzhenitsyn's novel *The First Circle* and his play *Feast of the Victors* were confiscated by the KGB from the flat of his friend V. Teush; and the writers Andrei Sinyavsky and Yuly Daniel were arrested and accused of having published their works abroad under the pseudonyms of Abram Tertz and Nikolai Arzhak. Their trial in February 1966, at which they were condemned to seven and five years of hard labour respectively, caused considerable indignation throughout the world, as it was the first trial against Soviet writers in which 'the principal evidence against them was their literary work'.[40] After the trial a special meeting convened in order that the judge could 'explain' the verdict to Soviet writers demonstrated the authorities' realisation that they had made a mistake.[41] An idea conceived by Vladimir Voinovich that Sinyavsky and Daniel should be released against the surety of the writers' community was taken up in a letter signed by 62 other Moscow writers, but the proposal was rejected. The Sinyavsky-Daniel trial was the catalyst which speeded up the process of disaffection of many liberal Soviet writers from the regime. The trial could, however, be seen as a compromise on the part of the regime because concerted efforts by neo-Stalinists failed to secure further arrests of intellectuals or the complete rehabilitation of Stalin at the Twenty-Third Congress of March 1966. Another slight lull from late 1966 to early 1967 was marked by the first publication in the USSR, in a shortened version, of Bulgakov's novel *The Master and Margarita* (written 1928–40);[42] although this could, perhaps, merely be ascribed to the authorities' recognition that Bulgakov's work had already been published abroad and would eventually have become known to the Soviet intelligentsia anyway.

After the appointment of Yury Andropov as chairman of the KGB in May 1967, a firm but more flexible line was taken on cultural and ideological matters. Solzhenitsyn took the unprecedented step of circulating an open letter attacking censorship to all members of the Fourth Writers' Congress in May 1967,[43] but although letters signed by 80 of the country's most distinguished writers asking that Solzhenitsyn's demands be discussed at the congress were sent to the Union Secretariat, the union leadership failed to respond or make any public mention of the controversy. Another watershed in Soviet literary politics was the year 1968, which saw the invasion of Czechoslovakia and the hardening of official policy after many writers had signed protests against the trial of the dissidents Galanskov and Ginzburg. In late 1969 Solzhenitsyn was expelled from the Writers' Union, and other writers, notably Voinovich and Vladimov, were subjected to increased harassment. The hopes of liberal writers were finally dashed at the end of 1969 by Suslov's dismantlement of the editorial board of *Novy Mir*, a move described in a powerful *samizdat* essay as 'the killing of *Novy Mir*',[44] which almost certainly led directly to the death of Tvardovsky in

1971. In 1970, at Suslov's instigation, the extreme Russian nationalism associated with the journal *Molodaya Gvardiya* since 1966 was also officially discouraged through dismissals and arrests. Firmly established in power by the end of the 1960s, the Brezhnev administration imposed more effective, less unpredictable controls on literature than Khruschchev. Brezhnev himself took little interest in literature, and was generally content to entrust this field to Suslov, who by 1969 had become reconciled to his position as 'Chief Ideologue' and number two in the party. The main factors determining Soviet policy towards intellectual and cultural matters in the Brezhnev era were, first, the desire to preserve tranquillity and stability, and secondly, the provision of support for intellectual activity which was likely to be useful economically and relatively neutral politically, and the rejection of intellectual activity which might prove to be politically dangerous and economically irrelevant. In Max Hayward's words, this led to a combination of 'marginal permissiveness' and 'selected terror'.[45] The Soviet leadership continued the policy which Khrushchev was pursuing in the last two years of his rule: the encouragement of the publication of mediocre, ideologically correct writing for the masses; an attempt to prevent the circulation of works which might be construed as actively anti-Soviet; and the desire to pacify the liberal intelligentsia by permitting the small-scale publication of some excellent books and articles. These include works on specialist subjects: for example literary criticism by D. S. Mirsky, Bakhtin and Lotman; pre-revolutionary and early post-revolutionary literature such as the 1973 editions of Bulgakov's novels and Mandelstam's poems, and the 1978 edition of Andrei Bely's *Petersburg*; or foreign literature in translation, including selections of Kafka, Proust and Joyce. The publication of such interesting works in small editions has led to a situation in which, as Klaus Mehnert observes, there are 'too many Russians chasing too few books'.[46]

The growing conservatism and repression from 1966 onwards led to the intensification of two phenomena which had emerged in the Khrushchev period: first, *samizdat*, the wide circulation of uncensored manuscripts and underground journals in typescript; and secondly, *tamizdat*: publishing 'over there', that is, in the West. From the 1970s the Soviet authorities have pursued a new policy towards dissident authors (and dissidents in general): they have either been permitted to emigrate, harassed so severely that they have virtually been forced to emigrate, as in the case of Brodsky

(1972) and Voinovich (1980), or, like Solzhenitsyn (1974), forcibly exiled. Emigration has proved a successful policy for the Soviet regime, first because dissident writers have less influence on Soviet citizens once they have left the USSR, and secondly, because they are not vital to the Soviet economy. Although some of their works may be smuggled back or broadcast to the USSR, they have less impact, because Soviet people regard *émigré* writers as having abandoned the struggle in favour of an easy life in the West.

Although the period since 1970 has been marked by greater caution and the absence of the unpredictable oscillations in cultural policy typical of the Khrushchev period and, to a lesser extent, the late 1960s, the image of the 'plateau' which George Gibian uses is not entirely apt.[47] In the first place, the period has been characterised by lively literary debates on such genres as 'village prose', 'everyday prose', 'production fiction', 'war prose' and science fiction, in the course of which a variety of conflicting views on literature and society has been expressed. Secondly, years of relative calm have been punctuated by periodic attacks on liberal and dissident writers, reflecting the regime's general policy towards dissent, which, in turn, is an indicator of the changes in the international situation, fluctuations in domestic policy and power struggles in the Kremlin. The periods of particularly harsh treatment for literary and other dissidents have been the years 1972–4, 1977, 1979–80 and the period since Brezhnev's death.

The bureaucratic organisations controlling literature have not changed much since Khrushchev's time, but an important development has been that, since 1971, the Congress of the Writers' Union has taken place every five years (rather than every four years) — that is just after the Party Congress which also occurs every five years. The purpose of this change was to make it difficult for writers to adopt any independent initiative. Traditional views of 'socialist realism' continue to be propounded in official publications on Soviet literature, in speeches by literary functionaries such as Georgy Markov, First Secretary of the Writers' Union since 1971, and the party leaders. The bulk of literature published in the USSR still conforms to socialist realist canons: prominent examples are Markov's Lenin Prize-winning novel *Siberia* (1971–3) and the works of Kozhevnikov, Chakovsky and Babaevsky. In the 1970s, however, some Soviet theoreticians have adopted a more flexible approach to the official doctrine, in an attempt to account for the widening gap between the theory of socialist realism and the practice of many Soviet writers, which had become largely apolitical, more akin to the 'critical realism' of nineteenth-century Russian literature. This can be largely attributed to the growing scepticism or indifference of Soviet writers towards ideology, and the greater sophistication of editors and censors.

There have been perceptible changes in the literary atmosphere at different times in the 1970s and 1980s. The slight relaxation in the harassment of writers in the years 1970–2 can perhaps be attributed to the election of Nixon in the USA and Brandt in West Germany which provided the framework for a new policy of *détente* and Ostpolitik. Another factor which influenced literary life in the years 1967–72 was a series of extended ritual jubilees, from the fiftieth anniversary of the October Revolution to the fiftieth anniversary of the formation of the USSR in 1972 which, according to the *émigré* writer G. Svirsky, provided such a 'stifling atmosphere' that they 'torpedoed the ship of literature and sent it to the bottom with practically everyone on board'.[48] One notable event was, however, the awarding of the Nobel Prize to Solzhenitsyn on 8 October 1970: Solzhenitsyn refused to attend the prize ceremony in Stockholm for fear that he would not be permitted to return; and an attempt to hold the ceremony in Moscow on 9 April 1972 was hindered by the Soviet authorities. A militant press campaign against Solzhenitsyn and the physicist Andrei Sakharov culminated in Solzhenitsyn's deportation in 1974.

By the mid- and late 1970s the Brezhnev regime seemed to be becoming more lax, both in its literary policy and its tolerance of corruption, perhaps initially because of the continuing policy of *détente* and subsequently because of the growing age and failing health of the party leaders. The height of *détente*, the years 1975–6, witnessed the publication of such interesting anti-Stalinist or critical works as Trifonov's *House on the Embankment*, Bondarev's *Shore* and Rasputin's *Farewell to Matyora*. By 1977, however, growing annoyance with Carter's 'human rights' policy led the Soviet authorities to take further repressive measures against dissidents. Extremely harsh attacks on *émigré* scientists and writers, unusual even in the Soviet press, appeared to herald a worsening political climate; and in 1978 Yury Lyubimov, the brilliant director of Moscow's Taganka Theatre, was subjected to severe criticism. Nevertheless, Lyubimov managed to survive, probably because of Andropov's protection (Andropov's daughter was married to

Alexander Filipov, an actor at Lyubimov's theatre); and in the late 1970s some interesting works on anti-Stalinist themes such as Kron's *Insomnia* (1977) and Gerasimovich's *The Effect of Position* (1979) continued to appear. The limits of official tolerance were, however overstepped in January 1979 with the unofficial printing in eight copies of the almanac *Metropol*, compiled by Aksyonov, Bitov, Iskander and others, a collection of hitherto unpublished Soviet writings, most of which had been rejected by Soviet publishing houses.[49] Appeals to the Union of Writers and to Brezhnev personally had already proved fruitless, but Aksyonov pursued the project as 'the last attempt at some sort of cultural compromise', undertaken in the hope that the authorities would then permit official publication.[50] In Sinyavsky's opinion, *Metropol* represented a possible 'point of convergence between dissident literature and the liberal wing of Soviet literature',[51] but the venture failed: *Metropol* was severely berated by the erstwhile 'liberal' critic Feliks Kuznetsov, now First Secretary of the Moscow Writers' Union, and the emigration of Aksyonov and Kopelev soon followed.

A new crackdown on dissidents occurred from late 1979 because of the invasion of Afghanistan and the desire to clear Moscow of subversive influences during the Olympic Games of 1980. The authorities wanted Voinovich to emigrate before the Olympics, but he managed to remain until September 1980. The deterioration of relations with the USA and the worsening crisis in Poland leading to the establishment of martial law in 1981–2 gave the party no incentive to change its hard line on literary policy. At the Twenty-Sixth Congress of 1981 Brezhnev attacked 'works that defame our Soviet reality' and reiterated the party's uncompromising attitude towards 'the ideological orientation of our art'.[52] At the Seventh Writers' Congress in June 1981 Markov endorsed Brezhnev's view, praising the Moscow Writers' organisation for exposing 'some self-styled publishers of utterly wretched, stinking works clearly inspired from abroad'.[53]

Although, as George Gibian has remarked, Soviet literature is engulfed in a 'great cloud of ignorance',[54] the literary climate in the second half of the 1970s and early 1980s is consistent with the theory that an ageing leadership under Brezhnev was attempting to steer a middle course on cultural policy, but occasionally adopted a very harsh line, perhaps under pressure from the chief ideologist Suslov or the KGB chief Andropov. It is possible that the KGB may sometimes have operated independently, exceeding the limits established by the party, for in 1977 Brezhnev himself felt the need to give a public assurance that there would not be a return to mass terror.[55]

In the years 1981–2, as Brezhnev became terminally ill, a conflict centred around the journal *Nash Sovremennik* between the so-called 'Russian party' of writers expressing nationalist sentiments, who may have enjoyed some protection from Suslov, and the more internationalist, technocratic tendency associated with Andropov and the KGB. Between February 1981 and January 1982 Russian nationalist works such as Soloukhin's *Pebbles on my Palm* and Belov's *Harmony* appeared in *Nash Sovremennik*, but after the death of Suslov on 19 January 1982 the journal was attacked in the press, and in April 1982 the key figure on the editorial board, Yury Seleznyov, was removed. The content of *Nash Sovremennik* from May to December 1982 showed that it was bowed, but not entirely broken, suggesting that the 'Russian party' (of which Chernenko was a prominent representative) continued to be influential within the Politburo.[56]

Andropov replaced Suslov as 'Chief Ideologue', and between May 1982 and Brezhnev's death in November became the most influential member of the Politburo. The clearest sign of Andropov's increasing impact on literature was a Central Committee resolution of July 1982, 'On Creative Connections between the Journals of Literature and Art and the Practice of Communist Construction'. This hard-line decree placed a renewed emphasis on traditional socialist realism, demanding that writers fulfil the tasks of the Twenty-Sixth Congress, selecting subjects of contemporary relevance, such as industry, agriculture, the army and navy, concentrating on depicting 'positive heroes' and inculcating worthy moral values such as patriotism, hard work, internationalism and disapproval of 'political indifference' and 'a consumer mentality'.[57]

Rumours that Andropov might be a liberal in cultural policy because of his liking for jazz and Western novels were soon scotched. He was, however, concerned to maintain his reputation as an intellectual, and in a conversation with Markov reported in January 1983 his views on Soviet literature were made explicit. Andropov criticised a popular writer, the late Yury Trifonov, for being too interested in the problems of everyday life; while admitting that talented writers should be allowed a degree of freedom of choice of theme and viewpoint, he advanced the traditional view that literature had the duty to help the party and state in its struggle for order. In furtherance of this policy Roy Medvedev was called in for questioning; theatres were instructed to pay more attention to socialist realism; and Vladimov was subjected to renewed harassment which led to his emigration. Although Chernenko, who also had a special interest in ideology and the arts, had tried to win a reputation as a liberal in his power struggle with Andropov, the repressive policy continued after he became First Secretary of the Communist Party in February 1984. In 1984 Soviet writers were instructed not to attend a reception at the American Embassy; Pasternak's family were evicted from their dacha in Peredelkino; Lyubimov delayed his return from a foreign tour and was stripped of his Soviet citizenship.

The present state of Soviet literature is far from encouraging. Up to 1980 works by Western scholars appeared bearing, somewhat prematurely, such titles as 'The Decline of Socialist Realism' and 'Beyond Socialist Realism';[58] but the evidence now lends more weight to Maurice Friedberg's assessment: 'Socialist realism is alive, even if not always well, although its health has shown remarkable improvement in recent years.'[59] Even though many writers may be sceptical about socialist realism as a literary doctrine, it still exists, in Voinovich's words, in the sense of 'the glorification of higher authority in a form accessible to it'.[60] Fiction continues to be published in vast quantities in all the languages of the USSR, although very little of what is published receives any critical attention at all. At the Seventh Writers' Congress of 1981 it was stated that there were 8,773 members of the Writers' Union, of whom at least 1,000 must be genuine writers (as opposed to critics, translators and bureaucrats), although in Aksyonov's opinion the literature of socialist realism is 'not literature at all, but some kind of surrogate' produced by 'graphomaniacs'.[61]

The post-Khrushchev period has witnessed the emigration of many controversial writers; the deaths of many others, including, most recently, Trifonov (1981), Abramov (1983) and Tendryakov (1984); while for years such well-known writers as Kazakov, Shalamov and Nagibin published nothing, or nothing of interest (and the first two have now died); but others, such as Iskander, Bitov and Okudzhava, have apparently surmounted criticism and appeared in print again in the 1980s. In 1980 Rasputin was reportedly mugged 'by four men who demanded his blue jeans',[62] and has produced little new work since.

Only a handful of internationally known writers now live in the USSR, and as yet few young writers have arisen to take the place of the 'third wave' of *émigré* writers, with the possible exception of the poet Gennady Aigi and the short story writer Yury Geiko. It is difficult for young writers to find advancement in the Union of Writers, and 45-year-olds such as Rasputin and Belov, who, in the words of the *émigré* Anatoly Gladilin, 'were young twenty years ago', are still regarded as 'younger writers'. Gladilin also claimed in 1979 that 'there may be individual good stories, but there's no new generation'.[63] However, one development of some interest is the emergence in the 1980s of the so-called 'Moscow school' of prose writers in their forties, which includes V. Orlov, A. Kim, V. Makanin and S. Rybas, who have been attacked, like 'everyday prose' writers of the 1970s, for concentration on trivia.[64] Perhaps even more significant is the appearance in the 1980s of interesting new dramatists like Lyudmila Petrushevskaya and Victor Slavkin, whose works were first produced in small studio theatres in uncensored amateur productions.[65] As yet it is too early to say whether such developments will continue, or whether Gorbachov's accession will be marked by any change in cultural policy, but, to adapt terms used by the *émigré* philosopher and writer Alexander Zinoviev, although the Khrushchev period was not as liberal as has sometimes been assumed, but was rather an 'epoch of confusion', the post-Khrushchev era has not been entirely a period of 'monolithic homogeneity'.[66]

Limitations of the Subject Matter

Several restrictions have been placed on the scope of this book. The word *nauka* ('science') has a much wider meaning in Russian than in English: like the Renaissance term *scientia* or the German *Wissenschaft* it is not restricted to the natural sciences, but encompasses most branches of scholarship. This study will, however, concentrate on the way in which the natural sciences and various fields of engineering have been treated in literature.

Because of the long time-span covered, less attention has been devoted to the literary treatment of specific sciences such as genetics, physics and chemistry than to general political, philosophical and moral problems connected with scientific development. Since it is difficult to view contemporary Soviet fiction in adequate historical perspective, all the literary works to be discussed were published before Brezhnev's death, although reference will also be made to political and cultural events which occurred up to the death of Chernenko in March 1985.

Since most of Soviet literature is of extremely limited literary value it cannot be judged according to purely aesthetic criteria; the discussion will, therefore, focus on subject matter rather than form or style. Preliminary work for the book necessitated a survey of a large number of literary works, including much fiction of poor quality, some of which probably did not enjoy a large readership even in the Soviet Union, and in the West has been almost totally neglected. For reasons of space, the book will not provide a descriptive survey of the lesser-known literature, but consider those passages of the works which possess significance for a given theme. It has not been possible to give a full analysis of recent genres such as 'village prose', 'urban prose', 'war prose' or science fiction, which all merit separate treatment in themselves. Certain exemplary works have been selected for detailed consideration; and greater emphasis has been placed, particularly in Part II, on literature of more generally recognised literary merit. The sheer quantity of literature published on the theme of science and technology since Stalin's death means that no hope can be entertained of encompassing the available material in its totality. There probably exist undiscovered novels and stories containing references to science and technology, but their very obscurity guarantees their unimportance to a study of general trends.

The Sources

Although all kinds of literature about science enjoy great popularity in the USSR, the present work will be primarily concerned with novels and short stories dealing with the theme of science and technology. A limited number of plays and poems have also been included, but, in order to restrict the field to a manageable size, only a few works of science fiction have been considered. One major Soviet genre which will be drawn upon for illustrative material is the 'production novel' (*proizvodstvennyi roman*) which deals with the social, managerial and technological issues of industry currently of concern to the party. This genre was particularly prominent in the Stalin era, but by the early 1950s the public's total lack of interest in this type of literature led some critics, and even the party itself, to censure the stereotyped character portrayal in certain works depicting heroes whose total attention was devoted to technical problems. There are no clearly definable boundaries between the conventional 'production novel' and the rather more interesting 'science novel', in which the banal industrial theme is replaced by a description of the work and dilemmas of an inventor or research scientist. This type of theme first emerged in the early 1930s in the works of Afinogenov, Gorky and Leonov, and continued in such post-war novels as Konovalov's *University* (1947). Both the 'production novel' and 'science novel' possessed a standard structure institutionalised in the Stalin era: a questing 'positive hero' overcomes personal, technical and socio-political obstacles on the way to achieving his goal. When Stalin died the structure was not abandoned, but used in a new way to investigate the phenomenon of Stalinism.

Science and technology are also featured in the *ocherk* or sketch, which consists of documentary reportage in quasi-literary form based on existing persons and events, usually on a topical subject, and sometimes containing invented incidents and characters. The *ocherk* may legitimately be regarded as a form of imaginative prose writing and will occasionally be drawn upon. Another genre which is sometimes mentioned is the lyrical science documentary, defined by Soviet critics as 'artistic-scientific literature' (*nauchno-khudozhestvennaya literatura*), which provides a poetic exposition of scientific ideas in a popular, journalistic style. Reference will also be made to memoirs, critical articles and reviews, and factual works by both Soviet and dissident authors.

The post-Stalin era was the first period since the 1920s when Soviet writers were able to express differing viewpoints in print. The literature to be discussed falls into four categories: first, conformist works adhering to the party line; secondly, more controversial works which have been variously described as 'liberal' or 'progressive', namely those in which writers extend the scope of their material to the limit of what is officially permissible at any given time; thirdly, works by 'conservatives' or 'dogmatists' which are neo-Stalinist in tone; and finally, works which have circulated within the Soviet Union in *samizdat* and have been published only in the West.

The inclusion of *samizdat* material can be justified on the grounds that published and *samizdat* fiction together comprise one Soviet literature: both conformists and dissidents use literature as a forum for the discussion of major political problems of the Stalin and post-Stalin periods, often in a realistic style. Moreover, in the post-Stalin period there has frequently been no clear distinction between what might or might not be published in the Soviet Union. Many of the works which later circulated in *samizdat* were originally submitted to Soviet journals before being obstructed by over-cautious or ill-disposed editors, or through the intervention of higher authorities on political grounds. A comparison between *samizdat* and published works allows us to measure the relative degree of censorship or freedom of expression in literature about science written at any given time. Since the 'third wave' of emigration in the 1970s it has not always been possible to measure how much material was written in the USSR and how much has been added in the West, but works written entirely in emigration will only occasionally be mentioned.

Methodology

Each chapter or section begins with a brief account of the political and scientific factors which have determined or influenced the literary treatment of certain themes, then goes on to consider the relevant works of fiction. The primary purpose of the factual summaries is to set literature dealing with science into its true perspective. Soviet literature cannot be approached in isolation from Soviet society, for many fictional incidents, characters and allusions are only fully explicable in relation to actual events. The second function of the summaries is to outline relevant facts in the history of Soviet science in order to contrast the propaganda about science promoted by the party with the real position of science in the Stalin and post-Stalin periods. A predominantly chronological approach has been adopted so that the treatment of each topic may be seen against the shifting political background.

Reference to the press and other sources aims to demonstrate how far Soviet writers have chosen — or have been forced — to follow the party's fluctuating interpretations of science policy. It has often been acknowledged in general terms that Soviet writers are acutely attuned to oscillations in the party line, but it is hoped to explore this process of adaptation in one specific field more fully than has hitherto been attempted. If Soviet literature is studied in isolation from the press and social trends, some works of fiction can be made to appear more original in their selection and treatment of themes than is really the case. Hence a comparison between literature and the press not only provides a valuable means of measuring the efficacy of literary controls, but also illustrates the degree to which Soviet fiction reflects the policies of the time in which they were written.

Notes

1. A. Hiersche, *Sowjetliteratur und wissenschaftlich-technische Revolution* (Berlin, 1976).
2. G. Gibian, *Interval of Freedom* (Minneapolis, 1960), pp. 29–73, 106–44; A. B. Murphy, 'Academic Life in Some Recent Russian Fiction', *SS*, 1981, pp. 421–32.
3. K. Armes, 'Daniil Granin and the World of Soviet Science', *Survey*, vol. 20 (1974), no. 1, pp. 48–54; K. Armes, 'Introduction' to A. Solzhenitsyn, *Candle in the Wind* (London, 1973), pp. 3–17.
4. R. Wells, 'The Genetics Dispute and Soviet Literature', *ISS*, 1980, no. 1, pp. 20–42.
5. V. G. Lartsev, 'Nauka i sovetskaya poeziya', unpublished doctoral dissertation, University of Samarkand, 1970.
6. A. Gavrilov, *Borets, sozidatel, novator* (M, 1971); V. Kovsky, *Literatura v izmenyayushchemsya mire* (M, 1974); N. Chornaya, *Uchonyi v sovremennoi sovetskoi proze* (Kiev, 1976).
7. *Review of National Science Policy: USSR* (OECD, Paris, 1969).
8. See the symposium in *Survey*, vol. 23 (winter 1977–8), nos 1, 2 (102–3); and Bibliography 1, section 2.
9. Zh. Medvedev, *Soviet Science* (Oxford, 1979); M. Popovsky, *Science in Chains* (London, 1980).
10. Two recent examples are Mary Seton-Watson's Radio 3 series 'Soviet Life through Soviet Literature' (1984); M. Crouch, R. Porter (eds.), *Understanding Soviet Politics Through Literature* (London, 1984).
11. N. Bulganin, *Pravda*, 17 July 1955.
12. *Pravda*, 2 Nov. 1961.
13. *Materialy XXIV Syezda KPSS* (M, 1971), p. 57.
14. *Pravda*, 18 Mar. 1976.
15. *Pervyi vsesoyuznyi syezd sovetskikh pisatelei* (M, 1934), p. 716.
16. M. Gorky, 'O temakh', *Sob. soch. v tridtsati tomakh*, vol. 27 (M, 1953), p. 108.
17. *Bolshevik* 1946, no. 15 pp. 11–14.
18. K. Clark, *The Soviet Novel* (Chicago, 1981), pp. 91–2.
19. Yu. Veber, 'Zhazhda yasnosti — zhazhda perezhivanii (o nauchno-khudozhestvennoi literature', *NM*, 1960, no. 4, p. 239.
20. G. Hosking, *Beyond Socialist Realism* (London, 1980), pp. 2–9.
21. G. Gor, *VL*, 1962, no. 1, p. 21; V. Aksyonov, *VL*, 1962, no. 9, p. 118.
22. V. Rasputin, *LG*, 16 Mar. 1977.
23. C. P. Snow, *The Two Cultures and the Scientific Revolution* (Cambridge, 1959), pp. 34–5.
24. A. Tertz (A. Sinyavsky), *Fantasticheskii mir Abrama Tertsa* (Trowbridge and London, 1967), p. 403.
25. See below, pp. 213–15; and the bibliography in R. Wells, 'Theme of Science',

pp. 596–6.

26. Hiersche, *Sowjetliteratur*, p. 223 contains a bibliography of the debates up to 1974. See also *VL*, 1976, no. 11, pp. 3–92.

27. Yu. Osnos, 'Literatura i NTR. Poiski. Obreteniya. Zabluzhdeniya', *VL*, 1977, no. 4, p. 9; D. Granin, *LG*, 4 June, 17 Dec. 1980.

28. A. Tvardovsky, *Za dalyu dal*, *NM*, 1953, no. 6, pp. 76–8.

29. V. Pomerantsev, 'Ob iskrennosti v literature', *NM*, 1953, no. 12, pp. 218–45.

30. E. Frankel, *Novy Mir* (Cambridge, 1981), pp. 50–1.

31. N. S. Khrushchev, *Pravda*, 15 Feb. 1956.

32. Khrushchev, *The Dethronement of Stalin* (Manchester, 1956).

33. S. Cohen (ed.), *An End to Silence* (NY, 1982), pp. 105–14.

34. For an abridged version of Khrushchev's three speeches on literature, see *LG*, 28 Aug. 1957.

35. Frankel, *Novy Mir*, pp. 107–21.

36. Khrushchev, *Pravda*, 24 May 1959.

37. A. Solzhenitsyn, *Odin den Ivana Denisovicha*, *NM*, 1962, no. 11.

38. R. Medvedev, *Khrushchev* (Oxford, 1982), p. 216; cf. P. Johnson, *Khrushchev and the Arts* (Cambridge, Mass., 1965), p. 8.

39. Medvedev, *Khrushchev*, p. 254.

40. M. Hayward, L. Labedz (eds.), *On Trial: The Case of Sinyavsky (Tertz) and Daniel (Arzhak)* (London, 1967), p. 36.

41. O. Matich (ed.), *The Third Wave* (Ann Arbor, 1984), pp. 140–1.

42. M. Bulgakov, *Master i Margarita*, *Moskva*, 1966, no. 11; 1967, no. 1.

43. L. Labedz (ed.), *Solzhenitsyn: a Documentary Record*, 2nd edn (Harmondsworth, 1974), pp. 110–16.

44. Cohen, *End to Silence*, pp. 201–5.

45. M. Hayward, *SSU*, vol. VIII (1969), no. 3, p. 4.

46. K. Mehnert, *The Russians and their Favorite Books* (Stanford, 1983), p. 13.

47. G. Gibian, 'New Aspects of Soviet Russian Literature', in S. Cohen, A. Rabinowitch, R. Sharlet (eds.), *The Soviet Union since Stalin* (Indiana, 1980), p. 254.

48. G. Svirsky, *A History of Post-War Soviet Writing*, trans. and ed. R. Dessaix, M. Ullman (Ann Arbor, 1981), p. 311.

49. V. Aksyonov, V. Erofeev, F. Iskander, A. Bitov, E. Popov (eds.), *Metropol: a Literary Almanac* (London, 1982).

50. V. Aksyonov, *RM*, 14 Aug. 1980.

51. A. Sinyavsky, 'Samizdat and the Rebirth of Literature', *Index on Censorship*, vol. 9, no. 4 (Aug. 1980), p. 12.

52. L. Brezhnev, *Pravda*, 24 Feb. 1981.

53. G. Markov, *LG*, 1 July 1981.

54. Gibian, 'New Aspects', p. 275.

55. Brezhnev, *Pravda*, 5 June 1977.

56. This paragraph is based on an account by Julian Graffy of a lecture in London by John Dunlop.

57. *Pravda*, 30 July 1982.

58. M. Hayward, 'The Decline of Socialist Realism', *Survey*, vol. 18, no. 1 (82) (Jan. 1972), pp. 73–97; G. Hosking, *Beyond Socialist Realism*.

59. M. Friedberg, 'Cultural and Intellectual Life', in R. Byrnes (ed.), *After Brezhnev* (London, 1983), pp. 277–8.

60. Matich, *Third Wave*, p. 48.

61. Ibid., p. 33.

62. Mehnert, *The Russians*, p. 84.

63. A. Gladilin, *The Making and Unmaking of a Soviet Writer*, trans. D. Lapeza (Ann Arbor, 1979), p. 147.

64. *LO*, 1981, no. 8, pp. 21–32; *LG*, 21 July 1982.

65. Based on information in a conference paper by Kjeld Bjørnager, Oxford, Sept. 1984.

66. A. Zinoviev, *The Yawning Heights*, trans. G. Clough (Harmondsworth, 1981), pp. 236, 706.

PART ONE

POLITICAL AND SOCIAL ASPECTS OF SOVIET SCIENCE:
THE LITERARY EVIDENCE

1   THE EFFECT OF STALINISM ON SCIENCE AND TECHNOLOGY

The impact of Stalinism on science and technology represents one aspect of the general investigation of the Stalinist past which constituted a major theme of the post-Stalin period, particularly in the years 1953–64 before the fall of Khrushchev. In Stalin's time scientific work was directed towards the immediate economic and military purposes of the Soviet state, and a centralised system of administrative and political controls was imposed on scientists and engineers to ensure their loyalty. Stalin and the Central Committee became the ultimate arbiters of scientific truth, so any scientific deviation was interpreted as a political deviation and punished accordingly. Innumerable scientists and engineers were persecuted; and the Stalin regime fostered little 'cults' in many branches of science on the model of the cult of Stalin's personality. A mediocre scientist, such as T. D. Lysenko in biology, would be proclaimed the supreme authority, immune to criticism. Scientific 'schools' holding opposing views about a particular theory were transformed into cliques who tried to destroy their opponents by political means. The content of many scientific disciplines was distorted and impoverished, and certain important subjects, such as classical genetics, the theory of relativity, quantum mechanics, resonance theory in chemistry, the 'big bang' theory in cosmology and the whole new field of cybernetics were banned altogether.

The decades of Stalin's rule had encompassed such revolutionary changes and caused such enormous suffering that his successors were obliged to come to some accommodation with the Stalinist past. In assessing the consequences of Stalinism they were, naturally, influenced by the policies which they themselves wished to pursue. Khrushchev, in particular, realised that it was necessary to reverse some of Stalin's repressive policies towards science and technology in order to win the support of scientists and engineers for his own drive to modernise the Soviet economy. Khrushchev's dethronement of Stalin and more flexible cultural policy thus permitted Soviet writers to criticise some aspects of science in Stalin's time. It was, however, impossible for fiction of the post-Stalin era to reveal the whole truth, since a profound exploration of Stalinism might have raised highly controversial questions about the role of

31

the current party leaders during the Stalin period, the responsibility of the party itself, the extent of the changes which had occurred after Stalin's death, and the whole issue of the relationship between science and politics in the USSR. Soviet writers were, therefore, obliged to treat this topic with circumspection, adhering closely to the lines of Khrushchev's de-Stalinisation policy.

Although Khrushchev's 'Secret Speech' of 1956 aroused great expectations which his subsequent actions failed to fulfil, it nevertheless marked the beginning of a new era, creating a changed psychological climate that encouraged writers to display greater frankness in their discussion of past abuses. This chapter will show that Soviet fiction, while following the version of truth sponsored by the party leaders, managed to impart some new information to the Soviet public, to tell more of the truth than was admitted in official pronouncements, and to raise important questions about the legacy of Stalinism.

The Cult of Personality

One new theme treated by Soviet writers after Khrushchev's denunciation of the cult of Stalin's personality at the Twentieth Congress of February 1956 was the deification of Stalin as a scientific genius. In April *Novy Mir* published the play *Did Ivan Ivanovich Exist?* by the Turkish communist Nazim Khikmet, which mocks ludicrous pronouncements on scientific subjects by an ignorant Stalinist official (and, by implication, by Stalin himself). Dogmatically applying to astronomy the Marxist principle of the superiority of the collective over the individual, the official pontificates: 'When observing the stars it is necessary above all to take care not to give preference to one particular star at the expense of the others.'[1] In a section of his poem *Horizon beyond Horizon* published in 1960, Tvardovsky extends the comparison made in Khrushchev's 'Secret Speech' between the adulation of Stalin and the worship of a deity, using it to suggest not only the former idolatry of Stalin, but also the profound, malign power which he exerted over the Soviet economy and all intellectual activities:

It had simply become convention . . .
That he . . . ordered all things, like a god;

And that these hands reached out . . .
To all industries, all science.[2]

Some writers disclose that Stalin was extolled as a genius in various specialised scientific disciplines such as physics and chemistry. In Vera Ketlinskaya's novel *Otherwise there is no Point in Living* (1960), a young chemist condemns a lecturer's habit of claiming that the development of Soviet chemistry was inspired by the directives of Comrade Stalin; he is sure that none can exist, 'as otherwise chemists would have known them by heart'.[3] Nevertheless, Ketlinskaya, a party member, continues to emphasise the positive aspects of Stalin's achievement. Evidently Soviet writers were unable to hint that people had actually seen through Stalin's pretensions to supreme wisdom, since this would have suggested complicity in falsehood on the part of both eminent scientists and high-ranking officials in charge of science.

The sincerity or otherwise of former encomia of Stalin by the intelligentsia and the *apparat* was a subject of controversy between 'liberals' and 'dogmatists' in the post-Stalin era. In 1963 the Stalinist critic V. Ermilov reprimanded Ehrenburg for suggesting in his memoirs that people had kept silent even though they had known about the arrests of innocent people.[4] Ermilov's attack may have been inspired by Khrushchev's hard-line opponents in the Presidium, Kozlov and Suslov, in an attempt to embarrass Khrushchev. At all events, Khrushchev combated Ehrenburg's revelations by propagating the 'new lie', as an anonymous Soviet writer has called it,[5] that the party leaders' support for Stalin had been motivated by genuine conviction and ignorance of Stalin's crimes.[6]

The harmful effect of Stalin's personal involvement in science could only be frankly presented in *samizdat* works written in the Khrushchev period but published later in the West. Alexander Bek's novel *The New Appointment* (accepted for publication by the editors of *Novy Mir* and prepared for printing in 1964, though eventually banned in the USSR and not published abroad until 1971) presents a realistic portrait of Stalin which is highly unusual in Soviet fiction. Bek attributes to Stalin a grandiose plan to industrialise Eastern Siberia in which, neglecting the advice of technical specialists, he insists on the use of electricity, rather than coal, to power blast furnaces.[7]

Solzhenitsyn's *First Circle* (begun in 1955, but first published

abroad in 1968 in an edition of 87 chapters after Tvardovsky had
been refused permission to publish it in *Novy Mir* in 1964) contains
a bitterly satirical portrait of Stalin, in which the author dissects the
poverty of thought and tedious style of Stalin's notorious 1950
article on linguistics,[8] which, he claims, was plagiarised from Professor Chikobava of Tbilisi University, who was about to be
arrested as an 'American agent'. Solzhenitsyn also affords interesting insights into the consternation created in academic circles by
Stalin's pronouncements on linguistics. The philologist Rubin, who
has worked for two years on a project influenced by the theories of
the Georgian philologist N. Marr (1864–1934), whose school has
now been denounced by Stalin, will, like many former disciples of
Marr who were forced to recant publicly, be obliged to abandon his
research. In actual fact this fate overtook the philologist Lev
Kopelev, the prototype of Rubin. The social consequences of
Stalin's articles could also be mentioned in published fiction in the
early 1960s. Granin's *Into the Storm* (1962) gives an idea of the
damage inflicted on Soviet science, industry and agriculture when
workers were obliged to waste months studying the problems of
linguistics.[9]

The Terror

Among the most controversial issues treated by Soviet writers in the
post-Stalin period was the effect of the purges on the scientific
community. Although Stalinist propaganda had constantly exalted
science and technology, in reality thousands of scientists and engineers had been dismissed, imprisoned or executed. Some had
suffered for their political views, others had attempted to defend
their disciplines against pseudo-scientific theories, while the persecution of many appears arbitrary and without rational motiva-
tion. In the post-Stalin period persecution of scientists ceased; and
many specialists who had suffered in the purges were released or
rehabilitated. At the height of Khrushchev's de-Stalinisation
policy, during the years 1962–4, a series of articles, memoirs and
literary works about the purges appeared, but no general history of
the Stalin terror has ever been published in the Soviet Union.
    Since science and technology were creative, officially approved
activities of great potential benefit to the Soviet state, authors
regarded the theme of science as a particularly suitable means of

exploring the detrimental impact of Stalinism on Soviet society in general. Moreover, as science had perhaps suffered less than other activities because of its national importance, it was a less controversial topic than either art or agriculture. Although comparatively few writers attempt to provide a general analysis of the effect of Stalin's terror on science, many refer explicitly to the persecution and arrest of individual scientists and engineers, sometimes basing their characters on real prototypes.

When dealing with the Stalin terror, Soviet writers of the post-Stalin period took pains to adhere closely to the oscillating version of reality sponsored by the party in its de-Stalinisation campaign. The first signs of change occurred in April 1953 when the Central Committee condemned the 'violation of Soviet legality' by the security organs and announced the rehabilitation of a number of Kremlin doctors — mostly Jewish — who had been arrested in January 1953 on charges of poisoning prominent party and military officials. In June 1953 Beria, the head of the secret police, was arrested; his execution was announced in December of the same year. Leonov's novel *The Russian Forest* (1953), which contains the earliest reference in published fiction to the ungrounded political accusations made against scientists in Stalin's time, represents a tentative response to this new policy.[10] Leonov manages to tell some of the truth through oblique allusions, despite the seemingly insuperable pressures of the years when the novel was written, including the censorship of his manuscript by Stalin himself.[11] Leonov was only able to treat this theme at all in the early 1950s because Stalin, in his 1950 article on linguistics, had issued a totally disingenuous denunciation of the 'Arakcheev regime' in science which he himself had created. (The name of Count A. Arakcheev (1769–1834), the director of domestic policy in the last years of Alexander I's reign, has become the symbol of repression in Russia.)

Stalin's ostensibly 'liberal' pronouncement enabled Leonov to depict the unscrupulous professor of forestry Gratsiansky, who takes advantage of the atmosphere of suspicion prevalent in the 1930s, accusing his rival, the honest scholar Vikhrov, of the political crime of attempting to 'limit socialist construction'. Leonov, perhaps rather disingenuously, suggests that such a deadly denunciation did not lead to 'the corresponding administrative measures' — that is, arrest — because of the intervention of the highest party organs. Although, before further de-Stalinisation,

Leonov could not have done otherwise than depict Vikhrov's eventual acquittal, he was nevertheless courageous even to hint that honest Soviet scholars had sometimes been unjustly accused. Leonov also exploits the figure of the Stalinist villain to launch a subtle attack on Stalin and Stalinist values. Gratsiansky possesses all the characteristics of a conventional villain of Stalinist fiction: a wealthy careerist, the son of a professor of theology, he once betrayed a Bolshevik friend to the Tsarist police and still has connections with counter-revolutionary foreign espionage within the USSR. Yet through his depiction of Gratsiansky's machinations, Leonov provides insights into the real history of Soviet forestry and the general corruption in Stalinist science. Gratsiansky's parasitism is finally exposed by his terror at Vikhrov's decision to abandon the ideological struggle, since this will reveal his inability to do any constructive research himself. Vikhrov realises that 'this man is afraid above all else of being left alone with the Russian forest' — the forest which throughout the novel symbolises the Russian land and people.

While Gratsiansky can by no means be totally identified with Stalin, certain features of his life — his theological background, activities as a Tsarist police spy, persecution of opponents and isolation from ordinary people — suggest known or alleged facets of Stalin's own biography. Moreover, his insistence that Russian forests are inexhaustible and can be felled ruthlessly in the interests of socialist construction can be interpreted as an allegory of the destruction of millions of people in Stalin's purges. There are scattered references to Dante throughout the novel, and the recurrent image of ice, culminating in Gratsiansky's apparent suicide in a hole in the ice, is reminiscent of the fate of Dante's Satan, lying eternally paralysed in a lake of ice in the deepest circle of *The Inferno*. Through this oblique parallel between Gratsiansky, Stalin and Satan, Leonov suggests that Stalin is the source of evil in Soviet society.

Leonov's novel is an exceptional case in which a liberal author used symbolism and imagery to express more than the party line permitted. Most authors were much more conformist: for example Bek's novel, *The Life of Berezhkov*, published in 1956 before the Twentieth Congress, traces the career of an aeroplane designer without mentioning the purges at all, even though the majority of Soviet aircraft specialists were arrested in Stalin's time.[12] The action of the novel ends in 1935 and the epilogue moves to the war years, avoiding the year 1937, when Tupolev and his group of aviation designers were imprisoned. An interesting variation to the general conformism of Soviet writers is the dilemma faced by neo-Stalinist writers after Stalin's death and Beria's execution. In *Youth is With Us* (1954)[13] the 'dogmatist' Kochetov ascribes rumour-mongering in scientific institutes to evil, untalented individuals, and depicts the exoneration of a professor who has been maliciously denounced through the good graces of a sympathetic MVD colonel and the Central Committee of the party. Thus, while obliged to acknowledge current party policy with occasional references to 'infringements of socialist legality', Kochetov nevertheless implies that the party has reformed itself from the top, and that the security services now contain humane and dedicated men.

The release and rehabilitation of former prisoners was a new theme introduced into Soviet literature by Part One of Ehrenburg's *Thaw* (1954), which welcomes the rehabilitation of the Kremlin doctors.[14] It is, however, only the dissident writer Abram Tertz (Andrei Sinyavsky) who exposes the limitations of the party's rehabilitation policy, which was initially very selective, concentrating mainly on influential party and government officials. In *The Trial Begins* (1960) he depicts the gynaecologist Rabinovich who was tried in connection with the doctors' case and still remains in the Arctic prison camp of Kolyma in 1956 because the authorities have forgotten to release him.[15]

Khrushchev's 'Secret Speech' played a vital part in extending the area of the influence of Stalinism on science which could be discussed in literature. However, Khrushchev had dethroned Stalin in such a way as to bring maximum credit on himself and maintain the people's faith in the party. He concentrated exclusively on communist victims of the purges in the late 1930s and the post-war period, and drew a distinction between the legitimate methods employed against non-party specialists and oppositionist communists before 1934 and the arbitrary terror used against party members after 1934. While criticising Stalinist excesses, Khrushchev praised the industrial and technological advances which had been achieved in Stalin's time, and emphasised the leading role of the party in promoting scientific development and correcting former abuses.

This was the usual line taken by writers throughout the Khrushchev period, but during the 'thaw' year of 1956 some authors went beyond Khrushchev's policy, depicting the purges as an arbitrary, wasteful destruction of scientific talent. One such work is Kaverin's *Searches and Hopes*, the final part of his trilogy *The Open Book*, published in the second volume of the outspoken anthology *Literaturnaya Moskva*. [16] Kaverin gives a good idea of the fantastic charges levelled against scientists: the doctor Andrei Lvov is arrested for allegedly having infringed a cholera quarantine in order to contaminate the Northern Caucasus, and for having introduced a typhus epidemic into his institute. Kaverin cogently demonstrates that the persecution of scientists harmed the very people whom the security services claimed to be protecting — it was madness to arrest Andrei, a talented epidemiologist, in wartime. Andrei's fate resembles that of P. F. Zdrodovsky, one of the country's leading epidemiologists, whom Stalin eventually released because he was frightened by the threat of epidemics.

Another character based on a real prototype is Dmitry Lvov, a microbiologist who gives brilliant but unsubstantiated lectures on the virus theory of cancer. In the 1930s Dmitry's research topic is disparaged as an abstract subject; but although his laboratory is subsequently closed and he himself is arrested, he continues work on his theory in prison. The virus theory of cancer was, in fact, a topic studied in the USSR by virologists in association with classical geneticists; and the portrait of Dmitry Lvov is based on Kaverin's own brother, the Jewish academician L. A. Zilber (Kaverin's real name is V. A. Zilber). The half-truth of Kaverin's portrayal is, however, highlighted by the fact that even in the 'thaw' year of 1956 he was obliged to give his character a Russian name, and that it was impossible for him to admit that Zilber was arrested three times and secretly sent his work abroad.

Moreover, Kaverin was unable, even in 1956, to mention the worst excesses of Stalinism, since he passes over the long period of Andrei Lvov's arrest and imprisonment. Kaverin does, however, go beyond conventional portraits of the rehabilitated specialist who never lost faith in the party even in prison and is eager to return to work, exposing the difficulties experienced by former prisoners in adjusting to the changed climate of the post-Stalin era. After his release in July 1953, Andrei finds it difficult to maintain 'true inner cheerfulness', as he feels resentment at the injustice he has suffered. Through the mouth of Andrei's wife Tatyana, Kaverin makes a poignant appeal for an end to the Stalin terror if future generations are to believe in Soviet justice. He implicitly urges the Soviet leadership to continue the policy of de-Stalinisation 'lest baseness should triumph — baseness and the lie'. Yet he concludes the novel with facile optimism: Tatyana is convinced that the Stalin era has gone for ever, and looks forward to a forthcoming event — the Twentieth Congress — which will change things for the better. Evidently it was still obligatory even for liberal writers in 1956 to emphasise the party's assiduity in rectifying past errors.

It was not until 1965, in the revised version of the trilogy,[17] that Kaverin was able to give a more explicit evocation of the abnormal atmosphere of suspicion in scientific institutes during the 1930s. He shows that scientists lived under the constant threat of anonymous denunciation and were so afraid of wire-tapping that they were obliged to cover a telephone with pillows before discussing the purges. Kaverin now emphasises that the arrest of scientists on ludicrous charges was extremely widespread: for example, all the staff of the Institute of Preventive Medicine are accused of being 'human monsters who have conceived the villainous plan of destroying the USSR'. The novel takes on a more tragic dimension in its depiction of the uncontrolled power of those in authority, the fear which percolates to all levels of the official hierarchy and the obsession with 'sabotage' and treachery. There is no machinery of justice to protect the individual: proper court procedure, such as legal defence for the accused and systematic rules of evidence, is ignored, and frequently the prosecutors, judges and appeal authorities are all interconnected. Moreover, the victim suffers from the panic which affects everyone when an acquaintance is arrested, preventing people from testifying in his favour for fear of arrest in their turn, and the defence mechanism which makes people believe that because someone is arrested he must be guilty. The omission of the epilogue from the new version of Kaverin's novel may, perhaps, reflect his growing pessimism about the party's ability to eradicate all the consequences of Stalinism.

The villainous scientists in Kaverin's novel differ from Leonov's Gratsiansky in that they are not products of pre-revolutionary Russian life, secret supporters or 'agents' of capitalism, but have been formed by the Stalinist system and have chosen to enter the privileged sphere of science to acquire personal power and its attendant advantages — prestige and material wealth. Another important distinction between these villains and the conventional figures in the earlier literary tradition is that they are not isolated individuals, but part of a powerful freemasonry which may include eminent scientists and highly-placed government officials. Like

Lysenko in real life, they have built up a scientific 'empire' by rewarding their supporters and persecuting their opponents. Kaverin's chief villain, who holds a high position in the field of microbiology and medicine from 1941 to 1956, is Professor Kramov, whose biography resembles that of Lysenko. He was once a talented scientist, but has contributed nothing new to Soviet scholarship since his major work of the 1920s. Realising that he is no longer capable of engaging in creative research, he seeks to protect his power and wealth by administrative manipulation and intrigue.

Kaverin adds a more explicitly political element in the 1965 version of his trilogy, showing that Kramov was able to take full advantage of the abnormal conditions of the 1930s, a time when 'pretence, flattery and suspicion' became — it is suggested — predominant features of Soviet life. He uses the purges to defeat his opponents, connecting members of his institute with the recently exposed 'Right Opposition' of Bukharin, Rykov, Tomsky and others. Through the mouth of his hero, Andrei Lvov, Kaverin makes a telling comment on the behaviour of prominent pseudo-scientists in Stalin's time: 'One has only to place an equal sign between one's own enemies and the "enemies of the people".' Kramov's motive force is envy of the talent of his younger colleagues; and, as Kaverin admitted in the 1956 version of his work, the envy of one powerful scientific administrator in the Stalin period could lead to far-reaching consequences: the dominance of a sinister conspiracy of hundreds, perhaps thousands, of corrupt scientists over Soviet biology and medical science for several decades. Kramov epitomises the entire caste of pseudo-scientists in the USSR, who, Kaverin implies, can only be defeated by forceful methods: 'Of course, these Kramovs must be beaten, or, if possible, killed.'

Another work of 1956, Vladimir Dudintsev's controversial novel *Not by Bread Alone*,[18] is the first in which it is explicitly stated that the central character, the inventor Lopatkin, is arrested on trumped-up charges and sentenced to a labour camp for eight years. Although Dudintsev passes over the period of Lopatkin's imprisonment, his hero came to epitomise the many creative people who suffered a similar fate. Lopatkin's defiant statement became widely known in the Soviet Union: 'The words "deprivation of freedom" are incorrect. A man who has learned to think cannot be completely deprived of freedom.' Dudintsev introduces a new dimension into the depiction of corruption in Stalinist science by his portrayal of the close collaboration between scientists and officials in the Ministry of Technology. He describes a group of powerful pseudo-scientists who, under their villainous director Professor Avdiev, work closely with bureaucrats to obstruct original inventions which might pose a threat to their established academic reputations. Avdiev, the supreme dictator over a chain of scientific institutes, is shown to possess even more influence than Kaverin's Kramov — Dudintsev constantly refers to Avdiev's scientific 'monopoly' which has replaced scientific research by authority and dogma. In his portrayal of Avdiev's accomplice, the bureaucrat Drozdov, Dudintsev goes beyond the criticism of industrial officials voiced in Khrushchev's 'Secret Speech'. Drozdov is an outstanding example of the new type of villain entirely formed by the Soviet period who caused untold damage to Soviet technological development. He defends the brutal realities of power against Lopatkin's idealism, regarding it as natural that an individual's ideas should be stolen by powerful administrators. Whereas Kaverin had strongly condemned one highly-placed bureaucrat, the Deputy Minister of Health Maksimov, for his 'indifference, secret contempt and striking lack of understanding', Dudintsev goes even further, showing that the collaboration between corrupt scientists and government officials enabled them together to exercise almost unlimited power.

The release from forced-labour camps of thousands of prisoners in 1956–7 made it difficult to contain the expectation of radical change aroused by the Twentieth Congress. This was especially true in Eastern Europe, where political unrest culminated in the Hungarian revolt of November 1956. Accordingly, Khrushchev adopted a more restrained approach to de-Stalinisation in the next few years, and writers were no longer free to paint such a black picture of Stalinist science. They adapted to this policy shift in several different ways. Nikolaeva, in *Battle on the Way* (1957),[19] praises Stalin's industrialisation campaign, which enabled the USSR to defeat Germany, while deploring the arrest and death of innocent scientists and engineers. Other works, such as Gennady Gor's *The University Embankment* (1959) merely attribute denunciation and intrigue in scientific circles to certain isolated individuals.[20]

Before Khrushchev's 'Secret Speech' had clearly designated Stalin as the main villain, the party leaders had implicated Beria as the chief instigator of the purges. During the confused period between the Twentieth and Twenty-Second Congresses, when the party had not yet issued a forceful public condemnation of Stalin, some writers reverted to the party's original explanation, emphasising Beria's alleged responsibility for the arrest of technical specialists. In Ketlinskaya's *Otherwise There is No Point in Living*, Beria is portrayed as Stalin's evil genius: he wishes to incriminate two young chemical engineers as 'wreckers' following an accident at their experimental station, whereas Stalin is depicted in a more favourable light as a defender of scientific initiative. In his memoirs Khrushchev later admitted that Beria had been a convenient scapegoat for Stalin's own crimes, and, somewhat disingenuously, condemned Soviet writers for their unquestioning acceptance of 'the Beria version'.[21] The conformism of Ketlinskaya's novel can, perhaps, be regarded as a consequence of the reprimand which she received after her support of Dudintsev in 1956.[22]

During the second literary 'thaw' of 1962, writers possessed greater freedom to discuss the problems of science in Stalin's time. In *Into the Storm* (1962), Granin provides interesting information about the relative immunity of atomic physicists from arrest because of the immense military importance of their work. The physicist Anikeev, engaged in research on 'the problem' (a term used to refer to the atomic bomb), comes into conflict with Beria, the director of the project. Anikeev is angry at Beria's 'ignorant, sometimes disastrous interference' with his research, and writes to the Central Committee asking them to 'protect "the problem" from the ignorant management of Beria'. Although such a challenge was 'positively suicidal' at that time, Anikeev's reputation and the importance of his work save him from 'swift reprisals'. When Beria orders him to leave his work on the bomb and go into exile to a northern pedagogical institute, Anikeev risks his life by staying on the project illegally for a while to finish testing the bombs. This portrait of Anikeev is probably modelled on the famous physicist Kapitsa who refused to collaborate on the atomic project and was kept under house arrest for eight years. It is a matter of some controversy whether Kapitsa's decision was prompted by moral opposition to nuclear weapons or a specialist's dislike of mismanagement and interference with his research, as evinced by Granin's Anikeev.

Although in 1963 Khrushchev was attempting to reimpose ideological orthodoxy on Soviet writers, and his support for Lysenko remained strong, a scientist, Vasily Mishnev, managed to publish his outspoken novel *The Academic Degree* in Minsk.[23] He portrays a genuine scientist, Professor Yunovsky, who rejects the teachings of the powerful 'Michurinist' Academician Verkhobasov at a time when, we are told, no conference can proceed without the expression of total loyalty to his theories and his name cannot be omitted from any article on biology. Verkhobasov's rise to power at the end of the 1940s with the help of opportunists and slanderers, the ensuing cult of his personality and his 'pretensions to a monopoly in biology' are highly reminiscent of Lysenko's career. Yunovsky condemns the Michurinists' naive conception of transforming nature and their abuse of scientific truth. In particular, he denounces Verkhobasov's theory of the absence of intra-species competition, which contradicts Darwin's theory of evolution and 'presupposes that plants possess a capacity for thought'. This was a direct attack on Lysenko, who in 1963 had reasserted his discredited theory of species.[24]

Khrushchev's renewed support for Lysenko probably prevented the appearance of Kaverin's novel *Dual Portrait* (written in 1963–4 but not published until 1966, after the fall of Lysenko and Khrushchev),[25] for it frankly admitted that well-known biologists had been imprisoned in Stalin's time as a result of pernicious denunciations by pseudo-scientific charlatans. Kaverin emphasises the inability of the eminent biologist Ostrogradsky to work on an important theory in the labour camp because of the incompatibility of research with 'humiliations, hunger, back-breaking toil'. Another possible reason for the failure to publish the novel was Kaverin's implicit criticism of Khrushchev's rehabilitation policy. Although Ostrogradsky is released, he is now incurably ill and finds it difficult to adapt to the new circumstances of the post-Stalin era. Moreover, although everyone knows he is innocent, the famous scientist is not allowed to live in Moscow, but is obliged to hide in the houses of his friends and acquaintances. Ostrogradsky's fate is probably modelled on that of Kaverin's brother L. A. Zilber, who died in 1966, and is also reminiscent of the eminent biologist Timofeev-Resovsky, who remained dedicated to science in prison and, although he was released in 1953, did not become a free citizen of the Soviet Union until 1955.

Conformist fiction published after the Twenty-Second Congress, such as Boris Dyakov's camp memoir *A Tale of Past Experiences* (1964), published in the 'conservative' journal *Oktyabr* to counter the realistic description of camp life in Solzhenitsyn's *One Day in the Life of Ivan Denisovich*, helped to sanction the new myth disseminated by Stalin's successors — the idea that, even under arduous conditions, communist specialists invariably remained loyal to the party in prison and were eventually released and rehabilitated.[26] All the scientists whom Dyakov depicts, for example the microbiologist P. F. Zdrodovsky and the mathematician P. A. Gelvikh, survived the camps and attained high positions in the post-Stalin era. Not surprisingly, Solzhenitsyn satirised Dyakov's one-sided account of camp life in *The Gulag Archipelago*.[27]

Stalin's Industrialisation Policy

Some Soviet writers undermine official claims about the excellence of Stalin's industrialisation policy, demonstrating in various ways that the Stalin terror had a harmful effect on Soviet technological development. L. Rotov's sketch *An Engineer in the Glavk* (chief department of a ministry) (1957) speaks frankly about the disorganisation of production caused by the need to give inexperienced young people jobs as chief engineers or factory directors after the arrest of their predecessors in the terror of 1937–8.[28] Sergei Snegov's novel *In the Polar Night* (1957) shows that the atmosphere of suspicion created by arrests for 'wrecking' had a harmful impact on industrial relations.[29]

Alexander Bek's *samizdat* novel *The New Appointment* calls into question another of Stalin's alleged achievements — the development of the heavy metal industry. Bek takes Khrushchev's revelations about the suicide of 'Sergo' Ordzhonikidze, Stalin's Commissar for Heavy Industry, even further, suggesting that Ordzhonikidze's death may have been directly occasioned by a quarrel with Stalin in 1937. Bek does not specifically mention the liquidation of Ordzhonikidze's brother and the arrest of his nephew Gvacharia, who had been responsible for the reorganisation of the Soviet foundry industry, but he discloses that by the autumn of 1938 a flood of arrests had swept away nearly all those who had been associated with Ordzhonikidze. Hence he no longer attributes the faults in Soviet industry to 'sabotage' by bourgeois specialists (as he had done in his earlier novel *The Life of Berezhkov*), but openly mentions Stalin's harmful personal involvement in industry and the large-scale arrests of competent managers and engineers in 1937–8, which led to very low productivity in 1939 and only a partial, slow recovery in 1940.

Even though forced labour greatly diminished in the USSR after

1953, its extensive exploitation on Stalin's great construction and industrial projects remained a delicate topic in the post-Stalin period. To this day no general study of the use of slave labour in Stalin's time has been published in the USSR. In the early 1960s Khrushchev's new campaign to send Komsomol volunteers to construction projects in Siberia led journalists to extol the heroic exploits of enthusiastic 'builders of communism' in Stalin's time without mentioning that prisoners had been employed.[30] As a contribution to this campaign, V. Azhaev's notorious work *Far from Moscow* was reprinted in 1961, without any explanatory introduction. This novel, first published in 1948, describes the construction of an oil pipeline on the island of Sakhalin, deliberately concealing the fact that it was built with prison labour under the direction of the Far Eastern Concentration Camps.[31] Not surprisingly, such works were regarded with considerable cynicism by the Soviet intelligentsia. In Bek's *New Appointment* the praise of Azhaev's novel by the Minister of Ferrous Metallurgy, Tevosyan, characterises him as a Stalinist; and in Solzhenitsyn's *First Circle* the work is satirised under the slightly disguised title *Far from Us*. A later work which evoked a similar critical reaction from the liberal intelligentsia was Yevtushenko's poem *The Bratsk Hydro-electric Station* (1965) which, in an attempt to extol the unbending faith of those who suffered in Stalin's purges, depicts the camps as strongholds of military and industrial power and the prisoners constructing a power station on the Volga as an enthusiastic communist labour brigade.[32]

It was only during the short interval between the publication of Solzhenitsyn's *One Day in the Life of Ivan Denisovich* and Khrushchev's fall in October 1964 that some writers were able to refer to the human cost of technological progress. Even at this time, however, their freedom was severely restricted, and there could be no suggestion that rapid industrial progress had been bought at the price of millions of lives. Khrushchev, who had apparently suffered considerable opposition from the hard-liners in the party as a result of his publication of Solzhenitsyn's novel, complained in a speech of March 1963 that publishing houses and journals had been inundated with manuscripts describing life in exile, prisons and camps. He advised writers to put an end to this flood, and editors to treat prison camp writings with extreme caution so as not to damage the work of the party. Immediately after Khrushchev's speech a ban was imposed on the publication of works exposing the arbitrary nature of

Stalin's terror. Any references to the labour camps in published works were therefore timid and guarded, but nevertheless imparted new and fascinating information to the Soviet public. Ivan Stadnyuk's *People are not Angels* (1962), for example, mentions that after his arrest the peasant Platon Yavchuk spent a year working on the White Sea-Baltic Canal before being transferred to a metallurgy combine. The author does not describe Yavchuk's experience in detail, but merely observes: 'His eyes saw a great deal there. He himself experienced many things. It seemed that he wouldn't have the strength to endure it.'[33]

A related theme treated in the early 1960s was the delicate issue of the abandonment of some of Stalin's great construction projects which had proved economically unviable. Yury Trifonov's novel *The Quenching of Thirst* (1963), which refers explicitly to 'the great MVD constructions on which prisoners were employed',[34] reveals that billions of roubles were wasted on the construction of the Turkmenian Canal from Takhia-Tash to Krasnovodsk, which was closed after Stalin's death. Alexander Pobozhy's sketch *Dead Way* (1964) purveys new and disturbing information to both Soviet and Western readers in an eye-witness account of the construction of the Salekhard-Igarka railway in Northern Siberia which was begun in March 1949 and abandoned after Stalin's death.[35] Free engineers, technicians and managers were employed on this project alongside prisoners and former camp inmates living in exile in the Far North. The prisoners laboured in up to 50 degrees of frost in the winter and were plagued by mosquitoes in the summer; after work they slept for five hours a day on the bare ground surrounded by notice boards proclaiming 'Camp Compound'. Pobozhy paints an unprepossessing picture of Antonov, the director of the Enisei camp, who arrives for a brief visit, commands the prisoners to work harder and feasts on a meal of fresh tomatoes and cucumbers specially flown in for his benefit.

Pobozhy stresses that the labour camps were a wasteful method of achieving technological progress. An engineer, a former prisoner, argues that although prison labour is cheap, prisoners require many guards; there are more opportunists who have acquired 'cushy jobs' than manual labourers; and the project cannot be organised effectively since convicts are forbidden to handle certain machinery. He contends that construction projects before 1937 were completed much more cheaply and efficiently by free workers earning good wages. Another engineer goes even further, maintaining that a cost-benefit analysis of the project would prove that the improvement of air and water transport would have been a more efficient means of opening up the tundra.

The Special Prisons

One of the most striking examples of the role of literature in breaking taboos and providing new factual information is Solzhenitsyn's novel *The First Circle*, which describes a hitherto unpublicised aspect of Stalin's penal system — the 'special prison' (known as a *sharaga* or *sharashka* in prison slang). The *sharashki* were secret research centres in which scientists and technologists carried out work in their fields under prison discipline. No reference to these institutions was permitted in published literature, although, as Svirsky has pointed out, the impossibility of describing the *sharashki* made such novels as Dudintsev's *Not by Bread Alone* unrealistic to those in the know.[36]

One work which exceptionally managed to evade the censorship was the memoir of the test pilot Mark Gallai, *Tested in the Sky* (1963), which suggested that eminent scientists had sometimes been allowed to continue research useful to the state in captivity.[37] Sergei P. Korolyov, the Chief Designer of the space programme, was arrested in 1938 on suspicion of wanting to launch a rocket attack on Stalin, sent to mine gold in Kolyma, subsequently transferred to a special prison to work on aircraft design until the importance of rocketry was recognised, and finally moved to a rocket *sharashka* until his release in 1945. Korolyov's identity was not revealed until his obituary appeared in 1966, although in the early 1960s articles about the anonymous Chief Designer had been published.[38] Gallai's account ventures further than conventional portraits of the Chief Designer in such literary works as Golovanov's *Forgers of the Thunder* (1964).[39] Gallai describes the modest though impressive man standing by the controls before the take-off of Gagarin's Vostok-1 whom he had first seen 15 years earlier at an aerodrome during the testing of his accelerator for the aircraft TU-2. While Gallai held a short technical conversation with this man a certain lieutenant — obviously a secret policeman — hovered around them, leading him to suspect that his interlocutor was a convict only allowed out of prison to supervise the testing of his invention. The Chief Designer is portrayed as a 'great man with a great, complex, contradictory, exceptional character, who could not be deformed by any external circumstances which had broken many other people like reeds'. Gallai's account is thus much more revealing than the official biography of Korolyov published in 1969 which does not mention his arrest, merely stating that the designer was unable to be present during the testing of two rockets in 1939 'through circumstances beyond his control'.[40] It has been suggested that Korolyov himself may have encouraged Gallai to include this section in his manuscript.[41]

An account of the aviation *sharashka* by a former inmate, G. A. Ozerov, published later in the West, vouches for the authenticity of Solzhenitsyn's description of the special prison of Marfino in Ostankino, a suburb of Moscow.[42] The precise name and location of the prison are given in the revised version of *The First Circle* published in 1978, which is based on Solzhenitsyn's original uncut manuscript.[43] Specialists imprisoned at Marfino were given 'special assignments' of extreme secrecy, usually connected with defence or internal security, sometimes commissioned by Stalin himself: for example, the design of a special telephone for Stalin fitted with a 'scrambler', or secret device to prevent his conversations from being understood even if they were intercepted. Many inmates of the *sharashki* were serving long-term sentences as political criminals and had been transferred from the concentration camps after undergoing long interrogations, torture and hard labour. Solzhenitsyn admits that he himself only managed to survive his eight-year sentence because he spent half of it working as a mathematician in the relative comfort of three *sharashki*. In several particulars Solzhenitsyn's account differs from descriptions of earlier prisons: by 1949 the prisoners slept in dormitories and the authorities only allowed visits once a year.

In *The First Circle* Solzhenitsyn explores the history and purpose of the *sharashki*. The first special prison was set up in 1931 after the Industrial Party trial; the most prominent scientist to be confined there was the energetics expert Ramzin. It was hoped that decent food and living conditions would make the specialists more productive. The experiment proved successful, since these scientists, deprived of their freedom, had nothing to do but concentrate on their work, with the incentive of possible release if they invented something important. Moreover, imprisonment eliminated the jealous secretiveness and competition for degrees and honours which hindered much academic work in the USSR.

Solzhenitsyn demonstrates that in some respects the Soviet regime achieved its objective: the specialists at Marfino have all their basic needs satisfied, and some men, such as Rubin and Pryanchikov, gain great pleasure from their absorption in scientific research, even in captivity. There is, however, a division of opinion about the effectiveness of the *sharashka* system: Sologdin is conscious that his engineering skill has developed enormously during his years as a prisoner away from worldly distractions, whereas the brilliant Bobynin complains that valuable scientific work cannot be undertaken unless men have freedom and peace of mind. Solzhenitsyn shows that research is hampered by the atmosphere of suspicion which necessitates innumerable security checks, and by the constant transfers of specialists back to the camps. The special prison has poor equipment, and security officials who know nothing about science, pressed by their superiors to promise results in as short a time as possible, impose unrealistic deadlines on the prisoners' work. Throughout the novel Solzhenitsyn emphasies that the creativity of the individual imprisoned specialist should not be confused with the sterility of the *sharashka* system as a whole.

Solzhenitsyn's portrayal of the *sharashka* is restrained in comparison with factual accounts. Ozerov considers that Solzhenitsyn actually understates some of the *sharashka*'s worst aspects; and it is true that he fails to stress the general depression caused by random transfers, the lack of recognition for valuable scientific research, the hostility between the prisoners and free workers, the ignorant interference of Beria and Stalin, and the demand that scientists make lists of their colleagues who are still at liberty. Moreover, unlike Ozerov, he does not explicitly point to the similarity between life in the prison and life in scientific institutes outside prison walls.

Nationalism

One feature of Stalinism which affected all scientists and technologists was the extreme nationalism prevalent from about 1944 to Stalin's death. In order to inflate national pride and counteract harmful Western influences, the accomplishments of Russian scientists were exaggerated and the achievements of Western science denigrated. Popov, not Marconi, was said to have invented the radio; the first aeroplane was allegedly built and tested by Mozhaisky 20 years before the Wright brothers; other claims for

Russian priority included electricity, the steam engine and the helicopter.

In Stalin's time many servile literary works extolled Russian science or attacked Western influences.[44] It was not until 1955–6 that Bulganin and Khrushchev publicly acknowledged the value of contacts with Western scientists;[45] yet fiction had, earlier, tentatively foreshadowed this change of policy. Vladimir Polyakov's *Fireman Prokhorchuk* (1953), a satire on the censorship of literature by cautious editors afraid of official reprisals, carefully challenges the exaggerated claims for the superiority of Russian science. When a budding author submits a story containing the phrase: 'Not a single electric light bulb was burning', the editor protests: 'What's this? Sounds as if in our country we make bulbs that don't work!'[46]

In 1955 the party leaders admitted that in some fields Western scientific achievements were superior and attacked the 'boastfulness and conceit' of institutes which had formerly denied the advances of foreign science.[47] This view is echoed in Lyubov Kabo's novel *The Difficult March* (1956), set in the years 1951–2. A schoolboy asks: 'Why, tell me, have all our text books been altered? All the foreign scientists have been replaced by Russians . . . Petrov's arc, for instance.'[48] This is a reference to the electric arc, which, commonly believed to have been invented by Davy and presented to the Royal Society in 1810, was alleged to have been invented by V. Petrov in 1803. Kochetov's novel *The Ershov Brothers* (1958), however, shows that conservatives still retained Stalinist attitudes. Popov is named as the inventor of the telephone, and the reader is assured that only former Nazi collaborators argue that 'people outside Russia dispute this statement'.[49]

Kaverin's trilogy *The Open Book* paints the most detailed picture of Stalinist scientific nationalism in published fiction. Some of the inconsistencies in the work can be explained by the fact that Kaverin began the trilogy at the height of the campaign against foreigners, whereas the last part was published in the more liberal atmosphere of 1956. In the early part of the novel, Kaverin follows Stalinist propaganda, presenting the microbiologist Tatyana Vlasenkova's work on penicillin as an authentic Russian discovery based on a pre-revolutionary theory about the protective properties of mould. The story of Tatyana Vlasenkova was modelled on the career of the Soviet scientist Professor Z. V. Ermolyeva, who began working on the extraction of penicillin from mould in October 1942 and isolated a concentrate named 'Soviet penicillin'. Although it was a similar substance to the penicillin which had been developed in other countries, official propagandists took the matter out of her hands and acclaimed her work as a major discovery; she was awarded a Stalin Prize and described as 'the discoverer of the new drug penicillin'. A *Pravda* article of 1945 referred to 'Ermolyeva's greatest discovery — Soviet penicillin' and added laconically, 'Penicillin was also discovered by Fleming.'[50] Kaverin initially praises Tatyana's nationalistic desire to develop Soviet medicine in advance of the science of the rest of the world, and presents British research on penicillin as a threat to Soviet supremacy. In the final part of the trilogy, however, Kaverin attacks Stalinist scientific chauvinism. When Tatyana wonders why it cannot simply be officially acknowledged that the English have won priority in the field, another character observes that such honesty would be considered unpatriotic in the prevailing climate of chauvinism: 'Don't you see how all around us people have simply gone mad over Russian priority? It appears that we invented the moon and stars, not to mention penicillin.'

Few writers admit that in Stalin's time scientists had been arrested on charges of collaborating with the West, since the practice had not been officially condemned by the party. In *The Thaw* (Part One) Ehrenburg merely hints that the factory director Zhuravlyov regrets that he can no longer take advantage of the 'trump card' that the wife of his antagonist left him years ago, married a foreigner and is now living in Belgium. This theme is treated more explicitly in the 1968 version of Solzhenitsyn's *First Circle*, which depicts the arrest of the diplomat Innokenty Volodin for his attempt to warn a professor against handing a sample of a new drug to a foreign colleague at a time when any meeting with a foreign scientist was considered a crime against the state. Solzhenitsyn also evokes the double-think of the communist Rubin, who, despite his belief that medical research should be shared internationally, tries to convince himself that 'if it were considered part of the vital interests of the state to claim that all scientific discoveries had been pioneered in Russia, then anyone who thought differently was objectively standing in the way of progress and must be swept aside'. Solzhenitsyn shows that the campaign against foreigners compelled Soviet scholars to make dishonest statements: an engineer is obliged to write an article affirming the impossibility of progress in Western science, and a postgraduate student has to rewrite her thesis in order to eliminate all references to Western specialists and bestow exaggerated praise on Russian scientists.

Anti-Semitism

In the climate of jingoism and xenophobia of the late Stalin period, it is not surprising that the old prejudices of anti-Semitism which lay near the surface flared up again. Stalin, alarmed at an enthusiastic demonstration of Moscow Jews during the visit of Mrs Golda Meir in 1948, initiated a militant campaign denouncing the state of Israel as a tool of Western capitalism and accusing Soviet Jews of failing to give undivided loyalty to their native land. Jews were very prominent in the academic world (nearly 20,000 held teaching posts in universities), in vital areas of science and technology such as nuclear research and in industrial management. The indispensability of some specialists enabled them to survive the campaign of terror, but many were regarded with mistrust and were liable to be branded as 'rootless cosmopolitans' and 'men of uncertain allegiance'; the culmination of the campaign was the notorious 'Doctors' Plot'.

In Stalin's time such literary works as Simonov's *Alien Shadow* (1949), which unmasked a Jewish scientist as a spy, contributed to the 'anti-cosmopolitan' campaign in science.[51] However, in 1963 Khrushchev publicly denied that anti-Semitism had ever existed in the USSR — a viewpoint totally opposed to the emphasis he later placed on Stalin's anti-Semitism in his memoirs. Perhaps Khrushchev was anxious to cover his own possible complicity in the 'Doctors' Plot'; he was certainly reluctant to suggest in public that the USSR had any features in common with the Third Reich; and he knew that if he had exposed anti-Semitism he would have had to seek to eradicate it. Khrushchev himself was always reluctant to criticise anti-Semitism in public, perhaps because he had inherited anti-Semitic attitudes from his native Ukraine, and because he regarded the Jewish population — estimated at two million by the 1959 census — as a serious security risk. Anti-Semitism was a useful safety-valve for the aggressive feelings of the population, and was particularly prevalent among the bureaucracy, many of whom despised the Jewish intelligentsia. To some extent Khrushchev himself institutionalised anti-Semitism by the 1961 law on economic crimes; most of those executed or imprisoned were Jewish. Anti-Semitic novels such as *The Ways of Our Life* (1963) by the Ukrainian writer A. Dimarov continued to be published; and the pressure which Khrushchev exerted to make Yevtushenko revise his poem *Babii Yar* (1962) demonstrates that anti-Semitism was still a controversial subject in the post-Stalin period.[52] However, some works of 1953–64, usually by Jewish authors, allude to the anti-Semitism prevalent in the scientific world under Stalin, although, as anti-Jewish feeling still persisted, references in published fiction are usually fleeting or oblique.

In Part One of Ehrenburg's *The Thaw* a patient asks a doctor — named Scherer — if she is sure about a diagnosis; she reacts angrily, then apologises, explaining that she is sensitive to any slight to her medical skill: 'Sometimes you have to hear such things nowadays . . .' The implication is that the accusations against Jewish doctors are on her mind. This appears to be the first reference to the effect of anti-Semitism on the scientific community in post-Stalin fiction; but almost contemporary with Ehrenburg's novel was an oblique allusion to anti-Semitism in Granin's *The Seekers* (1954). Daniil Granin, a Jewish writer whose real name is German, depicts an inventor with a no less obviously Jewish name, Reingold, who is dismissed because of a bureaucrat's accusation that he was in occupied territory during the war. Evidently Granin was unable, in 1954, to attribute Reingold's dismissal to the anti-cosmopolitan campaign, although this would have been a more credible reason in 1952–3, when the novel is set, as most of those accused of being in occupied territory had been dealt with more rapidly after the war. Although Granin does not state explicitly that Reingold is Jewish, the clearer reference to anti-Semitism in his later novel *Into the Storm* (1962), which will be discussed below, justifies this assumption.[53]

Dissident writers make franker references to the anti-cosmopolitan campaign. In *The First Circle* Solzhenitsyn depicts the Jewish engineer Adam Roitman, a major in the MGB and a warder at the special prison, who, during a sleepless night racked by fears of denunciation, recalls the origin and development of the anti-cosmopolitan campaign. Apparently this chapter was regarded as particularly controversial by V. Zaks, a cautious member of the editorial board of *Novy Mir*, when the possibility of publishing Solzhenitsyn's novel was discussed in 1964.[54]

Vasily Grossman's novel *Forever Flowing* gives a detailed account of the course and effects of the anti-cosmopolitan campaign in a scientific institute. This work was confiscated by the KGB, hastily reconstructed by the author and completed only a few days before his death in 1964; it circulated in *samizdat*, but was not published abroad until 1970. The main character of Grossman's novel, the mediocre biologist Nikolai, acquiesces in the anti-Semitic campaign which secures the arrest of many of his most talented colleagues and advances his own career. He convinces himself: 'What was involved was clearly a hostile attitude towards Jews among a section of party and government officialdom . . . Stalin, he felt, was not an anti-Semite and, no doubt, simply knew nothing about it.' Grossman shows how wild rumours made it difficult for Jewish doctors to continue their work after the communiqué on the 'Doctors' Plot': 'Several Moscow chemists had been shut down because the pharmacists — Jews and American agents — had sold pills consisting of dried lice. Tales were told about babies and their mothers being infected with syphilis in maternity homes.' Grossman evokes the ambiguous position of conformist biologists in Stalin's time: while believing that many Jewish scientists had been arrested unjustly, and deploring the fact that talented young Jews were being denied admission to university physics departments, postgraduate courses and positions in industry, Nikolai nevertheless publicly condemns the 'doctor-assassins' and approves the letter of congratulations sent to their denouncer, the police agent Lydia Timashuk.[55] Grossman does, however, make the point that it is not only Russian scientists who compromised their integrity: some Jewish scientists were particularly assiduous in denouncing their fellow Jews.

The Stalin Theme since Khrushchev

After Khrushchev's fall the new party leadership adhered to a middle course on the question of Stalin. On the one hand, the Brezhnev-Kosygin regime, composed of party and state bureaucrats, was more conservative than Khrushchev, and unprepared to disturb the security of its position by making any more revelations about Stalin and the 'Anti-Party Group'. On the other hand, the neo-Stalinist backlash associated with such figures as Alexander Shelepin and Sergei Trapeznikov, an old colleague of Brezhnev who in September 1965 was appointed head of the department of the Central Committee responsible for science and industry, failed to secure the rehabilitation of Stalin either at the Twenty-Third Congress of 1966, or on the ninetieth anniversary of Stalin's birth in

1969. Although foreign communist parties apparently prevented the total rehabilitation of Stalin in the post-Khrushchev period, it became easier to publish works containing qualified praise of Stalin rather than strong criticism of him; the phrase 'the period of the personality cult', frequently used in Khrushchev's time to refer to the period 1934–53, was banned; and there was a revaluation of Stalin's role, especially with relation to the war.

Alexander Rozen's novel *The Last Two Weeks*, published in 1965 shortly after Khrushchev's fall, was able to treat the controversial subject of the impact of Stalin's policy towards Germany on Soviet technology.[56] Set in the fortnight before the outbreak of war, when Stalin insisted that Germany would not attack, it provides a frank picture of the effect of Soviet-German relations during the period of the Molotov-Ribbentrop Pact of 1939–41. Rozen conveys the tension between the fear of an imminent attack and the need to maintain the pretence of unity, the weakening of the country through the continuing purges in the army and industry, and the general taboo, enforced during the period of the Pact, on anything considered likely to offend German susceptibilities. In the novel the factory director Podrezov is arrested as a provocateur for criticising the manufacture of an imported German turbine. Although the German owner of the turbine firm has admitted that the machine is defective (an allusion to the poor quality of the technology supplied to the USSR by the Nazis), Podrezov's guilt has already been established on political grounds, for Stalin himself has decided that Podrezov's case will serve as an appropriate illustration to his latest 'important document, which will show with the insight of genius that "Germany does not intend to fight the Soviet Union", and will give "provocateurs" their due'. By 1970, however, the resurgence of Stalinist attitudes towards the war years was demonstrated by an article by the dogmatist Vadim Kozhevnikov which complained that 'In A. Rozen's *The Last Two Weeks* people and events are depicted from incorrect positions.'[57] The vehemence of this attack and its publication in the official government newspaper *Izvestiya* suggest that Rozen's outspoken work may only have appeared because of an oversight by the censorship during the confused interval of transition after Khrushchev's fall.

Probably because of the threat of re-Stalinisation, some liberal writers returned to the subject of Stalin's harmful impact on science in the late 1960s. *Novy Mir* published *At the Testing Site* (1967),[58] a story by I. Grekova (the pseudonym of Elena Ventsel, a doctor of sciences and professor at the Zhukovsky Military and Air Academy, a lecturer in the science of ballistics). Grekova depicts the precarious position of General Sivers, a Stalin Prize winner involved in the research and development of nuclear missiles, in the tense atmosphere of 1952. Since his friend Professor Pavlovich, whose mathematical method he employed in his own work, is already in prison, he fears that his research may be branded as 'wrecking' at any moment. Sivers is also suspect because he does not admit the priority of Russian science in every field, and because of his name, even though he is not Jewish, but of Swedish origin. Grekova also alludes to the controversial issue of the hostility towards cybernetics in the late Stalin period. This was a subject which could not be mentioned even in the Khrushchev era: a novel on this theme completed by G. Svirsky in 1954, entitled 'State Examination', has never been published in the Soviet Union.[59] In Grekova's novel a scientist speaks of the need to apply principles of rational control, such as feedback, to the Soviet economy; and when his colleague, a party member, dismisses these ideas as 'a sort of cybernetics', he condemns the pejorative labelling of original scientific ideas and comments that he expects his interlocutor to accuse him next of being an 'apologist for bourgeois pseudo-science' or a 'fascist thug'. Evidently even in the late 1960s the subject of Stalinism could not be discussed frankly in published fiction, as Grekova was severely criticised by literary dogmatists, and subsequently found it impossible to publish a novel dealing explicitly with scientists engaged in work on cybernetics during the years of the ban.[60]

In the late 1960s anti-Stalinists continued to co-exist with neo-Stalinists. The influence of the Lysenkoites was again growing stronger in the scientific world; and one of the official reasons given for the incarceration of the biologist Zhores Medvedev in a psychiatric hospital in 1970 was that he had written a book on the genetics dispute.[61] Possibly in response to this new crisis, Granin hinted at the enduring power of Lysenko's disciples in Soviet science in his story *Somebody Must* (1970), in which an embittered inventor likens the corrupt scientists who obstruct his new design to the opportunists who suppressed genetics.[62]

Tvardovsky's dismissal as editor of *Novy Mir* in 1970 temporarily shifted the balance towards the dogmatists. The obscurantist Ivan Shevtsov, in his novel *Love and Hate* (1970), attempted to revive Stalinist attacks on new concepts in physics. Shevtsov's hero, the physicist Kobalyov, voices the contempt for Einstein common in Stalin's time in provocative anti-Semitic terms: he 'considered that the role of Einstein in science had been terribly exaggerated by publicity, that they'd made a Jesus Christ of him'. Kobalyov also rejects the theory of matter and anti-matter, maintaining that it contradicts dialectical materialism and could lead to idealism and religious superstition. The concept of anti-matter was uncongenial to the Marxist view that everything in nature is precise, patterned and comprehensible. Shevtsov's attempt to use the theme of physics to discredit the liberal intelligentsia is evident from his portrait of the physicist Dvin, a potential Nobel Prize winner possibly modelled on the independent physicist V. A. Fock, who is accused of taking the wrong side in the physics controversies under Stalin; one of his main defects is that he is 'a follower of Einstein himself' — that is, a poor physicist whose world reputation is undeserved.[63] Dvin, who was imprisoned in 1948 and subsequently rehabilitated, is doubly suspect because he wants to admit to his institute a scientist who has been imprisoned as a spy, and because he supports the progressive journal *Novosti*, an obvious reference to *Novy Mir*, which Shevtsov abhors as a stronghold of Soviet 'liberals'. Although Shevtsov occupies an isolated position in Soviet literature, expressing the views of some of the right wing, particularly of the upper echelons of the army, his work affords an insight into the bureaucracy's enduring suspicion of intellectuals.

The issue of Stalin and his rehabilitation was gradually shelved in the USSR; it was not mentioned at either the Twenty-Fourth or Twenty-Fifth Congresses. Yet since many aspects of the system Stalin created remained more or less intact in the 1970s, writers generally avoided any return to the controversial question of the effect of Stalinism on science and technology. Exceptions to this rule are three interesting novels: Kron's *Insomnia* (1977), Trifonov's *House on the Embankment* (1976) and Gerasimovich's *The Effect of Position* (1979). The past problems in Soviet science had become a topical issue again by the late 1970s, after the party's publishing house Politizdat had, in 1973, published an autobiography by Academician N. Dubinin which defended Lysenko and presented an extremely distorted history of Soviet genetics,[64] totally opposed to Zhores Medvedev's *samizdat* account, published abroad in 1969. Moreover, the persecution of geneticists could not only be treated as a thing of the past, because after the defection to Italy of one of the senior research scientists in the institute of the eminent biologist Boris Astaurov, several other members of his staff were demoted or dismissed on the recommendation of commissions on which Dubinin actively participated. Astaurov's health suffered, and political pressure may have been partly responsible for his death in 1974. Furthermore, in 1976 and 1977 a new dispute arose in Soviet genetics between Dubinin and D. Belyaev, Secretary General of the 1978 International Genetics Congress in Moscow.

These controversies — and the death of Lysenko in 1976 — may well have led liberal Soviet writers to return to the theme of biological science under Stalin. Their depiction of the past was relevant to the current situation in Soviet science, while creating less controversy than a frank exposure of contemporary problems. Alexander Kron, formerly a relatively orthodox writer, raises interesting questions in his novel *Insomnia*[65] through his portrayal of Uspensky, the director of a physiology institute. The narrator surveys Uspensky's career from the 1930s to the 1960s in order to build up a composite portrait of this complex man who is motivated throughout by a desire to further the proper pursuit of scientific research, but has at times been forced to make shoddy compromises to save his own skin, justifying his behaviour by claiming that he has always been trying to protect the essential aims of his institute. In the 1920s Uspensky attracted the notice of Stalin, who was pleased by his frankness and appointed him director of the institute; but, as Kron observes, Uspensky never argued with Stalin again. Uspensky played a full part in the two periods of greatest conflict in physiology: the late 1930s and the post-war period, which culminated in the All-Union Conference of Physiology in 1950 when all tendencies except the theory of higher nervous activity associated with the famous physiologist I. P. Pavlov (1849–1936) were banned. In the 1930s Uspensky approved of the political battle, but now realises that the dispute 'roused dark passions and for a long time poisoned the atmosphere in the institute'. In the 1940s Uspensky again bowed to political authority, allowing a talented, but outspoken scientist on his staff to be dismissed, while furthering the career of a party official on the basis of falsification and plagiarism. Although Kron claims that the situation changed radically in 1956, his depiction of Uspensky's remorse for his past crimes raises the general question, still relevant in the 1970s: how many men who held power under Stalin were able to keep a clear conscience? Kron's theme reflected on the many officials formed by the Stalin era who still held high positions in the Brezhnev period and continued to persecute such talented men as Zhores Medvedev, Efim Etkind and Alexander Zinoviev.

Another work of more general significance largely concerned with the last years of Stalin's rule is Yury Trifonov's *The House on the Embankment*. In this novel Trifonov returns to a theme which he treated from a relatively orthodox Stalinist point of view in his Stalin Prize-winning novel *The Students* (1950).[66] The contrast between the two works illuminates both Trifonov's own evolution and the development of Soviet literature since the Stalin period. In *Students*, academic conflicts at the end of the 1940s take on a great political importance, whereas in *House on the Embankment* academic battles are less important than moral issues: the exposure of egoism, fear and careerism. In the later work Trifonov has changed sides, supporting the victims of political persecution rather than the persecutors (although even in *Students* there were hints that his sympathies might lie with the 'negative' character, the professor censured for excessive sympathy towards the West, rather than with the 'positive' students who were hounding him).

House on the Embankment concerns an opportunist, Glebov, who has been helped by the eminent scientist Ganchuk and is engaged to his daughter Sonya, but, when already selected as a postgraduate, does not defend his former supervisor against the hatchet-men who are now trying to get rid of him. Glebov is forced into a complex moral dilemma: although his grandmother's death gives him a convenient excuse not to attend the first meeting designed to expose Ganchuk, he does participate in later meetings and allows Ganchuk to be dismissed; Sonya, who is no longer of use to him, has a nervous breakdown, falls seriously ill and dies.

Trifonov's novel is an interesting study in self-deception, revealing Glebov's slow acquiescence in betrayal, the selective operation of his memory and the gradual disintegration of his moral sense. The portrait of Glebov is a telling comment on many members of the Soviet intelligentsia who have made successful careers at the expense of a series of moral compromises. Trifonov's work provoked considerable criticism; and it is noteworthy that Vladimir Dudintsev, one of the 'radicals' of 1956, was in the forefront of the attack.[67] On the one hand, Dudintsev recognises that Trifonov has made a valuable contribution by unmasking insidious opportunists like Glebov who are more dangerous than outright villains; on the other hand, he claims that Trifonov's moral stance is not clear — an ironic accusation in view of earlier complaints about the excessive pessimism of *Not By Bread Alone*. Dudintsev argues that the conflict in biology had its villains and opportunists, but 'also had courageous soldiers who ensured the ultimate victory of scientific truth'. He undoubtedly had in mind Academician Nikolai Vavilov, who died in prison in 1943, and his own friend Zhores Medvedev. It is noteworthy that Dudintsev had for years been collecting material for a novel on the genetics dispute, apparently entitled 'The Unknown Soldier', which he said that he had almost completed in 1964,[68] but this work — whether for personal or political reasons — has never appeared in the USSR. It could be that Dudintsev was using this literary debate not so much to attack Trifonov as to stress the continuing need to fight careerists and pseudo-scientists who were still harming Soviet biology in the 1970s.

Trifonov's *House on the Embankment* was also denounced in a keynote speech by Georgy Markov at the Sixth Writers' Congress of 1976 for its failure to depict 'the presence of forces capable of changing the seeming irremediability of certain lives and situations'.[69] When obliged to defend his work at a commission chaired by the conservative critic Vitaly Ozerov, Trifonov claimed that his aim was to 'write about life in all its complexities'; and in a later interview of 1977 he stated that he expected the reader to make his own moral judgements, although he had been, perhaps, at his most judgemental in portraying the character of Glebov.[70] Frequent criticism of Trifonov's novel suggests that the work possessed unpleasant implications for highly-placed literary bureaucrats in the post-Khrushchev period. A more cynical view of Trifonov's position is, however, expressed by the *émigré* Grigory Svirsky, who claims that although Trifonov was at first censured by Soviet critics — if only mildly — he soon returned to favour and was allowed to go abroad, because his works, containing half-truths and editorial cuts, proved a useful 'lightning-conductor' directing Soviet readers' attention away from much franker works by Solzhenitsyn or Zinoviev.[71]

An interesting novel concerned more specifically with the genetics dispute is I. Gerasimovich's *The Effect of Position*.[72] This work shows that the past problems in Soviet biology were still an acceptable subject in the late 1970s, but its unusual frankness may reflect current controversies in genetics, especially the Dubinin affair. The likelihood that Gerasimovich had specific prototypes in mind is suggested by the author's somewhat disingenuous footnote: 'In the novel some events which took place in biological science are mentioned. However, the main characters are invented; all possible similarities are purely accidental.' Such a disclaimer, common in the West to avoid the possibility of libel action, is highly unusual in the Soviet context.

Gerasimovich shows that despite the improved situation in the 1970s, many Soviet geneticists are still adversely affected by the experiences they have suffered in the Stalin period. Gerasimovich's work is the first since Uspenskaya's Stalinist novel *Our Summer* (1953) to give a detailed account of the eight-day Session of the All-Union Lenin Academy of Agricultural Sciences in July 1948 at which Lysenko, with Stalin's support, established total dominance over Soviet biology and agricultural science, and forced many of his opponents to recant. Nevertheless, Gerasimovich's novel is also noteworthy for what it does not say: Stalin is not mentioned, and Lysenko is not referred to by name, only called 'the academician', or sometimes, 'the black academician'.

Gerasimovich's aim is to draw a parallel between past problems in Soviet biology and more recent events. The courageous Professor Kunitsyna, an opponent of Lysenko, stands up in public to a certain Dyunin, a man who had once staunchly defended genetics, but after his appointment as director of an institute began to cause harm to his science by dismissing people and appropriating their work. In view of the similarity in the names, and Dubinin's original opposition to Lysenko, it is possible that Gerasimovich had Dubinin in mind. Although Gerasimovich's treatment of the genetics dispute is only partial — he speaks, for example, of the temporary death of the science, but not of the death of scientists — he uses past events to highlight the plagiarism, intrigue and dictatorial behaviour in contemporary Soviet biology.

Possibly Gerasimovich's frank novel was only published because of the climate of opinion in the party which led to the appearance of two prominent articles commemorating the hundredth anniversary of Stalin's birth in December 1979, which mentioned Stalin's 'negative' sides and the 'harm' caused by his personal 'mistakes'.[73] However, the articles admitted that such mild criticisms had only been reluctantly wrung out of the authors because of persistent Western commentary on the Stalin years, and they are insignificant in relation to the praise of Stalin as a great national leader and benefactor in many official mass-circulation publications. The few anti-Stalinist literary works of the post-Khrushchev period (which also include the play by Aitmatov and Mukhamedzhanov, *The Ascent of Mount Fuji* (1973) and Yevtushenko's *Wild Berries* (1982)) have co-existed with neo-Stalinist novels by Kochetov, Shevtsov and Chakovsky which express attitudes prevalent not only among military and political officials who wish to return to the power and prestige of an earlier era, but also among broader sectors of the population. As one Muscovite is alleged to have said in 1978: 'Stalin today is less dead than he was twenty years ago.'[74] Such views are partly connected with the resurgence of Russian nationalism, and partly generated by a nostalgic desire to return to an age of law and order, stability and efficiency, to counteract what some perceive as the moral decay of contemporary Soviet society.

Since, with a few exceptions, critical analysis of the Stalinist experience has largely been banished from the official press and published fiction, dissident and *émigré* writers have felt the need to return to the theme of Stalinism in order that the past shall never be forgotten. Some, like Roy Medvedev, Solzhenitsyn and Zinoviev, have devoted themselves to a general analysis of Stalinism, but within this wider context the impact of Stalinism on science has remained a constant theme. New information on the fate of individual scientists and engineers has been adduced in Solzhenitsyn's *Gulag Archipelago*, Mark Popovsky's biography of Academician Nikolai Vavilov and Sergei Polikanov's autobiographical account of the history of the Soviet atomic scientists.[75] The 1978 version of Solzhenitsyn's *First Circle* and the memoirs of Lev Kopelev and Dmitry Panin have added to our knowledge of the *sharashka* of Marfino; and Grigory Svirsky's documentary novel *Hostages* (1974) contains an impassioned account of the persecution of Jewish scientists in the Stalin era.[76]

Apart from the recognition by Soviet *émigrés* that it is their duty both to the millions who died and to future generations to write the truth about the Stalin era, the anti-Stalinist themes which have surfaced in works of the 1970s suggest that this viewpoint still had adherents in the Soviet establishment. However, the symbolic re-admission to the party of Molotov, one of Stalin's closest associates, and the contrived return to the USSR of Stalin's daughter Svetlana Allilueva in 1984 indicated that the Soviet leadership under Chernenko was even more sympathetic than Brezhnev and Andropov to neo-Stalinist values. A new documentary film about Marshal Zhukov being shown in 1985 demonstrates the authorities' desire to portray Stalin in a favourable light in preparation for the celebrations of the fortieth anniversary of the defeat of Hitler.[77]

Notes

1. N. Khikmet, *A byl li Ivan Ivanovich?*, *NM*, 1956, no. 4, p. 44.
2. A. Tvardovsky, *Za dalyu dal*, *NM*, 1960, no. 5, p. 10.
3. V. Ketlinskaya, *Inache zhit ne stoit* (L. 1963), p. 665.
4. I. Ehrenburg, *Lyudi, gody, zhizn*, *NM*, 1962, no. 5, p. 152; V. Ermilov, *Izvestiya*, 30 Jan. 1963; *Izvestiya*, 6 Feb. 1963.
5. I. I. Ivanov, 'Letter from a Russian Writer', *Encounter*, June 1964, pp. 88–98.
6. Khrushchev, *Pravda*, 10 Mar. 1963.
7. A. Bek, *Novoe naznachenie* (Frankfurt, 1971), pp. 55, 112.
8. I. V. Stalin, *Pravda*, 20 June 1950; A. Solzhenitsyn, *The First Circle*, trans. M. Guybon (London, 1968), pp. 100–2.
9. D. Granin, *Idu na grozu* (M. L. 1964), p. 133.
10. L. Leonov, *Russkii les*, *Znamya*, 1953, nos. 10–12.
11. M. Dewhirst and R. Farrell (eds.), *The Soviet Censorship* (Metuchen, NJ, 1973), p. 17.
12. A. Bek, *Zhizn Berezhkova*, *NM*, 1956, nos. 1–5.
13. V. Kochetov, *Molodost s nami*, *Zvezda*, 1954, nos. 9–11.
14. I. Ehrenburg, *Ottepel*, *Znamya*, 1954, no. 5.
15. A. Tertz, *Sud idyot* (Paris, 1960).
16. V. Kaverin, *Poiski i nadezhdy*, *LM*, 1956, no. 2.
17. V. Kaverin, *Otkrytaya kniga*, *Sob. soch.*, vol. 4 (M, 1965).
18. V. Dudintsev, *Ne khlebom edinym*, *NM*, 1956, nos. 8–10.
19. G. Nikolaeva, *Bitva v puti*, *Oktyabr*, 1957, nos. 3–7.
20. G. Gor, *Universitetskaya naberezhnaya*, *Neva*, 1959, nos. 11, 12; G. Tropolsky, *Kandidat nauk*, *NM*, 1958, no. 12.
21. Khrushchev, *Khrushchev Remembers*, trans. and ed. S. Talbott (NY and London, 1971), pp. 343, 351–2.
22. *LG*, 26 Jan. 1957.
23. V. Mishnev, *Uchonaya stepen* (Minsk, 1963).
24. T. D. Lysenko, *Izvestiya*, 29 Jan. 1963.
25. V. Kaverin, *Dvoinoi portret*, *Prostor*, 1966, nos. 2, 3.
26. B. Dyakov, *Povest o perezhitom*, *Oktyabr*, 1964, no. 7.
27. A. Solzhenitsyn, *The Gulag Archipelago*, trans. T. Whitney (3 vols, Fontana, 1974–8), vol. 1, p. 540, n. 5; vol. 2, pp. 243, 334–5.
28. L. Rotov, *Inzhener v glavke*, *NS*, 1957, no. 2.
29. S. Snegov, *V polyarnoi nochi*, *NM*, 1957, no. 6.
30. Yu. Zhukov, *LG*, 5 Nov. 1963; *Izvestiya*, 14 July 1964.
31. V. Azhaev, *Daleko ot Moskvy*, *NM*, 1948, nos. 7–9.
32. E. Yevtushenko, *Bratskaya GES*, *Yunost*, 1965, no. 4; A. Sinyavsky, 'In Defence of Pyramids: Notes on the Art of Yevtushenko and his poem "Bratskaya GES" ', *PC*, vol. 18 (1968), no. 5, p. 90.
33. I. Stadnyuk, *Lyudi ne angely*, *Neva*, 1962, no. 12, p. 93.
34. Yu. Trifonov, *Utolenie zhazhdy* (M. 1963), p. 354.
35. A. Pobozhy, *Myortvaya doroga*, *NM*, 1964, no. 8.
36. Svirsky, *Soviet Writing*, p. 128.
37. M. Gallai, *Ispytano v nebe*, *NM*, 1963, nos. 4, 5.

64   *The Effect of Stalinism on Science and Technology*

38. G. Ostroumov, *Izvestiya*, 23 June 1963; N. Denisov, *Pravda*, 23 June 1963.
39. Yu. Golovanov, *Kuznetsy groma*, *Yunost*, 1964, no. 1, p. 34.
40. P. Astashenkov, *Akademik Korolyov, Moskva*, 1969, no. 12, p. 178.
41. L. Vladimirov, *Sovetskii kosmicheskii blef* (Frankfurt, 1973), pp. 27–9.
42. A. Sharagin (G. Ozerov), *Tupolevskaya sharaga* (Frankfurt, 1971), p. 7.
43. A. Solzhenitsyn, *V kruge pervom, Sob. soch.*, vol. 1 (1978), p. 36.
44. I. Shtok, *Pobediteli nochi (Russkii svet)* (M, 1951); V. Konovalov, *Universitet, Oktyabr*, 1947, no. 6; V. Kozhevnikov, I. Prut, *Sudba Redzhinalda Devisa, Zvezda*, 1947, no. 4.
45. Bulganin, *Pravda*, 17 July 1955; Khrushchev, *Pravda*, 15 Feb. 1956.
46. V. Polyakov, *Fireman Prokhorchuk*, trans. A. McAndrew, in P. Blake, M. Hayward, (eds.), *Dissonant Voices in Soviet Literature* (London, 1964), p. 271.
47. *Pravda*, 20 Jan. 1955; 8 July 1955.
48. L. Kabo, *Na trudnom pokhode, NM*, 1956, no. 12, p. 130.
49. V. Kochetov, *Bratya Ershovy* (M, 1960), p. 260.
50. E. Kononenko, *Pravda*, 8 Mar. 1945.
51. K. Simonov, *Chuzhaya ten, Znamya*, 1949, no. 1.
52. A. Dimarov, *Shlyakhami zhittya (Putyami zhizni)*. Dnipro (Kiev), 1963, no. 10; Johnson, *Khrushchev and the Arts*, pp. 12–13.
53. D. Granin, *Iskateli, Zvezda*, 1954, nos. 7, 8; see also below, p. 79.
54. A. Solzhenitsyn, *The Oak and the Calf*, trans. H. Willetts (London, 1980), p. 82.
55. V. Grossman, *Forever Flowing*, trans. T. Whitney (London, 1973), pp. 19, 21.
56. A. Rozen, *Poslednie dve nedeli, Zvezda*, 1965, no. 1.
57. V. Kozhevnikov, *Izvestiya*, 20 May 1970.
58. I. Grekova, *Na ispytaniyakh, NM*, 1967, no. 7.
59. A. Brumberg (ed.), *In Quest of Justice* (London, 1970), pp. 283–9.
60. L. Finkelstein, letter. Grekova herself decided not to circulate the novel in *samizdat*.
61. R. Medvedev, Zh. Medvedev, *A Question of Madness*, trans. E. de Kadt (London, 1971), p. 44.
62. D. Granin, *Povesti i rasskazy* (L, 1970), p. 55.
63. I. Shevtsov, *Lyubov i nenavist* (M, 1970), pp. 210, 241–2.
64. N. Dubinin, *Vechnoe dvizhenie* (M, 1973).
65. A. Kron, *Bessonnitsa, NM*, 1977, nos. 4–6.
66. Yu. Trifonov, *Dom na naberezhnoi, DN*, 1976, no. 1; cf. Trifonov, *Studenty, NM*, 1950, nos. 10, 11.
67. V. Dudintsev, *LO*, 1976, no. 5, pp. 48–52.
68. M. Mihajlov, *Moscow Summer*, trans. A. Field (London, 1966), p. 44.
69. G. Markov, *LG*, 23 June 1976.
70. *LR*, 2 July 1976; *LO*, 1977, no. 4.
71. Svirsky, *Soviet Writing*, p. 433.
72. I. Gerasimovich, *Effekt polozheniya, Znamya*, 1979, nos. 11, 12.
73. *Pravda*, 21 Dec. 1979; *Kommunist*, 1979, no. 18, pp. 25–46.
74. Cohen, *End to Silence*, p. 47.
75. M. Popovsky, *Delo Akademika Vavilova* (Ann Arbor, 1983); S. Polikanov, *Razryv* (Frankfurt, 1983).
76. L. Kopelev, *No Jail for Thought*, trans. and ed. A. Austin (Harmondsworth, 1979); D. Panin, *The Notebooks of Sologdin*, trans. J. Moore (London, 1976); G. Svirsky, *Zalozhniki* (Paris, 1974).
77. M. Frankland, *Observer*, 13 Jan. 1985.

2   SCIENCE AND TECHNOLOGY IN THE POST-STALIN ERA 1953–64

Inevitably, in demanding revelations about the past, Khrushchev was forced to invite discussion and potential criticism of his own government's policy towards science. Although fiction dealing with the contemporary post-Stalin era 1953–64 does not provide a systematic examination of the strengths and weaknesses of Soviet science, it nevertheless shows, by focusing attention on specific characters and situations, that there were a number of problems which remained to be solved. Some of these were a direct result of the Stalin era, while others were persistent difficulties endemic in the Soviet system itself.

As a result of Khrushchev's de-Stalinisation policy there was a gradual relaxation of the control formerly exercised over science and technology by the armed forces, ideologists and administrators. The party began to encourage technological innovation, develop new scientific centres and emphasise the need for more frequent meetings between Soviet specialists and their foreign colleagues. In the mid-1950s scientists ventures to criticise political dogmatism in scientific debate and to call for greater democratisation in science.[1] In the years 1953–64 scientific authority gradually returned to the scientists themselves.

Reforms of the scientific establishment in 1957, 1959, 1961 and 1963 aimed at improving the administration of a complex system and eradicating the worst aspects of the bureaucracy's influence on science under Stalin. However, party leaders and scientists continued to point out shortcomings in the system of organisation. In 1961 the President of the Academy of Sciences, M. V. Keldysh, censured duplication of research, concentration on unimportant work and delays in the application of scientific achievements, while A. N. Kosygin, First Deputy Chairman of the Council of Ministers, discussed planning problems and stressed the need for scientists to attain a higher academic standard and give value to the government.[2]

Such criticisms and the constant reorganisation of the scientific administration indicate the nature and scale of the major defects which persisted in Soviet research and development. First, the centralised direction of scientific research frequently led to the harmful interference of political leaders or bureaucratic bodies with little scientific knowledge. Secondly, scientists were still obliged to fit all their conclusions into the straitjacket of Marxist-Leninist ideology. Thirdly, the conservatism in Soviet industry and applied science meant that many valuable ideas and inventions were never developed to the stage of practical application. Fourthly, there were problems associated with the planning of scientific research. Work plans for the future were demanded, and scientists always had to demonstrate the material benefit to be derived from their work, even if they did not necessarily know where their research would lead. Because of this, they wasted time devising work plans convincing enough to gain official acceptance. The party did not approve of 'abstract' topics, so there was often a conflict between the needs of pure and applied science. Finally, individual scientists were not free to choose their own research topics, since a particular importance was attached to group and 'collective' work.

Many of these issues are facets of a general problem which Roy Medvedev has defined as 'the absence of democracy in science — the authoritarian atmosphere and lack of individual freedom, the dominating role of the censor'.[3] All these factors meant that the Soviet Union lagged behind the USA and Western Europe in terms of output of published scientific and scholarly work and in the number of inventions and discoveries by Soviet scientists, even though the USSR possessed as many scientists as any other country in the world. Apart from the discovery of Cherenkov radiation in nuclear physics and Zavoisky's electron-spin resonance, there have been relatively few important discoveries in Soviet research institutes since 1945; the Soviet Union, moreover, sometimes failed to exploit such original discoveries as were made.

This chapter seeks to explore how far literature conforms to the party-sponsored version of reality, and how far it affords insights into the continuing problems in Soviet science and the attitudes of scientists themselves.

The Legacy of Stalinism

Fiction is a unique source of information about the psychological effect of Stalinism on scientists and engineers during this contradictory transitional era when substantial changes occurred, but former attitudes conditioned by the Stalin period still persisted. In *The Thaw* (Part One), the engineer Koroteev is afraid to speak the truth about the dictatorial methods of the factory director Zhuravlyov because he has 'got used to keeping quiet'. He realises that the years of repression have left their mark on him, inculcating lack of principle, indifference to injustice and a discrepancy between belief and action; and he finds it difficult to adapt to the more liberal conditions of the 'thaw'.

Other works suggest that the fear conditioned by Stalinism cannot be easily eradicated among scholars and scientists either. Nagibin's *The Khazar Ornament* (1956) discloses that many scholars in Stalin's time, terrified by the purge of intellectuals, chose obscure fields of study in order to draw less attention to themselves.[4] In Granin's *Into the Storm* the elderly physicist Golitsyn acknowledges his inability to take advantage of the more liberal attitude introduced by the Twentieth Congress, which has allowed a wider range of research topics and a greater emphasis on interdisciplinary studies: 'Fear had eaten into him, penetrated into his brain. He had a certain timidity in the face of generalisations, unexpected associations.' Like Ehrenburg's Koroteev, Golitsyn envies younger men whose 'thought ranged widely, without hesitation'.

Fiction on scientific themes represents just one aspect of the general political debate between 'dogmatists' and 'liberals' about the wisdom of dwelling on the past. While such liberal works as Granin's *After the Wedding*[5] welcome Khrushchev's rehabilitation policy, maintaining that the return of purge victims has a beneficial effect on the style of industrial management and inspires young people to tackle difficult jobs in the Virgin Lands, 'dogmatist' writers voice suspicion of the new policy. In *The Ershov Brothers* Kochetov decries the efforts of irresponsible liberals to rehabilitate the engineer Vorobeiny, a former Nazi collaborator. Progressive intellectuals emphasised the need for honesty, the right of former purge victims and young people to speak the whole truth about the past and the imperfect present. The liberal view is expressed by the physicist Krylov in Granin's *Into the Storm*: 'The truth can never hurt.' The neo-Stalinist attitude is evinced by a 'positive' engineer in Kochetov's *Ershov Brothers*: when the 'revisionist' engineer Orleantsev says that it will take a decade or more to liquidate the 'personality cult', Kochetov's hero, speaking for the author, argues that too much attention is being paid to this question; it is more necessary to build up the Soviet economy, to 'produce steel'.

'Stalin's Heirs'

One of the major themes of fiction concerned with science and technology in the post-Stalin period 1953–64 is the continuing power of careerists and bureaucrats in the scientific world. Indeed, the evil bureaucrat, scientist, engineer or factory director appears to be an essential complement to the 'positive' scientist or inventor. The treatment of this theme in conformist fiction was largely a response to the party's criticism of bureaucratic methods of management. The predictable pattern of this kind of literature is the subject of ironic comment in Trifonov's *Quenching of Thirst*: when the journalist narrator is commissioned to write a sketch about the construction of an irrigation canal 'a familiar scheme took shape in his mind: a skirmish between innovators and conservatives. That would do for any article, sketch, film script, for anything you pleased.' However, the persistent criticism by Soviet writers of men who have attained high positions in the world of science and technology also affords illuminating insights into the real situation in Soviet science in the post-Stalin era. After Stalin's death the continuing power of scientific 'monopolies', the persistent need to subordinate science to communist dogma and the inertia of the bureaucratic system in many scientific institutes, together with the climate of secrecy, still tended to produce a special type of opportunist who masked his lack of creative talent by building a successful political career as an administrator or the party organiser of his institute. A career in science was particularly advantageous because, in comparison with other professions in the USSR, scientists and engineers enjoy great prestige, high salaries and desirable material possessions. The position of director of a scientific research institute is one of the most highly coveted in the Soviet Union, and is conferred only as a reward for services to the party and government. In the post-Stalin era many unworthy men who had attained such positions because they were adept at making politically orthodox speeches and censuring their more talented colleagues continued to hinder genuine scientific research.

The theme of bureaucracy also possesses wider political implications. The portrayal of such a large number of villains in Soviet fiction on scientific themes in the period 1953–64 can be attributed to the importance of the problem of 'Stalin's heirs'. The fundamental social conflict in the post-Stalin era was the struggle for de-Stalinisation and the increasing liberalisation of Soviet life. De-Stalinisation in science was not merely a question of abstract principles or of the methods employed by Stalin himself, but a more concrete attack on the powers and prerogatives of the tenacious 'Old Guard' of Stalinist functionaries in the Academy of Sciences, universities and economic ministries. Such men had built successful careers under Stalin and were concerned with defending their past records, present positions and the future of their children. Accordingly, that fiction of the post-Stalin era which treated the theme of the bureaucratic hindrance of scientific research touched directly upon one of the major political questions of the age.

The attack on bureaucracy in scientific fiction was, however, not confined to officials in the scientific world, but, by implication, extended to cliques of Stalinist dogmatists who occupied key positions in the party and administrative hierarchy and in literature — such men as N. Lesyuchevsky, director of the Sovetskii Pisatel Publishing House, A. Surkov, Secretary of the Writers' Union, A. Sofronov, Secretary of the Writers' Union of the RSFSR, D. Polikarpov, head of the Central Committee's Department of Culture, and, after the defeat of the 'Anti-Party Group' in 1957, such hard-line members of the Presidium as M. Suslov and F. Kozlov. Thus, literary debates about the presentation of bureaucrats in such works as Leonov's *Russian Forest*, Granin's *The Seekers* and Dudintsev's *Not by Bread Alone* reflected the deep division between 'liberals' and 'dogmatists' in Soviet society as a whole.

The character of the bureaucrat Drozdov in Dudintsev's novel possessed far-reaching implications for both neo-Stalinist literary officials and the party and government bureaucracy. For the Soviet intelligentsia in the 1950s, 'Drozdov' and 'Drozdovism' came to connote the most loathsome characteristics of the over-powerful, over-privileged bureaucracy. In an outspoken speech not published in the Soviet Union the respected writer Konstantin Paustovsky connected Drozdov with a widespread group of corrupt, highly-placed Soviet bureaucrats possessing anti-Soviet traits: 'a new group of acquisitive carnivores . . . which has nothing in common either with the Revolution, or with our regime, or with socialism' and uses weapons of 'betrayal, calumny, moral assassination and just plain assassination'.[6] Khrushchev himself cannot have been unaware that the growing power of the alliance between the state bureaucracy and the technical elite, to which Dudintsev had draw~ attention, had been clearly demonstrated in 1957, when the tʷ groups had pitted their combined strength against the party ʾ struggle for political power. He found it expedient to link e

writers such as Dudintsev with the 'Anti-Party Group' of politicians, while at the same time attacking the Group for allegedly
having denigrated such honest writers as the poet Maksim Rylsky.
Khrushchev asserted that Dudintsev 'is not imbued with concern
about the elimination of the defects he sees in our life; he deliberately lays it on thick, gloats over the defects'.[7] After his defeat of the
'Anti-Party Group', however, Khrushchev found it unnecessary to
continue attacking *Not by Bread Alone*, since Dudintsev had not
explicitly included the party hierarchy in his criticism of bureaucracy. At the Third Congress of Soviet Writers in 1959 Khrushchev
claimed that he had read Dudintsev's novel with interest, and that
although the author had exaggerated negative features of Soviet
society he 'was never our enemy and was not an opponent of the
Soviet system'.

   Two other works which were subjected to criticism in 1957 were
Granin's story *Personal Opinion* (1956) and Nikolai Gorbunov's
The Mistake (A Professor's Monologue) (1957) which both provide
radical, pessimistic treatments of the general corruption in Soviet
science and society.[8] Granin, a party member, appears to have been
chastened by the reprimand he received in 1957.[9] Mark Popovsky,
another pessimistic critic of Soviet science, considers that *Personal
Opinion* was a genuine attempt to depict the reality of Soviet
science, but that Granin subsequently 'changed' (presumably because of political pressure) and after 1956 became incapable of
writing the truth.[10] The unpalatable nature of Gorbunov's theme
for both scientific and literary dogmatists is demonstrated by the
censure of Yakov Elsberg, a critic notorious as a secret police agent
responsible for the denunciation and arrest of fellow writers, who
attacked *The Mistake* for creating a 'sceptical estimate of scientific
work' and painting a false picture of 'the degeneration and indifference of the new generation of scholars'.[11]

   The reason for such sharp polemics in literary debates on scientific themes in the years 1956–7 is that, while progressive writers and
scientists were united in their hope for a general investigation of the
adverse effects of Stalinism on both art and science, the literary
bureaucrats who still exerted great influence in the post-Stalin era
were the equivalent of Lysenko and Olshansky, the persecuters and
denouncers of honest scientists. The major issue which agitated
both the scientific and artistic intelligentsia was the problem of
responsibility for the purges of their colleagues. Would the men
of the imprisonment and death of such eminent scientists as

the geneticist Nikolai Vavilov be brought to trial and punished? In Vavilov's case a trial would, evidently, have implicated the highest party leadership — Molotov and the Presidium. This debate was one result of the ferment caused by the release and rehabilitation of millions of prisoners. Many of those returning from the prisons and camps sought some kind of retaliation against those responsible for their suffering: those who had compiled false evidence, conducted the interrogations, tortures and trials. Many people involved in such repressions still occupied high positions, and the Central Committee and Procurator General's office were inundated with petitions affirming the complicity of senior officials in the governmental and scientific hierarchies. It became known from underground publications, for example, that the then current Minister of Higher Education of the RSFSR, V. Stoletov, had been responsible for the arrest and execution of many scientists and selection specialists in Saratov, and that Lysenko had caused the arrests of many prominent geneticists. In the literary world such bureaucrats and police collaborators as Lesyuchevsky and Elsberg felt threatened by the changed climate. Sometimes the charges led to a minor demotion, as in the cases of Stoletov and Elsberg, but as Khrushchev and many of his closest associates had been involved in the Stalin terror, the radical demands of ex-prisoners for legal redress and safeguards against any possibility of a return to repression could obviously not be granted.

Kaverin touches on this delicate topic in *Dual Portrait*, illustrating the shock that the release of purge victims caused their former accusers. The pseudo-scientist Snegirev, who was responsible for the arrest of the talented Ostrogradsky, hopes to be able to bribe his rival into concealing his falsification of scientific data, relying on the humility and submissiveness which he will have learnt in the camp. The end of the novel is inconclusive: Ostrogradsky dies before he can be rehabilitated, and Snegirev retains his influence, although his position is becoming increasingly precarious. Anatoly Rybakov's *Summer in Sosnyaki* (1964) also testifies to the impact of Khrushchev's de-Stalinisation campaign, describing the suicide of an engineer out of remorse for having denounced his former superior under pressure from the secret police.[12] This theme would, for many Soviet intellectuals, have evoked the fate of Alexander Fadeyev, Chairman of the Writers' Union, who had been responsible for the arrest of fellow writers, and committed suicide in 1956 when those he had denounced began to return from the camps.

The most detailed treatment of the theme of 'Stalin's heirs' is contained in Bek's *New Appointment*. The central character, Onisimov, is modelled on I. F. Tevosyan, Minister of Ferrous Metallurgy under Stalin. Tevosyan's widow used her influence to prevent the publication of this novel, and even when Bek added a scene in which Tevosyan appears under his own name as a friend of Onisimov, accompanied by his charming wife, this could not save the work. One passage which apparently roused the ire of P. Demichev, head of the Central Committee's Ideological Department, and later of no less a person than Kosygin himself,[13] was the description of a quarrel between Stalin and Ordzhonikidze in 1937. On this occasion, although unable to understand a word of their argument conducted in Georgian, Onisimov betrayed Ordzhonikidze, his friend and immediate superior, by slavishly supporting Stalin's viewpoint. Subsequently, when Onisimov confesses that his half-brother has been arrested as an 'enemy of the people', Stalin writes on a scrap of paper 'I count you among my friends', and Onisimov is abjectly grateful. The controversy which Bek's novel caused in the higher echelons of the party leadership suggests that his picture of the incompetent minister who only managed to survive because of his extreme obsequiousness to Stalin was too realistic for comfort.

After Stalin's death Onisimov is demoted to the post of ambassador to a quiet North European country, and he dies from heart failure, a disease partly caused by the psychological impact of de-Stalinisation. Onisimov's last years are particularly reminiscent of those of his prototype Tevosyan, a prominent supporter of Malenkov, who became Soviet ambassador to Japan in 1956 and died in 1958. Bek's portrait might also have recalled the fate of Molotov, demoted by Khrushchev to the post of ambassador to Mongolia. The ban on the publication of Bek's novel shows that the Soviet authorities were unwilling to permit writers to provide a comprehensive analysis of the problem of 'Stalin's heirs'.

'Fathers and Sons'

Another delicate issue connected with the de-Stalinisation campaign was the conflict between 'fathers and sons'. First, this involved the scorn of the younger generation, many of whose fathers had perished in the purges of the 1930s, for the generation of 'fathers' who had either actively participated in Stalin's crimes or passively acquiesced in them and managed to survive. Secondly, young people felt contempt for older men who had adopted formal, bureaucratic attitudes under Stalin which they were later unable to discard. In both cases they had forfeited all moral authority for the future and, if de-Stalinisation were to become effective, would have to be made to retire, instead of dictating to the young.

From a more general standpoint, the 'fathers and sons' conflict illustrates the impatience of young people everywhere to replace their elders. In the Soviet Union of the early 1960s young people were exerting pressure to extend their influence on politics, science, the economy and the arts. The very vehemence with which the existence of any conflict between the generations was denied, even by Khrushchev himself, indicates the seriousness of the problem.[14] Clearly the 'fathers' had a psychological and ideological need to erect a defence mechanism in order to avoid the question posed by a young scientist in Granin's *Into the Storm*: 'How could you have allowed the events of 1937 to happen?'

Although in 1963 Tvardovsky denied that the concept of 'fathers and sons' was applicable to the scientific intelligentsia,[15] a number of literary works of the early 1960s dealt with this theme. In his story *A Piece of Glass* (1960), Kaverin points a contrast between the older generation of scientists whose experience of the Stalin era has taught them to manoeuvre and intrigue to maintain their positions, and younger scientists who pursue their research for its own sake and cannot understand the machinations of their elders. However, Kaverin advances the view that the main issue in contemporary science is not the traditional 'fathers and sons' dispute, or even the conservatism of the older generation, but a conflict between progressive and reactionary scientists of any generation.[16] Similarly, in Granin's *Into the Storm* the eventual reconciliation between the physicist Golitsyn and his young protégé Krylov reflects the alliance which began to develop from about 1962 between young scientists and prominent liberal scientists of the older generation.

Another permutation of the 'fathers and sons' dispute is highlighted in Alexander Popovsky's *Tale of Chlorella* (1963), an interesting study of the differences between the three generations of scientists in the 1960s.[17] The dispute between a respected elderly biologist, Professor Sviridov, and his middle-aged careerist son, an institute director whose outlook has been formed by the Stalin era, exemplifies the contrast between the 'fathers' and 'grandfathers' — the brave old men born before the Revolution who represented spiritual link with the West and the pre-Stalin era, both nineteen century Russia and the experimentally-minded Soviet Union of the 1920s. This was a topical issue in 1963, as Khrushchev had praised such men in a speech to Soviet writers, and many young authors had expressed their debt to such older men as Pasternak, Ehrenburg, Paustovsky and Kataev in answer to a questionnaire.[18] Popovsky shows that whereas Sviridov's son is an opportunist only concerned with pleasing the authorities, his idealistic young pupil Zolotaryov is a member of the generation of 'sons' who acts as a true disciple of Professor Sviridov.

Nationalism

In the post-Stalin era there was a steady, though not spectacular, increase of ties with foreign scientists. Fiction reflects the new party line, describing visits by foreign specialists to the USSR and trips abroad by Soviet scientists. Bylinov's sketch *An Engineer's Duty* is interesting for its portrayal of the visit of a group of Chinese engineers to a Soviet factory (a subject subsequently banned during the Sino-Soviet dispute). Bylinov demonstrates that honest engineers are no longer afraid of admitting the backwardness of Soviet technology to foreigners; it is only conservative officials who try to conceal the truth.[19] Trifonov's *Quenching of Thirst,* published after Khrushchev's visit to the USA, presents foreign approval as a criterion of the worth of a technological innovation: a new 'bulldozer method' of canal construction, attacked by Stalinist bureaucrats, is triumphantly vindicated when it is praised at a conference in America.

While recognising the need to learn from foreign specialists, Khrushchev was nevertheless convinced, both as a communist and as a Russian, of his country's superiority. He blamed Stalin's terror for the gap between Soviet and Western technology, and still emphasised the intensifying 'general crisis of capitalism' which would allegedly become sharper when the 'temporary factors' supporting capitalist industrial expansion in the 1950s were exhausted. It was claimed that the USSR could progress more rapidly in the pursuit of knowledge than the West and apply that knowledge in a more humane and effective way. Fiction of the post-Stalin era reflects this ambivalent attitude towards nationalism in science. Bek's *Life of Berezhkov*, for example, while presenting national pride and anti-foreign feeling as a powerful spur to a Soviet engineer's research, nevertheless emphasises the necessity and usefulness of assimilating Western technology.

The continuing struggle in the post-Stalin period between members of the intelligentsia who advocated scientific internationalism and dogmatists who still stressed the superiority of 'socialist' science is attested by the critical reception to Dudintsev's *Not by Bread Alone*. Dudintsev's own justification for his novel was a patriotic desire to make Soviet technology equal or superior to that of the West; his disillusionment during the war when he saw German Messerschmitts shoot down Russian planes convinced him that over-optimistic propaganda did no service to the cause of technological innovation.[20] Some critics, however, indignant at Dudintsev's apparent denigration of Soviet technology, enlisted the USSR's victory in the war, the design of Soviet aircraft, the invention of ballistic missiles and the launching of satellites to prove that the picture Dudintsev painted was incorrect.[21]

By the late 1950s it was possible for Soviet writers to express their own views about the need for international scientific co-operation, reflecting ideas prevalent among the scientific intelligentsia. The physicist Chukhlyaev in Gor's *University Embankment*, who visits Paris to study foreign methods, asks: 'What would happen if the physical and mathematical conceptions of the modern Japanese, Chinese, Russian, American and Frenchmen were based on different postulates? Science would not exist. Mathematics and physics are something objective, meaningful to everyone.' It was, however, still necessary for Gor to 'balance' such sentiments with the firmly expressed conviction that the Soviet system creates more favourable conditions for the development of science than Western capitalism. Because of the launching of the sputnik and other space missions, the cautious attitude of the party leaders gave way to a new surge of optimism about the USSR's technological capabilities at the Twenty-First Congress of 1959. This resurgent scientific nationalism was echoed by literary dogmatists: a character in Kozhevnikov's *Introduce Yourself, Baluev!* (1960) maintains that America would give millions of tons of steel in return for knowledge about Soviet sputniks and rockets.[22]

Although in the post-Stalin period lip-service was paid to the need to encourage contacts with Western scientists, the works of liberal writers indicate that the real situation in Soviet science did not in fact change all that radically after 1953, and that the bureaucracy still hindered international scientific co-operation. Granin's *Into the Storm* suggests that administrators with little knowledge of science were often sent to foreign congresses in the place of genuine scientists, and that many Stalinist attitudes persisted: the bureaucrat Lagunov, referring to meetings between Soviet and foreign scientists, states: 'This fashion will not produce any good results.'

Fiction of the period 1953–64 was unable to mention the negative side of Khrushchev's policy of duplicating foreign technology: the fact that, because they feared novelty and the risk of being held responsible in case of failure, conservative officials tended to prefer the adaptation of foreign models. The exploitation of Western scientific and technical knowledge was conducted on a large scale; an almost military-style operation was mounted to translate and summarise articles from Western scientific journals for the Soviet journal *Referaty*. The large-scale copying of American patents was known colloquially as 'translating from the American' (*perevod s amerikanskogo*); and there was a Soviet joke on this subject: 'Who is the greatest Russian scientist?' 'Reguspatoff' (the US Registered Patent Office).

Secrecy

Closely related to scientific chauvinism was another legacy of Stalinism which came under scrutiny after 1953 — the problem of excessive secrecy in the scientific and technical sphere. Soviet specialists worked in isolation from the outside world, and even from other Soviet research establishments and factories. Many books and journals, including most foreign periodicals, were withdrawn from general access in libraries and transferred to the *spetskhran* (library storage for forbidden literature). Soviet people were frequently very ill-informed about important issues, as the censorship forbade any mention of a large range of topics listed in a special handbook, the *Index of Information not to be Published in the Open Press*. The names of certain factories and institutes, breakdowns in experimental research, information about fires, explosions, aeroplane, naval and mine disasters, and even major catastrophes like the 1958 nuclear explosion in the Urals and the 1960 cosmodrome accident were concealed from the public. However, by 1955 both scientists and party leaders began to criticise the unreasonable secrecy which led to duplication of research and the absence of fruitful discussion.[23]

Kaverin took advantage of this official criticism in *Searches and Hopes*, attacking 'that fantastic secrecy, that gloom in which we could hardly distinguish one another!' Even in 1956, he claims, scientists 'haven't come to grips with that ignorant rubbish, that mysterious nonsense which was surrounded with protective barbed wire fences and preserved in sealed safes at the end of the working day'. Other writers suggest that the excessive secrecy in factories still prevented the free exchange of ideas about new technology. The Tartar writer A. Absalyamov asserts in *The Unquenchable Fire* (1959) that enormous government economies could be made if knowledge were shared among neighbouring Soviet institutions.[24] L. Rotov's sketch *An Engineer in the Glavk* makes a sharper criticism of an engineer who labels everything as secret, even insisting that ordinary foreign technical journals can only be made accessible to those with a special permit.

In the early 1960s specific Soviet research institutions began to be mentioned in literature. Khrushchev's willingness to lift the veil of secrecy was demonstrated by his decision to turn the town of Dubna on the Volga, a large centre for theoretical research in atomic physics established during Stalin's time, into an open town. Dubna forms the setting of Voznesensky's poem *Oza* (1964): and another prestigious open centre created by Khrushchev, Akademgorodok near Novosibirsk, is mentioned in Granin's *Into the Storm*. A further innovation in Soviet literature at this time was the depiction of secret research institutes. The number of such establishments had grown rapidly in connection with the space programme, but the censorship had formerly been under the strictest orders not to allow in print any oblique reference to these secret installations. However, this ban appears to have been relaxed for the first time in 1961, probably because of the self-confidence induced by Gagarin's first manned space flight in April. The first literary work on the subject was Grekova's documentary sketch *Beyond the Checkpoint* (1962), which makes no attempt to conceal the unimpressive look of the institute, situated in a dismal suburb and badly in need of repair.[25] Perhaps such general allusions to secret establishments were permitted in order to satisfy public curiosity about the people responsible for the party's military and space programmes without divulging any real secrets.

By the early 1960s the party leaders had also become sufficiently confident about the achievements of Soviet science to allow writers to introduce another new subject: the problem of accidents incurred in the course of scientific work. Grekova mentions the blinding of a scientist during an experiment; Chakovsky's *The Light of a Distant Star* (1962) depicts the death of a girl during the testing of a new rocket fuel in a secret chemical research institute; while Aksyonov's novella *A Starry Ticket* (1961) and Granin's *Into the Storm* portray scientists who die in plane crashes.[26] Since the party had introduced a new, stringent secrets law in April 1956, and the press was still forbidden to mention real accidents in the 1960s, it seems likely that the emergence of this new literary theme was due more to the attempts of writers themselves to widen their subject matter than to a significant change in party policy.

In the wake of the events in Poland and Hungary in 1956, and again in 1960, after the U-2 incident, ideologues and the secret police began to issue warnings about the dangers of liberalisation: the penetration of bourgeois ideology into the USSR; the risk of foreign espionage; and the possibility that the relaxed standards of secrecy might convey valuable scientific information to the enemy. This theme was taken up by the dogmatist Kochetov, who in *The Secretary of the District Party Committee* (1961) attempted to return to the mystique which surrounded secret scientific work under Stalin, portraying a chemical engineer who refuses to tell his mother the exact nature of his work, boasting that it is a state secret, and perhaps a military one too.[27]

Some liberal writers in the 1960s, however, criticised the caution of conservative officials and demonstrated that the problem of excessive secrecy remained serious. In *Tested in the Sky*, Mark Gallai derides the methods employed by vigilant officials in order to maintain secrecy: photographs given to him as souvenirs of his collision with a rook on a test flight are taken away because they show tiny parts of an experimental plane. More recent testimony by dissidents has corroborated such hints in Soviet fiction, emphasising that secrecy did indeed seriously hinder scientific research in the post-Stalin period.[28]

Anti-Semitism

Fiction shows that after Stalin's death anti-Semitism still existed among the bureaucracy responsible for science and technology. In his unpublished speech on Dudintsev's *Not by Bread Alone* Paustovsky described 'deputy ministers, very highly placed administrative officials and other very exalted personages' as 'cynics, obscurantists and anti-Semites . . . who had destroyed the country's most remarkable men and continued to weigh heavily on the country'.[29] Although the excesses of Stalin's anti-cosmopolitan campaign had ended and the indispensability of certain Jews prominent in physics and mathematics was recognised, it was still difficult for Jewish students to enter universities and institutes and to progress in a scientific career.

One published work which subtly touches upon this taboo subject is Granin's *Into the Storm*, which exposes the anti-Semitism of the Stalinist administrator Agatov who uses a common technique to embarrass the Jewish physicist Richard. Referring to the pseudo-scientist Denisov, Agatov asks Richard, who is not addressed by his Jewish surname elsewhere in the novel: 'Don't you like this *Russian* scientist, Comrade Goldin?' Discussion of anti-Semitism in the Khrushchev period is, however, mostly confined to dissident literature. In *Cancer Ward*, for example, Solzhenitsyn shows that the suspicion of Jewish doctors stirred up by the 'Doctors' Plot' still remained among the bureaucracy during the post-Stalin era.

Continuing Problems in Soviet Science

Post-Stalin fiction on scientific themes reflects both the party's attempt to reform Soviet science from above, and the lively contemporary discussions on the state of science by scientists themselves. De-Stalinisation and liberalisation raised scientists' hopes and expectations in much the same way as they had artists', encouraging some leading figures in Soviet science to speak their minds on the issues which perturbed them.

At the Twentieth Congress Khrushchev and Bulganin criticised the organisation of the country's scientific institutes, and it was proposed that all scientists be encouraged to discuss the future path of development of Soviet science. However, meetings of the Academy did not take their prescribed course, and such controversial issues as the methods of supervising scientific research were discussed, while interference with the free exchange of opinion and excessive political control over scientific activity came in for sharp censure. By 1957 the party had become afraid that the condemnation of the Soviet system of scientific administration had gone too far and was endangering dialectical materialism. Criticism was halted, and from 1957 onward the party directed scientific discussions.

Although Khrushchev, through his de-Stalinisation policy, had initially won support among Soviet scientists, by the 1960s he frequently came into conflict with the scientific community. His decision to reorganise the Academy in 1960 was strongly opposed for more than a year; and when eventually he was driven to introduce the reform without the Academy's co-operation, the President, Academician A. N. Nesmeyanov, was forced to resign. In the 1960s Khrushchev also clashed with individual scientists such as Sakharov, who opposed his decision to continue nuclear tests, and Kapitsa, to whom he refused permission to travel abroad. In June 1963 Khrushchev further alienated the scientific community by calling a special party plenum to discuss ideological orientation in science, literature and art.

Khrushchev's conflict with the scientific elite contributed to his downfall. In his report at the Party Plenum in October 1964 Suslov cited Khrushchev's attempted closure of the Timiryazev Agricultural Academy, his support for Lysenko and his decision to reorganise the Academy of Sciences into a Committee of Science in 1964 as among the reasons for his dismissal.[30] Other issues of concern to scientists which were not mentioned, such as Khrushchev's educational reform of 1958 and his exploitation of space technology for purely political reasons, probably also played a significant part. Naturally, literature published before Khrushchev's fall was unable to delve deeply into such questions. Some works, however, contain clues about certain areas of conflict between scientists and the Soviet authorities in the period 1953–64.

Administrative Problems

The organisation of science in the USSR created certain specific problems which can be deduced from Soviet fiction. In Bek's *Life of Berezhkov* an aircraft designer is taught the apparently obvious lesson that he should not duplicate other scientists' research — this implies that such duplication did in fact occur. Kaverin's story *A Piece of Glass*, which depicts the difficulties experienced by a physiologist in obtaining a small, but essential piece of glass for his research, leads us to infer that some Soviet scientists had difficulty in procuring adequate apparatus.

Perhaps because of the harsh attacks on writers in the years 1956–7, fiction published in the period 1957–64 did not provide such a frank condemnation of the bureaucracy in Soviet science as literature of the first 'thaw'. However, the persistent portrayal in Soviet fiction of individual bureaucrats and careerists, notably in Granin's novel *Into the Storm*, published in the second 'thaw' of 1962, indicated that many problems still remained in the structure of Soviet science. Granin's portrait of Lagunov, an eminent scientific administrator who was once a good scientist, but lost interest in research when entrusted with administrative responsibility, suggests that when science is highly organised and centralised, as it is in the USSR, there is a danger that scientists selected for important administrative posts may prefer the stability of power to the insecurity of a research laboratory.

Granin's novel also shows that even after successive reforms of the Academy in 1959 and 1961 there was still a conflict in science, as in industry, between the plan fixed by authority and the interests and initiative of individual specialists. An untalented bureaucrat imagines sitting in luxurious offices and conference chambers, concerned not with science, but 'the world of plans — plans which are approved, innovatory, grandiose, effective, efficient and overfulfilled . . . ' Granin does, however, express some sympathy for planners, emphasising that it is difficult to allocate resources and establish deadlines in scientific research, as it is impossible for a scientist to predict how long it will take him to achieve results. He disarms potential criticism of his exposure of administrative problems in science through his portrait of a 'positive' official eager to encourage scientific progress, who complains ruefully that a scientist's errors may be inevitable or even fruitful, whereas a government official has no right to make mistakes, since they waste the state's time and money.

Another topic treated in *Into the Storm* is the desire of scientists for greater freedom to pursue theoretical research. Throughout most of the post-Stalin period fiction had closely reflected the traditional emphasis on technology or 'applied natural science' directed towards beneficial and tangible ends. 'Pure science' is an unpopular term in the USSR because of its connotations of 'bourgeois individualism'; the preferred Soviet phrase is 'theoretical' or 'fundamental' science. After 1956 the Soviet scientific establishment gradually began to change; the more favourable attitude towards fundamental research, reflected in literature of the early 1960s,[31] sprang from the realisation that most of the really great discoveries in science originate from fundamental research, and that the USSR, with its insistence on the primacy of production and applied science, had remained backward in this area.

It was not until 1961, however, that official changes were made embodying scientists' demands that the Academy should concentrate on fundamental research: a State Committee for Theoretical Research was established, and applied research and development

institutes were transferred to the state organs. The changed climate
is evident from Granin's depiction in *Into the Storm* of an unconventional press conference in which the brilliant theoretical physicist
Dankevich defends the study of a scientific problem for its own
sake. When a journalist asks, 'What's the purpose of your
research?', he replies, 'We will obtain scientific results.' He refuses
to work for the utilitarian aim of benefiting Soviet industry: when
asked: 'What will that give our technology?', Dankevich states that
it will not 'increase the production of pig iron', but is 'simply an
interesting problem'. He realistically admits that he cannot predict
the results of his research, for 'If a research worker knew every time
precisely what he wanted to achieve, we would never discover
anything new.' Granin thus implicitly denies the value of scientific
planning and reflects the growing anxiety in the USSR that all the
greatest discoveries in contemporary science were being made
abroad. He shows that scientists continued to desire greater
freedom for theoretical research, although there was still much
prejudice against it: Dankevich's project is opposed by conservative
officials, his funds are cut and many of his staff desert him.

Granin was, however, unable, even in 1962, to give unequivocal
support to 'pure science' and completely abandon the conventional
notion of the relationship between science and technology. His
depiction of Dankevich's work, which quite rapidly proves to have
practical benefits for space navigation, radio technology and radio
astronomy, shows that in 1962 the party's criteria for judging
scientific research continued to be its ultimate success and potential
practical significance. Evidently scientists were still supposed to be
guided by the aim of using their completed research in the Soviet
economy; the pursuit of knowledge for its own sake was not encouraged. It was not until the 1963 reform that the Academy was
given more power in the planning and co-ordination of fundamental
research.

Although official propaganda favoured applied science and industrial production throughout most of the post-Stalin decade,
Soviet fiction suggests, rather surprisingly, that scientists harbour a
prejudice against practical work in industry, and that research,
theoretical work and teaching bring both greater prestige and
higher salaries. In Granin's *The Seekers* Lobanov, a gifted research
worker, disappoints his professor by leaving the scientific institute
to work in an industrial laboratory. A fellow scientist assumes that
Lobanov must have managed to keep the salary to which his candi-

date's degree entitled him as long as he stayed in a university or research institute, but Lobanov replies that he was willing to accept a reduction of 700 roubles a month for the opportunity of doing interesting work in industrial technology. Lobanov gains the sarcastic epithet 'altruist' for this attitude, and it is a fair assumption that such idealism was not particularly common among Soviet scientists. The prejudice against practical technicians is voiced even more clearly in Solzhenitsyn's *For the Good of the Cause* (1963). A party secretary asserts frankly:

In this country of ours they're always making such a fuss over the top scientists. They don't seem to think that anyone with less than an engineering degree has any education at all. But for us in industry it's the technicians who matter most of all. Yet technical schools get a raw deal.[32]

Here Solzhenitsyn appears to favour Khrushchev's controversial educational reform of 1958 which attempted to bridge the gap between manual and intellectual work by insisting that students should spend two years working in industry before entering an institute of higher education. Solzhenitsyn admits that *For the Good of the Cause* was one of the few works which he composed consciously and deliberately for publication in *Novy Mir*;[33] but it has not hitherto been emphasised by Western scholars that Solzhenitsyn was not averse, in 1963, to advocating views which were broadly in line with those of the First Secretary of the Communist Party.

The division between scientists and technicians represents one aspect of a wider problem which began to find reflection in post-Stalin fiction: the prejudice against manual labour and the superior status enjoyed by people with a higher education. In Victor Rozov's play *In Good Time!* (1955), the wife of a doctor of biological sciences threatens her son with the awful alternative open to him if he cannot have a scientific career: 'You'll be left with nothing, you'll go to a factory and work on a machine.'[34] Rozov indicates that there is great competition for places in scientific and technical institutes, and that highly-placed people use influence and intrigue to get their children accepted in these establishments.

The Individual and the Collective

A significant theme treated by Soviet writers in the post-Stalin era is the role of the talented individual, or the genius, in the scientific world. By the 1950s Soviet science had become a mass profession of about a million workers. The major benefits to the state of such large-scale scientific work are that science can be strictly controlled and that vast resources and manpower can be deployed on specific important projects. The disadvantages are that quantity of scientists does not necessarily produce quality of scientific research, and that scientists themselves may lose all sense of individual purpose and fulfilment. Conformist literature stresses the need for an individual, even the most gifted, to work as a disciplined member of a group and to obey the dictates of the party. However, some liberal works of the post-Stalin period imply that the talented man may be forced into a solitary way of life which places him in conflict with the party or government bureaucracy.

Bek's *Life of Berezhkov* and Granin's *The Seekers* testify to the dilemma afflicting all Soviet writers who attempt to portray a 'positive hero'. They are obliged to depict a character who is both docile and effective simultaneously, accepting without question the party's emphasis on disciplined collective work to create the communist future, while acting with vigour and initiative in the solution of all immediate problems encountered in the present. There appears to be a constant tension in Soviet fiction between the depiction of science as an heroic activity (exemplified by the frequent references to great Russian scientists of the past) and the exhortations to contemporary scientists to be modest servants of the party. Bek and Granin condemn the very characteristics which Western writers would appreciate in a talented man: inspiration, individualism, brilliance and eccentricity. Yet the need for Berezhkov and Lobanov to be politically re-educated by party officials is a tacit admission that the scientist's individualist desire to pursue his own research may sometimes conflict with the party's demand for collective scientific work performed for a practical, planned goal.

Granin expounds the conventional Soviet line that love of science, not the desire for personal fame, is the proper spur to a scientist's work. It is Tonkov, Lobanov's antagonist, who argues that the years of work and dedication which the inventor spends on developing his 'dream instrument' are wasted when another specialist improves it further. Although Lobanov repudiates this suggestion, contending that collective, perhaps anonymous scientific work is replacing the lone genius of the past, it may well be that

Granin is expressing, through the mouth of his negative character, the fears of some Soviet scientists about the insignificance of their research. Gifted Soviet scientists surely cannot be immune to personal ambition and the excitement of discovery depicted in such works as J. D. Watson's *The Double Helix*, which has been translated into Russian. Indeed, this inference is corroborated by Kochetov's *Youth is With Us*, which complains that, although group work is the most effective, scientists actually have a preference for individual research, disliking collective work because it prevents them from working independently and gaining fame and rewards.

While Granin's *The Seekers* had admitted that a talented inventor might be forced into 'temporary solitude' until his work received official recognition, Dudintsev's *Not by Bread Alone* goes even further, implying that an able individual in Soviet society is bound to come into conflict with a bureaucratic monopoly. The villainous Drozdov argues that Lopatkin's individualism is a relic of a past historical period, and that 'We worker ants are necessary . . . But you, a solitary genius, are not needed . . . ' Although Dudintsev makes it plain that Drozdov is cynically misrepresenting the party's emphasis on collective effort, there may be some truth in Drozdov's contention that the party always supports a powerful majority against the most brilliant individual. Mark Popovsky, for example, maintains that the Soviet bureaucracy prefers loyalty and mediocrity to brilliance and eccentricity, and that Einstein would have had no chance of building a career in Soviet science.[35]

During the second 'thaw' of the early 1960s Granin's *Into the Storm* once again raised the issue of the gifted individual's role in society, suggesting that some Soviet scientists felt discouraged by the proliferation of scientific workers and the loss of all sense of personal worth. The young physicist Tulin, depressed by the failure of his research, feels that there is no point in striving for scientific achievement: 'If only I were a genius . . . But the most I can do is to beat others by half a year. If I don't solve the problem others will. Hundreds of scientists are working on the same thing. There are enough scientists, nowadays.'

Granin also discusses the particular problems connected with scientific genius through his portraits of the eminent experimental physicist Anikeev, possibly modelled on Kapitsa, and the theoretical physicist Dankevich, perhaps based on Landau. His judgement is ambivalent: admiration and a reluctant acceptance of their individualism are combined with an awareness that fanaticism, inhumanity and dictatorial behaviour are the inevitable concomitants of genius, and that young scientists may have their creative originality destroyed by working for such men. Granin's portrayal of Anikeev and Dankevich reflects the disillusionment felt by some young Soviet scientists who complained that only academicians were allowed to have original ideas. While recognising the importance of collective work for scientists of average talent, Granin is bolder than other authors in stressing the role of individual ability in science.

Through his portrait of the brilliant physicist Dankevich thwarted by a collective of mediocrities, Granin suggests that some Soviet institutes may have been employing considerably more manpower than was justified by results. Dankevich condemns the practice of putting scientific questions to the vote, as the majority is always composed of mediocrities, and makes the controversial point: 'In view of our concern for people it's easier not to take on a good worker than to dismiss a bad one.' Granin's novel reflects the views of Kapitsa, who argued in a pamphlet of 1965 that there was a large and widening gap between Soviet and American science, and recommended that research supervisors should be given more freedom in appointing and dismissing staff.[36]

Ideological Interference with Scientific Research

As we have seen, Soviet science is both highly valued and subject to stringent political control. The Soviet leaders have continually proclaimed that their social and political theories are 'scientific'; therefore, if one were to take these statements literally, one would expect the empirical research of scientists to exert a great deal of influence on the theories of politicians. In reality, however, the opposite situation prevails: the Soviet leaders subject science to an active political interference unprecedented in any other modern state.

The tragic experience of the Stalin period made many Soviet scientists aware of the fundamental discrepancies between science and Soviet ideology; and after Stalin's death, as scientists became stronger and more conscious of their social prestige, they gradually shed the constraints of daily ideological control. It is, however, difficult to determine with any precision the attitude of Soviet scientists towards dialectical materialism in the post-Stalin era: probably some took it seriously, some less seriously, and others felt that it had no useful application to the natural sciences at all. Although many Soviet scientists still interpreted scientific concepts in terms of dialectical materialism,[37] it seems probable that some were merely paying lip-service to the official ideology in order to secure the publication of their work, while continuing to employ the scientific method common to Western tradition.

Most literary works published in the USSR during the post-Stalin period 1953–64, however, still upheld the official view that ideological considerations play an important part in inspiring the research of Soviet scientists, although fiction occasionally suggested that a certain confusion reigned as to the precise influence of ideology on science. The dedication of Soviet scientists, sometimes attributed, in works published before the Twentieth Congress, to the inspiration of Stalin, was later usually ascribed to the ideas of Lenin or to the leadership of the party. It is, moreover, necessary, even in conformist literary works, to draw a distinction between the roles assigned to the party and to Marxist-Leninist philosophy as a spur to scientific work. Following Khrushchev's own policy, the importance of the party is emphasised far more than the value of ideology; and the party is shown to have a political, social and moral, rather than philosophical influence on scientists. Most works on the theme of science and technology contain the stereotyped character of the 'positive' party official who is responsible for the assignment of scientific tasks, the allocation of resources and the ideological education of the scientist hero.

The Soviet public undoubtedly took a sceptical view of stereotyped portraits of the party secretary able to solve all problems at a stroke. In his sketch *Genya and Senya* (1956), Z. Paperny satirises such characters, depicting the official Partkomych (party committee-ich) as a *deus ex machina* — a saviour who arrives for the denouement in a chariot like a god.[38] Nevertheless, in view of the continuing myth of the omnipotent party secretary, it is noteworthy that Soviet writers made no attempt to suggest that party officials exerted any profound philosophical influence on science or played any part in the purely technical side of the scientist's research. There was evidently no place for the non-specialist, even a party official, when dealing with the complex concepts of modern science.

Soviet fiction affords indirect evidence that the desire for a relaxation of political control over their work was a widespread though hidden view among scientists and technologists in the post-Stalin period. The seriousness of this issue can be inferred from the very fact that it was mentioned in Soviet literature at all. Two sketches published in the mid-1950s, Bylinov's *An Engineer's Duty* and V. Kantorovich's *The Story of Engineer Ganshin* (1957), demonstrate that engineers are forced to waste a great deal of their time in political meetings, bureaucratic formalities and compulsory social activities.[39] They do not precisely denigrate the role of ideology, but imply that political control over Soviet engineers should be relaxed, allowing them to show greater initiative in the solution of technical problems.

In 1954 the Communist Party adopted two apparently contradictory philosophical attitudes towards science: first, rejection of any dogmatism in science; and secondly, criticism of philosophical neutralism and encouragement of the inculcation of scientific workers with dialectical materialist principles. As a result, the party recognised the defeat of dogma in many scientific disciplines, while at the same time encouraging a campaign against indifference to philosophy on the part of scientists. This campaign seems to have been far from successful, however, as the President of the Academy of Sciences found it necessary to condemn the 'revisionist' attempt to free science from ideology at the 1958 All-Union Conference on the Philosophical Questions of Contemporary Natural Science.[40]

Although post-Stalin fiction constantly reiterates the official claim that Soviet scientific achievements stem directly from their ideology, it furnishes little more than vague expressions of enthusiasm. In Gor's *University Embankment*, for example, a scientist merely states dogmatically, without explanation, 'A physicist cannot fail to be a philosopher. Of course, not merely a philosopher, but a dialectical materialist philosopher.' Soviet writers were unable to demonstrate precisely how or why ideology had helped scientists in their work, any more than scientists who repeatedly affirmed that they were guided by dialectical materialism could analyse exactly how it had contributed to their success; and party theorists failed to demonstrate a clear and consistent connection between the general laws of the dialectic and specific laws of science.

Soviet fiction reflects the topical discussion about the value of ideological control of science and of a 'philosophical' approach to scientific concepts in general. It leads us to infer that some form of mechanistic materialism, similar to that prevalent in the 1920s, was probably the dominant philosophy among Soviet scientists in the post-Stalin era; and that theoretical physicists and other specialists whose work lay in uncharted areas on the frontiers of knowledge realised that such physical concepts as probability and the finitude of matter had far-reaching implications which could cast doubt on some of the central tenets of dialectical materialism.

In the 1961 version of her novel *Elena*, Lvova depicts the young chemist Reshetov who, with his indifference to philosophy, epitomises all those scientists who, after the hardships of the Stalin era, just wanted to pursue their work without ideological interference. She also mentions a poor lecture on 'The Connection between Philosophy and Natural Science' which leads some students to maintain that a scientist's philosophy is irrelevant to his research, and even to conclude that 'materialism' and 'idealism' are fictions. Lvova's heroine, the research chemist Elena, concedes that the objections of scientists indifferent to philosophy are not easy to refute, and that when a scientist conducts an experiment, 'the processes develop of their own accord, independent of any philosophy'. She insists, nevertheless, that when theoretical assumptions have to be made a scientist's philosophy has a vital part to play, although she fails to demonstrate convincingly the actual value of materialist philosophy to scientists.[41]

The quantity of space in Lvova's novel devoted to a debate about the conflict between materialism and idealism shows that this was a serious contemporary problem. The 'positive' Professor Prokofyev's dogmatic assertion that Lenin's *Materialism and Empirio-criticism* is still a definitive refutation of all idealist philosophy, his declaration that materialism must be zealously defended, as idealism will lead to religious belief and a dead end in science, and his appeal for greater ideological vigilance indicate the depth of the anxiety felt by Soviet 'dogmatists' about the neutral attitude to philosophy prevalent among the scientific intelligentsia.

By the late 1950s there was a clear desire on the part of both scientists and philosophers to keep their spheres of influence separate. After 1960, provided they accepted the party's minimum requirements — the provision of the material foundation for building communism, the acceptance of Marxism-Leninism and guidance by party theorists — Soviet scientists were by and large able to devote themselves to research without constant ideological interference. At the Twenty-Second Congress in 1961 the writer Nikolai Gribachov, in a speech implying that writers should be given greater latitude, stated: 'Engineer-designers and physicists do not even have special party organisations [for their professions], yet are succeeding rather well — they are already in outer space.'[42] In

1963 the party acknowledged that it had no right to exercise complete control over 'the activities of the administration . . . [of] . . . the institutions of the so-called academic or theoretical category'.[43]

The second literary 'thaw' enabled some writers to denounce the dictatorial political control over science and technology imposed in Stalin's time and, by implication, the continuing power of Lysenko in the post-Stalin period. A young scientist in Granin's *Into the Storm* draws the general conclusion: 'We still have too many dogmas in science.' Here Granin echoes the view of Kapitsa, who in 1962 publicly attacked the regime's efforts to pronounce scientific theories true or false on the basis of Marxist dialectics.[44] Both Granin's novel and Grekova's *Beyond the Checkpoint* suggest that by the early 1960s Soviet scientists were not very interested in philosophical or ideological questions, preferring to devote themselves to their research, untrammelled by official dogma.

Science and Politics

The importance accorded to scientists, engineers and managers in Soviet fiction of 1953–64 shows that they were becoming a more influential pressure group in Soviet society. During the post-Stalin era scientists and engineers acquired greater bargaining power: there is evidence that scientists had access to the decision-making process through the State Committee for Science and Technology in the Council of Ministers and the Presidium of the Academy, and that experts were being given an increasing consultative role on government and party committees and commissions of the Supreme Soviet. Although much of this 'lobbying' was done behind the scenes, and little is known about the involvement of scientists in specific decisions, they had some influence over the formation of scientific policy: for example, they carried through the desired reorganisation of the Academy of Sciences, excluding engineers from this body, and a coalition of forces eventually reversed Khrushchev's education policy. Scientists had little impact on major political decisions, however, although there is some indication that they influenced Khrushchev during the Cuban missile crisis.

In the post-Stalin era the relaxation of ideological control was creating a certain division between the scientific elite and the party bureaucracy. There were two currents among the reforming technical intelligentsia which have been variously described as 'technocratic' and 'democratic', or the 'efficiency-seeking' and 'truth-seeking' intelligentsia.[45] The influence of the group of 'efficiency-seeking' intellectuals is apparent in the important role played by scientists and engineers from 1955 until 1961 in discussions about the improvement of the Soviet economy. Many specialists supported the proposal that profitability, rather than the fulfilment of a gross output plan, should serve as the main criterion of an enterprise's efficiency, a view which became associated with Professor Liberman of the Kharkov Economic Engineering Institute after a famous article of 1962.[46] The 'truth-seeking' intelligentsia is a term which has been used to designate the emerging alliance of people from many social groups, including writers, scientists and engineers, who were united in their hostility towards Lysenko and the Stalinist 'Old Guard' and later in formulating petitions for legal reform. In the 1960s party ideologues complained that scientists, engineers and technicians were not being governed tightly enough by the party. The Soviet press was, however, unable to discuss freely the idea that, as a result of education, industrialisation and technological progress, the technical intelligentsia might acquire an influence which could threaten the party's supremacy. Khrushchev himself was evidently aware of this danger, for he found it necessary to denounce as naive foreign propaganda the notion that an anti-communist or non-communist technocracy might displace the party bureaucracy.[47]

One positive aspect of the increasing influence of the Soviet technical intelligentsia was their greater independence and participation in economic decision-making. At a 1956 conference in the Academy of Sciences, scientists and engineers demanded improved criteria for rational economic decision-making,[48] because the absence of proper economic management hindered the introduction of automation and new technology, making it impossible to decide where new technical and capital investment could most advantageously be used. Moreover, without material inducements industrial managers had no incentive to innovate, even if new technology promised to yield great benefits to the Soviet economy.

Kantorovich's *Story of Engineer Ganshin*, published just before Khrushchev's reorganisation of industry in 1957, illustrates the division between 'technocracy' and 'bureaucracy'. The party sets Ganshin the task of constructing a new factory in order to demonstrate his 'scientific' methods of construction. He follows the rules laid down in economic manuals, obtaining a rapid supply of materials, switching off the telephone to avoid interference from his superiors, planning the construction efficiently and consulting with engineers and workers. Ganshin and another engineer are invited to write a paper for an economics seminar in Moscow about the advantages of the technical planning of construction work. Kantorovich emphasises the increasing influence of the technical intelligentsia after Stalin's death: it now 'seems natural that two ordinary engineers should have reflected on how to improve methods of managing the economy'.

Bakhirev, the chief engineer in Nikolaeva's *Battle on the Way*, makes even more radical suggestions about how to improve the Soviet economy. While remaining loyal to communist ideals, he is pained by Soviet technological backwardness, and realises that the free market system of capitalism possesses some economic advantages: 'In capitalist countries there is competition. Anyone who makes bad and expensive things fails and perishes. In our country ruin and failure threaten no one. Does that mean that one may produce bad things?' Bakhirev makes the controversial suggestion that abuses and inefficiency in Soviet industry may be caused by the failure to give people sufficient material incentives for their work, and considers a means of enlisting self-interest into the planned economic system. Nikolaeva thus advances views which had never before been discussed in Soviet literature, expressing in a popular form ideas similar to those of Liberman.

Solzhenitsyn's play *Candle in the Wind* (written in 1960, but published abroad in 1969)[49] suggests that Soviet specialists may have been increasingly attracted to the study of social cybernetics in the 1960s because the subject appeared to promise a 'scientific' reform of society in the direction of greater democracy. The argument of the social cyberneticist Terbolm that a society can only surmount the turbulent events threatening to destroy it — plagues, earthquakes, economic depressions, financial crises, wars and revolutions — if it possesses the three vital control factors of information, co-ordination and feedback, implies that a democratic structure and the free flow of information are vital to a society's survival. The far-reaching conclusions about Soviet society that could be reached by applying cybernetic principles to social and economic problems were later exemplified by *The Inertia of Fear* (1977), a work by the dissident scientist Valentin Turchin.[50]

Liberal Soviet writers such as Granin, Kaverin and Dudintsev depict the emergence of a 'truth-seeking' section of the scientific intelligentsia which was increasingly coming into conflict with the scientific and government bureaucracy. At the end of *Not by Bread*

Alone Dudintsev implies that the power of corrupt officials raises important political issues; the hindrance of technological progress and the attendant damage to the Soviet economy. He appears to favour the idealist Galitsky's belief that the only way to defeat the scientific bureaucracy is for specialists themselves to adopt a bold, independent line, and stresses the danger of the scientist's withdrawal from the political struggle once he has achieved his personal goals. Galitsky tells the inventor Lopatkin: 'This is a more important issue than the introduction of your machine. You wait, you'll become a politician yet!' One Western commentator has regarded this phrase as evidence of Dudintsev's belief that the only way to defeat such men is through political action;[51] yet the word *politik*, particularly at that time, was frequently used in the more restricted sense of 'cunning operator'. Dudintsev nevertheless hints that Lopatkin has begun to emerge from isolation and acknowledge a new duty — 'concern about people'. The implication is that Lopatkin realises that reform through science and technology is not enough; to achieve his aims he will have to yield power directly, to work for reform in the organisation of science. This action will be 'political' in so far as the enemy — the corrupt bureaucracy — is designated by the abstraction 'Drozdovism'.

Dudintsev's choice of an inventor as his hero, and the support which he subsequently gained from the delegates to the Inventors' Conference in 1956, testify to an increasing sense of common interest and purpose between the literary and scientific intelligentsia. At first, after Stalin's death, scientists were concerned only with their own problems, but such writers as Dudintsev and Kaverin initiated an alliance during the 'thaw' of 1956, exhorting scientists to social and political action. The alarm which the growing alliance between the technical intelligentsia and progressive writers aroused among the bureaucracy is revealed in Kochetov's *Ershov Brothers*, which satirises the relationship between the villainous engineer Orleantsev and a group of artistic intellectuals.

In the late 1950s some writers began to hint that scientists, unlike the party leaders, actually appreciated abstract art. In Gor's *University Embankment*, the physicist Chukhlyaev complains that he cannot understand the fragmented paintings of Miró which claim to reflect the contemporary world; he wants a cheerful, realistic art, not one which disturbs by depicting irrationality and disintegration. A French scientist, however, argues that the modern artist cannot fail to be influenced by contemporary scientific discoveries, and that socialist realism erroneously demands that the artist should see the world as in the time of Newton and Boyle. Although Gor attributes such sentiments to a foreigner, they correspond to the real opinions of some Soviet scientists who, since the early 1960s, have given their support to modern poetry, abstract paintings and sculpture. After Khrushchev's closure of the Manège art exhibition in 1962, the physicists Sakharov and Tamm were among the signatories of a letter to Khrushchev supporting abstract art. Khrushchev disapproved of scientists' support for controversial artists: when the sculptor Ernst Neizvestny said to him: 'You may not like my work, but it has the warm support of such eminent scientists as Kapitsa and Landau', Khrushchev replied, 'That's not why we admire Kapitsa and Landau.'[52] The sympathy between scientists and artists is also evoked in Granin's *Into the Storm*, in which the physicist Richard defends the abstract artists condemned by Khrushchev in 1962; it was, however, necessary for Granin to insure against criticism by admitting that Richard does not really like their paintings and only supports them out of youthful enthusiasm, because 'they are rebelling' and people are attacking them. Notwithstanding Granin's caution, however, scientists have continued to be among the most avid private art collectors, and physics institutes in Moscow have held unofficial exhibitions of art which could not be displayed publicly.

From the mid-1950s the *apparat* became alarmed that the increasingly influential technical intelligentsia might eventually escape from party control. Such works as Kochetov's *Ershov Brothers* and Lvova's *Elena* suggest that some Soviet intellectuals were becoming sympathetic to the ideas of 'revisionist' philosophers in Eastern Europe. The party evidently perceived the danger as real, for after the military intervention in Hungary hundreds of young scientists and student dissidents were arrested. Kochetov emphasises the threat posed by his villain Orleantsev, who does not even accept the authority of Lenin, and expresses the opinion that 'Our age . . . is the age of technology and science. That means that those who control technology and science should become the leading, ruling force. Engineers, my friend, engineers . . . ' He challenges the party bureaucracy: 'It is not we who should retreat from our positions, but they, they, these types made of reinforced concrete. Their time has ended, they are now living their last, they are dying out.' Orleantsev is attacked by a 'positive' worker who argues that his theory would lead to an abandonment of the dictatorship of the proletariat in favour of a pseudo-Dostoevskian dictatorship of 'strong personalities', and reminds Orleantsev that the present generation of engineers and technicians come from a working-class or peasant background themselves. Nevertheless, Kochetov's introduction of this subject at all suggests that a 'technocratic' view may have been fairly widespread among the technical intelligentsia, and was causing disquiet among party activists.

Literature and literary debates of the early 1960s also provide evidence that the party's emphasis on the 'NTR' was creating a new class of powerful technocrats who were beginning to challenge the old party bureaucracy. In 1964 Dudintsev argued that the nature of the villain had changed in contemporary Soviet society: 'Today's *meshchanstvo* ['bourgeoisie'] is against *meshchanstvo* . . . Nowadays the *meshchanstvo* is crazy about physics and cybernetics . . . '[53] The factory director Terekhov in Davydova's *The Love of Engineer Izotov* (1960), for example, is a typical representative of the rising class of influential technocrats who support technological innovation, not because it is encouraged by the party, but because it will bring them money, power and pleasure. Although such men were officially criticised, Stalin's daughter Svetlana has suggested that the privileges won by professional skill seemed more legitimate to the Soviet public than the similar advantages enjoyed by party officials.[54]

In 1956–7 only isolated members of the scientific and technical intelligentsia, such as Bukovsky, Litvinov, Orlov and Esenin-Volpin, were involved in dissident activities, but the situation changed around 1962–3, when a closer co-operation developed between the younger political dissidents and some liberal members of the highest scientific elite, including Academicians Tamm, Kapitsa, Sakharov, Semyonov, Engelgardt and Berg. This emerging alliance can be inferred from Granin's *Into the Storm* which states that young physicists only have respect for a few 'progressive' academicians; the others they consider to be 'sclerotics'. Granin's depiction of the self-confidence, reforming tendencies and sense of historic mission felt by young physicists in the wake of de-Stalinisation suggests that the climate of true creativity may produce men of an independent cast of mind differing considerably from the ideal of the 'New Communist Man'. They outrage bureaucrats with their outspoken ideas on 'the questions connected with the consequences of the personality cult' and they are 'confidently rebuilding this imperfect world. Together with Langmuir, Niels

Bohr, Kurchatov and Kapitsa, they commanded the era's most important field of specialisation. They believed that mankind's future depended on them; that they were humanity's prophets, benefactors, liberators.' Granin's description recalls the *émigré* journalist Leonid Finkelstein's portrayal of the inhabitants of a secret science town in Siberia (probably Akademgorodok) who longed for reform within the existing system.[55]

Published fiction of the post-Stalin era was, however, unable to discuss the vital issue of the relationship between scientists and the political leaders. Granin shows that only determined, influential older scientists can combat ignorant officials, and suggests no institutional solution to the problems in Soviet science. He appears to believe that scientists should devote themselves entirely to their research without any thought of participating in the decision-making process which devises work plans, allocates resources and controls the practical implementation of scientific discoveries. Although from 1958 onwards space and military experts demanded a significant role in political decision-making, this was not a topic which could be mentioned in literature published in the Soviet Union, where the state decides what use should be made of scientific and technological achievements. Only in science fiction did scientists' misgivings occasionally surface: for example the Strugatsky brothers' *Far Rainbow* (1963)[56] raises the question of which scientific research will be encouraged in an age when science has little bearing on man's needs. The implication is that the most successful research will be allocated the most resources — perhaps a veiled reference to the USSR's concentration on space and military research.

Notes

1. S. Sobolev, *Pravda*, 2 July 1954; A. Nesmeyanov, *VAN*, 1956, no. 3, p. 4.
2. M. Keldysh, *VAN*, 1961, no. 7, p. 22; A. Kosygin, 'Za tesnuyu svyaz nauki s zhiznyu', *VAN*, 1961, no. 7, pp. 90–106.
3. R. Medvedev, *On Socialist Democracy*, trans. E. de Kadt (London, 1975), p. 173.
4. Yu. Nagibin, *Khazarskii ornament*, *LM*, 1956, no. 2.
5. D. Granin, *Posle svadby, Oktyabr*, 1956, nos. 7–9.
6. H. McLean and W. Vickery, *The Year of Protest 1956* (NY, 1961), p. 158.
7. Khrushchev, *Pravda*, 28 Aug. 1957.
8. D. Granin, *Sobstvennoe mnenie*, *NM*, 1956, no. 8; N. Gorbunov, *Oshibka (monolog professora)*, *NS*, 1957, no. 2, p. 91.
9. *LG*, 19 Mar. 1957.

10. M. Popovsky, letter.
11. Ya. Elsberg, *LG*, 13 June 1957.
12. A. Rybakov, *Leto v Sosnyakakh, NM*, 1964, no. 12.
13. Svirsky, *Soviet Writing*, pp. 217–18.
14. *Oktyabr*, 1962, no. 11, pp. 172–91; Khrushchev, *Pravda*, 10 Mar. 1963.
15. *Pravda*, 12 May 1963.
16. V. Kaverin, *Kusok stekla, NM*, 1960, no. 8.
17. A. Popovsky, *Cheloveku zhit dolgo* (M, 1963).
18. *VL*, 1963, no. 4, p. 10.
19. A. Bylinov, *Dolg inzhenera, Oktyabr*, 1956, no. 7, p. 103.
20. *LG*, 19 Mar. 1957.
21. N. Fyodorov, M. Prilezhaeva, *LG*, 19 Mar. 1957; N. Shundik, 'Pisatel otvet-
stvenen pered narodom', *Neva*, 1957, no. 10, pp. 3–4.
22. V. Kozhevnikov, *Znakomtes, Baluev!* (M. 1960), p. 284.
23. A. Topchiev, *VAN*, 1955, no. 3, pp. 19–38; Bulganin, *Pravda*, 22 Feb. 1956.
24. A. Absalyamov, *Ogon neugasimyi* (M, 1959), p. 194.
25. I. Grekova, *Za prokhodnoi, NM*, 1962, no. 6.
26. A. Chakovsky, *Svet dalyokoi zvyozdy, Oktyabr*, 1962, nos 11, 12; V.
Aksyonov, *Zvyozdnyi bilet, Yunost*, 1961, nos. 6, 7.
27. V. Kochetov, *Sekretar obkoma* (M, 1961), p. 265.
28. Zh. Medvedev, *The Medvedev Papers*, trans. V. Rich (London, 1971), pp.
117, 120, 127; Popovsky, *Science in Chains*, pp. 69–91.
29. McLean and Vickery, *Year of Protest*, p. 156.
30. Zh. Medvedev, *Soviet Science*, p. 92.
31. A. Dementyev, *Prekrasna zima v Sibiri, Zvezda*, 1960, nos. 11, 12; V. Ketlinskaya, *Inache zhit ne stoit*, p. 172.
32. Solzhenitsyn, *Dlya polzy dela, NM*, 1963, no. 7, p. 79.
33. Solzhenitsyn, *Oak and Calf*, pp. 66, 90.
34. V. Rozov, *V dobryi chas, Teatr*, 1955, no. 3, p. 17.
35. Popovsky, *Science in Chains*, pp. 44–6.
36. P. Kapitsa, *Theory, Experiment, Practice* (1965), cited in *Business Week*, 24
Dec. 1966, pp. 74–5.
37. L. Graham, *Science and Philosophy in the Soviet Union* (NY, 1972), pp. 5–6
maintains that this proves that many Soviet scientists were genuinely committed to
dialectical materialism.
38. Z. Paperny, *Genya i Senya. Literaturnaya parodiya, Teatr*, 1956, no. 8.
39. Bylinov, *Dolg inzhenera, Oktyabr*, 1956, no. 7, pp. 99–100; V. Kantorovich,
Istoriya inzhenera Ganshina, NS, 1957, no. 1, pp. 165, 172.
40. A. Nesmeyanov, in P. Fedoseev *et al.* (eds.), *Filosofskie problemy sovremennogo estestvoznaniya* (M, 1959), pp. 5–8.
41. K. Lvova, *Elena* (M, 1961), pp. 163–5, 127 (first published *Almanakh: god
tridtsat vosmoi*, vol. 19 (1955), Part 1).
42. N. Gribachov, *Pravda*, 28 Oct. 1961.
43. *PZ*, 1963, no. 16, pp. 32–9.
44. P. Kapitsa, *EG*, 28 Mar. 1962.
45. D. Holloway, 'Scientific Truth and Political Authority in the Soviet Union',
Government and Opposition, 5, no. 3 (summer 1970), pp. 345–67; H. Skilling, F.
Griffiths (eds.), *Interest Groups in Soviet Politics* (Princeton, 1971), p. 398.
46. E. Liberman, *Pravda*, 9 Sept. 1962.
47. Khrushchev, *Izvestiya*, 20 May 1962.
48. *Pravda*, 17 Oct., 19 Oct. 1956.
49. A. Solzhenitsyn, *Svecha na vetru (Svet, kotoryi v tebe), Grani*, 1969, no. 71.
50. V. Turchin, *Inertsiya strakha* (NY, 1977).
51. Gibian, *Interval of Freedom*, p. 72.

52. Johnson, *Khrushchev and the Arts*, p. 11.
53. V. Dudintsev, *LG*, 21 May 1964.
54. S. Allilueva, *Tolko odin god* (NY and Evanston, 1970), p. 226.
55. L. Vladimirov (L. Finkelstein), *The Russians* (NY and London, 1968), pp. 214–23.
56. A. and B. Strugatsky, *Dalyokaya Raduga*, in *Novaya Signalnaya* (M, 1963).

3 SCIENCE AND TECHNOLOGY IN THE POST-KHRUSHCHEV ERA

Khrushchev's successors continued some of his policies towards science and technology, although they abandoned his more radical de-Stalinisation and reorganisation schemes, and adopted a cautious approach more clearly determined by needs of state. Lysenko's downfall in 1965 was caused by the leaders' realisation that he had seriously harmed Soviet agriculture. Similarly, greater freedom of discussion was permitted to economists and empirical sociologists because of their potential for improving management and economic performance. After Lysenko's fall, scientific research (as opposed to pseudo-scientific schemes) became more respectable, but applied scientific research corresponding to the state's needs was still favoured. The establishment of the State Committee for Science and Technology in 1965 led to greater party control over science, and the transfer of many institutes to ministries in the mid-1960s created unhappy scientists who wanted to work on basic scientific problems in the more prestigious setting of the Academy. The reform of procedures for awarding higher degrees in 1975, ostensibly designed to increase the quality of Soviet scientists, in practice also resulted in greater party interference in the selection and promotion of personnel.

The Soviet leaders realised that the USSR was still behind in almost all sophisticated areas of modern science, especially computer technology. They acknowledged that Khrushchev's policy of 'duplicating' foreign technology had proved unsuccessful, because by the time Soviet scientists had copied a model it had become obsolete. The USSR's decision in 1966 to join the International Convention on Patents, Licences and Inventions accelerated the use of foreign technology both for research and for industry, since the Soviet government usually considered it more economical to acquire the licence to manufacture many types of foreign equipment than to try to 'invent' something similar within the USSR. During the *détente* of the 1970s the USSR resorted to the wholesale importation of Western factories and technical experts, such as the Italian Fiat plant. Yet although the Soviet leaders have attempted to promote a gradual integration of Soviet science with international science and technology, they have continued to impose restrictions on foreign travel for some scientists and to limit the free exchange of information with the West. Repressive measures have been taken against dissident scientists, and Jewish specialists who have applied to emigrate to Israel have frequently been dismissed. For all its undoubted strengths, certain weaknesses remain endemic in the structure of Soviet science. It is not that the USSR is lacking in talent: the faults are largely a result of external constraints imposed on Soviet specialists. Perhaps the most serious is the persistent political interference with scientific work, which inhibits the scientists themselves and results in favoured treatment for the military, the slow diffusion of scientific information and over-dependence on the West. Secondly, a whole series of problems hinders the successful integration of science into the economy: the inflexible planning system, the stifling effects of bureaucracy, the lack of a unified scientific command, the resistance to technological change, and the absence of efficient management and adequate economic incentives.

The General Presentation of Scientific Themes

In the post-Khrushchev period the press and the speeches of party leaders have contained frank discussions of some of the faults of Soviet science.[1] Much criticism in Soviet fiction, therefore, merely echoes the explicit treatment of certain issues in the press. Post-Khrushchev literature has, however, generally avoided the more controversial topics which occasionally surfaced in fiction of the Khrushchev era: the prevalence of bureaucracy and corruption in the scientific world; the persistence of discrimination against Jews in higher education; the relationship between theoretical and applied science; scientists' indifference to ideology; and the relationship between scientists and the political authorities. Fiction dealing with life and work in scientific institutes displays less political sharpness than that of the Khrushchev period, but lays more emphasis on the moral, psychological and intellectual problems of the individual scientist. This change can be observed in such writers as Granin and Kaverin, who wrote mordant anti-Stalinist works in the 1950s and early 1960s, but whose later works are more concerned with the scientist's personal moral dilemmas and conflicts with his colleagues than with wider political issues. This reflects both the changing interests of Soviet writers and the more repressive atmosphere of literary politics in the Brezhnev era.

In post-Khrushchev literature about science there is a more realistic emphasis on everyday scientific work, as opposed to grandiose scientific schemes. Nikolai Amosov's *Thoughts and the Heart* (1969), for example, is a documentary account of a surgeon's work over several years, containing vivid reportage, including technical details of operations; and D. Konstantinovsky's *Ergo sum* (1974) describes daily life in a physics laboratory.[2] Soviet scientists have, however, continued to complain that fiction depicts scientific work in an over-glamorous light. Another feature of literature of the Brezhnev era is that it contains less obvious didacticism than fiction of the 1950s and early 1960s, and there is an attempt to invest novels with more 'human interest'. Some writers include certain elements of the Western 'thriller' in an attempt to appeal to a wider audience, especially to members of the working class. A novel by the Ukrainian writer Yury Shcherbak, *As if in the War* (1967), recounts a dramatic story of the incarceration of five scientists in a laboratory as a result of the escape of an encephalitis virus from a vacuum chamber.[3] Shcherbak describes their attempts to prevent infection using vaccine and interferon (which at that time was regarded as a new 'wonder-drug'). Similarly, *Gem of Pure Water* (1973) by the Georgian writer Georgy Pandzhikidze, a work whose original title in Ukrainian also meant *Honest Eyes*, includes certain sensational elements: Otar, the mathematician hero who is dying of leukaemia, witnesses a hit-and-run accident caused by the corrupt director of a lemonade factory who flashes 10,000 roubles around in a restaurant and subsequently hires a thug to shoot Otar for telling the police the number of his car. The publisher's preface criticised Pandzhikidze for the excessive 'publicist passion' of this work, but praised him for his sense of justice.[4]

The subjects treated in fiction show that there is a hierarchy in Soviet science: physics is perhaps the most popular subject; cybernetics also became fashionable; space technology retained its appeal, but medicine was not considered glamorous. More emphasis was also laid on the social sciences, especially economics and sociology, because of official policy to promote them.[5] 'Science towns' continued to form the setting of certain works, although real place-names were not mentioned: for example Boris Bondarenko's *Pyramid* (1976) is set in Dolinsk, 'a town in the forest' 100 kilometres from Moscow (an obvious reference to Obninsk).[6] There is, however, no suggestion that the inhabitants of such centres were becoming disillusioned with their environment, as Mark Popovsky implies.[7] Tragic themes are not avoided: Makanin's *Straight Line* (1967), for example, even treats such a seemingly taboo subject as the death of two people on a missile testing site because of a mathematical miscalculation caused by the need to rush the work.[8] Most writers show moral concern about the destructive potential of science and technology, although they were never again able to express disillusionment with the entire scientific establishment as frankly as certain writers of the post-Stalin 'thaw'.

Post-Khrushchev fiction treated visits abroad and the regular reading of foreign scientific journals as a matter of course, and there was no hint of the difficulties involved in obtaining scientific information and attending foreign conferences which have been graphically described in *The Medvedev Papers*. There are, however, indications in Soviet fiction that attitudes to foreign scientific work are still very sensitive; references to foreign science are often disparaging, or presented as an incentive to compete. The physicists in Bondarenko's *Pyramid* are frequently forestalled by foreign scientific achievements. They comb American and English journals, but when their equations are published in an Italian journal one of them remarks bitterly: 'Perhaps before working on physics we need to become polyglots?' On another occasion, when a theory is disproved by the Americans, Bondarenko's hero Dmitry comments philosophically: 'Such is scientific life.' On the third, more critical occasion an article appears in the American *Physical Review* which duplicates the findings of Dmitry's group. This defeat spurs the institute authorities to give them better facilities, and they engage in a race with American physicists to salvage about a third of their work. Although Dmitry sometimes wonders: 'What difference does it make who does it — we or the Americans? As long as it is done', he nevertheless continues the competition 'and, as in all Soviet fiction on scientific themes, achieves eventual success.

Soviet authors show that foreign scientific research may be either a hindrance or an inspiration to Soviet scientists, and the nationalist tone of fiction of the Khrushchev period is somewhat muted in literature of the era of *détente*. Writers indicate that US achievements were still regarded as an important criterion in measuring Soviet success, although they go nowhere near to suggesting that the gap between US and Soviet science was actually widening in the 1970s (as manifested by the increasing importation of Western technology).

Some works of the post-Khrushchev period emphasise individual talent and independent work in science more than earlier fiction. Bondarenko's *Pyramid* suggests that creative enthusiasm and official education may come into conflict: the physicist Dmitry and his friend Rudolf pursue independent research to the detriment of their university careers. Although they achieve original theoretical results, they are not allowed to take their university examinations because they have not attended courses regularly, and it is possible that they may lose their grants and university places. Their failure to take the course in political economy may well reflect the general lack of interest in ideology on the part of young Soviet scientists.

Bondarenko demonstrates the complexity of the relationship between individual and collective work in science. He emphasises that some research is too important and requires too many resources for scientists to pursue it on their own. However, Bondarenko also shows that the desire of a talented scientist to pursue an independent line of enquiry may be hindered by men of lesser talent, or such bureaucratic obstacles as the institute's annual plan. Dmitry's difficulties in establishing an independent group in his institute suggest that this may in reality be quite rare, but nevertheless feasible if a project is sufficiently important. The scepticism which Dmitry expresses towards traditional education may well reflect views current among Soviet physicists about the need for specialised education for talented people. Eventually, with the support of Dubrovin, a corresponding member of the Academy of Sciences, Dmitry and Rudolf achieve considerable success, and, bypassing the official channels, are awarded candidate's degrees when they write up their research. The implication is that although the procedure for obtaining degrees and promotion in the USSR is normally very well defined, in cases of exceptional talent bureaucratic formalities can be dispensed with. Zhores Medvedev confirms that before the reform of the degree structure in 1975 this was in fact possible, particularly in the case of geneticists who had formerly been suppressed by Lysenko.[9]

The last part of Bondarenko's novel seems to border on fantasy, but the extreme individualism which Dmitry is allowed to indulge may reflect the special conditions provided for scientific geniuses in the USSR. Dmitry asks Dubrovin for permission to leave the institute for one or two years to pursue a difficult scientific problem. Dubrovin shows great understanding in allowing him four months' leave with salary; he goes to the island of Sakhalin and lives in a fisherman's hut, spending all his time sitting on the beach thinking. The indulgence of Dmitry's superior and the isolated, hippie-like existence which Dmitry leads appear somewhat unrealistic in the Soviet context, but could conceivably reflect the experience of some real prototype. At the end of the novel the conflict between individual creativity and collective work is resolved: Dmitry writes a brilliant article, and a new department is created to continue his research.

Gerasimovich's novel *The Effect of Position* demonstrates that the greater emphasis placed in post-Khrushchev fiction on free creativity in science is not just confined to physicists. Gerasimovich makes an eloquent defence of the need to respect individual authorship through his portrait of Sasha, a young scientist who has decided to leave a genetics laboratory because his work has been plagiarised. Sasha states: 'However collective science is, individuals perform it, and I wanted to be an individual . . . In science I value freedom of thought above everything . . . ' Sasha maintains that the dictatorial regime established by the laboratory director demands the 'annihilation' of his staff, and emphasises that collective work may not produce beneficial results. Both Gerasimovich and Bondarenko imply that collective work may mean mediocrity, and that exceptional discoveries can only be achieved by exceptional individuals. The testimony of such dissidents as Zhores Medvedev, Popovsky and Zinoviev would seem to suggest that the tension between individual achievement and collective work has not yet been satisfactorily resolved in the USSR — but this is a general problem associated with contemporary science throughout the world.

While authors of the post-Khrushchev period have possessed a certain freedom in the treatment of themes and characters, most works do not venture beyond the party line. This has been becoming more evident in literature of the 1980s: even when at first sight a writer appears to be treating a daring theme, it often proves to be a contribution to a campaign sanctioned by the political authorities. In Anatoly Sofronov's play *The Heart Operation* (1981)[10] the surgeon Ryzheikin, an almost unbelievably evil character who intrigues to bring about the downfall of the world-famous head of his clinic, asks his mistress, one of the nurses, to find some women to write anonymous letters for three roubles. Her casual response that the rate has increased to five roubles suggests that the phenomenon is widespread in Soviet life. Ryzheikin arranges anonymous letters and telephone calls accusing his superior of causing deaths in the clinic, surrounding himself with favourites and lackeys, allowing negligence in operations and accepting bribes from patients. This exposure of bribery and corruption might imply that the hack writer Sofronov is speaking out frankly against faults in Soviet science and society. However, his close adherence to the party line is demonstrated by his association of Ryzheikin's negative qualities with those of treacherous Soviet *émigrés*: 'some of our former citizens who so easily change their fatherland'. Moreover, Sofronov's disclosure merely takes up one of the themes of Brezhnev's speech to the Twenty-Sixth Party Congress of February 1981: while welcoming sincere, honest 'letters and suggestions from the working people', Brezhnev added: 'As far as all sorts of anonymous vilifications are concerned, the party's stand is well known: there is no room for them in our life. Those who come out with truthful, businesslike criticisms have no need to hide their faces.'

Evidence that individualism in science is becoming a controversial theme in the 1980s is provided by the debate over *Thoughts on the Way*, the memoirs of a famous paediatric surgeon, Stanislav Doletsky. In 1981 the critic V. Gorbachov berated Doletsky for his view that there is 'no doubt that intellectuals are born', which he regards as tantamount to the Zionist concept of the 'chosen people'. Gorbachov takes particular exception to a passage in which the director of an institute refers to the faults of talented members of his staff, who are variously described as undisciplined, fanatical, proud, a womaniser, a narrow professional and a drunkard, but argues that they are all essential: 'They're enthusiasts. They're industrious. They see farther, and deeper. They possess the mysterious and inexplicable ability to produce something new. And that's the most important thing in science.' When the narrator complains about lax discipline and inadequate ideological supervision, the director replies that strict discipline may be useful in automated production or in the army, but 'By its very essence, such discipline is contrary to any exploratory activity. A creatively thinking scientist, like it or not, only achieves real success when he violates some codified rule — someone's postulate.' It is not surprising that scientists carry over this principle into their private life: 'It's not for nothing that people say talented scientists possess three qualities: an urge towards anarchy, exaggerated sexuality and hypertrophy of the personality.' The author is forced to concede: 'There was a great deal of truth in Sergei's words.' Gorbachov was indignant at this alleged apologia of the Nietzschean Superman, and, by implication, Doletsky's predilection for dissidence and deviance rather than communist morality.

Gorbachov's article was criticised in a *Literaturnaya Gazeta* editorial for allegedly distorting an opponent's views. However, the original editorial was unprecedentedly attacked by another critic in *Molodaya Gvardiya* in February 1982, who censured *Literaturnaya Gazeta* for publishing criticisms of the 'most spirited and impassioned articles' instead of 'supporting the invigoration and increased militancy of magazines' literary criticism sections that have been noted since the [Twenty-Sixth Party] Congress'.[11] This episode demonstrates not only that defence of individualism in science (which might imply dissidence) was becoming more difficult at the beginning of 1982, but also that Soviet criticism was becoming a battleground of conflicting ideas, perhaps reflecting the increasing influence of Andropov and the KGB.

Insights into Soviet Science

Most literature of the post-Khrushchev period treated questions of current concern to the party, but some works afford interesting insights into the problems of Soviet science and, in particular, reveal the different psychological types to be found in scientific institutes. It should be emphasised that the conflicts in academic life depicted in Soviet fiction are certainly not exclusive to the USSR: this is obvious to readers of the novels of David Lodge and Malcolm Bradbury, or indeed to any member of staff of a university or any other organisation where personality clashes occur. There do, however, appear to be certain specific problems pertaining to Soviet academic life.

The abuse most commonly mentioned in Soviet fiction is the plagiarism of a subordinate's work by an institute director or a high official. This theme emerges particularly clearly in Kaverin's novel *A Two-hour Stroll.*[12] A talented scientist, Konshin, writes a paper for a conference in Miami; his director, who used to be a well-known scientist, but has long become a mere administrator, wants his own name to be included as one of the authors, but Konshin refuses, even though he knows that 'writing in the name of one's boss is considered quite normal (the more so when he is director of the institute)'. This corresponds to the testimony of Mark

Popovsky, who cites the chemist Andrei Nesmeyanov, at one time President of the Academy of Sciences, who was credited with 1,200 works over 40 years — that is, an article or a monograph every twelve days![13]

The abuse of power is particularly evident in the case of dissertations. In Konstantinovsky's *Ergo sum* the narrator's boss, a candidate of sciences, has reached the limit of his abilities, but nevertheless arranges for his subordinates to write a doctoral dissertation for him, knowing that the defence will be a mere formality. It would seem that one difference between the Soviet and British systems is that scholars who choose to devote themselves solely to administration feel obliged to maintain the pretence that they are keeping up their research interests. An important stimulus to this is provided by the fact that a doctor of sciences in the USSR receives a tangible reward in money and prestige. As a character plainly states in Grekova's novel *The Department* (1978), there is a contemporary campaign for 'heads of faculties to be doctors of science'.[14]

The frequent treatment of this theme in literature of the 1970s was permitted as a result of the party's reform of the degree structure in 1975, but such liberal writers as Kron, Grekova and Kaverin suggest that corrupt practices had not been eradicated by this change. Indeed, the awarding of scientific degrees was still a controversial subject in the 1980s. A Candidate of Sciences proposed in 1981 that the candidate's degree and doctor's degree had outlived their usefulness, and should be replaced by a single doctoral degree, as in the West.[15]

Grekova's novel *The Department* provides a glimpse into the busy life of Soviet academic staff, the bureaucratic formalities they have to endure, and their problems with students. Grekova defines their life as a 'ceaseless floundering in a mass of urgent business, in a pile-up of things still to be finished'. There is some indication of the hours involved when the new director asks his staff to work a ten-hour day — that is 60 hours a week. Grekova condemns the bureaucratic formality of the lecturer's individual work plan, complaining that 'It is never read by anyone except the person who makes it up and the typist, but several copies of it are left to gather dust in various offices . . . On the other hand, it is no mean task to compose one . . . ' She shows that many types of work, such as preparation for class work, re-sit examinations for students, reviews, conferences and individual work with students simply cannot be put into a plan at all.

Grekova's work is one of the few novels directly concerned with students and the educational system. She admits that the admissions system to higher education is bad: the students accepted are not always those with the most talent or potential, but those who have been well coached. Many gain entrance to higher educational institutions not because of direct bribery, but because of *blat* — connections and acquaintances. The students, like the staff, are overworked: one Komsomol leader adds up undergraduates' commitments and finds that they would need 26 hours in a day to carry them all out. This inevitably leads to a search for ways of evading the rules, including cheating in examinations, which still seems to be widespread. Grekova's narrator is indignant at the dean's suggestion that the lecturers should fail fewer students and give the others higher marks, because if there are too many failures the university will be called to account by the political authorities. She suggests that the success rate should be increased by harder work on the part of students and teachers, not by lowering standards; and appears to favour a proposal that higher education should be a two-stage affair, reserving the second stage for those who would be able to undertake original work in the subject.

Scientists and Administrators

One theme which has remained remarkably constant in Soviet fiction on scientific themes is the conflict between the true scientist and the careerist or bureaucrat. In comparison with some works of the Khrushchev period, however, writers only depict individual villains, not a corrupt system. Moreover, even the 'negative character' has generally become less negative: for example Shumilov, the bureaucrat who impedes talented young physicists in Bondarenko's *Pyramid*, is not evil, but merely possesses limited abilities.

One particularly bitter conflict is, however, depicted in Kaverin's *Two-hour Stroll*. The director of Konshin's institute, who is envious of his talent, and his cynical deputy Oskolkov attempt to break up Konshin's research team by issuing a decree that all the places will be declared open to competition. Kaverin contrasts the unprincipled ruthlessness of the administrators with the tolerance and unworldliness of the scientists who are not always tough enough in fighting for the true interests of science. Eventually the scientists win, but only through what at first sight seems a rather unconvincing denouement: Oskolkov is exposed as the manager of a clandestine school of gamblers and arrested for his criminal activities. One Soviet critic, while admitting that 'This sort of thing does happen, of course, and it's always a timely topic', objected: 'Apparently Kaverin feels a need to give the brute Oskolkov some unusual trait, so he makes him a secret gambler. Shouldn't a bureaucrat and careerist be made to answer for being a bureaucrat and careerist, not for being a gambler?'[16] It seems, however, that Kaverin's novel was inspired by a true case history, and the characters were based on real prototypes. It has been alleged that the director of the institute in real life suffered a heart attack as a result of the novel appearing in print, and the deputy director was in fact a passionate gambler.[17]

Vladimir Komissarov's *Ancient Debts* (1979) is perhaps more typical of the majority of post-Stalin fiction in that it presents a more muted conflict between scientists and administrators.[18] Komissarov does not portray scientific administrators in such a negative light as Kaverin; rather, he regards them as a necessary evil. Two characters in particular deserve attention as representative types in Soviet scientific administration. Oleg, a relatively young, ambitious man who wants real power — as opposed to the indirect power wielded by pure scientists — leaves the institute for a job in the Central Committee where both his strengths and weaknesses are revealed. On the one hand, he wants to defend his thesis, which is five years out of date, although it is implied that it may eventually be accepted. On the other hand, he proves to be a clever administrator who secures a suitable future for a talented young scientist.

The most interesting character is the senior scientist, known only as 'Starik' ('the old man'). He has been ruthless in fighting his way to the top, but is motivated by a desire to serve the interests of science, rather than by any careerist considerations. Real-life prototypes for Starik might be the space scientist Korolyov or the aeroplane designer Tupolev who were uncompromising in pursuing their aims. It must be assumed that such administrators as Starik do hold powerful positions and maintain good relations with the political authorities — or how else could Soviet science have achieved any results at all? As Zinoviev contends in *The Radiant Future* (1978), if a good scientist in the USSR is to achieve anything, he must attain a position of power.[19] Soviet scientific administrators have occasionally complained in the press about their portrayal in literature. In 1972 the director of a cybernetics institute argued that although not everyone necessarily combines the qualities of a good scholar and a good administrator, like the extremely 'positive' hero of Mikhail Kolesnikov's novel *Atomgrad* (1966), neither do scientific administrators inevitably turn into careerists or bureaucrats, as Soviet writers tend to imply.[20]

The Role of Women in Science

Women scientists such as Kaverin's Tatyana Vlasenkova and Lvova's Elena had appeared in literature of the Khrushchev period, but, apart from the additional function of providing love interest, they were generally presented in the same way as male scientist heroes. By the late 1960s, fiction began to portray women scientific workers more realistically, reflecting increased concern about the role of women in Soviet society. It was recognised that, although women had equality with men in theory, in practice they bear a much heavier domestic burden than men, and hence find it difficult to rise to the top of their profession.

Natalya Baranskaya's story *A Week Like Any Other Week* (1969) played an important part in bringing the whole 'woman question' to public attention and sparking off a debate which is still continuing. Baranskaya gives a truthful account of the daily life of a woman laboratory worker in a plastics institute, Olga Voronkova, who tries to combine her career with family life and domestic duties. She lives in a new housing district over an hour's journey from the institute, and her whole life is spent 'running' between her job, the shops where she has to queue in her lunch hour and her home. It is implied that women cannot do their jobs properly: Baranskaya's heroine is reprimanded for failing to arrive at work on time; and she calculates that she had to take 78 days off work in the past year because of her children's illness. However, when her reasonably amiable husband suggests that she might give up her work, because he could earn another 200 or 220 roubles a month if he had fewer domestic chores, she reacts indignantly:

> But what you're suggesting means simply — extinguishing me.
> What about my five years of study, and the diploma I got, and my subject for a candidate's dissertation? You'd just be chucking that away. And what shall I be like, if I sit at home all the time? Cross as the devil, grumbling at you all the time![21]

Baranskaya implies that there is no solution, and the heroine's difficult life will continue as before.

Since the publication of Baranskaya's story and her famous article 'Men, Look After Women!' (1971)[22] a more sympathetic attitude to the problems of Soviet women has been expressed in fiction. Often women are shown to occupy fairly junior positions in scientific institutes: for example, the heroine of Sergei Zalygin's much-criticised novel *South American Variant* (1973), who works in the information department of an institute, does not find her work satisfying, and dreams of a 'great love'.[23] The low status of jobs performed by women in science is more clearly stressed in Pavel Nilin's story *Married for the First Time* (1978), which depicts an unmarried mother who works as a laboratory assistant in a scientific institute.[24] Her daughter is proud of her until she learns that her mother only washes test-tubes, bottles and even floors, and thus cannot be classified as a 'scientific worker'. The frank admission that some women have not been able to pursue their scientific ambitions to the limit of their abilities because of domestic responsibilities — suggested through the portraits of Inga in Tendryakov's *On Apostolic Business* (1969) and the shadowy figure of Tosya, the narrator's wife in Zalygin's fantasy *Oska the Funny Boy* (1973) — may reflect some guilt on the part of Soviet men.

Gradually in the 1970s, however, as Mary Seton-Watson has convincingly shown, there were signs of a male backlash.[25] The return to traditional values in fiction stems from more than conventional male chauvinism: it also reflects the concern of Soviet sociologists and the party leaders themselves about the growing demographic crisis in the USSR. The 1976 census recorded an increasing number of divorces (one for every three marriages), a mounting abortion rate and 1.5 million illegitimate births, and showed that throughout the 1970s Soviet urban mothers were increasingly restricting themselves to one child, or even having no children at all, with a result that the birthrate in European Russia was dropping at a significant rate, while the population continued to rise in the non-Russian republics, particularly in Central Asia. Since this issue was reflected in official statistics, noted by the authorities and therefore by the press, it found its way into fiction. Bondarenko's *What I have Lost* (1973) describes a physicist, Olga, who struggles with her mother for the right to study, leaves her village and eventually goes to Moscow, where she defends her dissertation brilliantly.[26] But the price of success is that she has become rather hard, even cruel — a quality which, her supervisor says, is not common for a woman, but useful in scientific research. After her mother's death Olga rethinks her life: she is disillusioned with being a mere cog in a great scientific machine, and dreams of being a mathematics or physics teacher in a village school. She is now incapable of making contact with her brother and sister or finding 'ordinary female happiness' in marriage. Olga's plight thus reflects two topical issues in Soviet society: the desire that Russian women should lay more emphasis on home and family, and the attempt to encourage intellectuals to return to their native villages.

Bondarenko's *Time Trouble* (1974) more obviously endorses the party's encouragement of Russian women to have babies.[27] Irina, a geologist who has reached the top of her profession, is obliged to spend most of the year in expeditions away from her husband, a computer engineer. When she becomes pregnant she decides not to have an abortion, but to leave her job and return to live with her husband (who is in danger of having an affair). Thus, even in the rather rare case of a writer depicting a very successful woman scientist, there is never any question of the husband leaving his job for the sake of his wife's work. In Bondarenko's *Pyramid*, the wives of the heroes Rudolf and Dmitry are merely helpers and sympathetic listeners who understand little about physics. Bondarenko blames the failure of Dmitry's marriage on the fact that his wife works in Moscow and only comes to see him at weekends. The author makes a powerful attack on the 'ultra-modern family' in which both partners possess complete independence, and asserts the need for children to hold the family together. The absurdity to which Bondarenko is prepared to go to make his point is demonstrated by the fact that when Dmitry is suffering from nervous exhaustion only the news that his new girlfriend Zhanna is pregnant can provide sufficient joyful stimulus to encourage him to work again.

Apart from the work of women writers such as Grekova's *The Department*, in which the semi-autobiographical character of Nina Astashova is convincingly portrayed, few recent literary works have depicted women who have reached high positions in the scientific world. Most literary heroines in novels by male authors are conventionally beautiful, and, although they may be highly intelligent, are ultimately dependent on their men for intellectual support. In Bondarenko's *Pyramid* this is true of Zhanna, who eventually becomes Dmitry's second wife: she is a candidate of physical sciences, but gives up her own subject to work in Dmitry's research team, because he is far more gifted than her. Asya, the heroine of Gerasimovich's *The Effect of Position* (1979), is a divorcée who does valuable independent work in genetics, but is willing to allow her supervisor Shtyrev to use her results because of his superior knowledge and ability to generalise. Subsequently, Asya enlists the help of her stepfather's friend, the talented geneticist Dmitry Ukladnikov; and when Shtyrev appropriates her work after Dmitry's death she considers continuing Dmitry's research rather than her own. The main plot of Gerasimovich's novel would seem to suggest that a woman scientist cannot succeed on her own, but the author attempts to provide a more balanced view of portraying a famous elderly geneticist, Professor Kunitsyna, a former opponent of Lysenko who feels an affinity with Asya and tells her: 'Don't ever give in to them.'

Such portraits of successful women scientists are, however, fairly rare in recent Soviet fiction, and somewhat unconvincing. This may merely be one facet of a much wider problem, common to all literature: the difficulty experienced by male writers in portraying female characters. Yet, as far as the USSR is concerned, the latent male chauvinism of many Soviet writers does appear to have been exacerbated by the party's emphasis on traditional female values. The Soviet woman's double burden does not seem to have been significantly alleviated by the 1981 decree allowing mothers to take paid leave to look after their young children.

Franker References to Soviet Science

Dissident writers, not surprisingly, provide the most revealing insights into the reality of Soviet science. Anatoly Gladilin's novel *Forecast for Tomorrow*, which circulated widely in *samizdat* and reached the West in 1972,[28] is not a particularly anti-Soviet work — indeed, it raises certain questions which have subsequently been mentioned in published fiction — but it was not published in the USSR because Gladilin had fallen into disfavour. Gladilin's main themes are the hero's search for scientific work which will be of genuine benefit to people, and his desire to express his human individuality, instead of being an insignificant cog in a huge machine. Gladilin condemns the unsatisfactory nature of top-secret scientific institutes, showing that secrecy can lead to duplication of research, even between two laboratories in the same institute. This is not a forbidden subject — duplication of work has been condemned in the Soviet press — but Gladilin is touching on a taboo area when he complains that scientists in secret institutes have no influence over, or even knowledge of, how their work will be used.

Gladilin also shows that unplanned scientific work is unacceptable in the USSR, and that the plan can kill initiative and enthusiasm. The scientists in the narrator's laboratory once took up an important problem on their own initiative, but their enthusiasm for unplanned scientific work rapidly waned when the laboratory was fined for failing to fulfil an insignificant order on time. Gladilin goes further than any writers published in the USSR when he claims that there are too many Soviet scientists with too little work to do: 'It is a difficult task for learned specialists to create the semblance of work when there *is* no work.' Gladilin claims that scientists in the USSR have a much easier life than their Western counterparts, because capitalists would have made many of them redundant. The narrator wants to pursue his own research in the slack periods, but realises that it is impossible to 'break out of the general monolithic rank. All talent is excluded.' He eventually leaves the institute, because in his opinion 'official unemployment is better than unofficial idleness'.

Similar themes are treated in Alexander Zinoviev's semi-autobiographical work *The Radiant Future*, which paints an even blacker picture of the trading of favours in Soviet scholarship. The narrator receives protection from a senior scientific official against a hostile review of his latest article before the elections to the Academy of Sciences. In return he will have to organise a doctoral dissertation to be written for this 'wily cretin' by one of the junior members of staff in the institute. Zinoviev demonstrates that mutual protection schemes operate well up into the higher reaches of the Academy of Sciences, and that people make careers in science by marrying the daughters of prominent party officials, or by informing for the KGB. Zinoviev claims that since the 'era of liberalism' came to an end in 1964 there has been a great resurgence of careerists and opportunists in the scientific world, and that people will do *anything* to be elected to the Academy of Sciences. He paints a bitterly satirical portrait of the 'symbolic figure' Academician Kanareikin, a typical opportunist who became director of a philosophical institute and a corresponding member of the Academy because of his glorification of Stalin, but whose name became linked with the anti-Stalin trend in philosophy after Stalin's death. He does everything possible to hinder the work of his subordinates, but they carry on as if he does not exist and give him copies of their books which he accepts with tears of gratitude before going off to the Central Committee, the KGB or the Town Party Committee to 'disseminate terror with threats against revisionists, warnings that he would sweep away deviationists and root out error'. Zinoviev presents envy and fear as the ruling passions in his institute. All the scholars censor themselves, and no talent or originality can survive, because outstanding ability only produces fear. In his essay *The Reality of Communism*, Zinoviev claims that the Soviet system cannot allow the existence of outstanding individuals, and that 'The very concept of scientist is in any case devoid of substance when used of the mass of bureaucrats who are employed in Soviet science.'[29]

Scientific dissidence

After Khrushchev's fall more members of the scientific and technical intelligentsia joined the 'human rights movement' in order to keep the cause of anti-Stalinism and democratic reform alive in the USSR. Such dissidents included two members of the privileged scientific elite — the nuclear physicist Andrei Sakharov and the mathematician Igor Shafarevich — and many younger scientists such as Chalidze, Tverdokhlebov, Turchin, Orlov and Litvinov. The mathematician Revolt Pimenov suggested an important reason for political involvement after a search of his flat in 1970: 'For some time now we scientists have lost our sense of personal security. Roughly since the end of 1966. It is the threat to personal security that makes us concern ourselves with politics. And it all began with those trials.'[30] Sakharov's memorandum of 1968, *Progress, Coexistence and Intellectual Freedom*, 'formed in the milieu of the Soviet Union's scientific and scientific-technological intelligentsia',[31] expressed anxiety about many aspects of Soviet foreign and domestic policy and the future of mankind, and advocated a truly 'scientific method' of directing policy. Throughout the 1960s many scientists and technologists gave their support to protests against legal injustices and petitions for reform on questions of civil rights and political issues such as the invasion of Czechoslovakia.

Scientists — particularly physicists and mathematicians — rank among the topmost professions in the USSR in terms of social prestige, yet, paradoxically, they have been unusually prominent among activist dissidents. This can be attributed partly to their desire that other groups in society should enjoy the relative freedom they had won; partly to their greater awareness of social issues; and, after 1966, to the increasing restrictions placed on the Academy of Sciences. The intervention of scientists in the political debate is also due to the realisation that they are necessary to the regime and therefore may have some chance of influencing policy. Yet throughout the 1970s the dismissal of such gifted scholars as the Estonian sociologist Yulo Vooglayd and the imprisonment of the physicists Yury Orlov and Anatoly Sharansky demonstrated the authorities' unwavering determination to crush dissidence among the scientific intelligentsia. The situation worsened in 1980 when Sakharov, who had previously appeared to possess some measure of immunity, was exiled to the provincial town of Gorky. The policy towards dissidents hardened under Andropov and Chernenko: in 1984 it was announced that Orlov and Sharansky would serve their full terms, and Sakharov's wife Elena was sentenced to five years' exile. One current of thought among the Soviet technical intelligentsia is, according to Leonid Finkelstein, the view that 'technocracy — rule by technologists and scientists' can be regarded as 'a transition stage before some new democratic system can be introduced'.[32] The belief that scientists and scholars should replace politicians in order to create a more rational, just way of life is not a new or exclusively Russian idea, but has been expressed throughout history by such thinkers as Plato, Campanella, Bacon, Saint-Simon and H. G. Wells. In the early 1960s some Soviet scientists even appeared to believe that this dream was coming true: Academician Artsimovich, at the 1963 Pugwash Conference, declared: 'We are voluntary advisers to our political leaders.'[33] A passing reference in a science fiction work by the Strugatsky brothers, *The Second Martian Invasion* (1968),[34] to rebels who discuss 'technocracy' suggests that this was still a live issue among Soviet scientists and managers — a supposition confirmed by a *Pravda* article of 1968 which warned of the dangers of rule by an academic elit.[35] An official work of 1979 on the period of 'developed socialism' in the USSR contains a more sanguine allusion by Georgy Shakhnazarov to 'rule by scientists' (*uchonokratiya*), showing that the debate is still continuing.[36]

Rule by party 'technocrats' is, however, a less controversial issue than the desire of Soviet scientists themselves to seize political power. The only writer to discuss this explicitly is Solzhenitsyn, who, in two chapters omitted from the original version of *The First Circle*, portrays the optics expert Gerasimovich as a rebel prepared to take up arms against the Soviet regime. Gerasimovich is moved by a description of Pavel Korin's pictorial series 'Vanishing Russia' which depicts many groups of people who once played an important part in Russian history but have now disappeared: statesmen, landowners, merchants, peasants, reformers, writers, scholars in the humanities, even revolutionaries. Gerasimovich feels that the only class capable of restoring Russia's greatness is the scientific and technical elite, and dreams of a new revolution which will create a rationally organised society ruled by a scientific oligarchy. Although Solzhenitsyn has, in *August 1914*, expressed considerable sympathy for the concept of a leading political role for scientists and engineers through his portrait of Obodovsky, the founder of the Union of Engineers, he nevertheless indicates the shortcomings and dangers of Gerasimovich's scheme: the lack of sufficient dedicated men, the excessive power of the Soviet regime, the tragic consequences of violent upheaval, the possible restoration of tyranny and the need to create a new society with ethical goals, not purely material ones.

In his more recent political writings Solzhenitsyn has expressed disillusionment with his earlier, politically naive belief in the possibility of technocratic rule. In his essay 'The Smatterers', Solzhenitsyn attacks the weakness of the Soviet intelligentsia's actual fight for freedom, condemning scientists who pursue their work peacefully, talking frankly in private, but lacking the courage to demand reform openly.[37] Similarly, Amalrik maintains that the most widespread sentiment in Soviet academic circles is 'conformist reformist ideology' — the comforting belief that gradual, piecemeal reforms and the substitution of more intelligent leaders for the present bureaucracy will eventually create a more humane society.[38]

Zinoviev, in *The Yawning Heights*, takes a cynical view of the enthusiastic espousal of cybernetics by the 'progressive forces' of Soviet society. Through his portrait of Teacher, a genuine cyberneticist, he suggests that liberals were originally attracted into the study of social cybernetics because they were 'suddenly presented with a means of ideological and organisational unification sanctioned from below'. Now there is a 'boom' in cybernetics, but when the enthusiasm wanes 'any scientists worthy of the name will have been eliminated and crushed', and cybernetics will be integrated into the Soviet scientific establishment. Teacher pessimistically predicts that the next stage will be total disillusionment with cybernetics as a force for social change. Zinoviev has been proved correct in so far as the outspoken social cyberneticist Valentin Turchin has been forced to emigrate. From the experience of cybernetics in the USSR Zinoviev draws a stern lesson for the dissident movement: 'The opposition must stop decking itself out in alien rags and tatters of science, art and economics. It must speak out in its own name without resorting to camouflage.'

In *The Radiant Future* Zinoviev gives an autobiographical account of the well-organised *prorabotka* or 'working over' which an errant scholar is obliged to undergo: a commission is organised to investigate his case; he is reprimanded at various public meetings and eventually dismissed. Zinoviev's picture of Soviet scholarship is particularly gloomy, and it is not surprising that he was compelled to emigrate. His analysis, however, goes further than mere personal animosity or a study of corruption in Soviet science: in some of his later works, such as *The Yellow House* and *In the Antechamber of Paradise*, he uses a study of the intrigue and power relationships in a scientific institute as a microcosm of Soviet society as a whole.[39]

Fiction on Production Themes

The post-Khrushchev period has been characterised by a tedious stream of conformist literature on production themes.[40] Poor writers endorse party policy actively and specifically; the better ones do it more subtly, in more general terms. One particularly orthodox writer on production themes is Mikhail Kolesnikov, whose series about the worker Altunin, who becomes a model industrial director and eventually a deputy minister, was praised by Soviet critics, although the public was less than enthusiastic.[41] In his novel *Altunin takes a Decision* (1976) Kolesnikov advocates a long-tried and tested area of party policy, the amalgamation of enterprises into large associations or 'firms' (*firma*, or *kombinat*). Similarly, in *School for Ministers* (1977), Altunin champions another idea which had been discussed in the press: arranging the production in Siberia of equipment for the mining industry especially designed for use in Arctic conditions.

Production literature of the 1970s and 1980s contains many of the same themes as earlier fiction, showing that the problems in Soviet industry have remained remarkably constant. Such continuity is not particularly surprising, as most Western observers agree that Kosygin's economic reforms of 1965–70, which gave individual factory managers greater autonomy and emphasised such capitalist 'economic levers' as quality and profits, did not have as significant an effect as was originally hoped. Although the Brezhnev-Kosygin regime managed the economy better than Khrushchev, their experience illustrates the difficulty facing a bureaucratic regime which wishes to modernise the economy without threatening ideological purity and political stability.

Literary works of the early 1970s such as V. Popov's *You Will Find Yourself in Battle* (1970), Lev London's *How to become Chief Engineer* (1970) and Kolesnikov's *The Right of Choice* (1971) make no direct reference to Kosygin's economic reforms, but evoke the perennial problems in Soviet industry: the difficulty of introducing technological innovation when plan-fulfilment is the basic criterion of success; slack periods in factories caused by poor supplies, followed by periods of rushed work or 'storming'; the persistence of dishonest practices; dictatorial methods of management and poor industrial relations; and the need for closer co-operation between science and production engineering. There are, however, certain new variations on old themes. In their portrayal of workers Soviet authors have tended to stress a new type, the so-called 'intellectual worker', in line with the party's emphasis on removing the distinction between manual and intellectual work. Bondarenko's *Time Trouble* updates the traditional conflict between innovators and conservatives by placing it in a new area of industry: the production of computers, which is shown to be very backward. Such writers as Popov, Kolesnikov and London contrast the old authoritarian style of management with new 'scientific' methods of direction based on technological innovation, concern for quality, cost-accounting, incentives, and the correct organisation of production. The entrenched opposition of bureaucrats to these new ideas suggests the hostility with which industrial managers regarded Kosygin's economic reforms.

Fiction of the post-Khrushchev period does not deal frankly with such controversial subjects as the stifling effects of the bureaucracy, the resistance to technological change and the conflict between the State Committee for Science and Technology, the Academy of Sciences and the ministries, which, in the opinion of Western observers, hampers both creative scientific effort and production efficiency. The speeches of the party leaders on such subjects are often more revealing than fiction: for example, Brezhnev at the Twenty-Sixth Party Congress stated:

> Research and design work should be more closely integrated with production, both economically and organisationally . . . one still encounters impermissible sluggishness in putting promising developments into production . . . We must look into the reasons why we sometimes lose our priority and spend large sums of money to purchase from foreign countries equipment and technologies that we are fully capable of producing ourselves, and often of a higher quality too.

Critics were constantly exhorting writers to create interesting novels on production themes,[42] but, perhaps because such works were not forthcoming, Dudintsev's *Not by Bread Alone* was republished in 1979 without alterations. This suggests that the theme of the inventor's struggle with bureaucracy was still topical, but because the novel was set in the distant past it no longer aroused serious controversy.

Some new issues have been introduced into literature of the 1970s and 1980s. The greater emphasis on consumer goods, symbolised by the Soviet government's decision at the Twenty-Third Congress of 1965 to encourage the production of private cars, has been reflected in literary works which no longer present cars as symbols of bureaucracy, but as possessions which it is natural for managers to acquire and for ordinary people to aspire to. Other topical subjects treated in fiction are an acknowledgement that the USSR produces too many engineers and that there are not enough interesting jobs for them; the need to give workers a 'polytechnic' education in order to prevent possible redundancy as a result of automation; demographic problems such as the rapid turnover of labour and the difficulty of encouraging people to work in Siberia; and the danger of introducing Western technology wholesale without reference to Russian conditions.

The Management of Industry

Drama was the most lively genre treating production themes in the 1970s. Major issues under discussion were the new type of industrial manager which the country needed and the relationship between 'efficiency' and 'morality' in industry. Discussions of fictional characters featured not only in literary magazines, but also in economics journals, demonstrating the seriousness with which literature was taken in economic debates.

Attention was focused on two plays, Ivan Dvoretsky's *The Outsider* (1972) and Gennady Bochkaryov's *Steelworkers* (1973), both of which enjoyed considerable success with the Soviet public.[43] The hero of *The Outsider*, Cheshkov, was the most discussed stage 'positive hero' of 1972. Superficially he seems to fit the traditional model of the innovator combating conservatives: he is a young, knowledgeable engineer who comes to a Leningrad factory as superintendent of a new casting shop where long-established methods are no longer in keeping with the demands of the time. He begins to introduce reforms abrasively, precipitating a crisis when 30 specialists ask to leave; but Cheshkov's radical reorganisation of management and labour is finally shown to be justified. Dvoretsky frankly exposes the hide-bound psychology of the factory collective which Cheshkov tries to eradicate. One problem is permissiveness: such practices as keeping on elderly secretaries who cannot do shorthand; indulgence towards drunkards and truants; time-wasting on lengthy reports; and allowing workers extra time off. Another difficulty is 'storming', a practice first criticised in the fiction of the 1950s.[44] Most seriously, Cheshkov has to deal with misinformation and the telling of outright lies for the sake of plan-fulfilment: the practice of signing that goods are completed when they do not yet exist, or producing the wrong materials and allocating them to false categories. It is interesting that the faults of the factory collective in this play, which derived from the maintenance of friendly relations established during the blockade of Leningrad, had become something like capital offences during the 'Leningrad Case' of the late 1940s. Since G. Kulagin, general director of the Sverdlov Machine Building Combine in Leningrad, stated that the actual factory described by Dvoretsky would be easily recognisable to any inhabitant of Leningrad,[45] it is rather surprising that such a situation could have persisted until the early 1970s.

Cheshkov tackles these production problems in the spirit of the party's economic reforms. He emphasises strict lines of responsibility; a rigidly scheduled work rhythm; precise, objective information; and an end to dishonest practices. He is primarily not a technical specialist, but an economist whose chief aim is profitability and a lower unit of cost of output. One critic saw Cheshkov, with his emphasis on economic efficiency and technical progress, as an important model to follow: 'The future of our economy lies with people like Cheshkov.'

Some Soviet economists, such as Academician A. Aganbegyan, Director of the Economics Institute at Novosibirsk, considered works like *The Outsider* to be an important method of influencing public opinion: a means of awakening people — including, perhaps, the party leaders — to faults in industry and preparing the way for economic reforms. At a discussion of production literature in 1974, after Kosygin's reforms had been virtually abandoned, Aganbegyan claimed:

> Economists now know what must be fought for. But public opinion has not sufficiently matured for many economic steps to be taken . . . What economics asks of literature is that literature use all its resources to prepare public opinion for changes connected with the scientific and technological revolution.[46]

Although economists wanted to enlist writers as their allies in promoting the cause of reform, literature did not always rise to the challenge. The production plays of Alexander Gelman continued to enjoy critical and public popularity in the late 1970s and early 1980s, but in 1982 a critic complained: 'The artistic representation of the man of affairs in our time seems to have come to a standstill.'[47]

Dvoretsky's play *The Outsider* also featured in the debate about morality in industry, as did Bochkaryov's *Steelworkers*, produced by the Moscow Arts Theatre in 1973–4. The play was successful both because of its visual impact and its unusual approach to the problem of the 'positive hero'. Bochkaryov raises an issue fashionable in literary discussions of the 1970s: the contradiction between the 'business-like' approach in industry — an emphasis on efficiency, modernity, discipline, order, even ruthlessness — and the 'human' approach — a concentration on people, whose interests are not always served by scientific progress. The hero of *Steelworkers*, Victor Lagutin, who seems at the beginning of the play to be almost a parody of the typical 'positive hero', has an unusual twist to his character — a point which attracted the producer O. Efremov to the play in the first place.[48] Victor is right, but wrong at the same time, and he clashes with a 'good' collective which is wrong, but right at the same time. The outcome is ambiguous in both the play and the production. Victor, a new employee, witnesses technical malpractices in the steelworks: ore is put into the furnace before it is hot enough in order to fulfil the plan and make sure of the prize money. Victor speaks out, and a glib deputy manager who is adept at mouthing all the current political slogans, such as the importance of quality and of eliminating dishonesty, persuades him into taking over, prematurely, the job of the foreman he has exposed. Victor is so convincing in his initial refusal of the job, and the injustice of his nomination is so obvious, that the audience in the theatre gasped with astonishment at his change of mind. As foreman, he alienates his brigade by calling them 'shopkeepers, not working class' because they express more interest in money than their jobs. He is infuriated by the sight of the bar which workers use between shifts, because his father died in an accident caused by a drunken driver; and he finally drives his bulldozer into it. In all this Victor acts as the standard positive hero, but his fanaticism has proved counter-productive: he has alienated the collective.

Towards the end of the play the workers are prepared to let Victor face responsibility for his actions at a factory meeting, to be followed by court proceedings. However, the last scene shows the workers passing a steelworker's helmet round to collect money to pay for Victor's destruction of the bar. This is an effective ending — but ambiguous. By analogy with Dvoretsky's *The Outsider*, the interpretation could be that the collective has decided to support Victor because the positive hero is right, despite his abrasiveness. But the producer Efremov interpreted it differently: the factory collective is bound by a code of unwritten laws which makes them recognise Victor's sincerity. Victor, seeing the actions of the collective, becomes aware that their rules are not wholly negative, and learns a lesson in humanity, or humility.[49]

The importance of a humane approach in industrial relations was stressed in discussions of these two plays. *Steelworkers* was generally welcomed, but Victor's moral extremism came under attack. Certain critics considered that the conflicts in the plays were wrongly presented, both from the moral and social points of view. While praising Cheshkov's managerial reforms in *The Outsider*, the critic Kuznetsov argued that 'technology' and 'humanism' need not necessarily be opposed in the 'era of the scientific and technological revolution'.[50] The industrial director Kulagin took exception to the fact that in both plays the hero, 'a man essential to society, becomes obviously stupid, not simply unsympathetic, but actually stupid'. In an ideal world Cheshkov's emphasis on honesty and labour discipline should permit him to triumph, but he is often rigid and incompetent in the real world. Similarly, Bochkaryov's Victor cannot perform the useful social function of encouraging reluctant Soviet people to become workers or inspiring them to fight indiscipline and unscientific methods, because he is presented in a disadvantageous light and opposed to the 'positive' collective. Kulagin quotes the comments of two workers who went to see the play: 'No, of course, a crank like him won't be able to do anything. They'll soon get rid of him.'[51]

These literary discussions demonstrate that, although Kosygin's economic reforms had largely been abandoned after 1971, economic officials, along with the party leaders, were still deeply concerned about managerial efficiency and more rational methods of running the economy. This again became evident in 1983, when Andropov made new attempts at limited economic reform.

Industrial Malpractices

Some of the most interesting works on technological themes published during the Brezhnev period ventured further than the official policy of making a general condemnation of corruption by describing industrial malpractices in detail. *Forty Years before my Pension* (1965), the first work of fiction by the scientific journalist Lev Vladimirov (the pseudonym of Leonid Finkelstein, who now lives in London), described how defective parts of a machine are used in order to keep the factory's conveyor belt going: the faulty machines will be kept in the factory and the defective parts replaced later. The narrator asks: 'Is this a normal practical approach or a crime?'[52] The persistence of dishonest practices in industry in the 1970s is illustrated by Alexander Avdeenko's *By the Sweat of his Brow* (1978),[53] which portrays Bulatov, the director of a famous industrial combine who retains his former prestige by resorting to inhumane or illegal methods. He allocates housing exclusively to people who work in his enterprise, so if their wives work elsewhere they have to pay him for the privilege of living in a flat owned by the factory; and he refuses to rehouse people living in a settlement which has been ruined by pollution caused by waste gases from his factory. He also indulges in illegal practices such as hoarding reserves of unconditioned steel which he uses to produce machinery above the plan. His chief engineer has to send 'pushers' (*tolkachi*) to acquire foreign machinery on the side in order to repair the damage caused by 'storming' and overloading machines. In Avdeenko's novel the problem is solved by the death of Bulatov and his replacement by the more humane, progressive chief engineer. The implication is that in real life such practices continue and cannot be so easily overcome. This supposition is confirmed by A. Kashtanov's novel *The Pedlars* (1981), which frankly describes the life of a 'pusher' in the car industry, and the bribery and corruption needed to acquire supplies and keep the industry moving.[54] Kashtanov's novel is an example of a literary work which raised important economic and moral issues before they had been publicly exposed and dealt with by the party. The narrator Yushkov, sent on a business trip to acquire special steel for his car factory, has to resort to giving the hotel manageress some expensive face cream; starting a relationship with Irina, an influential worker in the sales department of the metal combine; and wining and dining the foreman responsible for producing the steel he requires. He learns from more experienced 'pushers' that the only way to get what he wants is either to give the factory something it badly needs in exchange or to accept substandard metal. Later, when Yushkov changes places, becoming deputy director of a supply bureau, his boss, Belan, is arrested for taking large money bribes and sentenced to ten years in prison (it is also implied that Belan accepts sexual favours from female 'pushers'). Yushkov himself becomes head of the supply department, and tries to work in a purely legal manner, without bribery, but supplies very rapidly break down. The experienced director of the car factory, Khokhlov, remarks: 'If we begin like this, we'll be without engines altogether.'

The end of the novel is inconclusive: Yushkov does manage to acquire goods through official channels, for example by fining factories which are dilatory in fulfilling their orders, but he still occasionally has to resort to old methods. The novel ends with a reference to a new director, Buryak, who has abolished the practice of using 'pushers'. The implication is that the party is concerned about problems of poor supplies and corruption in industry. This was confirmed soon after the publication of Kashtanov's novel, in September 1981, when the party revived a practice virtually abandoned under Brezhnev of the confidential circularisation of party primary organisations telling them to stiffen measures against bribery and corruption. In 1981–2 a strict anti-corruption drive was organised by Andropov who, with Suslov's support, aimed at discrediting Brezhnev by compromising revelations about his daughter

Galina, his son Yury, his relative General Tsvigun, First Deputy
Chairman of the KGB, and other members of Brezhnev's party
circle. The hardening of the official attitude towards speculation
and corruption was also demonstrated in September 1982, shortly
before Brezhnev's death, by a frank article by the industrialist
Kulagin entitled 'How to Deal with Pedlars?'.[55] Conversations with
specialists had convinced him that the black picture which Kashtanov paints is true, but he distinguishes between those who are
obliged to sin in the state's interests, for the sake of their enterprise,
and those who, like Belan, take bribes for personal gain. Kulagin
proposes certain measures to improve this 'paradoxical situation',
including such radical solutions as the elimination of all deficits and
an increase in material reserves. However, he frankly admits that
the shadowy figure of the 'positive' director Buryak is a symbol
rather than a reality; and that the pragmatic director of the car
factory Khokhlov, who dislikes irregular methods, but can suggest
no alternative if the plan is to be fulfilled, is a much more realistic
character. The extent of the problem exposed by Kashtanov and
Kulagin's frank response suggest that it may be a long time before
the party can finally eradicate dishonest practices which oil the
wheels of Soviet industry.

Notes

1. *Pravda*, 9 Oct. 1976; Brezhnev, *Pravda*, 24 Feb. 1981.
2. N. Amosov, *Mysli i serdtse* (M, 1969); D. Konstantinovsky, ... *Sledovatelno, sushchestvuyu* (M, 1974).
3. Yu. Shcherbak, *Kak na voine* (M, 1967).
4. G. Pandzhikidze, *Kamen chistoi vody. Sedmoe nebo* (M, 1973).
5. On sociology, see M. Kolesnikov, *Pravo vybora* (M, 1971), p. 78; on economics, see Shcherbak, *Kak na voine*, p. 118.
6. B. Bondarenko, *Piramida* (M, 1976), p. 126 (written 1963–73 in Obninsk).
7. Popovsky, *Science in Chains*, pp. 158–79.
8. V. Makanin, *Pryamaya liniya* (M, 1967), p. 197.
9. Zh. Medvedev, *Soviet Science*, p. 179.
10. A. Sofronov, *Operatsiya na serdtse, Moskva*, 1981, no. 8.
11. *CDSP*, XXXIV (1982), no. 42, pp. 6–7, 42.
12. V. Kaverin, *Dvukhchasovaya progulka, NM*, 1978, no. 11.
13. M. Popovsky, *Science in Chains*, p. 33.
14. I. Grekova, *Kafedra, NM*, 1978, no. 9, p. 138.
15. L. Orlov, *LG*, 18 Mar. 1981.
16. V. Gusev, *LO*, 1979, no. 8, pp. 43–5.
17. Murphy, 'Academic Life', p. 424.
18. V. Komissarov, *Starye dolgi* (M, 1979).
19. A. Zinoviev, *The Radiant Future*, trans. G. Clough (London, 1981).
20. *LG*, 23 Aug. 1972.

21. N. Baranskaya, *Nedelya kak nedelya, NM,* 1969, no. 11, p. 53.
22. N. Baranskaya, *LG,* 10 Nov. 1971.
23. S. Zalygin, *Yuzhno-amerikanskii variant, NS,* 1973, nos. 1, 2.
24. P. Nilin, *Vpervye zamuzhem, NM,* 1978, no. 1.
25. M. Seton-Watson, 'Myth and Reality in Recent Soviet Fiction', *Coexistence. An International Journal,* vol. 19 (1982), pp. 213–19.
26. B. Bondarenko, *Poteryannoe mnoi* (M, 1973).
27. B. Bondarenko, *Tseitnot* (M, 1974).
28. A. Gladilin, *Prognoz na zavtra* (Frankfurt, 1972).
29. A. Zinoviev, *The Reality of Communism,* trans. C. Janson (London, 1984), p. 32.
30. M. Shatz, *Soviet Dissent in Historical Perspective* (Cambridge, 1980), p. 154.
31. A. Sakharov, *Sakharov Speaks,* ed. H. Salisbury (NY, 1974), p. 56.
32. L. Vladimirov, 'Soviet Science — a Native's Opinion', *New Scientist,* vol. 40 (28 Nov. 1968), p. 490.
33. A. Parry, *The New Class Divided* (NY and London, 1966), p. 171.
34. A. and B. Strugatsky, *The Second Martian Invasion,* in C. Bearne, (ed.), *Vortex* (London, 1970), p. 162.
35. V. Chkhivadze, *Pravda,* 10 Jan. 1968.
36. D. Kerimov (ed.), *Sovetskaya demokratiya v period razvitogo sotsializma,* 2nd, revised edn. (M, 1979), p. 171.
37. Solzhenitysn *et al., From Under the Rubble* (London, 1975), pp. 229–78.
38. A. Amalrik, *Will the USSR Survive Until 1984?* (NY and Evanston, 1970), pp. 27–8.
39. A. Zinoviev, *Zholtyi dom* (Paris, 1980); *V predverii raya* (Lausanne, 1979).
40. M. Kolesnikov, *Pravo vybora* (M, 1971); *Industrialnaya ballada* (M, 1972); V. Popov, *Obretyosh v boyu* (M, 1970); L. London, *Kak stat glavnym inzhenerom* (M, 1970); V. Kiselev, *Vesyolyi roman* (M, 1972); A. Krivonosov, *Gori, gori yasno, NM,* 1974, nos. 3, 4; Yu. Skop, *Tekhnika besopasnosti, NM,* 1977, nos. 2, 3.
41. M. Kolesnikov, *Izotopy dlya Altunina, Znamya,* 1974, nos. 1, 2; *Altunin prinimaet reshenie, Znamya,* 1976, nos. 1, 2; *Shkola dlya ministrov, Znamya,* 1977, nos. 10, 11.
42. Osnos, 'Literatura i NTR', p. 362.
43. I. Dvoretsky, *Chelovek so storony, Teatr,* 1972, no. 10; G. Bochkaryov, *Stalevary, Teatr,* 1973, no. 4.
44. F. Panfyorov, *Volga — matushka reka* (M, 1952), pp. 145, 178; A. Zlobin, *Pravda, kotoruyu ya skryval, LM,* 1956, no. 1, p. 686.
45. G. Kulagin, 'Cherty sovremennogo rukovoditelya promyshlennosti', *VL,* 1972, no. 8, p. 49.
46. V. Pertsovsky, A. Aganbegyan, cited in *CDSP,* vol. XXVI (1974), no. 37, pp. 6–7.
47. D. Tevekelyan, 'Sotri sluchainye cherty', *NM,* 1982, no. 5, p. 241.
48. O. Efremov, *VL,* 1973, no. 6, p. 16.
49. N. Volyanskaya, 'V tvorcheskoi laboratorii rezhissyora', *Teatr,* 1973, no. 10, p. 33; Efremov, *VL,* 1973, no. 6, pp. 14–15.
50. F. Kuznetsov, in *CDSP,* XXVI (1974), no. 51, p. 21.
51. Kulagin, *VL,* 1973, no. 6, pp. 28, 30.
52. L. Vladimirov, *Do pensii sorok let, NM,* 1965, no. 3, p. 28.
53. A. Avdeenko, *V pote litsa svoego . . . , NM,* 1978, nos. 1–3.
54. A. Kashtanov, *Korobeiniki, NM,* 1981, nos. 6, 7.
55. G. Kulagin, 'Kak byt s korobeinikami?', *Neva,* 1982, no. 9, pp. 150–6.

PART TWO

THE LITERATURE IN ITS WIDER CONTEXT

4 THE CULT OF SCIENCE

In the USSR Marxism-Leninism has bestowed on science an authority similar to that which believers confer on divine law. Science and technology, directed by the party, have been elevated to the level of a supremely important social value, the goal of which is the material improvement of human life, the defence of the state and the construction of the communist Utopia. It has always been in the interests of the party leaders to promote the worship of science in order to inspire respect for the Soviet regime, which claims to be based on science, to appeal to scientists and technologists whose skills are essential to the state and to provide the emotional impact necessary to create an optimistic faith capable of replacing traditional religion.

The Soviet cult of science is rooted in the 'Westernist' tendency of nineteenth-century Russian thought which led from the Decembrists of the 1820s to the 'nihilists' of the 1860s and eventually to the Russian Marxist movement. The Russian radical intelligentsia often borrowed ideas from the West which they had not always fully understood, expressing a passionate, uncritical faith in science as a panacea. Marxism claims that science provides the one true explanation of the world and the one guide to human action; and the Bolsheviks, armed with a Marxist determination to 'change the world', were committed to science from the very inception of Soviet rule. Lenin's enthusiasm for science and technology is also attributable to the voluntarist psychology demonstrated theoretically in his *April Theses* (1917) and practically in the October Revolution: the overwhelming desire to speed up the processes of history and hasten the advent of the socialist future through the application of man's reason and will-power. Lenin's views are illustrated by his enthusiastic pronouncement during the electrification project of the 1920s (GOELRO): 'Communism equals Soviet power plus the electrification of the whole country.' Stalin's doctrine of 'socialism in one country' and his exhortations during the First and subsequent Five Year Plans endorsed and extended the wishful thinking inherent in Lenin's theory of revolution. There is a striking continuity of thought from the 1920s to the 1950s, when Khrushchev too liked to represent himself as a Great Scientist, the infallible interpreter of

131

the single 'scientific' doctrine. Since Khrushchev's fall, party leaders such as Brezhnev, Suslov, Kosygin, Andropov and Chernenko have all been optimistic supporters of the 'NTR'.

Apart from the official current of Soviet ideology embodied by successive party leaders, there was another trend in Russian Marxist thought which contributed to the cult of science — the secular pseudo-religion of 'God-building' (*bogostroitelstvo*) which flourished in the left wing of the Bolshevik faction of the Russian Social Democratic and Labour Party in the decade after 1903 and was particularly associated with the names of Gorky, Lunacharsky and Bogdanov. The 'God-builders' believed that human history was a workshop for the creation of a biologically, psychologically and socially perfected breed of men, vastly surpassing the frail imperfect man of the present in power, creativity and beauty. Since this ideal human race would be supra-individual, 'immortal', a source of inspiration to ephemeral individuals and therefore truly divine, the creation of the perfected human culture of the future could thus be called the 'building of God'.

Although in 1909 the Bolshevik Central Committee officially condemned the doctrine of 'God-building', the Prometheanism of Plekhanov and Lenin differed less from that of the 'God-builders' in actual substance than in presentation and emphasis. While the latter emphasised the exalted, 'religious' dimension of man's historical task, Plekhanov and Lenin insisted on purging Marxism of every vestige of religious language and symbolism, however 'secularised'. Yet Lenin too sometimes spoke of the 'creation of heaven on earth' and was, like the 'God-builders', committed to the transformation of history through the medium of science and technology.[1] Influenced by his years in an Orthodox seminary, Stalin resurrected the vocabulary and symbolism of religion to make his ruthless social engineering more palatable to the masses. Perhaps unwittingly, he revived some of the ideas of Bogdanov, whom Lenin had discredited: the emphasis which he laid in 1935 on 'Socialist Man', 'a new man of a hitherto unknown species' whose will-power and political consciousness were to change the world; and his official adoption in 1948 of the theory of the 'two sciences' — the notion that there is an inevitable incompatibility between bourgeois and socialist science — which sanctioned Lysenko's scientific charlatanism and isolated Soviet science from the science of the rest of the world.

The 'God-builders' may have derived inspiration from the

writings of the religious philosopher Nikolai Fyodorov (1828–1903). Fyodorov believed that man's purpose was to transform mortal life on earth into an immortal existence in the universe through the application of human reason. He devised ambitious scientific plans designed to regulate the forces of nature and extend man's control over his own evolution and believed that mankind would ultimately be able to achieve the physical resurrection of the dead.[2] Fyodorov's ideas had a considerable impact on both Soviet literature and science. Views similar to those of Fyodorov can be discerned, for example, in Gorky's prose poem *Man* (1904), Mayakovsky's poem *War and the Universe* (1916), Platonov's stories *Descendants of the Sun* (1922) and *The Ether Way* (1927),[3] the works of Bryusov, Zabolotsky and Pasternak. Fyodorov was known to some Soviet intellectuals in the early 1960s, and a selection of his work was published in 1982 (without his religious writings). Fyodorov's ideas also exerted a powerful influence on such eminent scientists as the geochemist V. I. Vernadsky (1863–1945) and Konstantin Tsiolkovsky, the pioneer of Soviet space research, who both had faith in the limitless powers of human reason. Tsiolkovsky believed that scientific progress and man's conquest of space would ensure the immortality of mankind; and Vernadsky envisaged the development of the noosphere, the sphere of human reason, on a planetary scale. Soviet science has actually implemented certain proposals advocated by Fyodorov: the control of meteorological processes, the expansion of the Russian waterway system, the irrigation of desert areas, the utilisation of solar energy and the promotion of space travel.

Such grandiose projects sponsored by the Soviet authorities have provided the most tangible evidence of the cult of science in the USSR. During Stalin's Five Year Plans, the party's emphasis on the ability of man to become master of his fate was exemplified in industry by the 'Great Construction Projects of Communism' and in agriculture by the 'Great Stalin Plan for the Transformation of Nature' (1948). Since the Second World War the party leaders have channelled vast resources into military and prestige projects: the development of atomic energy, nuclear weapons and the space programme. Khrushchev's belief in scientific miracles inspired his agricultural and chemical campaigns, his extravagant claims that production of meat, milk and butter in the USSR would soon surpass that of the USA, and his exploitation of nuclear tests and 'space salutes' for purely political reasons. Since Khrushchev's fall each Five Year Plan has contained an ambitious project to capture the imagination: the Tenth Five Year Plan (1976–80) envisaged the construction of BAM, the Baikal-Amur Railway in Siberia, a 3,000-kilometre railway line linking Eastern Siberia to the Pacific with the aim of opening up the mineral resources of Siberia.

Although the Soviet authorities have consistently stressed the practical application of science and technology, there are certain fields in which theoretical work is encouraged because it reflects the basic tenet of dialectical materialism that the possibilities of science are limitless and that science can answer all the riddles of the universe by recognising the priority and eternity of matter. The aim of using natural science to refute the theological 'argument from design' — to prove that life, the universe and the human psyche can be explained without recourse to a supernatural intelligence — explains why the search for the origins of cosmic bodies and life figures so prominently in the plans of Soviet research institutes. The studies of protein and photosynthesis both satisfy Soviet scientific optimism and are concerned with long-term practical problems, such as the creation of new forms of plant and animal life and the improvement of existing ones.

Another theoretical sphere in which the Soviet cult of science has manifested itself is the search for a unified physical picture of the world — a consequence of the attempt to create a unified picture of the world as a whole. This is a problem of great importance to dialectical materialism, since it is the doctrine's claim to be a universal philosophy, equipped to answer all questions concerning the world and the processes occurring in it, which has the most effect on the psychology of the masses. Communist philosophy has always striven to prove that the laws of the development of nature, society and thought must objectively and inevitably lead to communism, and hence that resistance to communism is useless. The search for a unified picture of the world was particularly evident in the writings of communist theoreticians of the 'mechanist' tendency in the 1920s, such as A. Bogdanov who attempted to reduce all phenomena to a single universal science of organisation which he called 'tectology', and Nikolai Bukharin, who regarded society as a huge working mechanism operating according to the principles of a kind of energetics.[4] Although Bogdanov and Bukharin subsequently fell out of favour with the Communist Party, Lenin himself gave his blessing to a work by I. I. Skvortsov-Stepanov which also tried to explain the entire universe in terms of the laws of thermodynamics.[5] The dogmatism of the Stalin period rendered serious discussion of this subject impossible, but some physicists took up the challenge in the post-Stalin era, notably D. I. Blokhintsev, after 1956 director of the Joint Institute of Nuclear Research at Dubna. The main problem confronting Soviet physicists was Lenin's definition of matter in *Materialism and Empiriocriticism*, which, although directly opposed to the physics even of Lenin's time, was still accepted as authoritative.

Another striking feature of the Soviet cult of science is the desire to prolong life with the ultimate goal of achieving physical immortality — a result of two fundamental psychological problems affecting communists, who are men of atheistic convictions but religious temperament. They have the natural human fear of death, but at the same time wish to deify man, as their particular temperament requires a god, only one who does not conflict with Soviet ideology. They therefore hope that man will render himself physically immortal and become his own god-substitute. The search for resurrection is also firmly rooted in the Russian Orthodox tradition which lays great emphasis on physical immortality.

This current of thought had an impact on both pre- and post-revolutionary medical research. In the Soviet period the party leaders have encouraged medical research in three related fields: the prolongation of life, the resuscitation of the critically ill and the attempt to create life from lifeless matter. One prominent figure was A. A. Bogomolets (1881–1946), who believed that the 'connective tissue' was the key to ageing and developed a serum which, it is rumoured, was used to treat Stalin. In Stalin's last years, probably because of his own fear of death, official encouragement was given to the quack remedies of Olga Lepeshinskaya, an Old Bolshevik who had run a canteen for revolutionaries in Geneva before the Revolution, but in 1950, at the age of 80, won a Stalin Prize for her 'new cell theory', supported by Lysenko, which claimed that it was possible to obtain cells from non-cellular matter in 24 hours. Lepeshinskaya also maintained that life could be prolonged by soda baths or enemas; it is alleged that she treated Stalin in a small clinic in the Kremlin.

In the post-Stalin era, interest was aroused by the work of the Romanian scientist Anna Aslan, who claimed to have prolonged life by intramuscular injections of Novacain. Aslan was allowed to set up a clinic in Moscow, but the reasons for her failure to repeat her Romanian success in the USSR were not published because they were politically controversial: in Romania, Aslan had treated patients from old people's homes who benefited as much from hospital care as from her injections, whereas in the USSR the first people to undergo revitalisation therapy were top-ranking government and party officials, including Khrushchev himself. Nevertheless, although the treatment was not particularly successful, the interest taken in this subject by elderly political leaders led to the establishment of several institutes of gerontology and experimental pathology. Research into ageing has, according to Zhores Medvedev, received far more encouragement in the USSR than the West, where concern about the population explosion and the cost of supporting an ever-increasing proportion of old people in society has made gerontology an unpopular branch of science.[6] At a sub-scientific level Soviet people, including party officials, have always shown interest in the question of immortality:[7] they have, for example, expressed great enthusiasm and an inordinate credulity about the claims of centenarians living in the mountains of Abkhazia. In the post-Stalin era, Russian scientists writing popular articles on old age have often felt obliged to discuss immortality, whatever their personal convictions.[8]

Another result of the Soviet blend of scientific optimism, atheism and superstition is psychic research, which has been carried out in the USSR for a long time: the fields of investigation include telepathy, the movement of objects, eyeless sight, 'dowsing', the possibility of diagnosing disease from the 'psychic aura' before it occurs, UFOs and folk healing. In 1968 newspapers condemned parapsychology for its 'shocking seminars', 'specious theories' and 'lack of a clear political line', but research continues in many areas.[9] The *émigré* writers Topol and Neznansky suggest in their thriller *Red Square* that by 1982 the fashion for parapsychology had spread among the Soviet leaders.

In the post-Stalin era the party leaders had particularly urgent political reasons for promoting the cult of science, as Stalin's death and subsequent dethronement had created a spiritual void among the Soviet population. Previously science had been an acceptable object of faith as a handmaiden of the party and the god-like Stalin; yet since faith implies a belief in something greater than man which will explain the mysteries of life, science alone could not provide such an attractive focus of belief now that the 'Greatest Scientist of All Times' had been discredited. Scientific work performed by ordinary men could not appeal, in the words of Dostoevsky's Grand

Inquisitor, to 'mystery, miracle and authority', only to reason, method and objectivity. Hence it was in the interests of the party leaders to reawaken people's enthusiasm for science by devising new Utopian scientific projects which could be presented as a means of building communism. Although Khrushchev's prognosis that the era of 'full communism' would be attained by 1981 has been abandoned by his successors, the persistence of scientific optimism among the party leaders has been evinced by such projects as the Salyut space station and the recently completed BAM.

Yet quite apart from officially imposed optimism, there does seem to have been a genuine enthusiasm for science and technology in the USSR during the post-Stalin period.[10] Scientific Promethean-ism, the unacknowledged heir to the views of Fyodorov and the 'God-builders', provided a quasi-religious surrogate for Stalinism, a valid alternative to both Marxism-Leninism and traditional reli-gion. The cult of science was a current and growing view among the scientific and technological elite. It was an attractive philosophy for scientists, since it harnessed emotional and spiritual elements to an activity primarily based on reason, satisfying the scientist's desire to transcend his own ego and work for the good of humanity, and possessing much greater emotional appeal than the narrow materialism of Marxist-Leninist ideology.

Soviet literature since 1953 has been permeated with a faith in science which reflects both party policy and the views of Soviet scientists. Technological Prometheanism is a suitable philosophy for Soviet authors, since it corresponds to the party's requirement that the writer be an optimist. The worship of science necessitates an optimistic faith in the gradual improvement of human society; it banishes tragedy from man's existence and avoids any deeper dis-cussion of life and death, good and evil, the happiness and destiny of mankind, reducing all the dilemmas of human life to problems which can be solved by the application of science and technology.

This faith was exemplified by the new wave of Utopian science fiction which arose in the 1950s, resurrecting the Wellsian tradition of the 1920s which had fallen into abeyance in the Stalin era. The resurgence of this genre was inspired by the sensational achieve-ment of the sputnik, in conjunction with the Twentieth Congress which had destroyed Stalinist myths about society. The most dis-cussed work was Ivan Efremov's *The Andromeda Nebula* (1957)[11] which, with its heroism, socialist humanism and unlimited faith in science, appealed greatly to Soviet youth and the intelligentsia. The portraits of harmonious, physically and morally perfected people of the communist future are reminiscent of the ideal of the 'God-builders'. Efremov's work, although criticised by dogmatists who argued that it was 'too far from our times', won enormous popularity in the USSR, and has since been reprinted at least 30 times.[12] The genre of science fiction — both Soviet works and translations of foreign writers such as Stanislav Lem, Ray Bradbury, Isaac Asimov and Arthur C. Clarke — has achieved greater popularity in the USSR than in almost any other country in the world.

A characteristic feature of much Soviet poetry of the post-Stalin era, for example that of Voznesensky and Leonid Martynov, is an enthusiastic acceptance of scientific development, which forms a striking contrast with the rural nostalgia of much modern Western poetry. Voznesensky's poem *New York Airport at Night* (1962),[13] for example, is a direct descendant of Mayakovsky's *Brooklyn Bridge* (1925) in its expression of excitement at the beauty and power of the structures of the contemporary technological age.

The Soviet 'science novel', heir of Chernyshevsky's *What is to be Done?* (1863), also testifies to the impact of the cult of science on its themes, characterisation, structure and imagery. A quasi-religious belief in Soviet science and an unbounded confidence in man's ability to master any scientific problem, to subjugate the forces of nature and change the world are regarded as fundamental convictions for any 'positive' Soviet scientist. An extreme example of such faith occurs in the revised version of Lvova's *Elena*. When Professor Prokofyev praises Lenin's statement that science will enable man to exercise boundless power over nature, his words fire the imagination of his pupil Elena, who seems to hear a heavenly choir singing 'an exalted and majestic cantata to the triumph of human reason'. Since Prokofyev later complains that some scientists in the post-Stalin era are becoming attracted to 'imaginary philosophical freedom', like Bogdanov in Lenin's time, it is ironic that Lvova's depiction of Elena's ecstatic transcendence of her individual personality in communion with a higher principle actually corresponds closely to the ideas of Bogdanov and the 'God-builders'.

Implicit in the cult of science is the view that every problem has a solution, a notion which enables writers to fulfil the party's demand for happy endings. Soviet literature almost invariably describes the successful resolution of the scientific or technical questions confronting the hero, or, if the hero dies, as in Gerasimovich's *Effect of*

Position, the work concludes with a firmly expressed conviction that the problem will be solved in the near future.

In Soviet fiction of the immediate post-Stalin period 1953–64 the work of the scientist was usually idealised. Although there was a great interest in the psychological process of creativity in the USSR in the late 1950s and early 1960s,[14] the majority of Soviet writers give only a superficial idea of the scientist's thought processes. That they make no attempt to describe the 'hypothetico-deductive method' discussed in the writings of Karl Popper need occasion no surprise; but neither do most authors make any serious attempt to evoke the process of 'induction' considered by philosophers since Bacon to be the fundamental feature of scientific thought. In general, Soviet writers paint a somewhat romantic, impressionistic picture of scientific thought, providing little more than a layman's idea of how scientists think. Perhaps this emerges most clearly from one recurrent feature of Soviet novels, the sudden moment of inspiration when the final detail of an invention or scientific theory flashes into the hero's mind. Although Granin has effectively satirised such a naive interpretation of scientific discovery, his own novels *The Seekers* and *Into the Storm* are not entirely free of this defect.[15]

Soviet writers seeking a dramatic plot frequently structure their works around scientific projects which have to be completed by a certain deadline. This reflects the need of Soviet scientists to fulfil the annual plan of their institutes, and, particularly, the strict deadlines imposed on scientists engaged in work of vital political significance, such as atomic or space research. In Golovanov's *Forgers of the Thunder*, the deadline is portrayed as a source of inspiration to the team of space scientists rushing to launch a rocket on time; there is no suggestion that ignorant officials are demanding too much of talented specialists for purely political reasons, or that the insistence on speed in replacing a faulty rocket could cause a serious accident, as it did in the cosmodrome disaster of 1960. In the fantasy world of Soviet fiction, plans are invariably fulfilled on time, and there are no insoluble problems or major accidents.

While the heroes of post-Stalin literature about science were more interesting and varied than those of the Stalin era, they still generally conformed to the notion of the 'positive hero' who possessed qualities of courage, integrity, dedication and idealism. Such writers as Granin and Dudintsev emphasise the single-minded, obsessive quality of scientific work; others stress that a scientist must be prepared to sacrifice himself in the cause of science, like Andrei Lvov in Kaverin's *Searches and Hopes* who, in the course of investigating a diptheria epidemic, takes a risk and catches the disease himself. The constant references to Galileo and Giordano Bruno in Soviet fiction suggest that writers have a romantic view of the scientist as a hero and martyr. The deaths of such scientists as Richard in Granin's *Into the Storm* and Victor in Aksyonov's *Starry Ticket* are uniformly portrayed as noble, never gratuitous and wasteful like the deaths of scientists in Stalin's purges. When writers depicted scientists who displayed traces of weakness, sadness or disillusionment, such as Vikhrov in Leonov's *The Russian Forest* or the central characters of Granin's *Personal Opinion* and Gorbunov's *The Mistake*, they were attacked by Soviet critics.[16] Evidently, to reactionary opinion in the USSR, the cult of science meant uncritical admiration, not penetrating analysis, doubt and questioning of the conduct and aims of Soviet science.

Although Soviet writers constantly extol the power of human reason, they frequently depict science and scientists with imagery derived from the spheres of religion, art or magic. While partly a consequence of the genuine enthusiasm for science felt by some writers, such comparisons also have the advantage of satisfying the party's need to arouse an interest in science among the population. The application of religious imagery to scientific themes fulfils the party's demand that faith in science should be elevated into a universal world-view capable of inspiring support for the Communist Party and of forming an effective substitute for religion. If science were regarded as a supremely important occupation, this could prevent young people disillusioned with Soviet ideology from turning to real religion or free artistic creativity.

The use of religious imagery to depict the power of the scientist was a cliché of Soviet writing during the post-Stalin period. It was particularly evident in works dealing with atomic physicists and space scientists: in Gor's *The University Embankment*, for example, a physicist who uses a cyclotron to speed up atomic particles is presented as a more powerful god than the biblical God, since he is able to penetrate into the very essence of matter. In Soviet poetry the sputnik is extolled not merely as a great technological achievement, but also as a symbol of man's creative forces and the divine power of human reason.[17] The variety of Prometheanism expressed in literature of the post-Stalin era seems to occupy a position between the viewpoint of Plekhanov and Lenin and that of the 'God-builders'; although it is closer to the former, the frequent use of religious terminology shows that it owes something to the views of Gorky, Lunacharsky and Bogdanov, or, at least, to the adaptation of their ideas in Stalinist thought.

The presentation of science in terms of magic is an attempt to suggest the imaginative, intuitive aspect of science and the super-human power of the scientist. In Bek's *Life of Berezhkov* an engine is criticised because it lacks 'revelation, magic, the quality with which genius astonishes us'. A particularly extended image of magic is contained in the first chapter of Granin's *Into the Storm*, which portrays the physicist Tulin as an attractive 'magician' with the power to predict and control the weather.

The comparison of the scientist's work to that of the artist is a recurrent image, used to evoke the creativity of scientific research, its emotional impact and the spiritual fulfilment it can provide. This was not a new idea which arose in the 1950s, but was sanctioned by the Soviet classics: Gorky, for example, stated that the beauty of science was 'more than anything else worthy of admiration, amazement, enthusiasm'.[18] The 'poetry of science' is a vague phrase much used by Soviet intellectuals to express three distinct concepts: the aesthetic beauty of scientific theories or experiments; the similarity of scientific work to the creative inspiration of the poet; and the enthusiasm and idealism shown by dedicated scientists. Most fiction, however, manifestly fails to evoke the peculiar beauty of scientific concepts and the similarity of the scientist's work to a poet's creativity. Writers frequently describe scientific or technical subjects in images taken from the worlds of art or poetry, but these rarely rise above the conventional, as, for example, in Nikolaeva's *Battle on the Way* when the chief engineer, admiring the smoothly running, aesthetically satisfying factory machinery, likens 'the dream of an engineer' to 'the dream of a poet'.

Some writers, however, were more successful in conveying various aspects of 'the poetry of science'. In *The Seekers* Granin evokes the unusual splendour of a laboratory at sunset and the aesthetic pleasure gained from such experiments as the weighing of sunlight by the famous physicist Lebedev and the examination of light through a spectroscope. Leonov's *Russian Forest* includes the whole of an inspired lecture on forestry given by Ivan Vikhrov; the translucent green light which suffuses the lecturer suggests bio-genesis, the close relationship between nature and a scientist who has devoted his life to investigating nature's mysteries.

The imagery of religion, magic and art and the attempt to convey the 'poetry of science' contribute to the idealisation of the figure of the scientist. Although Granin's personal experience enables him to give a realistic account of an engineer's problems, in *The Seekers* he also expresses a lofty conception of the role of the engineer, regarding him not merely as 'a man with a higher education', but as 'a creative thinker', from Latin *ingenium* meaning 'skill', 'talent', 'genius'. In *Not by Bread Alone*, Dudintsev too presents his hero in romantic terms as 'a man with a most noble soul. A bold, intelligent man . . . a real hero.'

Soviet literature tends to depict the more grandiose aspects of science and technology, as a result of the conformist writer's function of supporting new ventures sponsored by the party leaders. This is particularly exemplified by literary works eulogising the extravagant agricultural campaigns of Lysenko and Khrushchev, the space programme or Khrushchev's 'Great Chemistry' campaign initiated in 1958,[19] by stories depicting life on construction sites in Siberia and, more recently, by the plethora of works extolling the construction of BAM.[20] The emphasis on great scientific schemes is also attributable partly to the writer's need to choose an exciting subject in order to arouse the reader's interest and partly to the Utopian direction of Soviet scientific thought. In the post-Stalin era fiction on scientific themes frequently deals with ambitious projects currently advocated by Soviet scientists which resemble schemes from the realm of science fiction: Ketlinskaya's *Otherwise There is No Point in Living*, for example, is concerned with a geophysical project to divert the Siberian river network; Granin's *Into the Storm* with climate control through the dispersal of storm clouds; Alexander Popovsky's *Tale of Chlorella* with the possibility of developing soil algae as a food for human beings in the future. Dudintsev's *New Year's Tale* (1960) depicts a scientist who is studying the condensation of the sun's rays in order to provide a permanent source of energy for the inhabitants of the eternally dark half of the universe.[21] Although the subject is fantastic, it nevertheless reflects the Soviet authorities' interest in the development of alternative sources of energy — a preoccupation also demonstrated by the many works which extol the exploitation of atomic energy for peaceful purposes.[22] The blurring of the distinction between fact and fiction is evinced by Efremov's *Andromeda Nebula*, which evokes many cherished Soviet dreams: the use of science to increase life expectancy, reverse the flow of rivers, change the climate and combat pollution.

Soviet literature also mirrors the dialectical materialist attempt to provide a total scientific explanation of the world. Gor's story *The Namesake* (1956) refers to two subjects considered particularly vital in the USSR: cosmology and the origin of life.[23] The view associated with Lepeshinskaya, that it may one day be possible to transform inert matter into life, is, however, denounced for conflicting with the theories of Academician Oparin. Nikolaeva's *Battle on the Way* reflects Soviet scientists' interest in the birth of the universe through the portrait of the cosmologist Geizman, who praises man's profound knowledge of cosmology, but talks enthusiastically about the research into the secrets of the universe which remains to be done. In general, however, cosmology and cosmogony do not figure prominently in Soviet fiction, possibly because the scientific problems are so complex and the philosophical implications uncomfortable: before Stalin's death any interpretation of the universe which could be turned into an argument for divine agency was automatically suspect. In Nikolaeva's novel Geizman is arrested for his allegedly uncritical attitude towards the theory of the expanding universe propounded by the 'idealist' astrophysicists Milne and Abbé Lemaître. Geizman's view resembles that of the astrophysicist V. A. Ambartsumyan, a prominent spokesman for dialectical materialism who in 1958 affirmed his acceptance of the concept of the expanding universe.[24] The wider political and philosophical significance of research into photosynthesis and the origin of life is made plain in Bek's *Life of Berezhkov*: N. Zhukovsky, the famous 'father of Russian aviation', is invited by a group of young Pioneers to give a talk on 'the origin of life on earth', and when he proposes to lecture on a subject closer to his field is told: 'You must not think only of yourself . . . Nowadays scientists must pay attention to general questions of world outlook.'

Soviet scientists' preoccupation with the question of developing a unified physical picture of the world, reflected in fiction of the post-Stalin period, suggests that they were unacknowledged heirs to the mechanistic world-view of Bogdanov and Bukharin. In Gor's *University Embankment* a physicist argues that scientists should work single-mindedly on one great idea, like Einstein on the unified field theory. In Lvova's *Elena*, the chemist Prokofyev quotes his conversation with a Dubna physicist Luchintsev, who feels that cyclotons are reaching the limit of their development, and that although physicists possess considerable knowledge about elementary particles, they have no unifying theory of matter. Luchintsev regards quantum mechanics as only a temporary limit to man's understanding; there is a need for a 'mad idea' transcending all known theories of space and atomic particles. In view of the similarity of their names and ideas, the portrait of Luchintsev is probably modelled on Blokhintsev, who argued in 1959 that it was necessary to discard all old concepts and create a completely new theory combining high energy physics and the physics of elementary particles.[25] Lvova, however, is unaware, or omits to mention, that Blokhintsev's radical conception was opposed to dialectical materialism which seeks to create a new theory using old models and insists on the infinity of matter in space which physics wishes to abandon.

The growing pessimism about the possibility of creating a unified picture of the world is reflected in Granin's *Into the Storm*, in which the physicist Krylov, who at one time longed to create a unified field theory, now admits that Einstein's work on this problem was a 'hopeless, inopportune venture'. This attitude is reminiscent of Blokhintsev, who in 1964 changed his view about the future of quantum mechanics.[26] Naturally, Soviet fiction was unable to mention that the outdated views of Engels and Lenin presented a serious obstacle to Soviet physicists working in this area.

In 1976 this theme was again treated in Bondarenko's novel *Pyramid*, which portrays the physicist Dmitry who wants to construct a new theory of elementary particles, starting again from first principles. Eventually Dmitry writes a brilliant article overturning all contemporary theories of elementary particles, but it is hinted that, like Einstein after the formulation of relativity theory, and Dirac after the discovery of anti-matter, he may never again have another 'great idea', although he has provided enough material for hundreds, perhaps thousands, of people to work on for a long time. This suggests either that Bondarenko's hero is based on Blokhintsev, or that Soviet physicists have not abandoned research in this area. In view of the ideological difficulties facing them, however, it seems unlikely that Soviet physicists will succeed in creating a unified picture of the world.

The subject of parapsychology is treated in such science fiction works as Emtsev and Parnov's *World Soul* (1964),[27] but only occasionally surfaces in mainstream literature and is usually negatively presented. In Konstantinovsky's *Ergo sum*, however, the popularity of this subject is suggested by the fact that many scientists flock to an advertised lecture on psychic research, although it subsequently proves to be a hoax. A more sympathetic attitude to parapsychology is expressed in Trifonov's *Another Life* (1975), in which the historian Sergei attempts to attain understanding of dead people by means of spiritual seances: 'Parapsychology is a dream-like attempt to penetrate into another person, to give oneself to a person, to be healed by understanding.'[28]

Soviet literature, particularly the poetry of Mayakovsky, has always been full of medical and non-medical references to physical immortality. In post-Stalin fiction this is, however, little more than a striking image, as, for example, in Yevtushenko's poem *Stalin's Heirs* (1962), which suggests that Stalin's spirit still communicates with his successors.[29] Nevertheless, the inordinate interest still felt by ageing Soviet officials in the possibility of prolonging life, epitomised by their acceptance of Lepeshinskaya's fraudulent theories, is illustrated by Kochetov's novel *Youth is With Us*, which depicts a group of biologists who 'talked about what was new in biology, about soda baths which, it was said, could rejuvenate people . . . ', but passes no judgement on this theory. Since the Soviet authorities were very sensitive about the discussion of areas of medical research in which the USSR was backward, writers generally bowed to the prevailing cult of science and selected some of the more spectacular Soviet medical advances as literary subjects: Kaverin's depiction of Professor Ermolyeva's discovery of penicillin and Academician Zilber's virus theory of cancer are prominent examples. It would seem that most Soviet writers do not attach much importance to extravagant claims about physical immortality: the imaginative pursuit of medical progress, with special emphasis on the prolongation of life, is probably considered sufficient.

One writer directly influenced by Fyodorov's views on resurrection was Boris Pasternak. Fyodorov was a friend of his father Leonid Pasternak, who painted the only portrait of him.[30] In *Doctor Zhivago* Yury echoes Fyodorov's fundamental belief when he asks: 'What is history? Its beginning is that of the centuries of systematic work devoted to the solution of the enigma of death, so that death itself may eventually be overcome.'[31] Pasternak's idea that death is 'old-fashioned' recalls Fyodorov's view that since man cannot understand death but can understand immortality, death is irrational and immortality rational. His disparaging reference to 'all that animal jostling', however, represents a clear awareness of the unpleasant Malthusian consequences of physical resurrection, a problem which Fyodorov proposed to solve by colonising other planets. When Yury is asked by the dying Anna Ivanovna to give his 'opinion as a scientist' on resurrection he rejects the idea of physical survival, envisaging spiritual immortality through work and the memory of others.

Science and Ideology

In 1894 Lenin claimed that the 'union of revolutionary zeal and scientific spirit' was the chief power of attraction in Marxism, and the Soviet authorities have always insisted that there is an indissoluble connection between science and Marxist-Leninist ideology. Soviet fiction of the post-Stalin era, however, suggests that by this time science and ideology were no longer regarded as almost identical concepts.

The whole body of literature implicitly reflects the contradiction between science and ideology: on the one hand, writers present science as a supreme value of Soviet society; on the other hand, they demonstrate the harmful effect of the political and ideological control of science. This ambivalence can be partly attributed to the policy of the party leaders themselves. By 1953 the Soviet Union had become the second most powerful country in the world, but its power was based on science and technology rather than on Marxist-Leninist ideology. Soviet scientific achievements had been largely due, not to the special influence of Marxism-Leninism, but to the liberal endowment of science and technology at the expense of other sectors of the economy. Moreover, the spectacular successes which the Communist Party had achieved in Russia stemmed from the fact that the Bolshevik experiment occurred at a time of unprecedented scientific and technological progress in the world at large. In 1961 official ideologists recognised that science was playing a new, qualitatively different role in Soviet society; as science was increasingly becoming a direct productive force contributing to communist construction, it was henceforth to be redefined as an essential element in the 'base', not merely part of the 'super-structure'.[32] Evidently the Soviet authorities now acknowledged that science and technology had become dominant forces in Russia, replacing Marxist doctrine both as a weapon of the party leadership for the increase of Soviet power, and as a hope of the Russian people for a happy life in the future.

Khrushchev himself contradicted Stalinist ideology by stressing the need to win support for communism through abundant production and a higher standard of living. Literature follows Khrushchev's personal viewpoint by emphasising scientific development, rather than ideological considerations, as a means of creating the communist future.[33] Kochetov adopts this new approach in *The Secretary of the District Party Committee*, in which the description of a machine-building factory evokes a fantasy of the communist Utopia, when advanced technology will free man to develop himself to his full potential.

The sources of inspiration for the scientist most frequently portrayed in Soviet fiction are Soviet ideology, patriotism and the humanitarian aim of promoting the welfare of mankind. Although most literary works affirm the indissoluble link between these three ideals, the ritual repetition of ideological clichés usually appears less convincing than the passages expressing patriotism or a concern for human welfare. Moreover, writers are much more successful at conveying the excitement of scientific work than at paraphrasing party ideology. Granin's *Into the Storm* evokes the obsessive interest which scientists take in their work, inspired by 'the ancient, inexhaustible thirst for knowledge, creation, which lay at the base of life'. Such tributes to science appear more personal and convincing than stale ideological formulae, suggesting that science is to some extent replacing ideology as an object of worship in Soviet society. This is also implied by some physicists in Granin's novel who make the half-humorous, half-serious suggestion that the portraits of scientific geniuses should be carried on the streets in May Day parades and demonstrations side by side with, or to the exclusion of, portraits of the party leaders. Fiction of the 1970s usually concentrates on scientific and moral issues; ideological questions are not generally mentioned at all, except in production literature. The absence of overt ideological content may also help to explain the great popularity of science fiction in the USSR.

The Scientist as Hero and Purveyor of Values

In the post-Stalin period, writers used the 'science novel' as a vehicle for the exploration of many of the major questions of the age. The theme of science and technology could either be treated as a safe, party-approved subject by dogmatists and hacks, or as a vehicle of moral protest by liberal writers. The figure of the scientist emerged as a positive hero in the works of both types of writer: in the case of the former he is seen as a faithful servant of the party, helping to staff missile and space programmes and performing other functions essential to the Soviet economy; in the works of the latter he is sometimes depicted as a lone idealist dedicated to the pursuit of truth, a role which may bring him into conflict with official values.

As we have seen, after Stalin's death Soviet scientists were struggling for greater freedom from party and government interference. They were trying to liberate themselves from the conception of science prevalent under Stalin — that of a science totally controlled by the party — to a conception more akin to that of 'bourgeois science', involving the impartial investigation of natural phenomena, the search for truth. This growing demand for the method and ideal of true science is highlighted in Gor's *University Embankment*, in which a character states categorically: 'In science truth is important, not authority. Only truth.'

The new type of scientist-hero who emerged in the works of such liberal writers as Kaverin and Dudintsev in 1956, while only partially liberated from didactic models, is a specialist dedicated to science rather than to the party, a man who responds inwardly to the goals he himself has set, not to the goals set for him by society. The scientist fighting for the right to pursue his scientific research and retain his integrity is elevated into a truly tragic figure who epitomises the fate of the Soviet intelligentsia in the Stalin era. The emphasis on truth in Soviet fiction transcends the world of science, reflecting the desire of Soviet intellectuals in the post-Stalin era for greater truth and sincerity in the scrutiny of Soviet history and society.

The portrayal of the scientist who remains steadfast in the pursuit of his vocation can sometimes also be interpreted as an allegory of the position of the artist in the USSR. Many of the problems discussed by Soviet writers — the fortunes of creative men, different attitudes to their work, the nature of the creative process itself and the role of the exceptional man or the genius in society — are attributed to the artist in Western literature. It should, however, be remembered that the artist would be too controversial a figure for most Soviet authors to depict, in view of the party's ideological supervision of art. There are a few exceptions to this rule — in *The Thaw*, for example, Ehrenburg contrasts a successful hack with a genuine artist — but the portrayal of an artist as an individual opposing powerful officialdom might result in such 'anti-Soviet' novels as *Doctor Zhivago*. Soviet writers were generally unwilling to depict an historian or a literary scholar, because many scholars in the humanities had been compromised by their servility to the party in Stalin's time. Only a scientist dealing with highly abstract concepts, or an engineer concerned with the practical task of designing a machine, could be sufficiently independent of party control to serve as a satisfactory image of the honest writer, while at the same time appearing conventional enough to be accepted as a 'positive hero' by editors and censors.

Although the relationship between the scientist and society is a safer topic for Soviet writers, it is, nevertheless, ambiguous. Some of the dedication which people in the USSR expend on science and technology may be a consequence of their disillusioned withdrawal from political or social action. Science can become an independent value; the ideals of the solitary inventor may be opposed to the interests of the party and government bureaucracy. Some important works of the post-Stalin period use the figure of the scientist in an unusual way as a means of upholding liberal, humanistic values common to the Western tradition: values of individualism, creativity and spiritual freedom which are applicable both to science and art, and which directly oppose the materialism and *meshchanstvo* of the Stalinist bureaucracy.

Dudintsev's *Not by Bread Alone* seeks not only to depict the struggle of the inventor against the bureaucracy, but also to explore the concept of 'the inventor' in a wider sense. Dudintsev emphasises the great value of an outstanding individual whose original ideas can contribute to the happiness of mankind. There is an effective contrast between the imagery of light and fire used to evoke creativity and the imagery of darkness and animality depicting 'the herd' of self-seeking people who oppose idealists. Lopatkin likens the genius to a comet which astounds people by its beauty and light; and the scientist's potential contribution to human welfare is conveyed by the reference to a line of the poet Bryusov: 'We shall carry lighted lamps into the catacombs, deserts, caverns.' Dudintsev compares the true scientist to Prometheus who, despite defeat and persecution by the evil gods (his bureaucratic opponents), still maintained his unshakeable resolution to bring fire to mankind. The spiritual nature of the scientist's work and its similarity to that of the artist is constantly stressed by the comparison of the inventor to a poet or a Christ-like figure. At a concert Lopatkin senses an affinity with persecuted artists and scientists of the past, and feels spiritually refreshed by the music of Rachmaninov. Dudintsev's frequent references to the eighteenth-century universal genius Lomonosov also show that he is drawing no distinction between artistic and scientific creativity. Dudintsev adds greater depth to his character portrayal through Dostoevskian allusions. Drozdov accuses Lopatkin of 'decadent moods, Dostoevskyism', but the inventor sees himself as a patriotic figure, 'that boy in *A Raw Youth* who outwitted the foreigner'. If, as the critic L. Slavin suggested in a comment not reported in the *Literaturnaya Gazeta* account of the Moscow writers' meeting of October 1956, Drozdov is a Dostoevskian ' "strong man" to whom everything is permissible',[34] Lopatkin, by contrast, is an idealistic dreamer like the hero of Dostoevsky's *White Nights*.

Lopatkin regards the inventor as playing a dual role: on the one hand, he is working for the good of the community, and on the other, his exceptional talents single him out as a non-conformist: 'The "inventor" is always someone who thinks differently in any field of knowledge. Because he has found a new, shorter path and rejects the old, customary one.' He emphasises the creative individual's uniqueness and need to differ from ordinary people, and contends that such men should not be persecuted by ignorant bureaucrats because 'like conscience, they are necessary to you'. It is significant that Dudintsev uses the word *inakomyslyashchii* ('man who thinks differently'), a term later used to describe Soviet dissidents. In the context of 1956 his novel can be read not only as a defence of talented inventors and scientists, but also as a veiled plea for tolerance towards liberal writers whose creative originality and imaginative insights should be regarded as valuable for the community, rather than condemned by literary dogmatists. Dudintsev's work runs counter to the 'Big Deal' — the alliance which Vera Dunham perceives between the Soviet authorities and the middle echelons of the technocratic and managerial class, exemplified in the philistine values of the Stalin Prize novel.[35] Although the Big Deal continued to exist after Stalin's death, for a short time in the 'thaw' period another alliance also emerged — between idealistic scientists and inventors opposed to bureaucracy and progressive writers defending free creativity against the *meshchanstvo* of successful literary hacks.

Another member of this new alliance was the poet Semyon Kirsanov, who in his satirical fantasy *Seven Days of the Week* (1956) uses a pseudo-scientific subject to defend human feelings and initiative and to attack some of the same abuses as Dudintsev.[36] The central theme of the poem is the attempt of the narrator, a medical research worker, to persuade a government ministry to sanction his invention of a new heart to replace those of people whose own hearts are failing. Certain elements in the hero's struggle against bureaucratic hostility evoke the position of the Soviet writer. The fine imposed on the inventor for daring to have original ideas without orders from the authorities suggests the penalties to which outspoken Soviet writers are subjected. The deception of the gullible public by the manufacture of cheap artificial hearts could refer both to the persistence of literary works of crude political propaganda and to the appeal of pseudo-scientific schemes backed by government authority. The commission's refusal of the doctor's request on the grounds that only useful, servile hearts are necessary, those prepared to execute the orders of their superiors without question, is relevant to officials in science, art and other spheres of Soviet life.

The main positive message of Kirsanov's poem is his emphasis on man's insatiable desire for creativity, and on the scientist's duty to pursue his altruistic endeavour. Kirsanov believes that in the final analysis it is impossible for bureaucrats to dam the tide of creativity:

> For you know
> that it is impossible
> to forbid the beating of the heart.

Kirsanov's poem, like Dudintsev's novel, suggests that creative individuals must be resolute in their fight to persuade the country to accept their original ideas. The criticism directed against Kirsanov in 1957, however, proved that this would be a long, difficult struggle.[37]

In his *New Year's Tale* Dudintsev also uses fantasy, symbolism and a pseudo-scientific subject to draw a contrast between conventional Soviet ideology and the individualist values of his hero, the bandit chief, and his double, the scientist. The Stalinist director of the personnel department contends that there 'are limits' to freedom of thought, whereas the scientist, speaking for the author, affirms the value of unconfined thought: 'The new, that which we are searching for, is nearly always to be found beyond the limits.'

Dudintsev inevitably makes concessions to conventional Soviet literary canons, introducing several stock themes — the Utopian scientific project, the deadline fixed for its completion, the enthusiastic collaboration of a research team and the scientist's eventual success in achieving an important discovery — but employs these orthodox features in a manner which is highly unusual by Soviet standards. The author's main point is that the content of time is more important than its duration, that love and friendship are essential to a human being and that creative originality can enable man to triumph over death and achieve immortality, like the lotus blossom which flowers from 2,000-year-old seeds.

Dudintsev may well have been influenced by the ideas of Boris Pasternak, whose novel *Doctor Zhivago* is a supreme manifesto for individualism, creativity and humane values. Of particular importance for our theme is an aspect of this work which has generally been neglected by critics: the reasons for Pasternak's choice of a doctor as his hero and the significance of this decision for the ideas of the novel, the title of which suggests that the profession of Pasternak's hero was a matter of some importance to the author himself. The depiction of an intellectual doctor-hero was an established tradition in Russian literature, as exemplified by such figures as Bazarov in Turgenev's *Fathers and Sons* and Astrov in Chekhov's *Uncle Vanya*. It is probable that Pasternak was conscious of this tradition, since Zhivago's resemblance to his literary predecessors was suggested by the author himself when he announced in 1954 that the hero of his forthcoming novel was a physician, 'a thinking man in search of truth'.[38] By portraying his hero as a doctor rather than solely as a poet, Pasternak turns him into a less exceptional man who is typical of the Russian intelligentsia as a whole. Moreover, as he embodies both the reason of the scientist and the emotions and imagination of the poet, he becomes representative of mankind in general.

Zhivago's profession is also significant from the point of view of the structure and style of the novel. It enables Pasternak to bring him in contact with a wide variety of people and to witness the major events of his time without being directly involved as a soldier, or restricted to the role of observer, like the war correspondent Misha Gordon. Zhivago's medical experience often leads him to make general observations on important topics as, for example, when the sight of the terrible wounds inflicted by modern weapons inspires him to draw conclusions about the horror and futility of war. His medical knowledge is sometimes the source of some striking imagery, notably his initial enthusiastic response to the October Revolution: 'What splendid surgery! You take a knife and you cut out all the old stinking sores.' The co-existence of Zhivago's scientific training and artistic temperament can create effective contrasts, as when the prosaic aspect of childbirth: 'Wounds, blood, antiseptics, not to speak of the psychological trauma', is juxtaposed with Yury's poetic vision of Tonya as a bark ferrying a new soul to the shore of life.

Pasternak's treatment of his hero's medical career was one of the features of the novel which aroused the wrath of Soviet critics. In orthodox Soviet novels, like those of Yury German, a doctor is frequently depicted as an idealistic toiler in the service of humanity; critics therefore found it particularly objectionable that Zhivago abandons medicine at difficult moments in his life in order to safeguard his own inner world and the welfare of his family.[39] Even Ehrenburg, who supported the publication of *Doctor Zhivago* in the USSR, argued: 'The choice of a doctor was a poor one. A doctor is a humanitarian — as Chekhov was. But Zhivago experiences the revolution and the civil war without doing anything to help anyone. If he were a poet rather than a doctor, he would be credible.'[40]

Soviet critics, however, failed to realise — or were unable to mention — the significance of Pasternak's use of one of the stock characters of socialist realism in a manner opposed to that of conventional writers. In the first place, Zhivago is not intended to be a totally admirable 'positive hero', but an ordinary, weak, suffering human being attempting to survive and remain true to himself in a time of historical upheaval. It is Zhivago's poetry, in which the essence of his thought and experience is crystallised, that gives shape and meaning to his life and death. Furthermore, Zhivago's abandonment of his medical profession only serves to emphasise the individualist message of the novel. The idealistic Zhivago does not regard art as a profession and originally chooses medicine because he possesses the traditional desire of the Russian intellectual to serve his people. The fact that such a man is eventually obliged to give up his work in order to preserve his soul intact highlights the intensity of his hostility to Soviet society. The whole of society is sick and the doctor is powerless to heal it; he can only struggle against unequal odds for the maintenance of his own spiritual values. Zhivago's death at the end of the 1920s is symbolic of the death of the old Russian intelligentsia, many of whose most eminent representatives — Berdyaev, Frank, Sergei Bulgakov and others — were forced to emigrate at this time. They were replaced either by fanatical revolutionaries like Pasternak's Strelnikov, who were unable to find a place in the Stalin era, and whose only course was, like Mayakovsky (whom the portrait of Strelnikov closely resembles) to commit suicide; or the conformist Soviet intelligentsia who, like Dudorov and Gordon, had been crushed by violence and bureaucracy and were forced to 'idealise their bondage'.

The depiction of Zhivago's artistic and scientific talents enables Pasternak to compare and contrast the role of the artist and scientist. Yury defines the forces at the source of progress in science and art as rejection and attraction, respectively: science moves by reacting against the ideas of the past, whereas art both imitates and re-expresses many features of the art of the past. In his autobiographical sketch *Safe Conduct* Pasternak had argued that in some respects science and art are similar: just as scientific discoveries reveal the immutable laws of nature, so artistic creativity unveils the eternal beauty of the world. Science and art uncover what is already in existence, regardless of man's knowledge of it, but it is the intervention of human creativity which enables man to perceive it. This view is implicit in the depiction of Yury Zhivago who, both as a doctor and a poet, is endowed with the gift of intuition — the ability to grasp the whole — manifested in his diagnostic ability and the precise, yet imaginative quality of his writing. Pasternak draws no significant distinction between science and art; for him the important thing is the possession of talent which throughout the ages has expressed itself through the scientific discoveries and artistic achievements of individuals. He feels repugnance for the uniform mediocrity of contemporary artists and scientists which springs from the conformism imposed by an authoritarian society hostile to individual creativity.

Unfortunately, Pasternak does not succeed in portraying Zhivago's medical career convincingly — its presentation is episodic, impressionistic and insufficiently concrete. Yury has a poetic rather than a scientific attitude towards medicine — as, for example, when the phosphorescent gleam of the body of a girl suicide on the dissecting table leads him to meditate on the enigma of life and death. Pasternak's failure to depict Yury as a plausible doctor is, however, an inevitable concomitant of his success in making him live on a symbolic plane.

The doctor's relationship with his patients is analogous to the poet's relationship with his readers: poetry is presented as a healing, life-giving force which is capable of stirring people's dormant senses and revivifying their spiritual powers. This is the message of the Epilogue to *Doctor Zhivago*, in which Yury's poems promise hope and consolation to Dudorov and Gordon, whose spirits have been crushed by the Stalin terror. Zhivago's dual role as an average man pursuing an ordinary profession and a prophet with outstanding poetic gifts contributes to his symbolic identification with the figure of Christ, characterised by Pasternak as a totally human, 'emphatically provincial' figure who, nevertheless, is also the Son of God. Throughout the novel, in episodes connected with both art and medicine — Yury's curing of the dying Anna Ivanovna; his suffering, decline and eventual immortality through art — Pasternak symbolically parallels the story of Christ's harrowing of hell, interpreted as a conflict between the destructive forces of death and disintegration and the positive, ultimately triumphant forces of life and resurrection. Zhivago, whose name suggests 'life', possesses both the ordinary doctor's ability to cure suffering people and the exceptional gift of faith-healing, indicating that art and the Christian religion, interpreted as 'love of one's neighbour, the idea of free individuality and the idea of life as sacrifice' can alone restore life to the human soul.

During the post-Khrushchev period the figure of the scientist was no longer used so explicitly to propound an alternative set of values to the 'party-mindedness' of the conventional 'positive hero' of socialist realism. Such writers as Kaverin, Trifonov and Gerasimovich, however, continue to emphasise the importance of moral integrity and the pursuit of truth. The hero of Bondarenko's *Pyramid* declares: 'Creativity demands freedom — if not absolute freedom, then the maximum approximation to it.' It is tempting to interpret this statement, in conjunction with Dmitry's frank admission of the difficulty of working under the constant surveillance of his superiors, as a veiled demand for creative freedom in the arts as well; but it perhaps merely reflects the fact that physicists possess greater opportunities for independent work than almost any other group within the USSR.

Science and Marxism

The view that Marxism is a 'science' is, naturally, implicitly accepted in literature published in the Soviet Union. Indeed, Khrushchev's de-Stalinisation policy stimulated writers to lay even more emphasis on the scientific nature of Marxism than before, as a result of the party's claim that it had returned to true 'Leninist norms' of behaviour, rejecting the irrational aberrations of the 'era of the personality cult'.[41] This attitude reflects both the desire of Soviet scientists to restore their right to objective scientific enquiry after the ignorant dogmatism prevalent in the Stalin period, and the hope of liberal Soviet intellectuals that the party would move towards a more democratic form of socialism.

The treatment of this theme in a few published works suggests that some members of the progressive intelligentsia in the years 1953–64 can be regarded as precursors of the 'liberal Marxist' trend in Soviet dissident thought now represented by Roy and Zhores Medvedev. Some writers used the technique of 'opposing' Leninism to Stalinism in order to contrast the encouragement of science which lay at the basis of Bolshevik rule with the stultification of intellectual life under Stalin. In Gorbunov's story *The Mistake*, for example, Lunacharsky, the Commissar for Education and Enlightenment in the 1920s, is depicted as a friendly man willing to chat amiably with a semi-literate sailor. Gorbunov stresses that the Leninist educational system made it possible for the son of a humble country blacksmith to become a professor, and implicitly contrasts the flourishing state of Soviet science in the 1920s with the careerism and intrigue in Stalin's time.

Published fiction very occasionally hints that Soviet society, particularly under Stalin, had been dominated by a 'godless theology' rather than a scientific outlook. Tvardovsky's poem *Tyorkin in the Other World* satirises Stalin's Russia where people claim that their world is:

> . . . the best and most advanced . . .
> It rests on a scientific foundation,[42]

although it requires an immense bureaucracy, secret police, prison camps and a Supreme One who erects monuments to himself.

The question of whether Marxism is a genuinely scientific doctrine is much too controversial an issue to be discussed in published literature, since this claim is one of the fundamental tenets of Soviet ideology, upon which the whole edifice of Soviet power is based. After Stalin's death, Marxist-Leninist philosophy continued to be inculcated at all levels of the Soviet educational system, but it was no longer found inspiring or generally felt to be a source of significant insights into the nature of reality. Nevertheless, although disillusionment with Marxist-Leninist ideology was widespread among Soviet intellectuals in the post-Stalin era, only a few dissident writers, each in his own distinctive way, explicitly challenged Marxism's claim to be a 'science'.

The whole individualist ethos of Pasternak's *Doctor Zhivago* is opposed to Marxist ideology. Pasternak does not reject science itself, but the debased concept of science which became current in the Stalin period; he attacks both the official claim that Marxism is a 'science' and the notion that natural science, linked with communist ideology, has the power to transform the world and human nature. When the pragmatic communist Samdevyatov advances the view that Marxism is 'a positive science, a teaching about reality, a philosophy of the historical environment', Zhivago replies that Marxism cannot be a 'science' because it is not based on objective facts, but on illusions manipulated by rulers to consolidate their own power: 'Marxism is not sufficiently master of itself to be a science. Science is more balanced . . . I don't know of any teaching more self-centred and further from the facts than Marxism.' Since Pasternak himself had studied under the rigorous neo-Kantian philosopher Hermann Cohen at the University of Marburg in 1912, and had decided to abandon philosophy because he felt that he did not possess a sufficiently 'disinterested interest in knowledge',[43] his own experience had qualified him to distinguish between genuine scientific method based on objectivity, patient questioning and the falsifiability of theories, and dogmatic Marxism-Leninism whose debatable tenets had to be accepted on blind faith in the authority of the party leaders.

Abram Tertz (Andrei Sinyavsky) approaches this theme more obliquely in his satire *Lyubimov* (1963) (translated under the title *The Makepeace Experiment*). He suggests that Soviet society (and indeed any society founded on the principles of Utopian socialism) is not scientifically based but teleological, since it exhorts men to serve a quasi-religious aim — the creation of an earthly paradise. Tertz uses gentle irony to rebut the claim that Soviet ideology is 'scientific'. Through his portrait of the bicycle mechanic Lyonya

Tikhomirov, a contemporary man with 'a passion for science and a talent for mechanical gadgetry'[44] who nevertheless takes over the town of Lyubimov by means of the ancient Oriental art of 'magnetism', the control of people's minds and wills, Tertz implies that 'scientific' socialism is in actual fact based on the age-old concept of charismatic dictatorial power.

Tikhomirov is a composite character embodying characteristics of several Soviet leaders: in him Lenin's 'scientific' outlook and revision of the theories of Marx and Engels co-exist with Stalin's ability to create myths and illusions. Like Lenin, Stalin and Khrushchev, Tikhomirov combines a fervent belief in science with a tendency to embrace pseudo-scientific schemes promising a rapid transformation of man and society, and a predilection for pseudo-scientific jargon masking the real source of his power, which is vested not in science, but in 'mystery, miracle and authority'. He has no need for real scientific progress, since he can imbue in people a new outlook which convinces them that the perfect future is already present to their touch, taste and smell — a subtle allusion to the intentions of Soviet propaganda. Tikhomirov's great scientific 'discovery' is that science itself can be dispensed with and replaced by thought control.

Solzhenitsyn's *First Circle* examines dialectical and historical materialism in a spirit of genuine scientific enquiry, displaying evidence of the close study of the works of Marx, Engels, Lenin and Stalin which the author undertook in order to refute them. The most extended attack on dialectical materialism and its application to the natural sciences is contained in Chapter 88 of the revised version of the novel entitled 'Dialectical Materialism — the Progressive World-View'. The subject is a lecture by an official from the District Party Committee on the essentials of dialectical materialism, as presented in Stalin's fourth chapter of the *Short Course of the History of the Party*. The staff of the special prison are depicted as a microcosm of all the people throughout the USSR who, on Monday nights, attended such political indoctrination sessions, not from choice but from an instinct for self-preservation. Solzhenitsyn achieves an estranging effect through devices of comic monologue and dogmatic assertion interspersed with accounts of the preoccupations of members of the audience, suggesting that Soviet Marxism is intellectually bankrupt, a barren, nonsensical ritual bearing no relation to anyone's life.

Solzhenitsyn contrasts the genuine scientific knowledge of some of the listeners with the extremely superficial ideas of the lecturer, who claims to be outlining the one true philosophy to all natural scientists. He satirises the lecturer's inability to demonstrate how the vague generalisation 'In nature everything is connected' and the proposition that science should study natural phenomena 'in spiral upward motion' will actually assist Soviet scientists. The lecturer fortifies his unproven assertions with puerile examples demanding a minimum of scientific knowledge: the transmutation of water into steam and ice is presented as proof of the law of the transformation of quantity into quality, and the creation of electricity from positive and negative charges is used to illustrate the omnipresence of the clash of contradictions leading to a higher synthesis, while the image of the sprouting seed is chosen to demonstrate the indestructibility of matter. Such examples, however crude and superficial, are, of course, among those used by Engels and Lenin (and also by Western apologists for Marxism).[45]

Solzhenitsyn demonstrates that modern science, far from corroborating dialectical materialism, actually contradicts some of its key concepts. The notion that matter forms the substance of everything in existence and is indestructible conflicts with Einstein's theory of relativity and fails to account for the disappearance of four million tons of solar matter per second; and the concepts of formal logic, which the lecturer rejects, constitute the basis of both modern mathematics and the new science of cybernetics. Solzhenitsyn seems to be coming close to Popper's view that the scientific method and ideal are incompatible with a totalitarian political regime. He evidently regards Marxism not as a 'science', but as a false belief: in *Letter to Soviet Leaders* he states that Marxism has now become an antiquated doctrine, but that 'even during its best decades it was totally mistaken in its predictions and was never a science'.[46]

Such apologists for Marxism as Roy Medvedev now argue, quite convincingly, that some of Solzhenitsyn's criticisms of Marxism are trivial or based on misconceptions: for example, the notion that Marxism was originally designed to be a static philosophy, or to predict the future with the accuracy of computers.[47] Nevertheless, even they acknowledge that Solzhenitsyn powerfully exposes the dogmatic Stalinist form of Marxism. Undoubtedly his critique also accurately indicates the unscientific nature of some of the fundamental assumptions of Marxist philosophy, and thus possesses relevance for modern Marxist scholars who still attempt to present

Marxism as a privileged 'science', rather than as just one political
The most comprehensive Soviet analysis of the difference
between science and ideology is contained in the literary works and
essays of Alexander Zinoviev. The distinction between science and
ideology constitutes the main subject of Slanderer's book in *Yawning Heights* and of the conversations between Scientist and Ideologist in *In the Antechamber of Paradise*.[48] Zinoviev clearly states his
own position in *The Reality of Communism*: 'scientific communism' — that is, Marxism — is quite distinct from a 'science of
communist society' — that is, a sociological theory for the analysis
of communist society, which he himself is trying to formulate.[49] He
hopes that his principles of scientific enquiry may eventually establish the 'universal laws' which, he believes, underlie all societies,
and may lead to the creation of a computer model of the Soviet
citizen and his society which will permit prediction of the future. His
purpose, however, is to establish facts, not pass value judgements.

Zinoviev's own works and a great body of other literature have
shown that it is a simple matter to demonstrate the unscientific
nature of Marxism. As he quite correctly states in *The Reality of
Communism*, however, this cannot invalidate Marxism as an ideology:

> Marxism is not shaken by this kind of criticism any more than by
> the disbelief of the population, and even of the rulers, in com-
> munism's earthly paradise. One cannot invalidate ideology. One
> can only weaken or strengthen it by weakening or strengthening
> its hold on people.

It is debatable whether Zinoviev has been able to provide a
sociological theory that will be adequate as an analysis of communist society. His recent decision to write essays rather than
fiction suggests that the fictional genre may have been less successful than he had hoped in conveying his serious sociological arguments. Moreover, although Zinoviev utterly rejects Soviet society,
he is himself a product of that society, with his view that only an
'insider' can make a serious study of the Soviet system, and his
belief in 'universal laws' and the possibility of prediction. Just like
the Marxism he rejects, his avowed purpose may prove to be based
on some of the fallacies of 'nineteenth-century scientism',[50]
although his skill in analysing Soviet society is unmatched by any
other Soviet *émigré*.

Notes

1. V. Lenin, *Sotsializm i religiya* (1905).
2. N. Fyodorov, *Filosofiya obshchego dela*, vol. 1 (M, 1905); vol. 2 (M, 1917).
3. Republished in A. Platonov, *Izbrannye proizvedeniya*, vol. 1 (1978).
4. A. Bogdanov, *Tekhtologiya: vseobshchaya organizatsionnaya nauka*, 3 vols (M, 1925–8); N. Bukharin, *Historical Materialism: A System of Sociology* (London, 1926).
5. I. Stepanov, *Elektrifikatsiya RSFSR v svyazi s perekhodnoi fazoi mirovogo khozyaistva* (M, 1922).
6. Zh. Medvedev, interview, Jan. 1980.
7. O. Kuusinen (ed.), *Osnovy marksizma-leninizma* (M, 1959), pp. 751–3.
8. V. Alpatov, 'O dolgoletii', *NZ*, 1960, no. 2, pp. 31–5, an article on old age, contains the subheading 'Does immortality exist?'
9. L. Ostrander, S. Schroeder, *Psychic Discoveries Behind the Iron Curtain* (London, 1973).
10. Zh. Medvedev, interview; L. Finkelstein, letter.
11. I. Efremov, *Tumannost Andromedy* (M, 1957).
12. On the 'Efremov debate', see D. Suvin, 'The Utopian Tradition of Russian Science Fiction', *MLR*, vol. 66 (1971), no. 1, pp. 153–6.
13. A. Voznesensky, *Antiworlds and the Fifth Ace*, ed. P. Blake, M. Hayward (London, 1968), pp. 144–9.
14. V. Kaverin, *LG*, 12 Mar. 1960; K. Zelinsky, *LG*, 18 June 1960; *Simpozium po kompleksnomu izucheniyu khudozhestvennogo tvorchestva* (L, 1963).
15. D. Granin, *LG*, 15 Aug. 1963.
16. On Vikhrov, see Z. Boguslavskaya, *Leonid Leonov* (M, 1960), p. 330; Ya. Elsberg, *LG*, 13 June 1957 criticised Granin and Gorbunov for failing to convey the 'poetry of science'.
17. See, for example, R. Rozhdestvensky, *Sputnik*, *Oktyabr*, 1959, no. 1.
18. M. Gorky, 'O temakh', *Sob. soch.*, vol. 27, p. 103.
19. See Wells, 'Theme of Science', pp. 121–39, 168–70, 177–9.
20. Crouch and Porter, *Understanding Soviet Politics*, pp. 172–3; *BAM — stroika veka*, 6th edn. (M, 1980).
21. V. Dudintsev, *Novogodnyaya skazka*, *NM*, 1960, no. 1.
22. D. Danin, *Dobryi atom*, *Znamya*, 1956, nos. 3, 4; V. Kozhevnikov, *Znakomtes, Baluev!*, *Znamya*, 1960, no. 4, p. 85; V. Orlov, *Bogatyrskii atom* (M, 1962).
23. G. Gor, *Odnofamiliets*, *Neva*, 1956, nos. 11, 12.
24. V. Ambartsumyan, in Fedoseev *et al.*, *Filosofskie problemy*, pp. 575–6.
25. D. Blokhintsev, 'Nekotorye voprosy razvitiya sovremennoi fiziki', *VF*, 1959, no. 10, pp. 31–4.
26. D. Blokhintsev, *Quantum Mechanics* (Dordrecht, 1964), pp. 41–4.
27. M. Emtsev, E. Parnov, *Dusha mira*, in *Uravnenie s blednogo Neptuna* (M, 1964).
28. Yu. Trifonov, *Drugaya zhizn*, *NM*, 1975, no. 8, p. 95.
29. E. Yevtushenko, *Nasledniki Stalina*, *Pravda*, 21 Oct. 1962.
30. See the frontispiece of N. Fyodorov, *Vselenskoe delo*, vol. 2 (Riga, 1934).
31. B. Pasternak, *Doctor Zhivago*, trans. M. Hayward, M. Harari (London, 1958), p. 19. See also the discussion of the views of Fyodorov and Tsiolkovsky on immortality in Yevtushenko, *Wild Berries*, trans. A. Bouis (London, 1984), pp. 291–6.
32. *Pravda*, 2 Apr., 2 Nov. 1961.
33. Khrushchev, *Pravda*, 26 Jan. 1959; 18 Oct. 1961.
34. L. Slavin, in *Moskovskii Literator*, 3 Nov. 1956.

162   *The Cult of Science*

35. V. Dunham, *In Stalin's Time* (Cambridge, 1976), pp. 3–23.
36. S. Kirsanov, *Sem dnei nedeli, NM* 1956, no. 9.
37. *LG*, 19 Mar. 1957.
38. Pasternak, *Znamya*. 1954, no. 4, p. 92.
39. See the 1956 letter by the *NM* editorial board, R. Conquest, *Courage of Genius* (London, 1961), pp. 143–7.
40. G. Sosin, 'Talks with Soviet Writers', *Survey*, no. 36 (Apr.–June 1961), p. 11.
41. See A. Kron, 'Zametki pisatelya', *LM*, 1956, no. 2, pp. 780–90.
42. A. Tvardovsky, *Tyorkin na tom svete, NM*, 1963, no. 8, p. 20.
43. B. Pasternak, *Safe Conduct and Other Works*, trans. A. Brown (London, 1955), p. 210.
44. A. Tertz (A. Sinyavsky), *The Makepeace Experiment*, trans. M. Harari (Fontana, London, 1977), p. 27 (first published as *Lyubimov*, Paris, 1963.)
45. F. Engels, *Anti-Dühring* (M, 1954), pp. 175, 188–9; J. Haldane, *The Marxist Philosophy and the Sciences* (London, 1938).
46. Solzhenitsyn, *Letter to Soviet Leaders*, trans. H. Sternberg (London, 1974), p. 4.
47. R. Medvedev, *Political Essays* (Nottingham, 1976), p. 148.
48. Zinoviev, *V predverii raya*, pp. 305–6, 312, 316–17, 420–1, 430–1, 444–5, 448–9, 455, 530–1, 539–40, 544, 546.
49. Zinoviev, *Reality of Communism*, pp. 16–18.
50. G. Urban, 'Portrait of a Dissenter as a Soviet Man. A Conversation with Alexander Zinoviev', *Encounter*, Apr. 1984, p. 16.

5   THE AMBIVALENT VIEW OF SCIENCE

Although Western philosophers recognise the importance of science, it is regarded as only one of several fields of enquiry. In the Soviet Union, however, as we have seen, science has been elevated into a quasi-religious cult; people have hesitated to express any reservations about the value of science, for fear of undermining the very basis of Soviet power. It is therefore significant that fiction was the first medium in the USSR to express any doubts about the development of science and technology. Whereas in the 1950s Soviet writers generally emphasised the triumphant march of science, by the early 1960s the conventional 'science novel' began to be replaced by stories and poems expressing a certain ambivalence towards science and technology, not in themselves, but towards the excessive emphasis on and even worship of science in Soviet society. This change of approach can be ascribed to three main factors: the political situation in the Soviet Union; the climate of opinion in the world as a whole; and the influence of the Russian literary and philosophical tradition.

Khrushchev's de-Stalinisation campaign initiated a widespread reappraisal of values associated with Stalin and the Five Year Plans, when men were exploited as mere tools of economic change.[1] There was a general revulsion against such Stalinist ideas as the subordination of man to machine and the sacrifice of the individual's present life for the sake of the happiness of future generations. In the 1960s writers' realisation of the limitations of mere social and economic change is implicit in their growing preference for the genres of lyric poetry and the short story which focused on the moral and psychological problems of the individual, as opposed to the grand social panoramas mandatory in the Stalin era. Soviet reality was increasingly regarded not as something to be extolled or criticised, but as a source of insight about human behaviour in general. Moreover, de-Stalinisation, which stimulated a demand for greater truth and sincerity in Soviet life, led to a certain disillusionment with the party's current policy towards science. It was recognised that science had been diverted into military and prestige projects: the party and government were still giving priority to the development

of atomic energy, nuclear bombs, weapons and the space programme. This resulted in an uneven development of Soviet science
and technology: biology, chemistry and various branches of technology remained relatively underdeveloped by the 1960s; the USSR
produced rockets and bombs, but had poor plastics, medicines,
glass, rubber and paper; it had electric power stations, but no cables
or distributing sub-stations in some villages. It is not surprising that
people should feel scepticism towards the 'NTR' which had failed
either to improve their standard of living or to bring them spiritual
fulfilment.

The growing ambivalence towards science and technology expressed in Soviet literature is partly a reflection of the mistrust of
science which has been felt since 1945 in the world at large. Together with an awareness of the immense advantages of modern
science has developed a profound concern over their possible implications. This anxiety, first expressed in the *Bulletin of the Atomic
Scientists* by participants in the Manhattan Project, increased in the
1950s, by which time a whole generation had reached adulthood
with the terrible knowledge that the destructive powers demonstrated at Hiroshima and Nagasaki could be unleashed at any
moment. Moreover, the appalling consequences of the misuse of
science had been graphically exemplified by the application of
scientific procedure and method to Hitler's 'final solution' for the
Jews; while in Stalin's Russia, military technology and scientific
surveillance devices had been used to maintain the position of those
in power and to extend Soviet influence over Eastern Europe.
Problems had also been caused by the development of biological
research. Although the USSR had signed the Geneva convention
against bacteriological warfare in 1925, since the late 1920s onward
research in this area had been carried out in a secret institute, the
first director of which was Professor Velikanov. By the early 1960s,
concern was being voiced about the consequences of the biological
revolution, which had brought the control of human genetics, and
hence of the evolution of mankind itself, within man's grasp.

The question as to whether scientific advances should occur is
rarely raised; it is usually assumed that society will learn to live with
new discoveries like genetic engineering, as it has learned to live
with computers and nuclear weapons. Yet, although the rational
methods of science have already become an integral part of modern
culture, much current political and philosophical writing in the
West has manifested a profound revulsion against science and a

movement away from rationality itself. One reason for this is the deep gulf between the research activities of scientists and the aspirations of ordinary people. Because of the dichotomy between the specialist and non-specialist, science is often viewed by the general public in a distorted manner, either with veneration or suspicion. Many people distrust new technology which threatens to replace man's labour, and reject the notion that the state's economic progress is an aim in itself. The decline in numbers of science students in the USA and Western Europe in the 1960s was also due to the antipathy among young people towards the abuse of science, especially in the service of war. Less coherently, the whole 'flower-power' movement of the 1960s represented a total rejection of science and rationality on the grounds that they provided no satisfactory aim in life. Some Western theorists have also expressed the fear that totalitarianism would be the natural framework for a society totally committed to the efficient application of scientific method.[1]

Although the Soviet leaders suppressed most disruptive foreign influences, Brecht's *Galileo*, staged at the Taganka Theatre in Moscow in 1956, must have stimulated Soviet intellectuals to consider the social and moral implications of scientific progress. Another work which influenced Soviet intellectuals two decades after its original publication was Aldous Huxley's 1947 essay *Science, Liberty and Peace* which circulated in *samizdat* in the 1960s. In this essay, written in the wake of Hiroshima, Huxley argues that science and its discoveries are being turned into instruments of totalitarianism, and discusses possible ways of overcoming authoritarian, centralised government. Soviet intellectuals may also have derived inspiration from the writings of revisionist philosophers in Eastern Europe, especially Leszek Kolakowski's *samizdat* essay of 1957 *I'll Tell You What Socialism Is . . .* which lists many definitions of what socialism is *not*, including prisons, intellectuals with 'captive minds' and a state which produces superlative jet-planes and poor quality footwear. It is also probable that the hippie generation had some impact on Soviet youth; and some of the 'youth prose' writers of the 1960s were influenced by the rebellious hero of Salinger's *Catcher in the Rye*.

Perhaps a more important influence on Soviet writers was the rediscovery of their native Russian literary and philosophical tradition. Just as the worship of science grew directly out of the Westernist tendency in nineteenth-century Russian thought, so the mistrust of science, reason and progress was a traditional pre-occupation of writers and philosophers representing the alternative, Slavophile current of thought. Perhaps a more immediate impact was made on young Soviet writers in the 1950s and 1960s by the selective re-publication or *samizdat* circulation of the works of writers of the older generation who possessed spiritual links with the pre-revolutionary period and the experimental Soviet Union of the 1920s, but whose voices had been silent in the Stalin era. Foremost among such writers were the quartet of great poets — Mandelstam, Tsvetaeva, Akhmatova and Pasternak. Of these, Pasternak probably exerted the most important influence, because he was still alive and active in the 1950s, and came to symbolise integrity and resistance to persecution during the Zhivago scandal of 1958. Soviet intellectuals must also have been aware that scepticism towards science was not a new theme in Soviet literature. Mayakovsky's play *The Bedbug*, Olesha's *Envy* and Zamyatin's *We* had all expressed considerable reservations about the 'brave new world' promised by science. The disturbing ethical implications of scientific progress had also been explored by Andrei Platonov, a former engineer, and by Mikhail Bulgakov, a doctor by training, in his fantastic philosophical fables *The Heart of a Dog* and *The Fatal Eggs* (1925). Although these stories by Bulgakov and the works of Platonov were not re-published in the Soviet Union in Khrushchev's time, some of Platonov's works were circulating in *samizdat* by 1960, and a selected volume of his stories was published in 1965.

It is natural for writers and artists who possess little scientific knowledge to feel a certain hostility towards the alien discipline of science and technology which sometimes appears to threaten their most cherished values — art, nature and human life itself. In Stalin's time, however, the censorship made it impossible for writers to express any reservations about the value of science, and even in the post-Stalin period such criticisms still had to be qualified and oblique. Nevertheless, while scepticism towards science has become a commonplace in Western literature, the very fact that this theme appears at all in Soviet literature of the post-Stalin period is significant. It may well be that the reaction against science has been more violent in some circles in the USSR than in Western Europe, because the cult of science has been imposed from above, and because there had been, in Stalin's time, a particularly striking contrast between the official praise of science and the profoundly unscientific political system.

Since the late 1960s officially sponsored enthusiasm for science has continued to exist, but an ambivalent or sceptical attitude towards science and technology has frequently been expressed in literary and political journals and has become more generally accepted in Soviet society. A questionnaire distributed by *Literaturnaya Gazeta* to Soviet and foreign scientists in 1971 asked: 'In your opinion, can the rapid development of science lead to any negative consequences?' The harmful aspects of scientific development most commonly mentioned in reply were pollution, nuclear weapons and genetic engineering.[2] By the 1970s, probably as a result of the growing awareness of popular indifference or scepticism towards science, it had become official policy to emphasise that science and technology must be used for the benefit of man. As the critic Kuznetsov stated: 'The scientific and technological revolution is made for man, not man for the scientific and technological revolution.'[3]

Although it is impossible to classify these subjects in mutually exclusive categories, the mistrust of science expressed in literature of the post-Stalin period can be conveniently examined under two main headings: first, a discussion of the social and political implications of scientific progress; and secondly, an exploration of the deeper moral and philosophical issues raised by the development of science.

Social and Political Implications of Science and Technology

Much of modern science has been shaped by the requirements and constraints placed upon it by the society in which it is performed. Science cannot be the impartial pursuit of pure knowledge, since it is the product of a specific social and political system, and the goals which society sets are never neutral. Although the direction of Soviet scientific policy could not be questioned in the official press, the de-Stalinisation campaign prompted some members of the creative intelligentsia to express concern in literature and literary debates about the proper goals of Soviet science and the sort of future society that was being created. Fiction also discussed wider issues which possess relevance not only for the USSR, but also for the world in general: the impact of technology on nature, village life and ancient culture; and the potentially destructive or dehumanising features of modern science.

Space Technology

Soviet writers and journalists are well aware that praise of the Soviet space programme, which is closely associated with the personal encouragement of the party leaders, is almost mandatory. However, there are occasional indications that some people have an irreverent attitude towards the achievements in space technology of which the Soviet authorities are so proud. In 1959 an anonymous correspondent to *Komsomolskaya Pravda* protested against the vast resources being spent on space exploration in view of the low standard of living in the USSR.[4] Such attitudes were officially condemned as 'bourgeois', but some liberal literary works of the early 1960s attest to their prevalence among ordinary people. In Aksyonov's *Starry Ticket* the 'nihilistic' adolescent Dimka and his friends express indifference to the launching of a Soviet satellite, as they are 'completely immunised against wonder'. Similarly, the loggers in Tendryakov's controversial story *Three, Seven, Ace* (1960) show no more interest in the launching of a sputnik than in snippets of local gossip.[5] Although such views are attributed to 'negative characters', the very fact that they are mentioned in literature at all suggests that the value of the space programme was a subject of dispute in contemporary Soviet society, as it was in the West. The Soviet authorities' dislike of such attitudes is demonstrated by the fact that in 1961 the KGB arrested V. Osipov and E. Kuznetsov, two young intellectuals from the group which congregated to read poetry in Mayakovsky Square in Moscow, because their meeting coincided with the 'day of celebration' of Gagarin's space flight.

A more stringent criticism of the Soviet emphasis on space research was voiced by dissident authors. In a poem of 1960 Dmitry Bobyshev, a mechanical engineer and editor of television programmes on mathematics (now an *émigré*), condemned the order of priorities adopted by the Soviet regime:

Men are still captivated by emptiness
And living bones
Deliberately adjusted in speed,
Spin about foreign planets . . .
So mend the railings here on earth
Repair the watchman's humble dwelling.[6]

The 'living bones' in the poem refer to the death of the Eskimo bitch Laika, launched into space on 3 November 1957. Alexander Ginzburg, editor of the Leningrad students' journal *Sintaksis*, which published Bobyshev's poem, was accused of 'speaking ironically about the space explorers and . . . scoffing at everything that is dear and sacred to Soviet people'.[7]

After a visit to the USSR in 1963 Sir Bernard Lovell, the director of the Radio-Astronomical Laboratory at Jodrell Bank, claimed that the Russians were not interested in a race to put the first man on the moon, but considered it more important to create an orbiting space station to investigate the solar system.[8] This change in Soviet propaganda was, however, probably inspired not, as Sir Bernard thought, by a more rational attitude to space research than that prevalent in the USA, but by a realisation that Soviet technology was incapable of sending a manned spaceship to the moon. After Korolyov had frankly admitted to Brezhnev and Kosygin that the Soviet Union was lagging behind America in space technology, journalists and writers were instructed at the beginning of 1965 to avoid all references to the USSR's forthcoming conquest of the moon, a common theme in Khrushchev's time. The prediction of the engineer Pryanchikov in Solzhenitsyn's *First Circle*: 'The first ones to fly to the moon will be the Americans!' may well reflect the increasing realism of Soviet scientists.

A sceptical attitude towards Soviet space achievements persisted into the 1970s. In the play by Aitmatov and Mukhamedzhanov, *The Ascent of Mount Fuji* (1973), the agronomist Dosbergen comments wearily on the launching of the Venus space station: 'What do I care about the universe? I can't plough or sow seeds out there. So who needs a planet where the grain won't grow?' Dosbergen's argument that scientists should concentrate on climate control to improve the crops is, however, countered by his friend Almagul who advances the official Soviet position: 'If you want to control the climate, you have to know what goes on around the earth. Space research is necessary.'[9]

The renewed emphasis on the space programme in the 1980s demonstrates that the Soviet leaders have by no means abandoned their dream of competing successfully with the USA. However, the persistent scepticism among the Soviet population towards both space research and the improvement of Soviet agriculture is attested by a ditty sung by the outspoken Bloke in Zinoviev's *Yawning Heights*:

From now on, who will take the rap
For shortages of grain?
Who will help us close the gap
When our space programme fails again?

Agriculture and Rural Life

Another area of official policy discussed, if only tentatively, by some liberal writers was the state of Soviet agriculture. In the Khrushchev period such writers as Ovechkin, Tendryakov, Dorosh, Troepolsky and Abramov depicted the economic problems of the collective farms and the need for scientific and technological progress in agriculture. To some extent Khrushchev himself mobilised Soviet writers and journalists, particularly Valentin Ovechkin, to give a frank picture of rural life in order to arouse the awareness of intellectuals and the party bureaucracy to agricultural problems.

However, since agriculture was vital to the party and Khrushchev's own prestige, a strict censorship applied to the discussion of agricultural questions in the press, and the subject of the destruction of crops by natural disasters like droughts, hailstorms and floods was banned altogether, in order to prevent the failures of Soviet agriculture from being known abroad. Some writers nevertheless ventured further than the official press, revealing that such disasters did occur, and that science and technology were only of limited value in improving Soviet agriculture. In Granin's *After the Wedding* (1956) a severe storm prevents successful sowing, and an agricultural official is 'obliged to look silently at this disaster, he who had all kinds of machinery, mechanisms, devices, knowledge at his disposal'. While Granin demonstrates the correct 'communist' reaction to this disaster, other writers display a more resigned pessimism about the inability of technology to compete with the weather: for example, Tendryakov's *Bad Weather* (1954) stresses that science is powerless to control a storm which ruins the crops, and Dorosh's *Rainy Summer* (1958) describes rain washing away aerially sprayed weedkiller.[10]

Some liberal writers attacked certain specific abuses in agricultural science before they had been publicly admitted by the Soviet authorities. In his *Country Diary* (1956) Dorosh brought out into the open the disastrous failure of Lysenko's afforestation scheme, which had previously only been condemned in academic journals;[11] and long before Khrushchev's decision, in 1962, to abandon totally the grass-arable system of crop rotation (*travopolye*) associated with Academician V. R. Vilyams and originally supported by Lysenko, Dorosh denounced the intensive campaign methods which caused it to be introduced everywhere in the most unsuitable conditions, then abandoned, even in areas where it was suitable. Dorosh's frequent criticisms of rash agricultural campaigns could be interpreted not only as an attack on over-zealous local officials, but also on Lysenko, and even on Khrushchev himself.

In 1963 there was a particularly disastrous harvest which forced the Soviet government, for the first time, to import large quantities of grain from the USA. Not surprisingly, this fact was not mentioned in literature, but Leonid Ivanov's sketch, *The Fate of the Harvest* (1963), attempts to account for the catastrophic harvest, emphasising the unavoidable losses caused by bad weather — late frosts and a summer drought.[12] The constant emphasis placed by conformist Soviet writers on man's powerlessness in the face of the elements perhaps represents an attempt to exonerate Khrushchev and other officials from all blame for the failures in Soviet agriculture. This was suggested by Valentin Ovechkin, who in a speech at the Kursk Party Congress in 1961 which was received 'very nervously'[13] condemned party-line critics who placed the blame for agricultural problems on the weather, and called attention to human factors. Ovechkin's view was shared by Fyodor Abramov, whose outspoken sketch *Round and About* (1963) depicts agricultural officials who issue orders without taking account of climatic and seasonal conditions.[14]

Some writers imply that the Soviet authorities have neglected to use science and technology to improve Soviet agriculture or to ameliorate the depressed condition of the majority of the collective farm peasantry. They show that collective farms sometimes lack essential equipment — L. Ivanov's *In Native Places* (1963) refers to the absence of the seed drills necessary in the boulder-strewn fields of North West Russia — or that machinery may be left out in the rain to rust.[15]

An even blacker picture is painted by dissident writers: for example, Shulubin in Solzhenitsyn's *Cancer Ward* depicts the primitive conditions of work in a collective farm chicken house and expresses scepticism about the value of Soviet science if it cannot direct its attention to such simple tasks as improving the lot of the peasantry. There is also an illuminating scene in Sinyavsky's *The Trial Begins* between the idealistic Seryozha, who is later arrested as a Trotskyite, and his grandmother, an Old Bolshevik who admits that 'there are still some shortcomings in certain kolkhozes', but is content to type out a book about a model farm with electric mills and ploughs 'in order that other farms can follow the example'. Seryozha categorically condemns such hypocrisy: 'I know those books. I've read them. It's a lot of model window-dressing — all lies.' There is a distinct difference between the approach of dissident writers and 'liberals' to the question of scientific progress in agriculture. While Sinyavsky and Solzhenitsyn attack the failure of Soviet policy as such, Tendryakov suggests that it is sometimes the peasants themselves who find it difficult to adapt to technological change.[16] While recognising that mechanisation in agriculture is indispensable, Tendryakov regrets that personal involvement in the work may be lost.

Some Soviet writers emphasise the reluctance of young educated people such as agronomists, engineers and doctors to leave the cities and accept compulsory postings to remote villages where they are most needed. The attitude of the coachman in Nagibin's *Get Down, We've Arrived* (1954) exemplifies the distrust felt by the peasantry towards the intelligentsia, who, it seemed to them, had no desire to use their knowledge and talents to improve the lot of the vast majority of the population.[17]

Some works of the early 1960s show that collective farmers enjoy none of the benefits of industrial civilisation. Certain backward kolkhozes have no club, radio or electric light; in other cases the planned electrification is delayed, or the service is poor. Both Solzhenitsyn's story *Matryona's House* (1963) and Yashin's *Vologda Wedding* (1962) were attacked for allegedly exaggerating the poor conditions in the Russian countryside.[18] Nevertheless, Soviet fiction shows that outside the main towns the life of the Soviet people in the period 1953–64 remained very primitive, and that this unchanging, traditional life co-existed with the immense scientific advances of the Soviet Union. The failure of Khrushchev's agricultural policies by the early 1960s disappointed many Soviet intellectuals. In 1962 Ovechkin submitted a memorandum to the CPSU Central Committee recommending that the collective farms be reformed 'on the Yugoslav model': that is, largely private farming co-ordinated by a network of state co-operatives. As a result of this action he was confined to a mental hospital, where he tried to commit suicide.[19]

Brezhnev reversed Khrushchev's agricultural policy, putting an end to reorganisations and unprofitable nation-wide 'campaigns', and supporting an intensification of production rather than an increase in the sown area. Agricultural investment substantially increased; prices for state purchase from the farms were raised; and greater encouragement was given to mechanisation and the private sector. All these measures led to an impressive improvement in agricultural production and peasant living standards compared with Khrushchev's time. It is this positive side of Soviet agricultural policy which the party wishes Soviet writers to emphasise. In Voinovich's words, critics favour works which depict 'the progressive movement of harvesters and other agricultural machines'.[20] Writers who were cited at the Seventh Writers' Congress of 1981 as having successfully depicted the 'scientific and technological revolution' in the countryside include such hack writers on rural themes as S. Babaevsky, Yu. Mushketik, Yu. Karanov, A. Yakubov, A. Krivonosov, Yu. Goncharov and Yu. Gribov.

The negative side of the picture is, however, the fact that the advance achieved in the post-Khrushchev period has been from very low levels and has been attained at a very heavy cost, both in investment and the high cost of production. There have been periodic agricultural failures — notably in 1972 and 1975 — and the persistent faults in Soviet agriculture include chronic distribution problems, the excessive size of farms, labour shortages, inadequate machinery, the short supply of animal fodder and the government's unwillingness to relax political controls on the collective farms. The 'Food Programme' of 1982 and the speeches of Gorbachov and Chernenko continued to afford great priority to agriculture in the 1980s.

Although the party leaders have admitted the existence of some problems in agriculture, writers of the post-Khrushchev period were not encouraged to dwell on them. Fyodor Abramov, however, in his novel *The House* (1978), the last part of his series *The Pryaslins*, provides a balanced appraisal of the problems of the contemporary *sovkhoz* (state farm) and its inhabitants.[21] By this time his hero Mikhail Pryaslin has built a new house with electricity and radio, the farm has sufficient machinery and the young people have motorcycles, but human problems remain. Abramov also suggests that the advances of science and technology may have certain adverse effects on agriculture and village life. The old women who carried the weight of the farm on their shoulders during the war now have no work because no one will employ them at the machine base. Moreover, machines have issued a 'death sentence' to horses, and until Mikhail Pryaslin is appointed supervisor of the stables, the horses are not looked after properly. Abramov subverts the conventional conception of the mechanic as the 'positive hero', presenting a conflict between Mikhail Pryaslin and a tractor driver, Victor Nesterov, who is ploughing badly, turning up the dead clay instead of the good topsoil and sowing rye seed in a drought. Abramov's criticism echoes attacks in the Soviet press on the irresponsibility of tractor drivers engaged in ploughing: because they are paid on piece-rates measured in terms of hectares ploughed and receive bonuses for economising on fuel and avoiding breakages, they have no incentive to plough properly (although, in contrast with Pryaslin's complaint, the usual criticism is that they plough too shallowly).

Abramov implies that the younger generation of agricultural workers take no pride in their work, which they regard as no different from a factory job, and are content to obey orders from above. Mikhail wonders why agriculture has not improved now that there are more men working on the farm in comparison with the post-war years, and concludes that the workers have forgotten the old ways, but have not yet learnt how to use the new machinery properly. Abramov merely suggests that it is the urban, technical psychology of young workers like Nesterov which prevents them from taking advantage of the party's policy of encouraging the rearing of private livestock, but the real reasons are economic: the peasant is now more highly paid for state and collective work, and may not want the bother of expanding his private activities, especially as there is not much to buy with the extra money in village shops.

Abramov also voices a serious critique of contemporary problems in the sovkhoz, which was in theory meant to be an improvement on the old *kolkhoz* (collective farm), bringing more investment and mechanisation. Abramov, however, shows that the era of 'kolkhoz democracy' and frequent meetings has now ended — all the power is vested in the director Taborsky who is appointed by the state, unlike the former kolkhoz chairman who was elected. Taborsky talks glibly about the way the 'NTR' has changed people's attitudes in the countryside, but Abramov implies that the establishment of the sovkhoz, with its gleaming new smithy, mill, electric power station, sawmill, garages, workshops and barns, has not necessarily improved Soviet agriculture. The new buildings have transformed the farm's appearance, but it is unprofitable: it is 25,000 roubles in debt to the government. Taborsky is quite happy with this situation, which is 'within the law', whereas Mikhail Pryaslin objects: 'But we can't live at the state's expense all the time!' Abramov thus suggests that the enormous subsidy paid to the inefficient Soviet agricultural sector (which in 1981 amounted for livestock products to 25,000 million roubles) may not always be spent in the wisest possible way. Eventually Mikhail's view is vindicated when a party commission replaces Taborsky with another more hard-headed chairman who makes no extravagant promises for the future. In reality, however, the problems of Soviet agriculture are proving more intractable than this optimistic conclusion would suggest. As Abramov's work shows, both managers and the younger generation of mechanics are using poor farming methods because of a fundamental lack of responsibility, and it is very difficult to stimulate initiative and enthusiasm among the workforce.

Abramov's criticisms of Soviet agriculture do not go beyond the speeches by Brezhnev and other party leaders, nor do they add any new information to Western studies of Soviet agriculture. Nevertheless, Abramov's novel is important for the clarity with which it states the problems, and for its evocation of the way changes in the countryside affect individuals. Even more significant is Abramov's tacit indication of a major flaw in the Soviet agricultural system, which has been described by Roy Laird as 'a distorted faith in technological advance that is an industrial fundamentalism'. In Laird's opinion, 'there has been no agricultural industrial revolution' in the USSR.[22] Certainly, Abramov's portrait of his hero, Mikhail Pryaslin, emphasises the need for the farmer to be a husbandman, not merely a machine óperator. His novel underlines the point made by a collective farm chairman in 1978: 'But how can one compare a mine or a factory to a collective farm? After all, the nature of production is entirely different.'[23] In view of the continuing emphasis on the 'NTR' in the countryside, it would appear that the party authorities have not taken full cognisance of this fact.

In a letter to *Pravda* in 1979, Abramov voiced some of the same complaints as in *The House*:

When was it known that able-bodied *muzhiki* go away at the time of the harvest? . . . The old pride in a well-ploughed field, in a well-sown crop, in well looked-after livestock, is vanishing. Love for the land, for work, even self-respect, is disappearing . . . [24]

Abramov's letter, which provoked a lively response, is a good example of an occasion when a Soviet writer was allowed to influence public opinion on important economic issues. Although Abramov was awarded the State Prize for his series *The Pryaslins* in 1975, *The House* received a mixture of praise and censure by Markov, Chairman of the Writers' Union, at the Seventh Writers' Congress in 1981. Possibly the honour may have been awarded to Abramov more in recognition of past services than because of the authorities' complete approval of his controversial series. Markov also instructed writers to uphold the agrarian policy of the CPSU, with its emphasis on 'the industrialisation of agricultural production'.

Industrial Development

In the 1950s conformist fiction such as Rozov's play *In Good Time!* and Granin's *After the Wedding* endorsed Khrushchev's policy of encouraging Komsomol volunteers to develop agriculture and new industrial projects in the Virgin Lands, depicting the easy resolution of a discontented character's personal problems by his decision to work on remote construction sites or machine tractor stations. Khrushchev's campaign appealed to young writers whose restlessness and desire for change inspired them to travel and work in distant regions of the country. Personal experience, however, led some of them to contrast the extravagant propaganda for technological progress with the reality of life in Siberia. Anatoly Kuznetsov was forced by Kataev, the editor of *Yunost*, to rewrite the end of his story *The Continuation of a Legend* (1957) in order to praise the feats of the Komsomol volunteers.[25] Similarly, Gladilin's *The Brigantine Raises Sail* (1959), which shows that the volunteers in the Biisk artillery plant in the Altai genuinely wanted a worthy manner of life, but were constantly given the dirtiest work or cheated on their pay, was rejected by *Yunost*, *Novy Mir* and the Sovetskii Pisatel Publishing House before eventual acceptance for publication.[26] Although Gladilin and Kuznetsov were only reflecting honestly what they saw with their own eyes, their attempts to shatter the romance of 'construction' were unacceptable to the Soviet authorities.

In another story, *Songs of the Gold Mine* (1960), Gladilin demonstrates, on the basis of personal experience of work in the gold mine at Chukhotka in Kolyma, that the Komsomol volunteers came for the good pay rather than to break production records and 'build communism'; since they were allocated the areas of the mine containing the most gold, people rushed into the 'communist brigades'.

Gladilin's harshest censure is reserved for the management of the gold mine, which fails to rectify chronic production and supply deficiencies, attempting to compensate for defects in planning and supplies by the enthusiasm of the masses, and withholding wages if production quotas are not met. When Gladilin's story appeared, it initially received a favourable review until the Magadan Regional Committee accused the author of libel, the Komsomol Central Committee approved their resolution and a hostile article appeared in *Komsomolskaya Pravda* accusing Gladilin of 'profaning' the communist labour brigade movement. A directive subsequently prevented his work from being printed anywhere for the next two years.[27]

Such works — and the semi-autobiographical novel by the dissident writer Valery Tarsis, *Ward No. 7* (1966)[28] — testify to the latent discontent felt by ordinary Soviet people who were becoming increasingly bitter about the low wages, inequalities in wealth and lack of essential consumer goods at a time when official propaganda was emphasising the great successes of Soviet scientific and economic development. This mood of disillusionment, demonstrated by a strike in a Moscow factory in 1956, reached a climax in the 'hunger riot' which broke out in Novocherkassk in June 1962 after Khrushchev had raised the prices of meat and dairy products; several hundred rioters were shot down.

Automation. In most Soviet fiction of the post-Stalin era, automation has been presented as a supremely positive development representing the very essence of the 'NTR', since it appeared to provide the principal means of changing the place and role of people in production. Yet the enthusiastic advocacy of automation in Alexander Sharov's *The Journey Continues* (1954) and the Utopian vision of a mechanised future depicted in Kochetov's *Secretary of the District Party Committee* avoid the more complex human problems raised by the automation of industry which were beginning to be felt in the USSR at this time. The seriousness of this issue is demonstrated in Panfyorov's *In the Name of the Young* (1960), which depicts a party secretary who knows that modern industry demands automation, but realises that this may cause personal tragedy for the men who are made redundant. A discussion in the District Party Bureau illustrates the difference between those who admire advanced technology for its own sake, regarding the dismissal of a million workers as a positive gain for the country, and those who deplore the human suffering it may cause. The party secretary concludes that it is necessary to consider each individual case on its merits and seek a solution in consultation with the workers so that automation can be used to serve man, but makes no practical suggestions about how this can best be achieved.[29]

Although this issue is treated only superficially in Soviet fiction of the Khrushchev period, the very fact that it is mentioned at all indicates that it was a topical problem in the USSR. The almost complete absence of any reference to the subject in the Soviet press suggests that it could not be publicly discussed because of the Soviet regime's emphasis on its policy of full employment. That such problems did exist, however, was conceded by Khrushchev himself who, in one of his economic speeches, complained about the failure of the central planning organs to pay attention to the question of forthcoming unemployment in the Kirghizian coal-fields.[30]

In the post-Khrushchev period Alexandra Koptyaeva proposed a rather facile solution to the dilemma in her novel *The Gift of the Earth* (1965), maintaining that, although the introduction of automation may cause unemployment in capitalist countries, in the USSR workers will be moved to new jobs with shorter working hours. Production fiction of the 1970s continued to treat automation as a positive benefit: Kolesnikov's novel *The Altunin Experiment* (1974) mentions, without adverse comment, a machine which replaced seven men at a stroke, and propounds the official view that automation will not replace 'all the human functions in industry', because 'Man will still have to set it all up, program it and supervise it.'[31]

Alienation. Another problem associated with industrial and technological development is the alienation of man from his work. Such romantic reactionaries as William Morris have argued that factory work is impersonal and inhuman, and that the machine is degrading to man because it dominates the pace of work, depriving the worker of any joy in the product he is making. Most socialists have held a more optimistic view: in particular, Marx believed that science and technology, harnessed to a new social and political system, would succeed in overcoming the deficiencies of the old, alienated order.

Some literary works, however, imply that this has not always been achieved in the USSR, where the reality of industrial work may be far removed from extravagant propaganda about technological progress. In the original version of Gladilin's *Songs of the Gold Mine*, for example, a worker gave a realistic account of the heavy production process which, predictably, proved too controversial to be retained in the published version of the story.[32] The dichotomy between hard, tedious work in the present and attractive propaganda slogans about working for the future is also highlighted in V. Nikitin's story *Thawed Earth* (1960) by the comments of a disillusioned young man working on a construction project in the Arctic: 'Is building communism only digging trenches?'[33] Another aspect of this problem is portrayed in Voinovich's *Two Comrades* (1967), which depicts the alienation of workers in a secret factory who do not even know the purpose of the spare part they are making.[34]

Ecological Problems

The problems of pollution and the conservation of natural resources began to be discussed in post-Stalin literature. This subject, largely ignored in the Stalin period, when the state stressed scientific and industrial development above all else, had been brought to public attention by the writer Leonid Leonov, whose 1947 article 'In Defence of a Friend' initiated a correspondence on forest conservation.[35] After Stalin's death some scientists, writers and journalists formed a pressure group whose aim was to arouse public concern about ecological problems and try to change party policy. They felt that it was important to fight for conservation while there still remained a fair amount of countryside and wild life to preserve.

Leonov's deep interest in forest conservation, exemplified by his many articles on the subject,[36] receives forcible expression in his novel *The Russian Forest*. The hero Ivan Vikhrov advocates planned, careful use of forests with continuous reforestation to conserve resources; the exploitation of the vast forest wealth of the European North, Siberia and the Far East; less wasteful, indiscriminate felling; the drying of marshy forests, protection of forests from fire and disease, and the replacement of wood by metal wherever possible. He believes that if these precepts are not followed, forest-farming will become forest exploitation with no regard for the needs of future generations. Vikhrov's pronouncements imply some criticism of official Soviet policy on forestry before 1948. Since 1929 forest utilisation had been completely subordinated to the general policy of rapid industrialisation, and the amount of lumber cut for domestic use and for export came greatly to exceed natural growth. Indeed, the industrialisation of the country had been financed largely by foreign currency gained from the export of timber supplied by the labour camps. Such unplanned felling and the failure to plant new trees led to a deterioration of the soil and the creation of marshland; in Stalin's last years unforeseen climatic and ecological changes were already making themselves felt. Leonov's novel provoked a lively debate about Soviet forestry: while most literary critics favoured Vikhrov's views, some forestry scholars argued that he expresses an incorrect idea of the balance between the number of trees destroyed and planted in one year.[37]

Although Leonov's criticism remained within the bounds permitted by the party, the themes of pollution and the predatory exploitation of natural resources are not favoured by the Soviet authorities, who assume that centralised economic planning will quickly and efficiently solve all such problems. Paustovsky ventured beyond the limits of officially tolerated criticism in his unpublished speech of 1956 which launched a powerful attack on the pollution of lakes and exploitation of forests by indifferent bureaucrats. Connecting the officials responsible for the devastation of fish stocks in the Black Sea and Sea of Azov and of forests along the River Oka with Drozdov, the villain of Dudintsev's *Not by Bread Alone*, he claimed that 'Quite knowingly, because of servility and, perhaps, stupidity, enormous damage was caused to our economy . . . The forestry protection belts have been laid waste. The water has been polluted. The Drozdovs don't care a damn. They want to fulfil the plan, so down go whole forests.[38]

The sensitive subject of environmental conservation is touched upon only rarely in literature published before 1964, but when it is mentioned it has a greater impact than the familiar complaints of ecologists in the West. Although environmental problems were perhaps still not as severe in the Soviet Union as in the USA and Western Europe, in the twentieth century the encroachment of technology on nature and human life has been more rapid in the USSR than in the West, partly because Western countries were more industrially developed than the Soviet Union at the beginning of the century, and partly because in the democracies people have not been compelled to change their way of life, as there has been a gradual spread and acceptance of urban life and attitudes. In the USSR, however, the pace of industrialisation has been forced, especially in Stalin's Five Year Plans, in order to drag people by brutal means into the modern world; and this rapid industrialisation has created a sense of impending doom.

Soviet writers usually attribute the destruction of nature to the irreversible advance of modern life. In *The Quenching of Thirst*, for example, Trifonov asserts that the spread of civilisation has impoverished the soil; deserts may soon encroach on fertile land unless forests are planted to avert the danger. Trifonov was obliged to confine himself to this mild criticism because the actual size of the problem and its real cause — the disastrous impact of Khrushchev's Virgin Lands policy — were too controversial to mention. Throughout the 1960s many millions of hectares of valuable land were ruined in the Soviet Union, and damage from soil erosion alone amounted to several billions of roubles every year.

In the 1960s scientists, writers and journalists were united in their protest against the pollution of Lake Baikal by a cellulose plant;[39] and in 1969 a government decree was issued affording special protection to the Baikal basin. Once the party had changed its policy on Lake Baikal, the ban on fictional treatments of the subject was lifted: in 1970 a film on this theme, Gerasimov's *In Siberia, by the Lake*, received a favourable review.[40] However, the pollution of Lake Baikal was a topic which was only permitted to appear in print for a short time; by 1971 the subject was officially banned,[41] illustrating the regime's sensitivity to any questioning of its industrial policy.

From 1970 onwards a heavily funded environmental programme was launched, aimed chiefly at preserving clean water. The dramatic rise of environmental issues to political respectability had little to do with the influence of public opinion. There were three main reasons for Brezhnev's great environmental programme, introduced in decrees of 1970 and 1973. First, there was an impending crisis in public health: cholera epidemics caused by untreated sewage broke out in the southern basins in the early 1970s. Secondly, pollution was causing problems in the fishing industry: catches of freshwater fish decreased greatly, including such important earners of foreign exchange as sturgeon. Thirdly, these problems coincided with a rapidly rising demand for clean water in the southern USSR caused by the spread of irrigated agriculture.

In 1973 annual investment for water quality abruptly jumped

fivefold; in 1974 environmental protection was incorporated into the National Plan; and at the Twenty-Fifth Congress of 1976 Brezhnev announced an enormous five-year, 11,000,000,000 rouble plan for environmental protection, mostly devoted to water. For the Eleventh Five Year Plan (1981–5), a further increase of more than 50 per cent was envisaged. So the environment, which 20 years ago had virtually no standing at all, has now been incorporated into every area of the Soviet government structure. Because of this, it has become an acceptable subject for literature and the arts. Kron's *Insomnia* treats the theme in an orthodox manner, depicting a scientist who acknowledges that scientists of all countries want 'to conserve life on our planet and prevent the disastrous costs of scientific and technological progress', but argues that the USSR has a greater chance of improving the ecological situation than the West, which is shackled by commercial interests. Boris Vasilyev's *Don't Shoot White Swans* (1973)[42] adopts a more lyrical approach, emphasising the need to preserve the environment to maintain man's moral and spiritual links with nature, and repudiating the senseless destruction of beautiful creatures, the exploitation of nature for personal gain. Vasilyev's story ends tragically: callous tourists camp in a protected forest and kill the swans which the hero, the forester Egor, has brought from Moscow zoo. Egor is beaten up by the tourists and dies of his injuries, but his predatory brother-in-law is punished, and hope is vested in the younger generation.

Although, since the 1970s, conservation has been a generally acceptable subject for Soviet fiction, some writers provoked criticism because they treated the issue in a different way from that sanctioned by the Soviet authorities. The Soviet environmental programme is not designed primarily to preserve wilderness or to protect natural beauty, but to improve public health and promote economic growth. Moreover, both Western observers and Boris Komarov, a Soviet ministry official in contact with the scientific and political establishment who still lives in the USSR, writing under a pseudonym in his *samizdat* work *The Destruction of Nature*, have raised serious doubts as to whether it is a really effective programme.[43] They ask whether the USSR can really manage balanced growth after two generations of nearly exclusive emphasis on heavy industry, and whether conservation is ever allowed to interfere with important economic targets. Some Soviet writers have touched upon these delicate topics, because they have emphasised the moral basis of the need for conservation, and have expressed a more pessimistic view about the effects of the NTR in the countryside than is admitted in official propaganda.

The most famous work on this theme is Valentin Rasputin's poetic story *Farewell to Matyora* (1976),[44] which depicts the gradual decline and death of a whole community, the island village of Matyora on the Angara River in Siberia, which is due to be flooded by the completion of a hydro-electric power scheme (the one hymned in Yevtushenko's poem *The Bratsk Hydro-electric Station*). Rasputin laments the passing of Matyora and provides no obvious redeeming feature or hope for the future. Everything is seen from the viewpoint of old Darya, who has lived on the island all her life and wishes to pass on her ancestors' traditions to her descendants. For her, the flooding of the village means the end of the old way of life and the spiritual values associated with it. If Darya exemplifies the general fate of old people in all rapidly modernising societies, her grandson Andrei, who decides to work on the hydro-electric power station, epitomises the brashness of the younger generation who exalt technological progress above moral and spiritual values. Andrei extols machinery and defends the flooding of Matyora: 'There's a demand for electricity, granny, electricity.' Andrei's enthusiasm for progress is presented with some sympathy, but Rasputin gives greater weight to Darya's view that 'Man thinks he's master of life, but he lost that mastery lo-o-ong ago . . . '

Darya's son Pavel, a kolkhoz chairman, occupies an intermediate position between the older and younger generations. He does not deny the importance of technological progress, but cannot accept the inhumane way the officials have dealt with the villagers, and the insensitive siting of the new sovkhoz settlement allocated to them. Although the multi-storey blocks of flats possess some advantages over their old huts — electric cookers and inside lavatories — they have not been designed with rural people in mind. Because of incompetent building there is water in the cellars, and therefore nowhere to keep food. There are no cowsheds or meadow land for hay, so it is impossible to keep cattle, and the ground is so rocky that topsoil has to be carted in from elsewhere for the gardens. Pavel wonders: 'Is the price to be paid for the change not too high?'

Pavel's reservations were precisely the points which caused most concern to Soviet critics. In a discussion of Rasputin's work in the journal *Voprosy Literatury* in 1977, several critics praised his sensitivity to change in the countryside and his concern for what remains constant in human life, but some considered that Rasputin was making a tragedy out of a non-tragic situation. The critic Salynsky, for example, complained that since there is no one to counteract Darya's views, an incorrect attitude to progress is expressed and the presentation of the new settlement is biased. A more sympathetic critic argued that Rasputin is not opposed to technological progress as such, but wishes it to be carried out in a more humane fashion. This more positive interpretation of Rasputin's work was not, however, entirely acceptable to the editors, who, while recognising Rasputin's great talent and concern with 'eternal questions', argued that the author should have defined his own position more clearly, avoiding identifying himself with Darya's retrograde point of view.[45]

In a 1977 interview, Rasputin made it plain that his concern for conservation was based on a deeper questioning of the ethical foundations of human progress.[46] *Farewell to Matyora* poses the question: should industrial and technological progress, advancing into regions as yet untouched by man, allegedly with the sole purpose of bettering the lives of the inhabitants, be carried out against the wishes of the people concerned? How much of the past should be sacrificed for the sake of some problematic future gain? In the ambiguous conclusion of the story Nature avenges herself on man by sending a dense fog in which Pavel's boat gets lost as he comes to take his mother away. The flooding of Matyora has religious overtones of a great calamity, a universal flood; Darya defends the value of conscience and 'the soul' against inhuman technological progress which threatens to engulf them.[47] Rasputin's work can be read on many levels: it suggests the futility of man's claim to be able to master nature, and implicitly poses the fundamental question about Soviet history: what is the point of the 'construction of communism' if people are hurt in the process?

Another interesting work touching on the theme of conservation was Victor Astafyev's *Queen Fish* (1976),[48] which was praised, in contrast with Rasputin's story, for demonstrating that 'a concern for what is unchanging in life does not by any means require an apologia for "immobility" '.[49] Astafyev's main theme is the inter-relationship and inseparability of man and nature in the author's native Enisei area of Siberia.

Astafyev makes a passionate plea in favour of forest conservation and is indignant about poaching, which depletes valuable fish stocks. He raises this theme to a spiritual plane by comparing a poacher of fish who speeds away from the fishing inspectorate to a 'poacher of the highways', a drunken driver who kills the fisherman's daughter. In the title story man, the alleged conqueror of nature, is dragged under by the Queen Fish, a powerful sturgeon which personifies nature, the feminine principle. While in danger of drowning the fisherman rethinks his life and, in particular, repents of his violation and ill-treatment of a woman in the past. Astafyev implies that nature is a woman who should not be violated by the poacher and hunter.

Astafyev wants to stamp out the age-old tradition of predatory behaviour in the taiga which leads to the extinction of animals and birds and the destruction of forests. His argument is that man himself becomes savage if he fails to respect life. Thus far, Astafyev does not deviate from official Soviet policy, suggesting that hunters and fishermen should keep within the law. However, Soviet critics go too far when they claim that Astafyev tends to stress the positive aspects of change; in fact, he questions the value of the rapid intrusion of progress into remote areas of Siberia. The transformation has led to certain ecological problems: hydro-electric stations have choked rivers and lakes with algae. Moreover, although modernisation has brought electricity and shops to Astafyev's native settlement, it has created ethical problems. Astafyev dislikes radio loudspeakers, the litter left behind by tourists and the horrors of 'urbanisation', and sees a connection between the damage which science is causing to nature and the disturbance to man's general moral outlook. A predatory attitude to nature leads to a deterioration in human relations. Like Rasputin, however, Astafyev feels that man cannot really control nature; the taiga is only wounded by man, and remains 'as majestic, as solemn and as imperturbable as ever'.

Although *Queen Fish* was generally welcomed by Soviet critics, a scientist repudiated Astafyev's view that a state of ecological balance once existed between man and nature; there were ecological crises in the past too. Only science is able to protect the environment; reverence for nature and the mere desire for conservation are not enough. Such characters as Astafyev's hero Akim, a humane fisherman, but a simple man and a drunkard, are unlikely to save humanity from a future ecological crisis. Another critic attacked Astafyev for an allegedly biased presentation of 'aggressive, soulless consumerism, simultaneously sated and insatiable' in the form of 'vacant-eyed transistor-carriers' and poacher-tourists armed with chainsaws and explosives.[50]

While most Soviet writers of the 1970s and 1980s treated conservation from an officially acceptable point of view, indicating Soviet achievements in this area, Rasputin and Astafyev are more pessimistic, and demand conservation for moral reasons which are not those which inspire official Soviet policy. It is perhaps significant that both authors are natives of Siberia, an area which is not a priority for Soviet ecological planners. Maurice Friedberg has suggested, quite convincingly, that Rasputin and Astafyev may have been allowed a certain leeway in their fiction because they write about Eastern Siberia, an area which is claimed by the Chinese.[51] Perhaps Soviet bureaucrats overlook their less than enthusiastic espousal of the 'NTR' because of their evident attachment to this disputed area, which, in their writings, they clearly regard as an integral part of the Soviet Union.

Soviet writers still manifest a deep concern for environmental issues. At the Seventh Writers' Congress in 1981 Yury Bondarev, known mainly as an exponent of 'war prose', made a passionate speech warning of the 'ecological catastrophe' threatening the world and arguing that the destruction of nature forms a natural subject for literature. Bondarev launched a powerful attack on the long-standing Soviet dream of reversing the course of northward-flowing rivers in order to send their waters south into moisture-deficient regions, a controversial project associated with Academician E. K. Fyodorov and favoured by the Brezhnev regime.[52] The doubts expressed by Soviet intellectuals have so far prevented the political authorities from implementing Fyodorov's scheme, which could markedly lower temperatures in the Arctic Ocean and therefore possibly alter the climate of the entire Western hemisphere.

The conservation debate raises the wider general question of whether public opinion has any power in the USSR. The economist Aganbegyan argued in 1972 that public opinion did eventually influence the Soviet government to change its policy on Lake Baikal, although he admitted that the problem had by no means been solved. Thane Gustafson, however, emphasises that scientists and writers cannot form independent groups or use courts and elections to put pressure on the political leaders, although he perhaps underestimates the capacity of Soviet journals and newspapers to publicise divergent opinions.[53] The dissident specialist Komarov states that a new commission reported in 1977 that the threat to Lake Baikal had not diminished, and the projected construction of new zinc and lead factories in the Baikal area by 1980 posed even greater dangers. He forcibly asserts that public opinion achieved nothing but the introduction of cosmetic, palliative measures, and the one lesson the Soviet authorities learnt from the Baikal debate was the need to impose rigid censorship on the discussion of environmental issues after 1975. Significantly, however, informed discussion of ecological problems in general and Lake Baikal in particular has again surfaced in the press in the 1980s. Both writers and scientists continue to participate in 'round-table' debates on conservation, showing that the Soviet intelligentsia still tries to influence party policy. A meeting held in 1982 to discuss the development of Siberia, for example, included the writers Sergei Zalygin (a former hydrologist), Granin, Rasputin and Astafyev.[54]

It remains a matter of dispute whether public opinion actually influences party policy on conservation, or whether the party line occasionally corresponds to the wishes of the Soviet intelligentsia. Komarov takes a very pessimistic view of the predatory exploitation of Siberia, especially by the prestige railway project BAM, and admits that in the literary works of Rasputin and Astafyev 'there is more of the tragic truth about the destruction of nature than in strictly scientific works'. It is, however, difficult to disagree with his conclusion that neither artistic images nor scientific statistics have the power to change the party's industrial plans.

The Destruction of Traditional Life and Culture

Society's enforced adaptation to a rapidly changing environment alters man's sense of a stable universe. The change effected by science and technology is both welcomed and resented; although it is hoped that change will be for the better, the change itself is often disturbing. It is natural that regret for the old ways should be felt particularly acutely in a country like the USSR where change has been exceptionally rapid and revolutionary. Since the early 1960s some literary works have expressed a nostalgic attitude to the countryside, traditional village life and customs which were becoming endangered by the encroachment of uniform Soviet rule and the 'NTR'.

Tendryakov's story *The Trial* (1961) depicts the disturbance caused to people whose moral standards have been formed by the relatively unchanging way of life of the Russian countryside, when confronted with technological progress and the administrative institutions of the modern world. Dudyrev, who has built a network of railway lines and bus routes through the Siberian forest and plans to construct an enormous timber factory in a peaceful village, comes into conflict with the old bear-hunter Semyon Teterin, who embodies the immemorial life of the countryside which Dudyrev will eventually destroy. Tendryakov has an ambiguous attitude to technological progress: while recognising its positive achievements, such as easier communications, the development of the country's resources and better housing, he at the same time regrets the destruction of nature and the moral stability associated with it.

Solzhenitsyn's *Matryona's House* manifests a less qualified nostalgia for traditional Russian village life than Tendryakov. In 1953 the narrator returns from exile to a remote village in the heart of Russia where he sits enjoying the silence of nature, away from the noise and bustle of modern civilisation. He regrets that a peat factory and neighbouring collective farm have ruthlessly felled the surrounding forests, and that the old peasant songs which used to be heard in the fields have been drowned by the noise of modern machinery.

In contrast to such writers as Ovechkin, Nagibin and Abramov, who express the 'Westernist' view that the primitive Soviet village is badly in need of modernisation, Solzhenitsyn and Yashin demonstrate a 'Slavophile' awareness of the beauty and traditional values of rural Russia which are threatened with destruction in the modern world. It should, however, be emphasised that the use of such terms as 'Westernist' and 'Slavophile' is only a convenient shorthand which simplifies the complex output of prose on rural themes and the varied positions taken in literary debates — and, as Max Hayward has shown, corresponds only approximately to the nineteenth-century meaning of these terms.[55] What might instead be called a 'Russophile' tendency based on Christian values shared some views with, but should not be confused with, the semi-official Russian nationalism which also began to emerge in the early 1960s; and the similarity perhaps helps to explain why works tinged with neo-Slavophile sentiments achieved publication in the USSR. The Russophile current of thought had certain significant social consequences: first, the contemporary interest in peasant arts and crafts; secondly, the discussion of natural medical remedies; and thirdly, the campaign for the preservation of the Russian cultural heritage.

Traditional Arts and Crafts. Towards the end of the 1950s a fashion arose among Soviet intellectuals for collecting icons, *objets d'art* and examples of peasant handicraft. Sinyavsky and his wife travelled extensively in the Far North of Russia, collecting peasant artefacts; and Soloukhin's *Byways in Vladimir District* (1957) lovingly depicts the lace-makers, icon-painters and artist-craftsmen of his native region who built ancient churches, decorated churches and carved window frames.[56] Similarly, in *Matryona's House* the narrator's photograph of Matryona at her spinning wheel suggests that Solzhenitsyn, like Gandhi and William Morris, believes that obsolete technology is in some way more desirable than the new. He implicitly invokes a past golden age when handicraft and hand-weaving were the dominant forms, allowing man to feel joy and take pride in his work. In a later essay Solzhenitsyn added a political dimension to this theme, depicting the spinning wheels thrown out of peasant cottages as a symbol of 'the people' of the past, destroyed by Soviet power in 1930.[57]

Natural Cures. Soviet literature provides evidence that there was a renewed interest in traditional peasant medical remedies in the 1960s, perhaps as a result of the back-to-nature movement and the mistrust of modern medicine aroused by the publicity given to the 'Doctors' Plot' and to the Soviet regime's support for such charlatans as Olga Lepeshinskaya. The most striking evidence of this is Solzhenitsyn's *Cancer Ward*, which expresses an ambivalent attitude towards modern medicine. On the one hand, Solzhenitsyn's own experience has led him to a rational acceptance of medicine and gratitude for the relief of pain; on the other hand, through the mouth of Kostoglotov he emphasises the psychosomatic origin of many diseases, expresses scepticism about the over-use of injections, pills and surgery, and a desire to leave recovery to 'the defensive forces of the organism'. Solzhenitsyn himself used both the folk remedies — the mandrake root from Issyk-Kul and the infusion made from a special birch fungus — which raise the hopes of some of his characters. In the novel, however, the belief in peasant remedies for cancer is invested with a deeper philosophical significance: Solzhenitsyn appears to regard it as natural that a sick man should turn for help to the earth, the source of man's being, which for Solzhenitsyn, as for Dostoevsky and Sergei Bulgakov, possesses an all-pervading spiritual power.

In published fiction the greater attention being paid by practitioners of orthodox medicine to popular remedies was reflected in

Dorosh's *Ancient Times are With Us* (1967), which expresses suspicion of textbook science coupled with respect for the traditional skills of country people — their knowledge of soil, wild life, plants and their medicinal properties.[58] Abramov's *Mamonikha* (1980) depicts a wise woman in a deserted village whose ancient chant cures a sick child of asthma.[59] Such works suggest that ancient peasant remedies and witchcraft are still alive in the Russian countryside, and, perhaps, assert as much power over people's minds as the miracles of the 'NTR'.

The Cultural Heritage. The most public and effective expression of 'Russophile' sentiments was the campaign of Soviet writers and artists for the preservation of pre-revolutionary architectural monuments and works of art. In 1956 a letter by Ehrenburg and some other writers complained about the destruction of ancient monuments, especially the sudden demolition of a famous cathedral in Ufa.[60] The growing interest in this subject among the Soviet population led to the establishment in 1964 of the officially approved 'Rodina' ('Motherland') Clubs and in 1965 of the All-Russian Society for the Preservation of Historical and Cultural Monuments.

Soloukhin's *Letter from the Russian Museum* (1965) presents a powerful defence of ancient Russian architecture, listing numerous old buildings — mostly churches — which had been demolished in Moscow alone, and referring to the hundreds of icons kept unseen in the cellars of the Russian Museum in Leningrad.[61] Soloukhin's essay, animated by a desire to return to the long-lost values essential to the identity and spiritual life of the Russian people, contributed to the campaign launched in 1965 by the Komsomol journal *Molodaya Gvardiya* to preserve old historic buildings. Similarly, Solzhenitsyn, in *Zakhar-Kalita* (1966) and in other literary works not published in the Soviet Union, makes a plea for the preservation of historic monuments and offers an indictment of the desecration of ancient buildings by the encroachment of ugly new features of Soviet life.[62] In *The First Circle* he depicts a beautiful ruined church standing next to 'the site of a future skyscraper', a symbol of the construction of the communist future. An interest in the conservation of urban areas of outstanding natural beauty continued to be expressed in literature of the 1980s. Granin's novel *The Picture* (1980), for example, evokes a provincial party official's bitter struggle to conserve a picturesque inlet and a timber merchant's house depicted on a painting of his town, an area designated as the site of a computer factory.[63]

'*Village Prose*'. In the post-Khrushchev period some of the more interesting authors of what came to be known as 'village prose' depicted the peasant and his way of life as possessing a value of their own, worth analysing and preserving for the moral and spiritual principles they represent. Soviet writers themselves link the importance of 'village prose' in the 1970s to the 'NTR'. Abramov said at the Sixth Writers' Congress of 1976 that the 'truly unprecedented revolution' caused by science and technology in the countryside involved 'not only a fundamental restructuring of rural production and the entire way of rural life, but also 'a change in Russian geography, a change in the face of the Russian land . . . '[64] Abramov considered village life to be such a prominent theme in contemporary Russian fiction because the old village and its thousand-year history were disappearing, and young people were losing the moral and spiritual values espoused by their grandparents.

To some extent, therefore, the very choice of village life as a literary subject by so many writers in the 1970s implies some rejection of the 'NTR' and modern urban Soviet values. It is not the rural innovators — tractor drivers, electricians or agronomists — who are the heroes of some of the most interesting 'village prose'; the main figures are ordinary peasants like the simple Ivan Afrikanovich in Vasily Belov's *That's How It Is* (1966)[65] and old Darya in Rasputin's *Farewell to Matyora*. The constant recurrence of the word 'soul' in such works emphasises the search for spiritual values on the part of writers from the newly urbanised generations who want to retrieve, before it is too late, the memory of a past which appears to offer a sense of tradition and moral stability that modern urban civilisation lacks. Debates about 'village prose' in the post-Khrushchev era to some extent replaced political discussions about agricultural questions, and became a forum for a general debate about the place of moral values in a society where they were threatened by urban and industrial civilisation. This was evident from a discussion in *Literaturnaya Gazeta* in 1967–8 when such critics as V. Kamyanov took exception to the humble passivity and Christian morality of the heroes of some 'village prose' who, they claimed, were not adequate as models for Soviet man in a rapidly changing world. Other critics, including V. Kozhinov and F. Levin, however, contended that man is particularly in need of moral guidance in the modern world, and that the peasant possesses an integrity which urban man would do well to emulate.[66] Debates about 'village prose' were also used as a forum by such 'nationalist' critics as V. Chalmaev to exalt the 'Russian soul' and aspects of pre-revolutionary Russian culture, and by the critic L. Anninsky to assert an almost Christian or neo-Kantian view of the primacy of individual values over the impersonality of modern technology and society.[67]

In 1973 the critic Kuznetsov attempted to strike a balance between two extreme attitudes towards village life, arguing that the writer should avoid a superficial nihilism towards peasant life and nature, but should also shun an equally superficial idealisation of patriarchal peasant life. He praises Belov's *That's How It Is* which 'represents a kind of emotional reaction to the upheavals caused by the NTR', but attacks Russian nationalist critics who cite Soloukhin as their spiritual mentor for the doctrine that 'the patriarchal Russian village is the sole "source" of moral and spiritual values for our time, and that the traditional peasant is a morally unique representative of the people'. He draws the conclusion that such a doctrine, embodying social and national isolation, involves 'the opposition of city to countryside and the rejection of scientific and technological progress'. The attitude of such critics is merely a romantic illusion, since profound changes have been taking place in rural life in recent decades: modern farm machinery, electricity, radio, television and improved education all mean that 'today's villagers are in tune with the times'. Kuznetsov claims, with some validity, that the views of the 'romantics' do not correspond to the true needs of Russian villagers in the 1970s who want 'their own t.v. sets, an evening at the cinema or the theatre, and beauty shops, libraries and sports arenas nearby. They will even give up their celebrated Russian stoves if they can have gas in their homes.'[68]

The fact that Abramov was permitted to address the 1976 Writers' Congress on the subject of 'village prose' suggests some degree of official acceptance of the genre. However, Abramov made a fiery speech which must have annoyed conservative literary officials. He satirised ignorant critics who wish writers to depict the 'NTR' and choose a 'young machine operator' as their hero, censuring Belov, Astafyev and Rasputin who write about simple peasants and old people. He argued that such works are not anti-intellectual or a passing fad, but a sign of the maturity of Soviet literature, and made a poignant plea for the conservation of spiritual values as well as nature and ancient monuments.

In the 1980s, 'village prose' writers continued to be criticised for allegedly failing to present 'the real problems of today's real countryside'. *The Last Wizard* (1980), a collection by the young Arkhangelsk writer, Vladimir Lichutin, was berated for its over-pessimistic view of the White Sea coastal region in a process of transition wherein the old is dying away and the new is yet to be born.[69] In a pugnacious speech at the Seventh Writers' Congress in July 1981 Abramov attacked a recent ill-informed discussion in *Literaturnaya Gazeta* in which some critics pontificated about 'village prose' without having ever set foot 'from the asphalt on to the bare ground'. He defended the concentration on moral values in literature: such ancient but still vital concepts as 'conscience, goodness, sympathy, compassion, mercy, pity' need to be emphasised because 'for a long time these concepts were not highly respected in our country, to say the least'. He deplored the fact that such 'pearls' of contemporary literature as Belov's *That's How It Is* and *A Carpenter's Tales* had not yet achieved a wide circulation by being published in the popular 'Roman-gazeta' series.[70] Evidently there are still difficulties facing those writers who adopt a nostalgic view of the passing of the old ways and point out the moral and spiritual costs of the 'NTR' in the countryside. Unfortunately, because of constant criticism and the severe party line, 'village prose' does not now exist as a genre in the way it did previously. Abramov died in 1983, and some of the best writers have been diverted into other themes.

Urbanisation

A theme related to the nostalgia for the traditional values of the countryside is the growing dislike of urbanisation. In V. Rozov's play *In Search of Joy* (1957) the sceptical 15-year-old Oleg argues that although people spend their time building enormous cities, they constantly try to escape out into the country at weekends. When his more conventional brother Nikolai, who is about to enter a scientific institute, maintains that the only problem is that towns are not properly planned, and tells his impatient brother: 'Wait for atomic power. Wait for the push-button age', Oleg answers irreverently: 'What a bore that will be . . . !' He envisages the towns of the future as mere assembly points where people will come for only a few hours a day to work: 'And we'll live outside, more simply, close to nature.' Such hostility towards modern cities, the product of the latest Soviet scientific and technological achievements, implies an indirect criticism of Soviet housing policy, a feeling shared by many ordinary Soviet people. This fact did not escape one Soviet critic, who condemned young playwrights for their fondness for 'lyrico-psychological emotions' which she defined as an inexplicable preference for ancient buildings rather than blocks of modern Soviet flats.[71] The apartment blocks constructed during the Khrushchev period were in fact of particularly poor quality, and known popularly as 'Khrushchev slums' (*Khrushchoby*).

One theme running through Solzhenitsyn's work is the dehumanising influence of modern cities, a view diametrically opposed to that of Marx, who believed that the urban environment enriched man more than the 'idiocy of rural life'. Solzhenitsyn's description of the cottages of Matryona and of Uncle Avenir in the revised version of *The First Circle* suggests that he considers the most pleasant type of living accommodation to be a small house with a garden. This view received fuller expression in his *Letter to Soviet Leaders*, where he blames poor planning for the creation of cities, which he regards as 'anti-human, multi-million concentrations of people' where people are forced to 'clamber on top of one another in multi-storey blocks'. Solzhenitsyn advocates the future development of a small-scale economy with an advanced technology which will necessitate the construction of new towns of the old type, with fewer cars, cleaner air and houses no more than two storeys high. It would, however, appear that Solzhenitsyn vastly overestimated the Soviet population's dislike of urban life; in the USSR there is a persistent and continuing influx of people into the cities from the countryside.

The growing convergence between dissident views and those published in the USSR is highlighted by an article of 1977 by the 'neo-Slavophile' critic Vadim Kozhinov, who claims that 'millions of people' have felt, at least temporarily, the desire to break away from the 'artificial' conditions of the city and live in an 'untouched' corner of nature. It is now more appropriate, paraphrasing Marx, to speak of the 'idiocy of urban life', with its air pollution, smog, incessant noise and the need for city-dwellers to waste hours each day travelling to and from work. Kozhinov regards such factors as evidence of universal conflict between man and an artificial environment — a problem by no means confined to the USSR. Kozhinov is not opposed to the 'NTR' as such, because it frees man from mechanical labour, but he believes that 'Literature's main task with respect to the NTR is to address this question of just what we are losing and what we are gaining in the modern world.'[72] Kozhinov's article was published with an editorial note mentioning that its subject matter was controversial and in need of critical appraisal, but the fact that it was published at all suggests that Kozhinov's views represent a significant strand of thought in the USSR in the 1970s.

Nuclear Weapons

Since the subject of the USSR's attitude to nuclear weapons was intimately connected with military and foreign policy, and a special military censorship vetted all literary references to nuclear research, Soviet writers on this theme adhere closely to the party line. A notable feature of post-Stalin literature is that, despite occasional changes of rhetoric, it has continued to express a remarkably consistent attitude towards nuclear policy. In the successive eras of Khrushchev's 'peaceful co-existence', the reaction caused by the Vietnam War and the invasion of Czechoslovakia, Brezhnev's period of *détente* and the tension of the 1980s, fiction has, despite occasional changes of rhetoric, faithfully reflected the ambiguous Soviet position, which can be defined as the combination of an avowedly defensive policy with an offensive posture. Within this broad framework of agreement, however, liberal writers have laid more emphasis on peace; dogmatists on confrontation.

A horrified reaction to nuclear weapons has been common in both the Soviet Union and the Western world since the Second World War. At no time, however, has protest in the USSR approached the proportions of the CND marches in Britain. Between 1945 and 1953, as the USSR was racing to produce the atomic and later the hydrogen bomb, discussion of this subject was kept to a minimum, while the Soviet authorities encouraged propaganda for peace. It seems that the physicists Sakharov and Tamm, who were working on the H-bomb project, both believed at the time that they were 'working for peace' — that an equal nuclear deterrent would maintain the balance of power and prevent world destruction. However, Sakharov later admitted that he deplored the sight of the huge material, intellectual and nervous resources of thousands of people being poured daily into the creation of a means of total destruction potentially capable of annihilating all human civilisation. He realised that the project was controlled by people who, though talented, were cynical: until the summer of 1953 the chief of the nuclear project was Beria, 'who ruled over millions of slave-prisoners'. Yet it was not until the late 1950s that Sakharov got a clear picture of 'the collective might of the military-industrial complex and of its vigorous, unprincipled leaders, blind to everything except their "job" '.[73]

The dangers of nuclear radiation were not publicly admitted until 1954, when the adverse consequences of the American nuclear test on Bikini Atoll were publicised in connection with the Soviet government's decision to reopen disarmament negotiations. With some reservations, Khrushchev approved Soviet participation in the Pugwash international conferences, at which prominent scientists discussed world political problems and the social implications of different scientific projects. Although these conferences did not exert much influence on the activities of politicians, they raised the consciousness of Soviet scientists about their role in Soviet society and the world in general. Indubitably, the Urals nuclear disaster of 1957–8 also contributed to the revulsion felt by some Soviet scientists against the Soviet authorities' continuation of nuclear tests.

By 1960 Sakharov became convinced that further testing of nuclear bombs was no longer necessary on scientific grounds, but was being undertaken for purely political reasons. He attempted to halt the series of nuclear tests planned for 1961–2, but although he convinced the head of the project, Igor Kurchatov, his challenge to Khrushchev proved unsuccessful. Subsequently, liberal scientific opinion must have been at least partially satisfied by the 1963 Soviet-American agreement to halt tests in the atmosphere, in space and under water. According to Nadezhda Mandelstam, however, it would seem that a fear of nuclear war, a sense of approaching doom, has been spreading among the Soviet people, all the more so because it was originally artificially suppressed by the Soviet authorities.[74]

From 1954 to 1964 a number of Soviet writers laboured hard to present the contradictions of Khrushchev's policy of 'peaceful coexistence' in a plausible manner, combining propaganda for world peace with a justification of the arms race and a desire for the overthrow of capitalism. Granin introduced this theme into *The Seekers*, although it is only tenuously related to the rest of the novel. The hero Lobanov, looking through American journals concerned with the development of the H-bomb, reflects: 'Those people would have dropped their bombs if we hadn't got similar bombs. So we will have exactly what they have, and even more.' In 1959 the Central

Committee of the party exhorted writers to discuss the problems of nuclear war, disarmament and the maintenance of world peace;[75] and the new concern felt by Soviet intellectuals about the social consequences of atomic research is reflected, if only obliquely, in the literature of the late 1950s and early 1960s, in which an emphasis on nuclear weapons usually still had to be connected with anti-American propaganda.[76] Tendryakov's story *An Exceptional Event* (1961) raises this issue, omitting the anti-capitalist bias. When a school debate is held on the topical 'physicists and lyricists' question, the manifesto of the 'lyricists' asserts that science has produced atomic bombs as well as peaceful sputniks, and that the scientist has a moral responsibility to ensure that his discoveries are not misused.[77] In the early 1960s Soviet writers were obliged to adapt to Khrushchev's professed and probably real desire to achieve relaxation with the USA to ensure Soviet internal development, while at the same time taking account of Khrushchev's actions, which periodically placed a strain on Soviet-US relations. Encouraged by the U-2 incident of 1960 and the continuing Berlin crisis, such dogmatist writers as Kochetov, Kozhevnikov and the neo-Stalinist Ukrainian writer Natan Rybak began to express virulent anti-American feeling in their work.[78] A more moderate approach was adopted by Granin, who, somewhat incongruously, inserts at the end of *Into the Storm* a didactic passage avoiding crude chauvinism, but emphasising the value of the Soviet nuclear deterrent and the government's desire for peaceful co-existence.

By the 1960s the ideas of Sakharov and other scientists were reflected in the growth of a certain internationalist, pacifist sentiment among young people. Yet although the USSR genuinely desires arms limitation as a means of freeing scarce resources for economic development, it seems that Soviet peace propaganda is largely for foreign consumption only. Yevtushenko was censured for remarks made on the eve of his departure from Germany in 1963 expressing support for world unity and apolitical humanism.[79] Okudzhava's *Good Luck, Schoolboy!* (1961), which presents war in a starkly realistic way, was accused of 'Remarquism' — a reference to Erich Maria Remarque, the author of *All Quiet on the Western Front* — that is, of painting war in such dark colours that the work implied that war itself was wrong.[80] Absolute pacifism is opposed to Soviet ideology because it fails to distinguish between just and unjust wars. In 1964 the Ministry of Defence called a special conference for writers, artists and film-makers at which Marshal

Malinovsky upbraided authors for composing unheroic, pacifist works.[81] Their failure to respond adequately is demonstrated by further accusations of 'Remarquism' against Grigory Baklanov for his novel *July 1941* (1965) and against the Byelorussian writer Vasil Bykau for *The Dead Feel No Pain* (1966).

The harmful impact of Soviet nuclear tests was a subject forbidden by the censorship. Nevertheless, Andrei Voznesensky, in some poems inspired by his journey to the USA in 1961, uses the Aesopian device of referring to America in order to highlight the horror of nuclear war. His *Beatnik's Monologue* (1962) evokes the terrifying effects of nuclear fall-out:

> Women will give birth to Rolls-Royces throughout the nation
> Radiation.[82]

A significant variation on this theme is treated by M. Lvov (the pseudonym of the Kazan poet Rafgat Dovletshin) in his poem *Products of the Disintegration of Uranium* (1960). Lvov voices concern that nuclear waste may endanger mankind, and that 'it is not too soon' to think about its safe disposal.[83] Lvov's anxiety may have been aroused, not by the 'monstrous dreams' mentioned in the poem, but by a real event — the Urals nuclear disaster of 1957–8.

Soviet sources date the beginning of the Brezhnev regime's policy of *détente* to the Declaration on Strengthening Peace and Security in Europe issued by the Political Consultative Committee of the Warsaw Pact powers in Bucharest in July 1966; but there seems to be no noticeable change of attitude towards the West in literature of the late 1960s and early 1970s. Indeed in 1969 there was a resurgence of neo-Stalinist intransigence in Kochetov's *What Do You Want, Then?* which depicts foreigners as agents of an international anti-Soviet conspiracy attempting to undermine the USSR ideologically by the export of suspect films, novels, pop singers and dancers. Kochetov's appeals for political vigilance and the strengthening of the Soviet economy, and his emphasis on the need for high military expenditure to prevent another war, which could overturn the Soviet regime and lead either to a fascist order or domination by the NATO powers, played on deep Soviet fears and insecurities. After the defeat of the neo-Stalinists in December 1969, however, Kochetov was attacked for his overt chauvinism, even though such views continued to be held by certain elements in the party, the managerial class and the army.

The real beginning of detente can be dated to the Twenty-Fourth Congress of April 1971 when Brezhnev outlined his Peace Programme, further elaborated at the Twenty-Fifth Congress of 1976, which laid down the basic principles of Soviet *détente* policy in the 1970s. There is some debate about whether *détente* sprang from a position of Soviet weakness or strength, although the argument that Brezhnev's policy resulted directly from the USSR's achievement of strategic parity appears highly plausible. The USSR always regarded *détente* as a relationship of both co-operation and conflict: while agreeing that co-operation in such areas as arms control and trade was mutually beneficial, the Soviet leaders never contemplated changing their political system or modifying their foreign policy. In Brezhnev's words at the Twenty-Fifth Congress: '*Détente* does not in the slightest abolish and cannot abolish or alter the laws of the class struggle.'[84]

Soviet fiction did not immediately respond to Brezhnev's peace initiative. M. Kolesnikov's novel *The Right of Choice* (1971), for example, displays little difference from the propaganda of the 1950s and 1960s. The working-class hero praises peaceful Soviet atomic research and compares it with the imperialists' preparation for atomic, chemical and biological warfare against the USSR. He implicitly links German Nazism with the contemporary menace of the USA and Western Europe and clearly asserts his own position: 'I believe in peaceful coexistence. But I don't believe an imperialist can become tame, harmless in class terms.'[85] Kolesnikov's explicit statement of the view that it is necessary at the same time to fight for peace and to prepare for war, militarily and psychologically, could be regarded as either a pre-*détente* party position or a realistic interpretation of *détente* by a conformist Soviet writer.

By 1972, with Nixon's visit to Moscow in May, the impact of Brezhnev's Peace Programme was beginning to be felt. The edition of *Literaturnaya Gazeta* celebrating the twenty-seventh anniversary of the victory over fascism published Pavlenko's *Maria*, a work written in the early post-war years, which presents a relatively balanced view of the Germans.[86] In the 1970s, expressions of horror about the destructive power of nuclear weapons remained constant; but although references to the American bomb and the pangs of conscience suffered by the scientists Robert Oppenheimer and Leo Szilard and the bomber pilot at Hiroshima were still common in literature and criticism, the decrease in anti-American rhetoric reflects Soviet writers' response to the new *détente* policy.

Throughout the Brezhnev era, 'war prose' continued to account for a significant proportion of the programmes of Soviet publishing houses; the very prevalence of the theme in Soviet fiction, like the well-kept cemeteries, is a reflection of the terrible trauma war caused in the USSR and the desire that it should never be repeated. Bondarev and Bykau, for example, do not mention nuclear weapons directly, but implicit in their writing is a warning against future wars and a concern about the moral questions of peace.

Certain works use historical events to highlight more recent social and political developments. One such is Bondarev's *Shore* (1975)[87] which, like the Helsinki Agreement of the same year, recognises the reality of the existence of the two German states, but also manifests the deep ambiguity of the Soviet attitude towards *détente*. It represents a new departure in Soviet fiction in that it is set entirely in Germany; its action takes place 26 years apart: partly in May 1945, the concluding days of the war, near Berlin; and partly in 1971, in Hamburg. The hero Nikitin, a young artillery officer who had an affair with a German girl, Emma Herbert, in 1945, has by the 1970s become a famous Soviet writer whose books are published in West Germany. Frau Herbert, now proprietor of several bookshops, issues an invitation to Nikitin to visit a literary society in Hamburg for a discussion on the subject 'The Writer and Contemporary Civilisation'. The very structure of the novel reflects the view that the war can never be forgotten, but that it is time to make an attempt at new, friendly contact between the West and the East.

Bondarev's main theme, however, is the difficulty of making contact between the two 'shores'. On the one hand, Nikitin's companion, the Soviet writer Samsonov, is an intransigent dogmatist whose deep suspicion of the Germans makes understanding impossible. Samsonov is shown to possess many sterling virtues, but his 'excessive harshness' towards his foreign hosts finally precipitates a quarrel between him and Nikitin. Bondarev's portrait of Samsonov may be partly attributable to his own skirmishes with dogmatist critics which date back to 1962, when Lev Nikulin denounced his first novel *Silence* to the Central Committee and the KGB.[88] On the other hand, Bondarev paints all the negative sides of the West in lurid colours: pornography, licensed prostitution, financial exploitation of tourists, the unlimited pursuit of money and pleasure. Yet Bondarev also allows his German characters to make the valid point that Russians do not know the new Germany very well. Modern West Germans are quite different from the Nazis: they want peace and, unlike the Russians, do not even want to think about the war because of the guilt complex it inspires.

In discussions with his German hosts about such controversial topics as the pursuit of truth and the impact of the consumer society Nikitin takes a conciliatory line, attempting to find some 'general human truth' which will unite them, but these discussions are often vague and inconclusive, suggesting that Bondarev himself does not have any easy answers to the questions he raises. The author has to some extent disarmed criticism by putting the most interesting arguments into the mouth of a German journalist, Dietzman, who approves of homosexuality and prostitution. Bondarev shows that the Russians and Germans strive to come closer together, but the two 'shores' are separated by an unbridgeable chasm. The philosophical dilemma is paralleled by the personal: Emma has treasured the memory of her first love, whereas for Nikitin it was merely a passing episode.

Nikitin's visit to the West ends in failure: his rupture with Samsonov seems final, and he apparently suffers a heart attack in the aeroplane going home. Bondarev later said that he was sorry to part with his hero, but could not imagine another ending for him; the title *Shore* would have been meaningless otherwise. He argues that it is not quite true to say that Nikitin fell ill because he could not endure the psychological tension of his visit to Germany; nor does he admit that his hero actually dies on the plane. Yet the ambiguity of the ending perhaps suggests that Bondarev could not bring his hero back to Moscow, where his moral questioning and searching for an individual meaning of life could have appeared ideologically suspect.

Bondarev's novel was much discussed in the press in 1976, and most critics did not see Nikitin's views as an adequate expression of Soviet ideology.[89] Bondarev defended himself, claiming that the philosophical discussions presented in *Shore* were a concentrated version of similar debates he himself had experienced in the West, which were not 'discussions', or even political arguments, but a vitriolic attack on the Soviet way of life based on preconceived opinions. He asserted that the new wave of 'anti-Sovietism' in the West was connected with support for the so-called 'dissidents'.[90] This statement would seem to have been induced — either willingly or reluctantly — by political considerations, since Jimmy Carter's election to the presidency in 1976 had led to a new approach to international relations and, in particular, to an emphasis on linking *détente* with human rights in the USSR.

From 1976 onwards international relations deteriorated considerably, leading to what can now be seen as a new 'Cold War'. The failure of arms control talks, Soviet-American rivalry in the Third World, the Soviet invasion of Afghanistan in 1979, the rise of Solidarity in Poland and the US-led boycott of the Moscow Olympics in 1980 all contributed to what Brezhnev characterised at the Twenty-Sixth Congress of 1981 as a 'complex and stormy' period in Soviet-US relations. Brezhnev did not exactly renounce the *détente* policy announced ten years earlier; indeed, he still tried to portray the USSR as the champion of the world peace, while at the same time expressing his dislike of the worsening political climate.

In the 1980s Soviet writers had to adapt to the new situation, expressing more hostility to the West than before, while continuing to stress the Soviet desire for peace. However, an analysis of two philosophical novels, Chingiz Aitmatov's *The Day Lasts More than a Hundred Years* (1980) and Alexander Chakovsky's *Victory* (1980–2), demonstrates that, within limits, writers were still able to treat this theme in very different ways. The more liberal Aitmatov lays greater emphasis on the need to preserve world peace. He juxtaposes a story about the humane Kirghiz workman Burannyi Edigei, with his humanity, love of ritual and ancient legends, with elements of science fiction. Aitmatov depicts a Soviet and an American cosmonaut co-operating on the space station 'Parity' which has been set up to work on an energy programme designed to help the whole of mankind. With a glance back at the Apollo-Soyuz space mission of 1975, Aitmatov postulates a future of even greater international scientific and political co-operation, but the name of the space station suggests that this can only occur when the USA and the USSR maintain strategic parity. The cosmonauts unexpectedly receive a communication from extra-terrestrial beings and journey to another planet, where they meet an advanced civilisation which wishes to make contact with Earth. The people are friendly, do not believe in war or weapons, and want to help solve the earth's problems, such as the energy crisis. The cosmonauts are excited, but do not know if the new civilisation will bode good or evil for mankind. However, when the cosmonauts wire back to base asking if the planet can make contact with Earth, both the Soviet and American authorities refuse; Earth is so unprepared for a meeting with a harmonious extra-terrestrial civilisation that it avoids the challenge. This science fiction tale, which is not successfully integrated with the rest of the novel, was pronounced 'debatable' by Georgy Markov at the Seventh Congress of Soviet Writers, although the novel itself won considerable praise for its 'humanist' values. Soviet critics objected to the 'cosmic theme', not merely on aesthetic grounds, but also because it suggested that the USSR and the USA were equally responsible for poor international relations, and that Soviet society (as well as the modern Western world) could by no means be considered an advanced, harmonious civilisation. Aitmatov had evidently failed to disarm criticism by adding a preface to his novel which not only condemned 'pointless conflicts between peoples and the waste of material resources and mental energy on the arms race' as 'the most monstrous crimes against mankind', but also contained ritual references both to imperialism and the Chinese cultural revolution, and attacked the Olympic boycott of 1980 as 'an excuse for Cold War'[91] (a statement which now sounds ironic in view of the 1984 Olympic boycott by the Eastern bloc).

Aitmatov's genuine commitment to peace and international co-operation was again demonstrated in his speech at the Writers' Congress of 1981 which made no ideological points, but expressed the hope that man would 'avoid technological barbarism and not dare to press that nuclear button in which all lives are connected.'[92] Aitmatov's emphasis on the total catastrophe of nuclear war has been official party policy since Brezhnev's speech at Tula in January 1977.[93] The decrease in annual military expenditure in the USSR from 1976 to 1981, the replacement of Grechko by Ustinov as Minister of Defence in 1978 and the extensive discussion of nuclear war in the press were all signs of a reformulation of Soviet military doctrine. At the Twenty-Sixth Congress Brezhnev made it clear that the USSR did not want nuclear war or military superiority: 'To try to outstrip each other in the arms race or to expect to win a nuclear war is dangerous madness.'

The three-volume blockbuster *Victory* (1980–2) by the influential Alexander Chakovsky, editor of *Literaturnaya Gazeta*, reflects the main elements of Soviet nuclear policy in the early 1980s and represents a dogmatist's response to a bleak international situation.[94] Like Bondarev's *Shore*, the action of Chakovsky's novel takes place in the West at two different times: the Potsdam Conference of 1945 is juxtaposed with the Helsinki Conference of 1975. Chakovsky's main theme is the conflict between the two opposed worlds of capitalism and communism. The Soviet journalist Voronov, who attends both the Potsdam and Helsinki conferences, sees a significant connection between the two events. First, Helsinki represents a peaceful recognition of the Potsdam agreement which 'the West sabotaged for 30 years'. On the other hand, both conferences raised great hopes for world peace, but at Potsdam Churchill and Roosevelt frustrated Stalin's wise plans and sowed the seeds of the 'Cold War'; and at Helsinki, despite the fine speeches by Western leaders in favour of peace, the threat of a new 'Cold War' exists if the principle of non-interference in the internal affairs of other countries is not upheld. Chakovsky is writing with hindsight: the Helsinki Final Act of 1975, which ratified the existing territorial boundaries in Europe and called for expanded cultural and scientific links, did not create a new pattern of East-West relationships in Europe; and the two follow-up meetings in Belgrade (1977–8) and Madrid (1980–1) proved acrimonious, especially on the issue of human rights.

   Although Chakovsky presents a reasonably objective account of the Helsinki Conference itself, he expresses virulent anti-American feeling through the stereotyped figure of the capitalist newspaper proprietor Stewart, who interprets the Helsinki agreement on economic co-operation as an opportunity for American business and advanced technology to improve the Soviet standard of living, with the proviso that the USSR and Eastern Europe should abandon their planned economies. Voronov sees Stewart's proposal as a means of undermining the Soviet system, comparing it to the Marshall Plan of 1947 which the USSR rejected. Here Chakovsky echoes the accusations of Soviet leaders about the USA's 'economic and technological' offensive against the USSR and the socialist camp (a possible reference to the 1975 Jackson-Vanik Amendment to the Soviet-American Trade Bill which linked the export of grain to the USSR with permission to Soviet Jews to emigrate to Israel). Chakovsky's hero faithfully expounds the main lines of the party's military doctrine. He admits that a nuclear war would be catastrophic for all mankind; discounts all Soviet responsibility for the failure of *détente*; expresses the view that Soviet weapons are based on a defensive and deterrent strategy; and claims that the USSR — especially Brezhnev, who is presented as a 'cult' figure — is the main champion of peace in a troubled world. Chakovsky's novel, which suggests that the USSR desires peace but is preparing for war, reflects the ambiguity of current Soviet military doctrine: an emphasis on deterrence, coupled with a refusal to espouse the doctrine of mutual assured destruction, which means that the USSR will prepare and wage a nuclear war if necessary. Chakovsky's hard-line views received even more forcible expression in an 'Open Letter' addressed to 'Mr President' in *Pravda* in 1980 which attacked President Carter's 'human rights' policy and his meeting with such dissidents as Vladimir Bukovsky.[95] The difference of emphasis in the novels and articles by Aitmatov and Chakovsky reflects the continuing debate in the USSR between 'doves' and 'hawks'.

War continues to be an important theme in the Soviet literature of the 1980s. Patriotic themes had been publicised again in 1978 by Brezhnev's war memoir *Little Earth*, for which he was awarded the Lenin Prize for Literature in 1979. Astafyev's novella and film *Star Shower* was praised in 1982 by a critic who defined its message as 'War is terrible . . . it's no joking matter';[96] but further evidence of the party's dislike of pacifism was provided by the harassment of Bykau and the arrest of members of the independent dissident 'peace group' in July 1982. After Brezhnev's death both Andropov's peace initiatives and the original intransigence of the new party leadership under Chernenko signalled changes of style in the Kremlin, but no basic change of policy; and the party continued to use the arts to prepare public opinion for policy shifts. In 1984, during a period of intense anti-capitalist propaganda, Yevtushenko's film *Kindergarten*, which presented a 'good' German soldier, was, contrary to its creator's expectations, allowed to be shown (although the authorities expressed their reservations about the film by confining it to slightly out-of-the-way cinemas),[97] thus helping to keep alive a spirit of *détente* which could be re-emphasised when the Soviet leaders launched a new peace initiative timed to coincide with the re-election of President Reagan.

A view totally opposed to official Soviet nuclear policy is expressed in the works of Solzhenitsyn. Although he scarcely mentioned nuclear war in his earlier literary works, in his protest against expulsion from the Writers' Union in 1969 he spoke of the need for a sense of man's common humanity, since the Marxist concept of the class struggle would be irrelevant after the nuclear holocaust, 'when the few surviving bipeds will be wandering over the radioactive earth, dying'.[98] *The Gulag Archipelago* and the revised version of *The First Circle* show that Solzhenitsyn had in fact been concerned about nuclear weapons for many years. One reason for his confinement in a *sharashka* was that he put 'nuclear physicist' as his profession on the prison registration card in 1946, when the bomb was desperately needed, relying on his knowledge of the Smyth Report, the US Defence Department's official record of the first American atomic bomb. The new edition of *The First Circle* restores the controversial 'atomic theme' which existed in some form in the original manuscript begun in 1955, but was omitted from the fifth version which the author submitted to Tvardovsky in 1964. Innokenty's crime is no longer a humane act of personal friendship, but a bold political challenge: the decision to telephone the American Embassy in Moscow with a warning that Koval, a Soviet agent, is about to obtain information about the atomic bomb in New York. This incident is based on the case of a real Soviet diplomat, Ivanov, who rang the American and Canadian embassies about Koval in December 1949, and whose voice Kopelev and Solzhenitsyn were required to identify in the *sharashka*. Since Ivanov's act may have been motivated merely by considerations of personal gain, and the Soviet government's practice in questions of espionage and the acquisition of military secrets was not significantly different from that of other governments, Innokenty's decision to betray a Soviet agent to a foreign power renders his moral stance more equivocal than it was in the 1968 version of the novel. Although Solzhenitsyn himself and other dissidents eventually reached the point where they totally condemned the acquisition by the Soviet state of any more powerful weapons, there were few Soviet citizens still at liberty who could have accepted that position in 1949 (indeed, Solzhenitsyn himself at that time cursed the caller and willingly co-operated with Kopelev).[99] Moreover, as most of the research and the first Soviet A-bomb tests had been successfully completed by the autumn of 1949 (although deliverable bombs were not tested until 1950), and Innokenty is aware that a nuclear test is imminent, his act appears merely futile and self-destructive.

Solzhenitsyn's attitude to disarmament negotiations presents a striking contrast with that of conformist writers. He emphasises that Stalin unwisely rejected the 1946 Baruch Plan to ban further research on nuclear weapons and place the American bomb under the control of an independent United Nations Atomic Energy Committee. He implies that the Soviet bomb is not merely a deterrent to capitalist aggression, but also a powerful means of internal control in the hands of the Soviet regime. Innokenty's Uncle Avenir states that if Stalin has the bomb, 'we shall never see freedom'. Solzhenitsyn takes a sceptical view of peace propaganda by both the USSR and the USA: in *Candle in the Wind* a journalist preparing for a congress declares: 'The idea is that every country should have the right to have nuclear weapons, but we have to serve it up as part of the struggle for peace. It's a very subtle business.'

Scientific Methods of Social Control

In the 1960s some Soviet writers began to express concern about the dangerous implications of modern biological and psychological techniques. Although most research in biocybernetics was classified, by the early 1960s the USSR was several years ahead of the USA in this type of research. The project to 'neuro-stabilise' a human being depicted in Solzhenitsyn's play *Candle in the Wind* was fictional, but potentially possible: in the USA biofeedback techniques were already being used in medicine and as a means of inducing relaxation and a feeling of euphoria. Solzhenitsyn's theme also reflects the view of some enthusiastic Soviet proponents of cybernetics that the evolution of matter, from the simplest atom to the most complex of all material forms, man, may be seen as a process of accumulation of information.[100] From here it is a small step to the concept of transforming a human personality from a chaotic to an ordered state. Since Solzhenitsyn's work is set in an imaginary society of the future combining capitalist and socialist elements, it also issues a more general warning about the consequences of unlimited scientific development in any society where science is unchecked by moral restraints.

In a later essay Solzhenitsyn described the prospect of controlling psychological processes and heredity as 'close to our idea of hell on earth'; and Sakharov has also warned of the threat to basic human values inherent in biochemical and electronic control of psychic processes.[101] The fears of the scientific and artistic intelligentsia may have been aroused by the research being conducted in Alma-Ata by the biophysicist V. M. Inyushin, whose aim was to construct a 'psychogenerator', an apparatus which could work at a distance to curb the passions of some individuals, instil courage and optimism into others and ultimately create a harmonious society by scientific methods. Such themes occasionally surface in science fiction published in the USSR. The Strugatsky brothers' novel *The Inhabited Island* (1969),[102] which contains the apparently fantastic theme of the use of mind control by powerful generators operated by the ruling elite of 'All-Powerful Creators', may have been inspired by

Inyushin's work or by research into ESP funded by the military in the hope that it may be of use in espionage. A related theme treated almost exclusively by dissident writers is the misuse of science by the Soviet security services. In his *samizdat* story *The Second-Hand Bookseller* Shalamov depicts a prisoner nicknamed 'Fleming', a former NKVD interrogator, who admits that the suppression of the will of the accused in the 1930s purge trials was achieved by the use of drugs: 'The secret of the trial was the secret of pharmacology.'[103] This is an admission unique in Soviet fiction, although the use of drugs and hypnotism by the secret police is also posited in Solzhenitsyn's *Gulag Archipelago*. Another practice forcibly condemned by Solzhenitsyn as 'spiritual murder' is the Soviet authorities' confinement of dissidents in mental hospitals.[104] This method was first used in the late 1930s, but became more widely applied from the beginning of the 1960s, after Khrushchev had abandoned the mass terror of the Stalin era. The writer and mathematician Alexander Esenin-Volpin, first confined in a psychiatric hospital in 1949, was recommitted in 1960; Valery Tarsis was incarcerated in a mental hospital in 1962; and the poet Iosif Brodsky was subjected to a psychiatric examination before being exiled as a 'parasite' in 1964.

The first literary work to deal with the Soviet authorities' abuse of psychiatry was Valery Tarsis's fictionalised documentary *Ward No. 7*. In a parallel with Chekhov's story *Ward No. 6*, Tarsis implies that it is the doctors who are mad, while the patients are perfectly sane, although unsuited to a life of slavery. In ward No. 7 people are not cured, but permanently crippled; the hospital is a prison and the doctors police spies and jailers. The majority of doctors know nothing about psychiatry, but establish diagnoses arbitrarily and give every patient the same treatment — the anti-psychotic drug aminozin or a painful injection. Tarsis denounces Soviet psychiatry as charlatanism and pseudo-science. First, it has pretensions to cure the sickness of men's souls, although it denies the existence of the soul. Secondly, there can be no satisfactory definition of mental illness in Soviet society, because there is no acceptable definition of mental health. The Stalin period has distorted the human personality through decades of terror and violence, creating a persecution complex which has affected successive generations of Soviet citizens; and Soviet reality, with its poverty, fear and lack of hope, has intensified feelings of depression and paranoia. There can be no truly 'normal' people in such conditions and no possibility of cure, since such psychological traumas can only be treated by giving people an alternative, acceptable manner of life, which would involve the introduction of democracy and freedom in the USSR. As the Soviet authorities cannot countenance this, they use anti-psychotic drugs to violate the personalities of sane people, leading to loss of memory, distorted vision, impotence and apathy. Tarsis contends that the Soviet regime is happy with such methods, because its aim is to turn people into obedient robots and force the whole population to think in an identical manner.

The exploitation of advanced technology by the secret police was another subject unmentionable in published literature. In his poem *Oza*, however, Voznesensky hints at the possibility that science may be used to spy on people through his grotesque vision of the cyclotron which screws an ear in the middle of one man's forehead, enabling him to look and listen through keyholes at the same time. Voznesensky's preoccupation with the theme of surveillance is also evident in the poem *An Obligatory Diversion* (1962), which alludes to bugging devices and secret cameras, and employs the Soviet term *stukachi* (informers) in such a way that the portrayal of FBI agents shadowing him in New York can be read as an indirect reference to the Soviet secret police.[105]

Abram Tertz (Andrei Sinyavsky) also expresses revulsion against the misuse of science and technology for political purposes. In *The Trial Begins*, set in 1952, he portrays two secret policemen who envisage the Orwellian possibility that the KGB might design a machine called a 'psychoscope' capable of reading men's criminal thoughts and feelings and controlling them automatically at any hour and at any distance. Every 'harmful element' would then have all his 'ideologically negative' thoughts projected on to a screen at the District Psychoscopic Point. Despite every effort to empty his mind, the criminal would be unable to deceive the machine or to deny his guilt, and would be obliged to confess to imaginary crimes. The implication is that advanced scientific methods would merely be used to perfect a technique which was already in operation in Stalin's time, when the security forces used spies, denunciations and listening devices to extort confessions.

It is ironic that Sinyavsky's own trial paralleled this theme in his fiction: the judge stated that his allusion to the use of 'bugging devices' by the secret police was a 'slander', although he allowed in evidence a tape-recorded conversation of Sinyavsky acquired by means of such a device. In Tertz's later novel, *The Makepeace*

Experiment, the two plain-clothes men reappear as Vitya Kochetov and Anatoly Sofronov (a satire on the neo-Stalinist writers Kochetov and Sofronov). Kochetov praises the method of 'magnetism' used by the dictator Tikhomirov which possesses the advantage over the psychoscope of directing people's thoughts on to the right path from the start. In this way Tertz suggests that Soviet ideological propaganda and socialist realist literature may be even more effective techniques of thought control than listening devices.

Zinoviev's *Yawning Heights* is permeated with a similar awareness that science can be used to enslave people. He imagines an 'Institute of Penology' which leads the world in such radical scientific discoveries as 'techniques of Execution'; depicts the horrific physical and mental suffering inflicted on dissidents by psychiatric techniques; and suggests the ultimate in scientific development: a receiver implanted in the brain which will make all citizens hear and see anything the authorities want, and which cannot be switched off.

Moral and Philosophical Implications of Science and Technology

Soviet propaganda has always claimed that science and humanism are indissolubly linked. Humanist considerations have, however, had somewhat contradictory effects on the development of science and technology. On the one hand, the desire to contribute to human welfare can have a beneficial effect on the scientist's work, acting as a spur to research. On the other hand, science and humane values may frequently come into conflict. First, the scientist's eagerness to help humanity may lead him to avoid the more complex areas of theoretical research on the grounds that the objective search for truth is less important than practical, utilitarian projects; or to accept false scientific theories if they promise to promote human welfare. Secondly, science may clash with moral values, since science and technology in themselves provide no basis for ethics. Thirdly, science, with its emphasis on reason and objectivity, cannot fulfil the emotional or spiritual needs of the human being. Fourthly, scientific research into nature and the universe may actually make man appear less important than he seemed in the ancient religious view of the world. Finally, the growth of human knowledge may actually increase man's uncertainty, rather than his power over nature, and may release destructive forces which could escape from human control.

Post-Stalin literature began to manifest an awareness of some of these issues, exploring the deeper moral, psychological and philosophical implications of the development of science and technology. Two main currents of thought can be distinguished: an awareness of the limitations of science in relation to other facets of human life; and a deeper questioning of the value of science, leading in the case of some dissident writers to a rejection of uncritical devotion to science as a panacea.

Science and Love

In the early 1950s Stalinist 'production literature' was criticised for its cursory or stereotyped treatment of human feelings.[106] A new theme introduced into Soviet literature during the first 'thaw' was the acknowledgement that a man's dedication to technological progress need not preclude affection and love, which also play an important part in human life. Pogodin's play *Petrarch's Sonnet* (1956) depicts Sukhodolov, the director of a large construction works, who now feels that he has devoted his life to a half-truth, as 'in the world there are not only great construction sites, but great feelings too'.[107] After 20 years Sukhodolov is prepared to abandon construction for personal love and an uncertain future. The criticism to which Pogodin was subjected suggests that it was still controversial to imply that communist construction is insufficient to fill a man's life and that personal life is a private domain which should not fall under party scrutiny; but the literary treatment of this theme perhaps helped to prepare public opinion for the debates of the late 1950s, in which lawyers discussed whether people's personal affairs could slip from beneath the net of legal control, so that divorce could be dealt with outside the courts.

Nikolaeva's *Battle on the Way* gives a sensitive depiction of the affair between two engineers, Tina Karamysh and Dmitry Bakhirev, both of whom are already married. When eventually the lovers are parted they continue, despite personal sorrow, to find satisfaction in working to build communism; but Nikolaeva leaves unanswered questions about the limitations of a materialist Utopia: although communism may end economic exploitation and produce great scientific achievements, it may be powerless to create perfect marriages and good mothers or to abolish love outside marriage. Nikolaeva was subsequently attacked for her portrayal of adultery, which was very frank by Soviet standards, and was obliged to omit certain outspoken passages from the second edition of the novel, published in 1958. In the 1950s it was evidently still unacceptable for Soviet writers to imply that a man might value love more highly than scientific work, as Pasternak did in *Doctor Zhivago*. By the early 1960s, however, literature began to devote more attention to the individual's personal life. Granin's *Into the Storm* satirises the futile attempt of young people to deny the importance of love in the 'atomic age'; and Voznesensky was criticised for his poem *The Skull Ballad* (1962) which uses 'Aesopian language' to attribute the neglect of love in Soviet literature and society to the psychological impact of the Stalin era.[108]

The subject of love in the 'era of the NTR' created further controversies in the 1970s. Critics continued to complain that love was not adequately depicted in such works of 'production literature' as Kolesnikov's 'Altunin' series. Zalygin's novel *The South American Variant* (1973), an evocation of the love affair and day-dreams of a middle-aged woman engineer, provoked a storm of criticism: some critics ignored Zalygin's use of irony and fantasy, condemning him for portraying a 'philistine milieu' and for wishing to transport his heroine 'from a computer in a research institute to a cave', while the sociologist Perevedentsev went to the other extreme, suggesting that Zalygin's heroine embodies 'the best features of a female intellectual in an era of scientific and technological revolution'. A more balanced view closer to the author's intention was expressed by F. Kuznetsov, who argued that the banality of the affair set amid computers and other technology suggests that 'Zalygin is quite conscious of the fact that spiritual and moral progress does not always keep pace with scientific and economic progress.'[109]

Science and Nature

In the post-Stalin period some writers, influenced by Pasternak, resurrected another traditional poetic theme: the relationship between man and nature. Soloukhin's work is reminiscent of Rousseau and Tolstoy in its exaltation of the wonders of nature above man's scientific achievements. In *Byways in Vladimir District* he states that 'the cow remains, as before, a more valuable aggregate than, for example, a jet plane'. In his poem *The Apple* (1961) he evokes the apple which allegedly fell on Isaac Newton's head, prompting him to formulate his theory of gravitation; the poet is convinced that Newton also admired the apple's beauty and eventually ate it.[110] Soloukhin implies that nature has always existed independently of man, and that its function is not merely to furnish man with phenomena worthy of scientific investigation.

In his *Letter from the Russian Museum*, Soloukhin remarks that man is very arrogant to consider himself superior to the animal kingdom, especially as many animals have faculties which human beings lack: birds find it easy to fly, whereas man requires a clumsy aeroplane; bats have the power of echo-location, whereas Soviet scientists have only recently acquired cumbersome locators; other species can predict the weather better than we can. This is an unusual theme in Soviet literature, particularly in view of official approval for Gorky's dictum: 'Man whose name has so proud a sound.'

Science and Art

During the years 1959–64 the question of the relationship between art and science in the modern world, a subject which had preoccupied Soviet writers in the LEF disputes of the 1920s, again became a topical issue. The discussion was opened in 1959 by Ehrenburg's article answering a letter from a certain Nina V. who had left her boyfriend Yury, an engineer, because he scorned art and literature, claiming that only science and technology are relevant to contemporary society. In reply Ehrenburg endorsed Chekhov's view that there need be no conflict between art and science, but maintained that man cannot live solely in order to produce material goods and increase factual information, since socialism demands an all-round development of the human personality.[111] In response to Ehrenburg the engineer I. Poletaev argued that science and technology mould the consciousness of modern man, and that art and literature have become irrelevant to contemporary society:

> We live by the creativity of the reason, and not of feelings, by the poetry of ideas, theories, experiments, construction. This is our epoch. It demands the whole of a man, and we have no time to exclaim: 'Oh, Bach! O, Blok!' Naturally, they have grown obsolete and have not kept pace with the development of our life. Whether we like it or not, they have become a leisure activity, a diversion, not life . . . [112]

Poletaev's letter sparked off a lively exchange in *Komsomolskaya*

Pravda: while some correspondents agreed with him, the majority argued that art and science are not mutually exclusive, that 'a branch of lilac is necessary even in space'.[113] *Literaturnaya Gazeta* raised the central issue in 1960:

> The question of the relationship between contemporary art and the scientific revolution, the mutual influence of scientific and artistic creativity, today arouses widespread interest. Will they become antagonistic? Or will they peacefully share out 'spheres of influence'? Or perhaps somewhere the boundaries between them will disappear?[114]

Interest was also aroused by C. P. Snow's *The Two Cultures and the Scientific Revolution* (1959), which maintained that the increasing specialisation required in the contemporary world inevitably leads to a division between arts specialists and scientists.[115]

In a poem whose title, *Physicists and Lyricists* (1960) was widely used to describe the whole debate, Boris Slutsky suggested that the popularity of science in an era of atomic energy, cybernetics and space travel had overshadowed the popularity of poetry, and that Soviet poetry had failed to rise to the challenge of reflecting the contemporary age. Slutsky was, however, attacked by some indignant poets for undermining the significance of contemporary poetry.[116] The 'physicists and lyricists' debate was also a common theme in Soviet prose. Naturally, while showing a certain sympathy for the extreme views of some young scientists, writers defend the value of art against the ideas of men like Poletaev. In his story *A Piece of Glass* Kaverin portrays the young physiologist Petya Uglov who, like many intellectuals of the post-Stalin period, came from a humble background, specialised in science at an early age and did not acquire a wide general culture. Another young scientist, Valka, who is interested in art and literature, accuses him of resembling 'that engineer whose letter was printed in *Komsomolskaya Pravda*'.

The friendship and mutual support between many Soviet scientists and artists show that the rigid distinction between 'art' and 'science' was largely a false problem. Andrei Voznesensky, for example, came from a scientific background: his father was a scientist and he himself graduated from an architectural institute. In *Lyrical Religion* (1963) he defends the relevance of poetry in the modern age;[117] and his poem *Oza*, which refers to his scientist friends as 'gods', has been popular among Soviet scientists since its first appearance. When asked in an interview of 1962, 'Who are your readers?', Voznesensky answered, 'The people who especially like modern poetry are the young physicists, the young scientists, men who, while they appear very uncomplicated and ordinary, do complex things and are complex people.'[118]

While Soviet intellectuals clearly had a genuine interest in the relationship between art and science, and some liberal writers used the discussion to propound their own views on the importance of literature, it is also quite possible that the 'physicists and lyricists' debate was artificially sponsored, or at least encouraged, by the party authorities in order to create the semblance of intellectual ferment,and to divert people's attention from more controversial political issues such as the problems of 'fathers and sons' and 'Stalin's heirs'. This is implied by Voznesensky's poem *Who are We?*:

> Who are we?
> There is no physicist no lyricist blood . . .
> You're either a poet or a Lilliputian.[119]

Voznesensky's words were interpreted by his young audience as an allusion to the major moral conflict in Soviet society between petty Stalinist bureaucrats and those who upheld genuine art and spiritual values.[120] The Soviet regime's direct involvement in the 'physicists and lyricists' debate was demonstrated by its organisation of the June 1963 Ideological Plenum for the discussion of problems of artistic and scientific creativity — an event regarded with suspicion by Soviet intellectuals as possibly heralding a more repressive cultural policy. Yet the genuine and continuing interest of Soviet intellectuals in the relationship between art and science — a subject to which little attention is now paid in the West — is attested by the numerous press debates on this subject in the 1960s and 1970s.

Science and Humane Values

The relationship between science and humane values constitutes just one aspect of the wider conflict between morality and Soviet ideology, which has received a fuller treatment in general studies of post-Stalin fiction. While literature usually propagated the official view that humanism and party policy are identical concepts, it was occasionally acknowledged that scientific values and humane values might come into conflict.

The Twentieth Congress aroused a longing among the Soviet population for the revival of morality and humanism, for the removal of the political constraints deforming human feelings. Alexander Yashin's controversial story *The Levers* (1956) used technical imagery to evoke the dehumanisation of Soviet man through bureaucracy, and to suggest that human beings and moral values were being sacrificed in the cause of technological progress.[121] Party members also began to express such sentiments in their fiction. Tendryakov's story *Potholes* (1956) highlights the distorted system of values created by Stalinism, demonstrating that the prevention of the unauthorised use of agricultural machinery is valued more highly than the preservation of a man's life.[122] Margarita Aliger's poem *The Most Important Thing* (1956) depicts a strong 'positive hero' of the type portrayed in Stalinist production novels who is subsequently exposed as a liar, coward and slanderer. The poet implies that such qualities as integrity and sincerity are more important than technology, and that this man is 'not necessary to humanity'. Aliger was, however, subsequently forced to recant because of her disparaging comments about the impersonal 'builders of communism'.[123]

In the early 1960s Khrushchev himself encouraged writers to place a new emphasis on 'humanism', as opposed to the development of science and technology for their own sake: the new party programme of 1961 went beyond materialism to assert the importance of 'humane relationships and mutual respect between individuals'.[124] Some liberal writers, however, ventured beyond the party line, portraying elderly scientists who emphasise the limitations of scientific research and technological progress, and the greater importance of the permanent values in human life. The physicist Dankevich in Granin's *Into the Storm* verges on a gradualistic ordering of values in which science and technology are seen as possessing only a relative validity in relation to the moral and spiritual world: 'What, in your opinion, distinguishes people from animals? Atomic energy? The telephone? I would say — morality, imagination, ideals. Men's souls won't be improved because you and I are studying the earth's electrical field.' Evidently Granin endorses the moral values upheld by members of the older generation of scientists such as Tamm, Kapitsa and the biologist and philosopher A. Lyubishchev (1890–1972).

The rejection of the cult of science and the search for a new morality were particularly evident among Soviet youth in the 1960s.

The spiritual vacuum created among young people by the dethronement of Stalin led to what Soviet Komsomol leaders described as
'nihilism',[125] whether it found expression in drunkenness and hooliganism or in a return to spiritual or religious values.
Such soul-searching shows that young people no longer regarded
science and technology as acceptable objects of belief. This mood is
reflected in the controversial story by the Latvian writer V.
Eglons *Smoke is Rising* (1960), which depicts a nihilistic young man who
'contemptuously' pushes aside books on applied science as irrelevant to his needs, searching for the meaning of life in world literature.[126] Similarly, Yevtushenko remarked in his *Precocious Autobiography*, which he published abroad in 1963: 'To this day I can't
understand what electricity is or where it comes from!' He was
criticised for this casual dismissal of science and technology by both
the physicist A. Aleksandrov and the cosmonaut Yury Gagarin
(although an eminent scientist apparently sympathised with
Yevtushenko, claiming that he too had never solved the enigma of
electricity).[127]
The nihilism of Soviet youth deprived ideologues of the argument
that young people were enthusiastically 'building communism'.
Indeed, one cause of the younger generation's disillusionment with
scientific progress was the unwillingness of Soviet theorists to
describe the ideal society which Soviet science and ideology were
allegedly creating, and their failure to explain adequately whether,
when the stage of full communism was attained, society would
continue to evolve or whether the dialectical process would cease.
A poll organised by *Komsomolskaya Pravda* in 1961, asking 'What
do you think of your generation?', established that many young
people wanted a personal aim in life in addition to (or in contradis-
tinction to) the social aim of using their scientific and technical skills
to 'build communism'.[128]
In the early 1960s such writers of 'youth prose' as Dubov,
Aksyonov and Rozov depicted a generation reaching adulthood
and choosing their first employment who often counter conventional ideology with scepticism and a desire for personal integrity
and independence. In particular, they evince a mistrust of false
ideals and bombastic speeches about using science to build the
communist Utopia. Nikolai Dubov's story *The Difficult Test* (1960),
for example, depicts the narrow-minded worker Victor who
declares that the aim of life 'is the same for all — to build communism', and a girl who asks him, 'What about your personal

aim?'[129] In Victor Rozov's film script *A, B, C, D, E* (1962) a young
nihilist expresses a more explicit scepticism towards technological
progress: 'People invent colour television and the tape recorder, are
just about to discover the secret of protein and fly to the moon, but
this does not make them any more honest or happy . . .'[130]

In *A Starry Ticket* Aksyonov contrasts two brothers — Victor
Denisov, a physicist engaged in confidential work for the space
programme, and his seventeen-year-old brother Dimka who is
sceptical of all conventional Soviet values and wants to find a
personal aim in life. Dimka despises his brother's life, which has
merely continued 'through all the other regular motions on the
great road that leads to the Academy of Sciences . . . that is, to
being a corpse which has earned the general respect of the community'. Although this work was considered too controversial to be
re-published in a separate edition, the conclusion differs little from
a conventional 'production novel', as the rebellious Dimka, chastened by his brother's death, settles down as a zealous construction
worker. However, the orthodox conclusions of Aksyonov's stories,
which were probably a product of self-censorship, or added because
of the insistence of Kataev, the editor of *Yunost*, make less impression on the reader than the interesting insights which they offer into
the feelings of young people in the 1960s.

Aksyonov's *Colleagues* (1960) demonstrates more explicitly that
scientific values and humane values are not easily reconcilable,
suggesting that man is an aim in himself, not a means to an end, and
that concern for the individual human being in the present is more
important than concern for mankind in a hypothetical future. The
sceptical young doctor Aleksei Maksimov disparages people who
deceive themselves with propaganda slogans about 'planning for
the future' and 'creative labour', and claims that only a handful of
idealists work for the joy of creativity.[131] Since Aksyonov's emigration to the West he has made it plain that he deliberately censored
himself while writing *Colleagues* in order to ensure its publication,
and that his own sympathies lay with the 'anti-Stalinist' Maksimov
rather than with the 'positive hero' Zelenin, whom he now characterises as an 'idealistic fool'.[132]

The 'youth prose' of the 1960s could be regarded as the precursor
of what came in the 1970s to be called 'everyday prose' — a genre
which raises the problem of the ethics of the contemporary Soviet
urban intelligentsia. The works of Trifonov, Zalygin and other
'everyday prose' writers imply that man's psychology and morality

do not necessarily change, despite scientific progress and improved living standards. Trifonov's work poses the crucial question: can a perfect communist society be built when the essence of man remains unchanged?

Negative Aspects of the Cult of Science

The cult of science has had contradictory effects on the development of Soviet science and technology. On the one hand, it has provided the inspiration behind the great scientific and technological achievements of the USSR. On the other hand, the pervasive Soviet belief in the ability of science to remake the world has led to the acceptance of pseudo-scientific theories which aim at changing the world before it has been properly understood. This is a result of the need for quick practical results and the wishful thinking inherent, if not in Marxism itself, in Lenin's theory of revolution and the doctrine of 'socialism in one country'.

While some works published in the USSR, such as Fazil Iskander's story *The Goat-Ibex Constellation* (1966),[133] were able, within certain limits, to expose the charlatanism of Lysenko, Vilyams, Lepeshinskaya and other quacks who had at one time found favour with the Soviet authorities, dissident authors more explicitly challenged the cult of science in Soviet society. Yuly Daniel's satirical story *The Man from MINAP* (1963) depicts a young member of the Moscow Institute of Scientific Profanation who claims that he can predetermine the sex of children before conception.[134] Daniel defended himself at his trial by stating that his story was designed as an irreverent comment on the 'practice of making sensational publicity about scientific discoveries' and was inspired by the example of the pseudo-scientist Boshyan.[135] G. M. Boshyan was a supporter of Lysenko whose fraudulent research on the origin of viruses from microbes and vice versa received wide publicity in 1949–51, but whose work was the object of official investigation and refutation in 1954, after which Boshyan was exposed as a charlatan and stripped of his doctor's degree. Daniel's story, however, contained a clear reference to Lysenko: a scientist, suggestively addressed as 'Trofim Denisovich' (Lysenko's name and patronymic), claims that the young adventurer's ludicrous pseudo-scientific theory can be easily reconciled with Marxism. Daniel's work also possesses much wider implications for the general attitude to science in the USSR, implying that a failure to believe in science is tantamount to ideological deviationism in the

USSR. The Soviet authorities' exaltation of 'science' by means of ideological jargon is shown to be closer to an irrational faith in pseudo-science; theories formerly stigmatised as 'idealist' are considered acceptable if they can be of practical benefit to the bureaucracy. Through his depiction of the eagerness with which Soviet officials allow the young scientist to impregnate their wives, Daniel exposes the exploitation of scientific discoveries by a narrow circle of political leaders in order to increase their prestige among the Soviet people (as occurred, for example, in the case of Aslan's rejuvenation therapy).

In the post-Khrushchev period some published works began to criticise the extravagant claims for science made in the Soviet press: for example, a physicist in Konstantinovsky's *Ergo sum* pokes fun at the 'vast promises on global questions' which scientists are expected to make; and in Kron's *Insomnia*, a scientist working on the problems of premature ageing objects to the title 'The Struggle against Death' which a journalist foists on his article. Zinoviev, in *The Yawning Heights*, takes a cynical view of current experiments aimed at prolonging life to the age of 100 or 200 years:

> Just imagine what would happen if the elixir were discovered! Who would be allowed to live 200 years? Who would carry out the treatment? How could it be set out in ideological, moral and legal terms? You can imagine what lengths people would go to to win the prize of 200 years of life.

Other dissident writers made a more fundamental criticism of the anti-intellectual attitudes created by the cult of science and reason in Soviet society. In his essay *A Leaf of Spring* (1961) the mathematician and philosopher Esenin-Volpin attacks all monistic faiths, including a faith in reason, since they can do violence to the individual, and comments laconically, 'It is not enough to *believe* in reason. For a thinking man it is enough to be reasonable.'[136] Similarly, in *The Yawning Heights* Zinoviev declares:

> A faith in reason is not a scientific phenomenon. It is faith — in other words, the fundamental basis of ideology. By striving to appear scientific, official ideology destroys the foundation of the foundations of everything that is most human in humankind — belief in one's own reason.

Science and Death

Another new subject considered in Soviet fiction was the value of science in relation to man's inevitable death. Death is not mentioned by many Soviet writers, both because it is a taboo subject in Soviet society, and because authors are required to depict reality in an optimistic light. In the post-Stalin period, however, authors were able to treat more tragic themes as long as they followed the precept outlined in 1958 by Krivitsky, a member of the editorial board of *Novy Mir*: 'Draw us a zebra — black stripe, bright stripe, black stripe, bright stripe. Step back and you've got an objective picture.'[137]

In Dudintsev's *New Year's Tale*, the hero's hesitations in the face of the news of his approaching death reveal a profound questioning of the value of science rarely found in works published in the USSR. His first thought is the conventional view that he must hurry to finish his work in his one remaining year; although man is ephemeral, human thoughts live on. He then reflects, however, that ideas will exist only as long as human life on this planet, which may be for thousands of years, or for just a short time if there is a nuclear war in the near future, but in either case the scientific ideas written down in books will not survive. After the holocaust a new race may gradually evolve, but it will be a primitive society which will turn to religion, not science, for an explanation of the universe. The hero's doubts raise the question: if all human life must inevitably cease, can man without God ever attain true immortality, either through scientific achievements or through art? Although Dudintsev himself may not have been aware of the full implications of his work, he was, quite understandably, attacked by dogmatist critics for asking many 'extraordinary questions'.[138]

Grossman's *The Elk* (1963) is a more pessimistic story which shows that both science and ideology are irrelevant in the face of death.[139] Grossman depicts a retired turbine engineer who is dying alone; his research and the life of the institute now seem meaningless, as his only technical innovation has been superseded and his work will possess no lasting value. As he gazes at the head of an elk which he shot many years before, he feels that his solitary death is a just reward for this crime against love and humanity. In this understated story Grossman suggests that all is vanity in relation to death: official propaganda for the building of communism, revolutionary zeal and scientific research. Grossman's story was, predictably,

attacked for its evocation of 'man's boundless solitude' which was
judged inappropriate in 'a time of struggle for the best in man'.[140]
Such pessimism may well have reflected Grossman's own despair
after the KGB's confiscation of his manuscripts in February 1961
and the sense of his own approaching death.

In *Cancer Ward* Solzhenitsyn confronts the dedicated geologist
Vadim with the prospect of imminent death. Vadim epitomises the
noblest legacy of Stalin's rule; intelligent, energetic, committed to
science, he resembles a 'positive hero' of socialist realism. By
emphasising the extreme malignancy of Vadim's tumour,
Solzhenitsyn parallels the device of the deadline for the completion
of scientific work used in conventional Soviet novels. Vadim feels
that he must use the short time remaining to him to complete some
original work — the use of radioactive water to locate ore
deposits — in order to bequeath something valuable to the Soviet
people. Solzhenitsyn uses this orthodox framework to undermine
the Marxist-Leninist attitude to the value of science with which
Vadim has been indoctrinated. He shows that Vadim's growing
inability to concentrate on his work as the disease progresses runs
counter to the ideal of will-power epitomised by the heroes of
socialist realism. Moreover, Solzhenitsyn stresses the tragic irony of
Vadim's predicament: officials representing the regime whose
mineral wealth he is attempting to increase fail to send him a
mineral which he desperately needs — radioactive gold — to cure
his secondary tumours and enable him to complete his work.

Vadim's position is also undermined by Shulubin, who asks if he
is not deceiving himself by spending his time reading geology and
chemistry books. Why does he need that and not something else?
For once Vadim fails to answer with the 'correct' ideological slogan,
responding with a simple personal statement: 'It's the most interesting thing I know!' Shulubin, however, complains that many selfish,
unethical occupations such as making money might also be considered interesting; work done merely for the sake of its intrinsic
interest will never create anything ethically good. Through the
portrait of Vadim, Solzhenitsyn illustrates his own firm conviction,
expressed by the old doctor: 'Modern man is helpless when confronted with death . . . he has no weapons to meet it with.'

The Ultimate Purpose of Science

The Soviet leaders have always claimed that politics and morality
are synonymous, and that the scientist's role is to serve the Soviet

state and people. From the 1930s to the 1950s the doctrine that the entire purpose of a scholar's life should be measured in terms of social and political utility does indeed appear to have been accepted by some of Russia's greatest scientists. By the post-Stalin period, however, although this view was still sincerely propounded by such eminent scientists as N. Semyonov, A. Aleksandrov, D. Skobeltsyn and N. Amosov, Soviet scientists had come to hold a wide variety of opinions on the question of science and morality. Some were fanatical believers in science who denied that morality played any part in human progress; others, perhaps the majority, were indifferent to moral and social issues, either because their sole aim was personal advancement, or because they chose to avoid social evils and moral responsibilities by devoting themselves to their work. Many young scientists had been brought up to believe that scientific research was its own justification, or felt that their duty was to obey orders from their superiors. This attitude is epitomised by the team of young scientists depicted in Grekova's *Beyond the Checkpoint*: although some of them behave ethically in relation to each other, they never question the ultimate value of their research in space or military electronics.

The Soviet authorities evidently did not welcome a deeper investigation of the moral responsibilities of the scientist, for the censorship banned both an article of 1956 by Professor Lyubishchev advising young people embarking on an academic career to remain independent of dogma and authority and later works by Mark Popovsky and E. and G. Abelev asserting the need for morality in science.[141] Only a few scientists were brave enough to adopt high moral standards and defend them in public, since any moral protest was interpreted as a political one; but Lyubishchev's essay circulated in *samizdat* and helped to reawaken scientists' interest in moral questions. Nadezhda Mandelstam testifies to the questioning of the value of science among young scientists and engineers who were 'a little embarrassed at having become technocrats', since they were no longer considered to be the spokesmen of their age or the people most in touch with modern life.[142]

Voznesensky's *Oza*, which reflects views current among Soviet scientists, presents the fullest exploration of the moral and philosophical implications of the development of science and technology in literature published in the USSR during the Khrushchev period.[143] The poet's attitude towards scientific progress is ambivalent: he praises the nuclear research station at Dubna, but condemns the depersonalisation of man through modern technology. Voznesensky goes further than other writers in explicitly attributing the neglect of humane values in Soviet society to the Stalin era. He alludes to the bright hopes for humane values raised by the Russian Revolution which were dashed by Stalin, the 'Great Engineer',

> Nuts and bolts surveying
> Blind to human beings.

He expresses the hope that scientific progress and industrialisation will no longer be valued above human life:

> Of Stalin do not sing
> We are more than nuts and bolts;
> And no more shall we choke
> On his blue-bearded smoke.

The clearest reflection of the poet's own position is in the words:

> All progress is retrogression
> If the process breaks man down.

Voznesensky expresses values similar to those of Pasternak, defending love, nature, poetry and the free human spirit against the worship of technological 'pseudo-progress' for its own sake; science is meaningless unless it is used to serve man. Technology and politics are transient, whereas the human soul, expressed in love or poetry, is eternal.

> Technologies and states live for a day
> Then go their way and pass us by.

> Only one thing on earth is constant
> Like the light of a star that has gone
> It is the continuing radiance
> They used to call the human soul.

Solzhenitsyn's works show that he had, since the 1950s and early 1960s, been concerned about the moral and philosophical issues raised by the development of science and technology, both in the USSR and any modern society. In *The First Circle* he demonstrates that scientific research is insignificant in relation to personal integrity and human suffering. In the brief time-span depicted in the novel, each imprisoned scientist is required to make a personal decision to accept or reject the regime's plans and methods. If he is prepared to do scientific work for the security services he may receive an early release, a pardon and a flat in Moscow; refusal to comply will mean a certain transfer back to the labour camps. Nerzhin is asked to do research into codes and cryptography; the image of the Rosicrucians suggests an arcane secret society of initiates for whom science and mathematics represent an absolute value in themselves. Nerzhin, however, realises that science is not morally neutral, and refuses to compromise his human dignity by collaborating with the secret police.

Solzhenitsyn's rejection of the view that intellectual interest and personal fulfilment are sufficient justification for scientific research is demonstrated most clearly through the tragic figure of the communist Rubin, who misuses his own talent, becoming absorbed in his attempt to devise a new science of 'phonoscopy' which will enable an individual's voice on the telephone to be identified from its 'voice prints'. The secret police, however, are interested only in the practical results of Rubin's work which leads to the arrest of Innokenty and an innocent colleague. The socio-political implications of Solzhenitsyn's viewpoint were clarified in the revised version of *The First Circle*, which condemns the scientists who agreed to create nuclear weapons for Stalin, thus tacitly censuring, among others, his political opponent Andrei Sakharov. In *Letter to Soviet Leaders*, Solzhenitsyn attributes the emergence of amoral scientists to the false values propagated by the Soviet educational system: 'School leavers rush into military electronics like flies to a honeypot — is it really for such sterile pursuits that we have been developing these last eleven hundred years?'[144] Through the figure of Philip in his play *Candle in the Wind*, who represents the amoral scientist in any society of the future, Solzhenitsyn also implicitly repudiates Sakharov's view about the desirability of 'convergence' between the capitalist and socialist systems; in his opinion both societies, dedicated to the blind, unethical pursuit of 'perpetual progress', are doomed to perish unless they achieve total economic reconstruction and moral renewal.

In *Candle in the Wind* Solzhenitsyn also raises the fundamental question: why is science necessary at all? The hero Alex is dissatisfied with the answers he has received about the purpose of science — that it is interesting, that it is an irreversible process, or that it creates material goods — and the view that one must work for work's sake and live for society seems to him a circular argument which begs the vital question 'What are we living for?' It is the social cyberneticist Terbolm who defends science in the most convincing manner. Although he does not agree with Alex's conviction that the scientist has a moral duty to consider the 'external aims' of science — what direction it takes and how it is used — as science has often developed in a way completely independent of man's desires, he believes that science possesses a mysterious inner purpose like art, and is as necessary to the human spirit as conscience. Terbolm's words suggest that Solzhenitsyn is not opposed to science as long as it is subordinated to morality. Alex's eventual decision to work in social cybernetics implies that science can and should be used to make society more efficient, but should not interfere with man's inner life. There is, however, a tragic irony in the fact that Terbolm's optimistic message is recorded while he is lying in hospital with paralysed legs; while it demonstrates the power of his belief in science, it also shows that science will always be powerless to control the element of chance or fate which intrudes in human lives. Although Solzhenitsyn's play was not published in the Soviet Union, he read selected passages from it to audiences in scientific institutes in the 1960s.[145] The interest aroused testifies to contemporary awareness among Soviet scientists of the fundamental questions which Solzhenitsyn raises about the purpose of science and its relationship to life, death and human suffering.

In the post-Khrushchev era many issues connected with the development of science and technology have also been explored in fiction published in the USSR. The growing concern about morality in science is reflected in Granin's biography of Professor Lyubishchev, *This Strange Life* (1974) which has, however, been disparaged by Mark Popovsky because of the amount of information about Lyubishchev's life which it omits.[146] Soloukhin, in his collection of thoughts *Pebbles on my Palm* (1978), repeats a question posed by the poet Fyodor Glinka 130 years previously: 'What about people? People will become gods', and asks whether modern man, with his 'everyday, moral and social problems', has in fact become a god. Some of the negative sides of contemporary life which Soloukhin mentions — drug addiction, unemployment, pornographic and horror films — are designed to incriminate the capitalist West, but he also refers to such universal problems as 'the hypnotic reign of television' and poses the general question: 'Have we simply become better than the poet Fyodor Glinka . . . and in thirty years' time will people on earth be better than us?'[147] He advocates a balanced approach to progress, encompassing not only technological change, but also intangible moral and spiritual values.

In the post-Stalin period some of the most interesting questions about scientific progress have been raised in works of science fiction and fantasy, which are able to shed the constraints of realistic writing. Zalygin's *Oska the Funny Boy* (1973) is an unusual work subtitled 'A fantastic narrative in two periods' in which, as the author admits in his introduction, 'fantasy exists for its own sake'.[148] Much of the action of this strange tale takes place in the mind of the main protagonist Aleksei Drozdov. In the first part he is a young man daydreaming as he observes meteorological and natural phenomena in the Far North; while in the second part he is a professor and doctor of geographical sciences dying of a heart complaint, trying to solve in fantasy problems that cannot be solved in reality. Zalygin raises certain questions connected with scientific progress in an allusive, paradoxical fashion. Various philosophical hypotheses are represented by imaginary figures who are all facets of Drozdov's own subconscious. Through the figure of the robot Alpha-Omega, which regards the whole planet as nothing but raw material for further development by science and technology, Zalygin suggests that modern technology can distort ordinary human values and man's relationship with nature. The Cockroach, which symbolises the destructive potential of science, suggests that biochemists who seek to create an artificial living cell may first produce a virus which could destroy life on the planet. In the 1980 book version of the novel Zalygin made his fears about genetic engineering more explicit, claiming that biologists 'always choose not between good and evil, but between evil and evil, that is the least of all evils'.[149] Zalygin may also be using the figure of the Cockroach, whose only desire is to multiply, to suggest that after a nuclear war only insects will be able to survive. The Integral, which symbolises the power of abstract thought, suggests that concepts will remain when inventions and people die, but the dying Drozdov refuses to regard himself as nothing but pure reason. The Integral is defeated, and Drozdov comes closer to the view of Oska, a boy who realistically accepts technological change in his native Siberia, but also epitomises the need for humanity and individuality in the contemporary scientific age.

The message which eventually emerges from this puzzling story is the need for a balanced approach to scientific progress; man must conserve the environment and not misuse science in a way that harms the essence of human life: individual emotions and moral values. Zalygin's unorthodox work, which raises issues similar to those treated by such dissident writers as Sinyavsky and Solzhenitsyn, was greeted with almost complete silence by Soviet critics, probably so as not to draw attention to it. As Zalygin promised in his apologetic introduction, this was to be an 'experimental story', and he subsequently returned to realism.

Science fiction is also able to treat political and ethical issues which are otherwise taboo, using devices like the parable, the allegory and the grotesque. The Strugatsky brothers, the most interesting writers of science fiction in the USSR, have explored many of the complex consequences of scientific progress. Arkady Strugatsky (born in 1925) is a specialist in Japanese language and Boris Strugatsky (born in 1933) is an astronomer at Pulkovo observatory, so the authors combine an interest in both science and the humanities. The development of their work illustrates a general trend in Soviet society: the transition from the Utopian idealism of the 1950s to the waning of confidence in science and technology from the mid-1960s. Their work has evolved from direct dependence on science towards what the authors themselves term 'social fantasy':[150] a genre which creates hypothetical worlds within which recognisable elements from the present reappear in an estranged form in order that they can be observed from a new, critical angle, and in which the protagonist increasingly comes into conflict with an alien environment which cannot be tamed by science.

Since the early 1960s their work has displayed a heightened awareness of ethical and political concerns, reflecting the influence of Khrushchev's de-Stalinisation campaign, the publication in Warsaw of Lem's *Solaris* (1961) and translations of Western science fiction. *Far Rainbow* (1963), which depicts a small planet overwhelmed by a black wave, an unforeseen side-effect of the constructive experiments performed by a happy community of physicists, is a parable of the negative consequences of scientific progress such as the creation of nuclear weapons and, perhaps, also a warning of the price which must be paid for all man's scientific and historical experiments.

The novels *An Attempted Escape* (1962), *It's Hard to Be a God* (1964), *Predatory Things of the Age* (1965)[151] and *The Inhabited*

Island (1969) all provide models of a totalitarian society, showing how science and technology can be misused in the service of tyranny. They depict a Utopian protagonist who comes into conflict with a fantastic totalitarian setting which may combine elements of Stalinism and Nazism, as well as aspects of contemporary Soviet and Western society, but is presented as a remote, inferior stage of mankind's development which shocks the more advanced hero. In *It's Hard to Be a God*, one of the most popular works of science fiction in the USSR, the hero Anton argues that scientists, scholars and artists, whose mentality is totally alien to bureaucratic officialdom, will eventually survive persecution and create a more advanced society. Yet the whole burden of the novel is that human nature cannot be changed by science, and the tragic ending, in which the feudal kingdom of Arkanar descends into obscurantism, suggests that predictions of inevitable progress (as, for example, in Marxist theory) may be wrong, and that Utopian attempts to change society in a beneficial direction may be futile.

The Inhabited Island (translated under the title *Prisoners of Power*) contains an anti-Utopian setting which perhaps bears the closest resemblance to contemporary Soviet society, with its anonymous collective leadership whose main objective is to stay in power, its bureaucracy, interest in high technology, control of the public media and suppression of dissent; and once again, the Utopian protagonists are powerless to change the oppressive system. This work was probably heavily censored because it was published in the mass circulation journal *Neva*, although it still contains much interesting material. The island, a world of dirty factories, radioactive rivers, ugly houses with metal roofs and vicious metal robots, provides a graphic warning about many of the potentially harmful consequences of scientific progress.

Another of the Strugatskys' major themes is a criticism of bourgeois consumerism and a philistine mentality. In *Predatory Things of the Age* (translated under the title *The Final Circle of Paradise*), the Strugatskys depict the 'Country of Fools' whose inhabitants are satiated with consumer goods and addicted to an artificial stimulant which renders them completely passive. According to the didactic authors' introduction, this is meant to be an allegory of 'the spiritual death which bourgeois ideology brings to man'. However, the novel is not merely an attack on contemporary Western societies, particularly the USA; since the improvement of the material conditions of life was also a goal of the Soviet 'NTR' it can also be interpreted as a warning against the growth of materialism within the USSR. In an article of 1976 Arkady Strugatsky stated that one of the new types of man created by the 'NTR' was the 'well-fed uneducated man of the masses' — a man whose material needs can never be satisfied, and whose philistine emphasis on consumption is not accompanied by an improvement in intellectual and spiritual development.[152]

Since the mid-1960s the Strugatskys' work has suggested a waning of confidence in the limitless possibilities of Soviet science. In *Monday Begins on Saturday* (1965) they use the genre of the contemporary folk tale to attack a bureaucratic approach to scientific research,[153] depicting a Research Institute of Sorcery and Magic where magic is measured and analysed in a bureaucratic manner reminiscent of a real Soviet research institute. The Strugatskys attack scientific charlatanism and imply that modern science, with its incomprehensibility and alienation from the mass of the population, is equivalent to magic. *Tale of a Triumvirate* (1968), which features some of the same characters, attacks authoritarian administration by pseudo-scientists.[154] The Strugatskys' depiction of the triumvirate of bureaucrats who try to explain away incomprehensible phenomena and mask their desire for unlimited power in pseudo-scientific jargon is reminiscent of the three-man tribunals of the Stalin era. It may, however, also have been interpreted as a political satire against the current Soviet authorities, as the work has not been re-published in book form, and Samsonov, the editor of the journal *Angara*, was dismissed. The *émigré* critic Grigory Svirsky has also provided a purely political interpretation of this story;[155] but the refusal of bureaucrats to meet a highly intelligent extra-terrestrial civilisation has wider philosophical implications, suggesting that contemporary man, with his degenerate power structures, is unprepared for contact with a Utopian future.

In 1976 Arkady Strugatsky spoke of the emergence of a new type, 'the scientific worker of the masses', who constitutes a decline of the 1950s ideal of the scientist.[156] He argued that the scientist no longer possesses the narrative interest he had in the early days of the space programme, since it is now recognised that scientists possess ordinary human weaknesses, and that the atmosphere of a research institute exerts a negligible influence on the human personality. This disillusionment with science is reflected in two controversial works, *The Snail on the Slope* (1966–8) and *The Ugly Swans* (1972), which create deliberately irrational worlds in which man is seen as an estranged creature subjected to forces of modernisation beyond his control. This subject ventured beyond the bounds of the permissible: after the publication of the second part of *The Snail on the Slope* in the journal *Baikal* in 1968 the editorial board was dismissed;[157] and *The Ugly Swans*, which was accepted for publication by the Molodaya Gvardiya Publishing House in 1968, has never appeared in the USSR.[158]

After a period of disgrace the Strugatskys seem to have come back into favour in the 1970s with such works as *Roadside Picnic* (1972) (the basis of Tarkovsky's film *Stalker*), *A Billion Years before the End of the World* (1976–7; translated under the title *Definitely Maybe*) and *The Beetle in the Anthill* (1978–9), all of which raise the issue of the desirability of scientific and technological change and whether it should be limited.[159] The Strugatskys suggest no easy solutions: it is simply demonstrated that control could prevent potentially beneficial as well as evil consequences of scientific development.

The best of the Strugatsky's works raise complex issues reflecting disillusionment with the vision of the Utopia conventionally associated with the development of the 'NTR'. They show that science and technology either do not alter man's life, or do not improve it in any significant sense. The critic Gromova contends that the anti-Utopias portrayed by the Strugatskys (and in Emtsev and Parnov's *World Soul*) are less pessimistic than the visions of such Western science fiction writers as Ray Bradbury;[160] yet Soviet science fiction arguably produces an even greater impact, because of the officially-sponsored cult of science in Soviet society. When the Strugatskys have come close to the pessimistic views of Western or dissident writers in their evocations of alienated man in a universe which is not rationally explicable, they have aroused the wrath of the Soviet authorities. Their very popularity, however, ensures them a measure of immunity; they have survived temporary setbacks, and in the 1980s have been permitted to publish demands for more meaningful science fiction.[161] The Strugatskys' work has the same purpose as much of Western science fiction: in Ray Bradbury's words, 'The function of science fiction is not only to predict the future, but to prevent it.'

232   *The Ambivalent View of Science*

Notes

1. J. Ellul, *The Technological Society*, trans. J. Wilkinson (London, 1965); H. Marcuse, *One-Dimensional Man* (London, 1964).
2. *LG*, 17 Nov. 1971; 22 Mar. 1972.
3. F. Kuznetsov, *CDSP*, XXVI (1974), no. 51, p. 21.
4. Letter by Aleksei N., *KP*, 11 June 1960.
5. V. Tendryakov, *Troika, semyorka, tuz, NM*, 1960, no. 3, p. 5.
6. D. Bobyshev, *K zapusku kosmicheskoi rakety* (1960), *Grani*, no. 58 (1965), p. 164.
7. I. Ivashchenko, *Izvestiya*, 2 Sept. 1960.
8. *Survey*, no. 52 (July 1964), p. 78.
9. Ch. Aitmatov, K. Mukhamedzhanov, *The Ascent of Mount Fuji*, trans. N. Bethell (NY, 1975), pp. 93–4.
10. V. Tendryakov, *Nenastye, NM*, 1954, no. 2; E. Dorosh, *Dozhdlivoe leto, Moskva*, 1958, no. 3.
11. E. Dorosh, *Derevenskii dnevnik, LM*, 1956, no. 2, p. 611.
12. L. Ivanov, *Sudba urozhaya (zametki pisatelya), Oktyabr*, 1963, no. 9.
13. V. Kantorovich, 'Delat pravdu. Valentin Ovechkin i sovremennyi ocherk', *VL*, 1974, no. 6, p. 154.
14. F. Abramov, *Vokrug da okolo, Neva*, 1963, no. 1, p. 110.
15. L. Ivanov, *V rodnykh mestakh, NM*, 1963, no. 3, p. 187; Granin, *Posle svadby, Oktyabr*, 1956, no. 8, p. 6.
16. Tendryakov, *Podyonka — vek korotkii, NM*, 1965, no. 5, p. 125; *Sud, NM*, 1961, no. 3, p. 49.
17. Yu. Nagibin, *Rasskazy 1954 goda* (M, 1955), pp. 473–91.
18. Solzhenitsyn, *Matryonin dvor, NM*, 1963, no. 1; A. Yashin, *Vologodskaya svadba, NM*, 1962, no. 12; criticised in S. Pavlov, *KP*, 22 Mar. 1963.
19. D. Pospielovsky, 'The "Link" System in Soviet Agriculture', *SS*, vol. 21 (1970), p. 415.
20. V. Voinovich, 'Author's Foreword', in Voinovich, *In Plain Russian*, trans. R. Lourie (NY, 1979).
21. F. Abramov, *Dom, NM*, 1978, no. 12.
22. R. Laird, 'The Political Economy of Soviet Agriculture under Brezhnev', in D. Kelley (ed.), *Soviet Politics in the Brezhnev Era* (NY, 1980), p. 68.
23. K. Kozhevnikova, *LG*, 24 May 1978.
24. F. Abramov, *Pravda*, 17 Nov. 1979.
25. A. Kuznetsov, *Prodolzhenie legendy, Yunost*, 1957, no. 7; Kuznetsov, *Daily Telegraph*, 7 Aug. 1969.
26. A. Gladilin, *Brigantina podnimaet parusa, Moskovskii Komsomolets*, 1959; discussed in Gladilin, *Making and Unmaking*, pp. 32–5.
27. A. Gladilin, *Pesni zolotogo priiska, MG*, 1960, no. 6; discussed in Gladilin, *Making and Unmaking*, pp. 67–8, 70–1.
28. V. Tarsis, *Palata No. 7* (Frankfurt, 1966), pp. 44, 90, 115.
29. A. Sharov, *Puteshestvie prodolzhaetsya* (M, 1954), pp. 59–60; F. Panfyorov, *Vo imya molodogo, Oktyabr*, 1960, nos. 7, 8.
30. Khrushchev, *Stroitelstvo kommunizma*, vol. 7, pp. 268–9.
31. A. Koptyaeva, *Dar zemli* (M, 1965), pp. 362–3; M. Kolesnikov, *School for Ministers*, trans. L. Tudge (M, 1980), p. 16.
32. Gladilin, *Making and Unmaking*, p. 68.
33. V. Nikitin, *Talaya zemlya, Yunost*, 1960, no. 6, p. 71.
34. V. Voinovich, *Dva tovarishcha, NM*, 1967, no. 1.
35. L. Leonov, *Izvestiya*, 28 Dec. 1947.

The Ambivalent View of Science   233

36. L. Leonov, *LG*, 22 Jan., 30 Mar. 1965.
37. M. Shcheglov, ' "Russkii les" Leonida Leonova', *NM*, 1954, no. 5, pp. 220–41; M. Kuznetsov, *Pravda*, 28 Mar. 1954.
38. McLean and Vickery, *Year of Protest*, p. 158.
39. A. Merkulov, *Pravda*, 28 Feb. 1965; the letter from 30 scientists, artists and writers, *KP*, 11 May 1966.
40. G. Kapvalov, *Pravda*, 14 May 1970.
41. Svirsky, *Soviet Writing*, p. 303.
42. B. Vasilyev, *Ne strelyaite v belykh lebedei, Yunost*, 1973, nos. 6, 7.
43. B. Komarov, *Unichtozhenie prirody* (Frankfurt, 1978).
44. V. Rasputin, *Proshchanie s Matyoroi, NS*, 1976, nos. 10, 11.
45. *VL*, 1977, no. 2, pp. 3–81.
46. V. Rasputin, *LG*, 16 Mar. 1977.
47. Yu. Seleznev, 'Zemlya ili territoriya?', *VL*, 1977, no. 2, p. 56.
48. V. Astafyev, *Tsar-ryba, NS*, 1976, nos. 4–6.
49. *VL*, 1977, no. 2.
50. *LO*, 1976, no. 10, pp. 50–7.
51. M. Friedberg, 'Cultural and Intellectual Life', p. 283.
52. Yu. Bondarev, *LG*, 8 July 1981.
53. A. Aganbegyan, in *CDSP*, XXIV (1972), no. 23, p. 1; T. Gustafson, 'Environmental Disputes in the USSR', in D. Nelkin (ed.), *Controversy. Politics of Technical Decisions* (Beverley Hills, 1979), p. 79.
54. *Ekonomika i organizatsiya promyshlennogo proizvodstva*, 1982, no. 3, pp. 147–94.
55. M. Hayward, *Writers in Russia: 1917–1978*, ed. P. Blake (London, 1983), pp. 301–3.
56. V. Soloukhin, *Vladimirskie prosyolki, NM*, 1957, nos. 9, 10.
57. Solzhenitsyn *et al.*, *From Under the Rubble*, p. 265.
58. E. Dorosh, 'Razmyshleniya v Zagorske. Iz knigi *Drevnee ryadom s nami*', *NM*, 1967, no. 5.
59. F. Abramov, *Mamonikha, Neva*, 1980, no. 9.
60. I. Ehrenburg, K. Fedin, E. Dorosh, *LG*, 23 Aug. 1956.
61. V. Soloukhin, *Pismo iz russkogo muzeya, MG*, 1966, nos. 9, 10.
62. Solzhenitsyn, *Zakhar-Kalita, NM*, 1966, no. 1.
63. D. Granin, *Kartina, NM*, 1980, nos. 1, 2.
64. F. Abramov, *LG*, 30 June 1976.
65. V. Belov, *Privychnoe delo, Sever*, 1966, no. 1.
66. V. Kamyanov, *LG*, 22 Nov. 1967; V. Kozhinov, *LG*, 31 Jan. 1968; F. Levin, *LG*, 17 Jan. 1968.
67. V. Chalmaev, 'Neizbezhnost', *MG*, 1968, no. 9, pp. 259–89; L. Anninsky, 'Tochka opory', *Don*, 1968, no. 6, pp. 168–81.
68. F. Kuznetsov, 'Sudba derevni v proze i kritike', *NM*, 1973, no. 6, pp. 233–50.
69. V. Lichutin, *Poslednii koldun* (M, 1980); criticised in *LO*, 1981, no. 1, pp. 33–6.
70. F. Abramov, *LG*, 8 July 1981.
71. I. Vishnevskaya, *LG*, 15 Sept. 1962.
72. V. Kozhinov, 'Avtoritet istorii', *LO*, 1977, no. 3, pp. 63–7.
73. Sakharov, *Sakharov Speaks*, pp. 8, 31–3.
74. N. Mandelstam, *Hope Abandoned*, trans. M. Hayward (London, 1974), p. 103.
75. *LG*, 23 May 1959.
76. V. Soloukhin, *Zhitelyam zemli, LG*, 24 July 1958; I. Ryadchenko, *Na ulitse Zhanny — vesna!, Oktyabr*, 1959, no. 3, p. 47.
77. V. Tendryakov, *Chrezvychainoe proisshestvie*, in *Izbrannoe*, vol. 2 (1963), p.

234   *The Ambivalent View of Science*

563.
78. Kochetov, *Sekretar obkoma*, p. 269; Kozhevnikov, *Znakomtes, Baluev!*, *Znamya*, 1960, no. 4, p. 87; N. Rybak, *Pora nadezhd i svershenii* (M, 1961).
79. E. Yevtushenko, *Die Zeit*, 8 Feb. 1963; criticised in G. Oganov, V. Pankin, V. Chinkin, *KP*, 30 Mar. 1963.
80. B. Okudzhava, *Bud zdorov, shkolyar!* (M, 1961).
81. R. Malinovsky, *Krasnaya Zvezda*, 9 Feb. 1964.
82. Voznesensky, *Antiworlds*, p. 159.
83. M. Lvov, *Produkty raspada urana, LG*, 5 Nov. 1960.
84. Brezhnev, *Pravda*, 25 Feb. 1976.
85. M. Kolesnikov, *Pravo vybora* (M, 1971), p. 156.
86. P. Pavlenko, *Mariya, LG*, 9 May 1972.
87. Yu. Bondarev, *Bereg, NS*, 1975, nos. 3–5.
88. Svirsky, *Soviet Writing*, p. 301.
89. *VL*, 1976, no. 3.
90. Yu. Bondarev, *LG*, 30 Mar. 1977.
91. Ch. Aitmatov, *The Day Lasts more than a Hundred Years*, trans. J. French (London and Sydney, 1983), pp. 6–7.
92. Ch. Aitmatov, *LG*, 8 July 1981.
93. Brezhnev, *Pravda*, 19 Jan. 1977.
94. A. Chakovsky, *Pobeda*, 3 vols (M, 1980–2).
95. A. Chakovsky, *LG*, 6 Feb. 1980.
96. T. Ivanova, *LG*, 14 Apr. 1982.
97. *The Times*, 13 July 1983.
98. Labedz, *Solzhenitsyn*, p. 224.
99. L. Kopelev, *Utoli moi pechali* (Ann Arbor, 1981), pp. 95–7, 101.
100. A. Kolmogorov, 'Automatic Machines and the Life Process', *Soviet Review*, vol. 3, no. 7 (July 1962), pp. 40–56.
101. Solzhenitsyn et al., *From Under the Rubble*, p. 16; Sakharov, *Sakharov Speaks*, pp. 89–90.
102. A. and B. Strugatsky, *Obitaemyi ostrov, Neva*, 1969, nos. 3–5.
103. V. Shalamov, *Kolyma Tales*, trans. J. Glad (Toronto, 1980), p. 210.
104. Solzhenitsyn, *Oak and Calf*, p. 495.
105. Voznesensky, *Vynuzhdyonnoe otstuplenie, Znamya*, 1962, no. 4, p. 68.
106. *Pravda*, 7 Apr. 1952; A. Sofronov, *LG*, 27 May 1952.
107. N. Pogodin, *Sonet Petrarkha, LM*, 1956, no. 2, p. 335.
108. Voznesensky, *Antiworlds*, pp. 18–21; criticised in V. Nazarenko, 'Nastuplenie ili otstuplenie?', *Zvezda*, 1962, no. 7, pp. 181–8.
109. *CDSP*, XXV (1973), no. 48, pp. 8–10.
110. V. Soloukhin, *Kak vypit solntse* (M, 1961), pp. 14–15.
111. Ehrenburg, *KP*, 2 Sept. 1959.
112. I. Poletaev, *KP*, 11 Oct. 1959.
113. See Elvira Popova's letter, *KP*, 11 Oct. 1959; and *KP*, 25, 29 Oct. 1959.
114. *LG*, 18 June 1960.
115. Snow expressed a similar view to a Soviet audience in *LG*, 24 Sept. 1960.
116. B. Slutsky, *Fiziki i liriki, LG*, 18 June 1960; criticised in S. Shchipachev, 'O chuvstve sovremennosti', *Moskva*, 1960, no. 7, pp. 177–92.
117. Voznesensky, *Akhillesovo serdtse* (M, 1963), p. 229.
118. Cited in Parry, *New Class Divided*, pp. 120–1.
119. Voznesensky, *Antiworlds*, p. 107.
120. Gladilin, *Making and Unmaking*, p. 80.
121. A. Yashin, *Rychagi, LM*, 1956, no. 2.
122. V. Tendryakov, *Ukhaby, NS*, 1956, no. 2.
123. M. Aliger, *Samoe glavnoe, Oktyabr*, 1956, no. 11; for Aliger's recantation,

see *LG*, 8 Oct. 1957.
124. *Pravda*, 2 Nov. 1961.
125. S. Pavlov, *Pravda*, 16 Sept. 1961.
126. R. Ekmanis, 'Realism in Place of Socialist Realism', *Bulletin*, vol. 8, no. 9 (Sept. 1961), pp. 45–54.
127. E. Yevtushenko, *A Precocious Autobiography*, trans. A. McAndrew (London, 1963), pp. 31–2; A. Aleksandrov, *Izvestiya*, 10 Mar. 1964; Yevtushenko, *Wild Berries*, p. 10.
128. *KP*, 6 Jan., 21, 22 July 1961.
129. N. Dubov, *Zhostkaya proba, NM*, 1960, no. 9, p. 14.
130. V. Rozov, *A, B, V, G, D, Yunost*, 1961, no. 9, p. 14.
131. V. Aksyonov, *Kollegi, Yunost*, 1960, no. 6, p. 22.
132. *Kontinent*, no. 27 (1981), p. 434.
133. F. Iskander, *Sozvezdie kozlotura, NM*, 1966, no. 8.
134. N. Arzhak (Yu. Daniel), *Ruki. Chelovek iz MINAPa* (Washington, 1963).
135. Hayward and Labedz, *On Trial*, p. 175.
136. A. Esenin-Volpin, *A Leaf of Spring* (London, 1961), p. 186.
137. Gladilin, *Making and Unmaking*, p. 34.
138. See R. Gul, 'V. Dudintsev. Novogodnyaya skazka', *Novy Zhurnal*, Mar. 1960, pp. 286–8.
139. V. Grossman, *Los, Moskva*, 1963, no. 1.
140. L. Saltovskaya, 'Shchemyashchaya nota', *Oktyabr*, 1963, no. 8, pp. 216–18.
141. M. Popovsky, *Science in Chains*, pp. 218–19.
142. N. Mandelstam, *Hope against Hope*, trans. M. Hayward (London, 1971), p. 249.
143. Voznesensky, *Antiworlds*, pp. 200–45.
144. Solzhenitsyn, *Letter to Soviet Leaders*, p. 40.
145. Solzhenitsyn, *Oak and Calf*, p. 142.
146. D. Granin, *Eta strannaya zhizn* (M, 1982); M. Popovsky, letter.
147. V. Soloukhin, *Kameshki na ladoni, NS*, 1978, no. 11, p. 90.
148. S. Zalygin, *Oska — smeshnoi malchik, DN*, 1973, no. 9.
149. Zalygin, *Sob.soch. v chetyryokh tomakh*, vol. 3 (M, 1980), p. 326.
150. A. and B. Strugatsky, 'Cherez nastoyashchee — v budushchee', *VL*, 1964, no. 8, p. 74.
151. A. and B. Strugatsky, *Popytka k begstvu*, in *Fantastika. 1962 god* (M, 1962); *Trudno byt bogom*, in *Dalyokaya Raduga* (M, 1964); *Khishchnye veshchi veka* (M, 1965).
152. A. Strugatsky, 'Novye chelovecheskie tipy', *VL*, 1976, no. 11, pp. 16–18.
153. A. and B. Strugatsky, *Ponedelnik nachinaetsya v subbotu* (M, 1965).
154. A. and B. Strugatsky, *Skazka o troike, Angara*, 1968, nos. 4, 5.
155. Svirsky, *Soviet Writing*, pp. 224–6.
156. A. Strugatsky, 'Novye chelovecheskie tipy'.
157. A. and B. Strugatsky, *Ulitka na sklone*, not published as a book in the USSR: Part I appeared in *Ellinskii sekret* (L, 1966); Part II in *Baikal*, 1968, nos. 1, 2.
158. A. and B. Strugatsky, *Gladkie lebedi* (Frankfurt, 1972).
159. A. and B. Strugatsky, *Roadside Picnic* (London, 1978); *Definitely Maybe* (NY, 1978); *The Beetle in the Anthill* (NY, 1980), all trans. A. Bouis.
160. A. Gromova, 'Introduction' to Bearne, *Vortex*, pp. 28–9.
161. *LG*, 27 Feb. 1980.

6

SCIENCE AND RELIGION

A significant theme which appeared in Soviet literature towards the end of the 1950s was the relationship between science and religion. Many people in the West now share Popper's view that the nineteenth-century conflict between science and religion has been superseded. In the USSR, however, the party leaders have always considered science to be a powerful means of combating religious belief among the population, and have frequently contrasted 'progressive science', which allegedly endorses the Marxist view of the unlimited power of the human mind, with the 'reactionary, obscurantist' forces of religion.[1] The present study does not attempt to provide a general analysis of religious and spiritual themes in literature, but is exclusively concerned with the place of religion in literature to the extent that it complements, highlights or acts as a foil to the presentation of scientific themes. The emphasis will fall on two contrasting areas of investigation: the portrayal of science in anti-religious literature; and the depiction of the relationship between science and religion by writers who adopt a more sympathetic approach towards philosophical, spiritual and religious themes.

In the post-war and post-Stalin periods the party decided that anti-religious propaganda should concentrate on an advocacy of atheism founded on natural science, with the premiss that science and religion are antithetical and irreconcilable. One of the main functions of science, in the view of the Soviet authorities, has been to destroy the religious superstitions created by man's ignorance of the natural forces controlling his life. They point out that, from the time of Bruno and Galileo to that of Darwin, the Church has regarded the spread of scientific knowledge as a threat to faith, and they encourage the dissemination of scientific facts as a means of combating the backwardness of the Russian peasantry. The Museum of Religion and Atheism in the former Kazan Cathedral in Leningrad contains exhibits designed to illustrate the conflict between science and religion: for example, an alchemist laboratory, and a diagram depicting the evolutionary process juxtaposed with a picture of the Garden of Eden. Soviet scientists are expected to contribute to the popular press, explaining such problems of the natural world as the origin of life and the universe in dialectical materialist terms opposed to the religious interpretations of believers and the 'idealist' theories of some foreign scientists.

The Soviet authorities have also assumed that the Russian people, especially the peasantry, would be impressed by scientific discoveries, new machines and technical devices which would seem to them superior to any biblical miracle. They have attempted to exploit various technological achievements such as the tractor and the aeroplane as proof that man alone is the arbiter of his own destiny. After Stalin's death this type of propaganda, which had little effect on believers, intensified as a result of Soviet achievements in space. The launching of the first sputnik in 1957 gave rise to the claim that Soviet man had proved that there were no gods in space. The director of the Moscow Planetarium said: 'Now that the first two sputniks have appeared in the cosmos . . . it is possible to say that we have visited heaven . . . We have been where the eyes of the believer have always been directed with religious awe.'[2] Official propaganda declared that after the launching of the satellites believers could not fail to admit their errors and renounce their faith. However, believers reacted quite differently, regarding the sputniks and rockets as no argument against God, or even denying their very existence.[3]

In the post-Stalin period the press constantly reiterated the view that scientific theories directly refute religious belief, and atheist propagandists have laboured hard to make science an adequate emotional substitute for religion. The Moscow Planetarium in Easter week 1963 tried to provide a scientific martyrology opposed to that of Christian religion, presenting Giordano Bruno consumed at the stake while churchmen looked on. Another sense in which 'science' is invoked in opposition to religion in the USSR is highlighted by the phrase 'scientific-atheistic propaganda', which denotes not merely the arguments of natural science, but also the acceptance of Marxist-Leninist ideology, the economic and political policies of the Communist Party and the whole complex of Soviet views hostile to religion. It was expected that 'scientific Marxism-Leninism' would provide a comprehensive vision of the universe and man's place in it that would replace the worship of supernatural beings under the guidance of priests by faith in progress towards an earthly paradise under the guidance of the party.

The emergence of the theme of science and religion in literature of the post-Stalin period can be regarded both as a reflection of the general resurgence of interest in religion in the USSR at this time, and as a response to the party's concern about this development, demonstrated by the militant anti-religious campaign instigated by Khrushchev in the years 1957–64. Khrushchev's campaign achieved only limited success, as violence and the forcible closure of churches tended to make clandestine religious groups more widespread and to antagonise believers against the state. Khrushchev's successors, faced with two new phenomena — the growth of religious dissent and a religious revival among the population — were obliged to continue his policy, although in a less violent form. The Brezhnev-Kosygin regime continued anti-religious propaganda on as wide a scale as before and did not withdraw the legal regulations limiting religion, but it also adopted a new policy of elevating a docile church leadership, while continuing to persecute dissenters and schismatics of all denominations. In 1980 the government intensified its persecution of religious dissidents, and such prominent figures as Father Gleb Yakunin and Father Dmitry Dudko were arrested. In November 1980, however, the tax paid by clergy was cut by 15 per cent in an effort to reassure believers that the campaign against dissidents did not mean an all-out attack against religion.

Up to the present day the Soviet authorities have proved incapable of destroying religious belief, despite half a century of intensive anti-religious propaganda and radical social change. The main reason why the worship of science has failed to replace religion in the minds of many Soviet people is that material progress cannot form an effective substitute for spiritual values. The quasi-religious cult of industrial productivity sponsored by the party leaders has been achieved by investment in heavy industry at the expense of consumption, facilitated by the development of political despotism, bureaucracy and mass terror. The 'Great Construction Works of Communism', which were exploited by anti-religious propagandists as proof of man's mastery of his own destiny, probably exerted more influence against 'scientific atheism' than in its favour.

There are also serious intellectual objections to the Soviet claim that science and religion are incompatible. First, some of the discoveries of modern science such as anti-matter, black holes and irrational particles suggest the presence of a principle of irrationality in the physical universe itself. Secondly, there need be no inevitable conflict between science and religion, since they are concerned with totally different spheres of investigation. Science seeks to analyse how the universe functions, and is by definition concerned with things perceptible to the senses, whereas religion attempts to explain why things are as they are, and is concerned with the intangible world of the spiritual and the supernatural.

Although Soviet intellectuals could not have been impervious to such arguments, they began to turn towards religion primarily for emotional and spiritual fulfilment. The deepest appeal of Christianity is its personal aspect: the idea that God created man and cares for the individual. If Soviet communism were to succeed in replacing religion completely, it would have to fill the spiritual void left by the absence of religion. The Soviet authorities, however, have found it impossible to replace religion in a few decades either with the abstract theory of dialectical materialism, which is concerned only with the temporal world, or with rational scientific method, which may attract scientists and engineers, but possesses little appeal for ordinary people. Lenin himself once admitted that 'apart from the theatre, i.e. art, there was "not a single institution, not a single organ which we could substitute for religion" '.[4] The need to believe in a personal god perhaps helps to explain why the spiritual vacuum created by de-Stalinisation could, for many former communists, only be filled by religious faith. Another attraction of religion was that it did not claim to be a science, to offer a complete explanation of everything, which, even if it could be explained, would be too difficult to understand; it just offered the peace of God and guidance on how to live.

Atheist propaganda has proved ineffective in the USSR for four main reasons. First, it provides no satisfactory emotional substitute for the religious rituals which mark the great events of human life — birth, marriage and death — and has created nothing to equal the fine religious art of the past. Secondly, intellectual questioning is not satisfied by the naive, uninspiring atheist propaganda in the USSR which has introduced no new arguments since the 1920s. Thirdly, science and Soviet ideology provide no basis for ethics. Fourth, atheism does not, for many people, offer sufficient spiritual nourishment. The eternal enigmas of life, death and human conduct, so powerfully presented in nineteenth-century Russian literature, are still problems for every human being to resolve in his own way.

In the post-Stalin period the constant criticism of the work of the Society for the Dissemination of Scientific and Political Knowledge, and the appeals for increased struggle against religion[5] demonstrate that the authorities were aware of the vitality and persistence of religious belief among the population. Reports were published about the expulsion of school-children and students because of religious belief;[6] and at the end of 1961 a writers' conference acknowledged that the younger generation, who had been brought up in the post-war period when the influence of the Orthodox Church had greatly increased, were deeply concerned about the meaning of life and happiness.[7] It was, moreover, officially admitted that religion had changed its form: priests no longer fought science directly, as they had done in the past, but pretended to support it, preaching that science and religion were complementary, and interpreting scientific discoveries in an 'idealist' way.[8] The press also provides evidence that educated Soviet people were turning to religion by the early 1960s: thus a teacher, disturbed by the creation of nuclear weapons, argued in 1960 that 'science should submit to religion, because without the control of religion it begins to work towards destruction'.[9] It was even discovered that religious beliefs had not been eradicated among scientists: for example, a well-known Leningrad physiologist working in the Academy of Medical Sciences was exposed as a secret believer, notwithstanding his membership of the party, when he refused to give a lecture about the incompatibility between science and religion;[10] and Oleg Lenchevsky, a specialist on salt-water conversion, defected from the Soviet Union in 1961 for religious reasons. It had already become known among the Soviet intelligentsia by the late 1950s that many Soviet scientists were believing Christians, including the anatomist A. A. Abrikosov, the geochemist V. I. Vernadsky, the ophthalmologist V. P. Filatov, and many professors, notably the surgeon S. S. Yudin and the astronomer Kozyrev.

The Theme of Science in Anti-religious Literature

During Khrushchev's anti-religious campaign the authorities constantly stressed the value of science in atheist propaganda. The importance which they attached to the role of science in combating religious faith is highlighted by the title of the Moscow monthly *Nauka i Religiya (Science and Religion)*, which began publication in 1959. Emphasis was also laid on the ability of literature to counteract the emotional and psychological power of religion over men's minds. Yet the frequent criticism of Soviet writers for failing to treat this theme adequately[11] suggests that anti-religious works could be a double-edged weapon: they attacked religious faith, but could also demonstrate the weakness of 'scientific' ideology and the vitality of religion in the Soviet Union, leading the reader to sympathise with the 'negative' believers rather than with the 'positive' atheists.

Evidence of the party's failure to inspire the younger generation with faith in science and a 'scientific' world-view is provided by literary works which show the attraction exerted by religion over young people who either persist in beliefs held in childhood or turn towards religion at a later stage.[12] In reality there were three main reasons for this: a tragic personal experience such as bereavement; the influence of older members of their families; and the frustrations awakened in young people by Soviet society and its ideology. Soviet propaganda, however, only admits the first two of these reasons.

Some authors also concede that anti-scientific attitudes still remain among the rural peasantry, either because they live in remote areas untouched by modern technology,[13] or because they have not 'fully overcome the dependence of man's activities on the play of elemental natural forces'.[14] In Solzhenitsyn's *One Day in the Life of Ivan Denisovich*, for example, the educated Captain Buinovsky is astounded at the barely literate Ivan Denisovich's belief that there is a new moon each month, and that God crumbles up the old moon into stars. When asked if he believes in God, Ivan Denisovich replies, 'Why not? Hear Him thunder and try not to believe in Him.' While giving a sympathetic portrayal of the religious views of the Baptist Alyosha, Solzhenitsyn nevertheless suggests that religious superstition among the peasantry is still based on fear of incomprehensible natural forces such as thunder and lightning, and demonstrates the low level of scientific education of broad sectors of the population.

Belief in magic among the peasantry is illustrated in Vera Shaposhnikova's sketch *On the Lyunda* (1957). Shaposhnikova describes a patron saint's festival during which pilgrims flock from miles around to Lake Svetloyar in Vladimir Region in which, according to legend, the town of Kitezh was submerged.[15] Old Believers credit the lake with miraculous powers of healing: there is a superstition that if a sick person takes an oath to go to the lake and crawl round it on his knees he will be cured, but if he fails to keep his vow he will be struck down. The local intellectuals and party officials seem reconciled to the fact that the ancient Russia of superstition co-exists with the new, 'scientific' society of the Soviet Union. A similar picture is painted in Kaverin's *Youth* (1949; re-published in 1965) and German's *The Cause You Serve* (1958), which depict the belief in witchdoctors still prevalent in primitive areas of the Far East and Mongolia.[16]

In *The Miracle-working Icon* (1958) Tendryakov suggests that science can disprove primitive superstitions which induce religious faith.[17] Rodka, a 12-year-old boy, starts to believe in God when he confirms for himself the rumour that there is a terrible noise in the dome of the local church at ten minutes to midnight, but his teacher explains that the noise is a common phenomenon known to physics: an acoustic resonance in the dome caused by passing trains, which can be heard in the daytime too. Thus Rodka learns that superstition is nothing but a primitive attempt to explain phenomena without reference to scientific fact. Other writers tried to maintain the illusion that scientific achievements could directly refute religious faith: Bek's *Life of Berezhkov*, for example, refers, evidently with approbation, to 'Aviation versus religion' as the possible title of a lecture. Among the plethora of journalistic verses written in praise of the sputnik and first manned spacecraft, Soviet man's glorious triumph over the old gods is a frequent theme.[18]

Some works, however, show that this kind of propaganda could misfire. In *The Goat-Ibex Constellation* Iskander indicates the pitfalls of using Lysenko's pseudo-scientific theories for purposes of anti-religious agitation. Other writers demonstrate that religious believers reject scientific arguments: the Pentecostalist Mikhail in Evdokimov's story *The Sinner* (1960) ridicules the view that the launching of sputniks into the sky has disproved the existence of God, as it is impossible to see Him; while another Pentecostalist in Polukhin's *Whirlpool* (1960) regards space travel as a contribution to world peace and a confirmation of the commandment 'Thou shalt not kill', and contends that man's reason itself is directed by God.[19] An incident in Sinyavsky's *The Trial Begins* is intended to demonstrate that science cannot destroy religious faith: although the Moscow Planetarium claims to illustrate a universe without God, a sceptical old man insists that there is a God all the same. This scene was directly inspired by a real event — the reaction of a Moscow workman on leaving the Planetarium in 1934: 'Well, well, who would have believed how wisely God has organised the universe?'[20]

Although arguments from the spheres of natural and social sciences are used to combat religion in some Soviet stories, they are usually superficially presented or employed against weak opponents. Most writers make the point that a personal approach to believers is vitally important; their faith cannot be destroyed by scientific theories alone, but must be gradually eroded by a more humane attitude on the part of the community which should exert an influence on their emotions as well as their reason.

Although the Church's attempt to adapt to modern scientific advances is usually satirised in anti-religious propaganda,[21] some authors concede that the relationship between science and religion is complex, and that many contemporary priests see no incompatibility between them. In *Save Our Souls* (1960), Sergei Lvov emphasises that theological students use electric light in their seminary and are excited by the launching of the sputnik; and the student Pavel accepts the view that 'Religion and science are two different books. In one man searches for knowledge, in the other — faith.' Lvov frankly admits the difficulties facing Soviet anti-religious propagandists. Pavel's girl friend Asya understands that scientific theories alone are not sufficient to change his attitude. She rejects the shallow view of the electronics expert Gennady that 'from the point of view of physics there's simply no place for God in nature', for, in her opinion, 'man is more complex than a television set'. After presenting quite an evenly balanced case, however, Lvov finally weights his argument against religion, depicting a fundamentalist history teacher who threatens Pavel with expulsion for expressing the view that science and religion are not incompatible. This denouement would seem to suggest that anti-clerical arguments could be more powerful and, perhaps, more effective in the USSR than 'scientific-atheistic propaganda'.

Pavel's decision to leave the seminary is motivated not by scientific or rational argument, but by his love for Asya and growing disillusionment with the religious life. Lvov admits that Pavel still feels the power of religious faith, which lvas offered people comfort for centuries and been espoused by many great scientists. Asya's superficial contention that the questions which Pavel raises are all 'long dead' is contradicted by the logic of the story, which indicates that young people are still attracted into the Church in the Soviet Union.[22] Lvov does, however, touch on the essence of the relationship between science and religion when he acknowledges that science alone cannot destroy religion, and shows that the fundamental problem, common to all religions, is that faith demands an abdication of reason. It is for Pavel himself to decide whether he wants to be free to think and understand, rather than allowing his reason to be fettered by religious belief.

Vladimir Tendryakov is the Soviet writer who has provided the most profound analysis of the relationship between science and religion in published fiction. Tendryakov's works reflect his increasing sophistication in the treatment of this theme, and afford indirect evidence of the party's failure to eradicate belief among young people and intellectuals. Tendryakov's early story, *The Miracleworking Icon*, is a conventional anti-religious work which was, nevertheless, subjected to some criticism because the priest, Father Dmitry, was not presented in a sufficiently negative light. Believers may well have interpreted his character in a more favourable manner as a spiritual leader who carries on his work in spite of the hardships inflicted by an atheistic, totalitarian state. Tendryakov was berated for portraying only two representatives of the 'scientific-atheistic' viewpoint in his story,[23] although he was merely reflecting the real indifference of local party officials towards anti-religious propaganda. Such absence of opposition to believers was not confined to rural Russia: a poll organised by *Komsomolskaya Pravda* in 1961 showed that the majority of people considered adherence to religion among the 'least of social evils'; and many industrial workers agreed with the believers' argument that religious convictions are a private matter which should not conflict with the allocation of jobs and benefits.[24]

Tendryakov's later story, *An Exceptional Event* (1961), treats the theme of religion and science with greater complexity. It contains some elements which go beyond the permitted bounds of official policy and could even be interpreted as showing sympathy to 'idealist' tendencies. The publication of the first part of the story may, perhaps, be ascribed to the fact that Tendryakov, a party member, had previously proved useful to the authorities by writing forcible anti-religious articles,[25] and had won the right to treat the theme of religion with greater subtlety in his literary work. Yet it is evident that Tendryakov's depiction of a party functionary's daughter who comes to believe in God excited official disapproval, as the planned publication of the story in the August 1961 edition of *Novy Mir* was postponed, and its subsequent publication in the journal *Nauka i Religiya* was suspended. It has been said that L. Ilyichov, the Central Committee Secretary responsible for culture, disliked the story.

Tendryakov depicts Evgeny, a mathematics teacher who believes in God in the sense of 'a certain spiritual principle' which set the universe in motion. He explains his faith using mathematical terminology: he once believed in materialist doctrine without proof, just as one accepts in Euclidean geometry that parallel lines never meet. However, although experience of life confirms Euclid's axiom, Lobachevsky's theory that parallel lines do meet when extended to infinity has proved to be no less correct than Euclid's. Since it is impossible to prove whether there was a beginning or will be an end of the universe, materialism is no more concrete than idealism. Evgeny asks: 'Why can I not refute the axiom of the materialists and believe in a spiritual power which created the world?' This speech is remarkable, as, regardless of whether the ideas are true or false, it contains views which had never previously been advanced in Soviet literature and form a basis for new modes of thought. The teacher's views closely reflect reality, for by the early 1960s at least one mathematics teacher, Solzhenitsyn, had embraced religious faith, and a mathematician who was a corresponding member of the Academy of Sciences subsequently wrote an essay, widely circulated in *samizdat*, on the theme that mathematics by its very existence bears witness to God.[26]

The headmaster offers no serious challenge to Evgeny's opinions: he reacts in a conventional manner, expressing confidence that scientific research will eventually elucidate the mysteries of the universe, and advancing the simplistic argument that all scientists, whether believers or not, are really materialists. Nevertheless, Tendryakov questions the usual hard line of the party at a time when Khrushchev was intensifying the severest anti-religious campaign since the 1930s. The headmaster criticises the way in which such complex issues as the correct way of dealing with believers are decided by the party in the interval between conversations about economic matters. The headmaster is forced to accept Evgeny's dismissal, although he regrets that harsh administrative measures and unsubtle atheist propaganda will replace the more personal approach which he had recommended. The headmaster's attitude reflects the general view of the Soviet intelligentsia, who did not on the whole collaborate with the official anti-religious propagandists, regarding them as 'a sort of atheist sect' which had 'assimilated the worst features of intolerance and fanaticism'.[27]

The failure of such harsh methods to suppress persistent spiritual questioning among Soviet intellectuals is attested by Tendryakov's later story, *On Apostolic Business* (1969), which portrays Yury

Rylnikov, a 32-year-old scientist working as a journalist on a popular scientific magazine, who comes to recognise the limitations of the NTR, both in its aim of creating an abundance of material goods, and its faith in the pursuit of scientific knowledge for its own sake.[28] In this work Tendryakov raises many interesting questions about the relationship between science and religion which are otherwise only treated by dissident authors.

Yury comes to sense the insatiability of man's desire for material possessions and the ephemerality of earthly joys; and realises that science is powerless to make men happier or morally good. Moreover, science is unable to give precise answers about the world. Tendryakov contrasts the true scientific spirit of rational doubt and the provisional acceptance of hypotheses with Yury's thirst for certainty. A prominent theoretical physicist admits that he is prepared to accept the Zeldovich-Smorodinsky hypothesis of the origin of the universe until a better alternative is proposed, but Yury is distressed at the impotence of man's reason. He is also dissatisfied by the argument that science can only answer the question how?, not the question why?, because if man only lives 'in order to live' he is no different from inanimate objects or the animal kingdom. The humanist argument in favour of science is also inadequate, because Yury regards all work for the good of others as futile unless he is convinced that other people's lives have meaning too. He finds that he cannot continue his job, because he can no longer answer a letter from a physics teacher 'aggressively proving that science and religion are not contradictory'. In a last effort to reconcile religion with his former Soviet ideals, he investigates Einstein's views, but is disillusioned to find that Einstein's 'faith' was merely a 'cosmic religious feeling' which sees no need for God or a higher purpose to man's existence, the 'ecstasy of a natural scientist' founded only on a sense of wonder at the grandeur of nature — a feeling which Yury himself could share without invoking religion. In fact this pantheistic or 'pre-theistic' view is perhaps the most common form of belief among Soviet scientists.

In his exploration of Yury's 'illness' Tendryakov suggests that it is the very extravagance of his enthusiasm for science and the 'unbalanced nature' of his character that are responsible for his sudden disillusionment with science. Yury's disenchantment resembles not an intellectual doubt, but the process of falling out of love. Yury is not a scientist involved in the daily pursuit of knowledge, but an enthusiast whose job is to 'extol science'. Thus Tendryakov suggests that the Soviet-sponsored cult of science may produce an illusory faith which may be easily shattered, and that people may be encouraged to expect too much from science.

Alone in the boundless universe, tormented by the apparent worthlessness of his pleasures, reason and morality, Yury attempts to build up a new set of values. He comes to the conclusion that there is nothing worse for man than the unknown, and that no one can prove that God does *not* exist. His inability to comprehend the universe leads him to feel that he needs religious faith to give meaning to his individual life. Yury's 'faith' is thus an abdication of human reason in favour of God's 'mysterious ways', an intellectual construct born of his sense of inadequacy and need to believe in a higher purpose: 'Whether he exists or not, one thing is certain — I need that god.' Yury's attitude, as a character remarks later in the novel, is 'not so much faith as the desire for faith'. It is reminiscent of Voltaire's dictum: 'If God did not exist, it would be necessary to invent Him.'

Significantly, both the Western critic Hosking, writing from a Christian standpoint, and the Soviet critic Kuznetsov have, for different reasons, commented on the unconvincing nature of Yury's 'faith'. However, both are agreed that Tendryakov has presented a realistic analysis of the reasons why many Soviet intellectuals have in recent years experienced a spiritual crisis and sought relief in some kind of religious faith.[29] And this, surely, is the main point: Tendryakov provides a penetrating investigation of the type of individual 'faith' that a Soviet scientist brought up in an atheist society might tentatively embrace when he becomes disillusioned with his former Soviet ideals. There are many different kinds of religious faith, and although Yury's belief may not be the faith of Hosking himself or of Sergei Bulgakov, because it 'implies the actual abdication of human faculties, not merely a recognition of their inadequacy', it certainly represents one type of belief held by intellectuals in any society as an escape from the corrosive power of doubt. Hosking maintains that the God in whom Yury claims to believe is 'not at all the God of Pascal or Dostoevsky', and this is, of course, true in the sense that no one person's idea of God is the same as any other's. Yet Yury's anguished cry: 'I need God. I need to inspire myself to believe and the imaginary God will turn into a reality' is somewhat reminiscent of Pascal's advice to the unbeliever to go through the motions of religious observance in the hope that true faith will come. And did not Dostoevsky, who posed so many 'accursed questions', himself embrace a reactionary kind of religious faith in order to banish his doubts and suppress his unanswerable questions?

The second part of Tendryakov's novel is conducted along more traditional anti-religious lines. In Krasnoglinka, the village to which he escapes for spiritual fulfilment, Yury discovers that scepticism about science and lack of material possessions do not necessarily make better people. Nevertheless, while condemning bigoted Christians, Tendryakov also attacks unsubtle atheist propaganda — the 'working-over' session to which Yury is exposed by a neo-Stalinist party secretary. He also shows that anti-religious lectures, even if they contain sophisticated new scientific arguments, have little impact on believers. Yury's 'faith' is, however, undermined at the first serious test, when the kolkhoz chairman Gusterin opposes him with humanist arguments. He stigmatises Yury's belief that man needs a higher being possessing a purpose incomprehensible to him as a desire for 'despotism'; and argues that religion offers a 'goal' — the Day of Judgement — which can only inspire man with horror. Using an analogy with chess, Gusterin contends that even if man has no possibility of checkmate, the point is in the playing of the game, in the continuation of human life on earth. Yury comes to realise that the 'fairy story' in which he took refuge ignores the true value and complexity of human life.

At the end of the novel, although Yury's tentative 'faith' has been undermined, he has nevertheless attained greater wisdom: he believes in the Christian values of mutual love and understanding; and has a more balanced attitude to science, recognising its potential for destruction and its inability to offer men happiness or love without allowing this understanding to make him despair of man's creative activity as a whole. He retains a secular, humanist belief in the immortality of the human soul, as expressed in a work by the psychologist Bekhterev, 'The immortality of the human personality from the scientific point of view.' He comes to a conclusion similar to that of Pasternak's Zhivago and the narrator of Belov's *Carpenter's Tales* that 'The spiritual side of man never disappears completely, but lives on in his descendants.'

Although Soviet critics at first chose to pass over Tendryakov's work in silence, perhaps so as not to draw attention to it, in June 1970, after the disbandment of the editorial board of *Novy Mir*, the editors of *Izvestiya* claimed to have received 'several indignant letters' about Tendryakov's story which complained that there were not enough atheist arguments to balance the false religious ones, and that Yury returns to his wife and daughter only because of a 'movement of the heart', not because he recognises the superiority of Soviet ideology.[30] The journal *Nauka i Religiya* was severely reprimanded for allowing Tendryakov's work to be published. In 1972, however, the novel was reprinted and subsequently received a more favourable mention by the critic Kuznetsov, who, while berating Yury as a 'bourgeois who does not possess a true spiritual life', admits that such types, who can also be encountered in Trifonov's work, do exist in Soviet society.[31]

Tendryakov evidently came into conflict with the Soviet authorities over his controversial story, because it only reappeared in 1980, perhaps as a contribution to the renewed campaign against religious dissidents. The fact that it was re-published at all shows that the problems it treats are still topical; but the editions of 1980 and 1982 differ both from the original and from each other, altering the spiritual and political implications of the story.[32] Hosking claims that in the original version of the story Tendryakov's conclusion was 'not merely open, but genuinely ambiguous',[33] and this is true up to a point, because it is not clear whether Yury will be accepted back by his wife, or will be able to resume his work again. Hosking, however, omits to say that the spiritual position which Yury has reached at the end of the work is clearly stated, even if it is only a temporary haven: 'I have rejected God — if only for the time being.' In the 1980 version, this statement was strengthened: 'I have rejected God — it appears, completely.' However, in the 1982 edition this passage is omitted altogether, making Yury's changed views far less clear.

Another reason for the greater ambiguity of the 1982 edition is the omission of many arguments advanced by the kolkhoz chairman Gusterin, which Kuznetsov originally saw as the main positive — although somewhat 'prosaic' — message of Tendryakov's work. In the 1969 version Gusterin had opposed Yury's faith by his belief in the division by the inhabitants of Krasnoglinka of their collective income, a process which he hopes will create greater mutual understanding. This passage was retained in the 1980 edition; and its omission from the later version was probably motivated by political, rather than moral factors: Tendryakov's strong attack on the management of collective farms, and on the dogmatic presentation of Soviet ideology. Gusterin had originally associated Yury's belief in a despotic god with the reasons why people leave the collective farms to go to the towns; but Tendryakov was forced to omit from both subsequent editions Gusterin's attack on the incompetent orders issued from above which prevent collective farmers from having a sense of their own dignity and an interest in social and civic matters. Gusterin's criticism of Yury's tyrannical God could also be seen as a veiled allusion to the relationship between the Soviet people and the political authorities.

Never again in literature published in the USSR were the questions of religion, science and ideology discussed as frankly as in the 1969 version of *On Apostolic Business*. The textual revisions Tendryakov was obliged to introduce made the story less sharp politically but, at the same time, more ambiguous from the spiritual point of view, suggesting that religious faith still possesses an appeal for Soviet intellectuals in the 1980s.

Tendryakov was again drawn to the theme of science and religion in his work *The Eclipse* (1977),[34] which also stresses the limitations of a purely scientific, rational view of the world, but, perhaps because of the criticism to which he had been subjected, presents religious faith in a less favourable light than *On Apostolic Business*. Tendryakov depicts a conflict between a scientist, Pavel Krokhalev, who believes in logic and the search for truth, and his wife Maya, who longs for spontaneity and emotional intensity and leaves him for Goshka, a drop-out and itinerant 'anarchist' who subsequently becomes a religious preacher. Both Maya and Goshka undermine Pavel's faith in science. He has a sober view of such negative sides of science as pollution and the creation of nuclear weapons, but nevertheless dreams of discovering a strain of 'super-bacteria' which will enrich the soil. Goshka, however, argues that agrochemistry cannot be an acceptable faith for him, first because he does not understand it, and secondly, because it cannot provide a universal aim. Maya is disillusioned to discover that Pavel and his colleagues are far from achieving the fantastic discoveries he has boasted about; they just concentrate on facts and do not think about the ultimate practical application of their work. Maya asks in astonishment: 'But why do you do all this, then?'

Pavel's conflict with his mentor Lobanov also makes him sceptical of the value of scientific progress. Lobanov, a chemist who once made an important breakthrough in fertiliser production, complains that during the years 1949–68 in the USA the production of grain per head of the population increased 6 per cent, whereas the use of fertiliser increased 648 per cent. To Lobanov this proves that 'chemical fertilisers are like drugs; the more they are used, the larger the doses that are needed'. Lobanov also stresses that many twentieth-century scientists, such as the nuclear physicists Szilard and Oppenheimer, have judged their own achievements very harshly. Lobanov too abandons his research in favour of participation in pressure groups for environmental protection.

Pavel comes to feel that science cannot be a support for modern man because it has destabilised and polluted the whole planet; moreover, contemporary physical theories render the world incomprehensible, beyond reason. He reads the latest cosmogonical theory of the Dubna physicist Academician Markov which suggests that the immense universe, with its millions of galaxies, could contract to the size of a few elementary particles, creating 'a universe in a cup of tea'. In his distress Pavel feels that the whole universe has lost its reason and that Satan is laughing at man, as in the nightmare visions of Hieronymous Bosch which so impress his wife.

The ending of Tendryakov's story is tragic; Pavel finds no solution either to the personal or the philosophical dilemmas confronting him. The story is set between two lunar eclipses in 1974, emphasising that Pavel's personal and professional lives both end in darkness. He feels that the only people interested in the making and breaking of worlds are 'learned fools like Academician Markov'. Science offers no salvation, and he is left with 'just one eternal question: can man understand, respect and love his fellow man?'

Tendryakov's later stories discuss religion, science and ideology more frankly than any other published work. They are remarkable for the complex questions they raise and for their absence of easy solutions. Tendryakov undermines the Soviet cult of science from many angles, while not doubting the limited value of everyday scientific work. Hosking's criticism that Tendryakov distorts the ideology he wishes to refute is not entirely fair, because religious faith is a very individual matter, and the views of Yury, Pavel and Maya may be more typical of the questing Soviet intellectual than more traditional forms of religion. This is suggested by Zinoviev in the section of *In the Antechamber of Paradise* entitled 'About God and the Soul', an episode somewhat reminiscent of Dostoevsky's 'Legend of the Grand Inquisitor' in which a 'Commission' composed of scientists and secret police chiefs interrogates a young man who has invented a new religion.[35] While not necessarily sharing his character's views, Zinoviev makes an interesting attempt to devise a religious creed which will be adequate for an advanced scientific and technological age. This was something specifically rejected by Tendryakov's Yury who had argued: 'One should not have an individual God! . . . Your God is a general God, don't try and invent some new pocket religion for personal use!'

However, some aspects of the young man's concept of God do resemble that of Yury, especially his view: 'If you want a God, create him yourself – that's the principle. The desire for God is also a primordial and spontaneous state of the soul.' It would appear that the idea of creating a God tailored to suit one's own individual needs may be a typical feature of the Soviet intellectual bereft of a traditional religious upbringing and easy access to religious literature. In his essay *Communism, Religion, Morality*, Zinoviev expands this point, arguing that 'the image of the believing atheist in my books is therefore not a deliberate literary paradox, but a reflection of a very real situation for a definite category of people in communist society'.[36] While advocating that people should have a good knowledge of science, Zinoviev is, like Tendryakov, critical of 'the exaggerated scientism of our age' which has even influenced man's concept of God so that he is seen in terms of 'extra-terrestrial beings' or 'waves'. When eventually, like Christ in *The Brothers Karamazov*, the young man is led away because his teaching poses a threat to the collectivism of Soviet society, the members of the Commission desultorily discuss the possibility of God's existence, referring to flying saucers and the hypothesis that man is nothing but an experiment performed by some higher beings. Zinoviev concludes laconically: 'They were not troubled by conscience. They simply did not have one.' Zinoviev points out that morality is a far more important aspect of religious teaching in the contemporary world than mere faith in a higher being or beings which may be little more than a reflection of the contemporary enthusiasm for science fiction, and does not necessarily have any effect on man's moral or social behaviour.

Religious Themes in Literature

The renewed interest in both religious pantheism and traditional religion in the USSR by the early 1960s was stimulated by the general re-examination of values initiated by the de-Stalinisation campaign, the disillusionment caused by the failure of Khrushchev's attempt to reform the communist system, and the profound sense of spiritual emptiness in the technological age. Scientists who had been brought up to believe that science and religion are incompatible were surprised to learn not only that some eminent Soviet scientists were believing Christians, but also that religious faith still persisted among Western intellectuals. Another source of inspiration for the spiritual revival was the rediscovery of Russian literature on religious themes, particularly the works of Tolstoy and Dostoevsky and the poetry of Mandelstam, Tsvetaeva, Akhmatova and Pasternak. In literature of the early 1960s, whether published in the USSR or disseminated in *samizdat*, there was a marked increase in religious vocabulary, imagery and themes. Such writers as Voznesensky and Kazakov manifested the influence of Pasternak in their concern for man's spiritual welfare, with man portrayed as a solitary, suffering individual, not as a tool of Soviet ideology and economic progress.[37]

While for some Soviet intellectuals in the 1960s access to Russian religious philosophy was limited to its reflection in literature, there is also evidence of a growing interest in the Russian religious and philosophical renaissance of the early twentieth century. The works of such philosophers as Berdyaev, Solovyov, Sergei Bulgakov, Frank, Florensky, Rozanov, Shestov and Fyodorov were sought for and read avidly. Although such works were kept in 'special sections' of libraries and only issued to people with a special permit certifying that they were required for 'scientific purposes', some must have remained in private family collections, while Tarsis regularly received works by such religious thinkers as Rozanov and Berdyaev from abroad. By the mid-1960s many works by Russian religious philosophers, and the *Herald of the Russian Student Christian Movement*, published abroad, were available in the USSR. In 1974–5 personal contact with Moscow intellectuals established that they were eager to acquire volume two of Zenkovsky's *History of Russian Philosophy*, which deals with twentieth-century religious thought.

Solzhenitsyn and other writers were particularly influenced by *Landmarks* (1909),[38] a powerful critique of the secular Messianism of the Russian intelligentsia. Dissident Soviet intellectuals felt a particular affinity for the contributors to *Landmarks*, since they too had originally accepted Marxism, then rejected it on the basis of personal experience. Struve, Bulgakov, Berdyaev and Frank re-examined Marxism from a Kantian point of view, emphasising the fundamental value of free individuality. They believed that the human spirit was ultimately rooted not in class or society, but in God himself, and that history was progressing towards the reunion of God and man in Godmanhood (*bogochelovechestvo*). Read avidly many decades after its original publication, *Landmarks*, with its appeal for moral self-perfection and advocacy of a new, creative spirituality, held a powerful attraction for dissident Soviet intellectuals.

The influence of the Russian religious tradition can clearly be discerned in the attitude adopted to the relationship between science and religion in the works of some writers in the 1960s. An eccentric essay written in the autumn of 1963 by D. Blagov (the pseudonym of Solzhenitsyn's friend V. Teush) testifies to a profound consciousness of the spiritual barrenness of the contemporary scientific world where man has lost the revelations of both art and religion.[39] In 1966 Aleksei Dobrovolsky, another dissident writer of the Russophile tendency, suggested that science only provides a collection of truths, whereas religion is eternal because it corresponds to man's greatest need – to commune with absolute truth.[40]

By the 1970s the religious revival among intellectuals had developed further, and many, including scientists, became practising believers and members of the Russian Orthodox Church. In literature of the 1970s and 1980s Soviet writers have generally adopted a more sympathetic approach towards spiritual and religious values. Whereas Trifonov, through his portrait of Rita in *Taking Stock* (1970), shows that an obsession with old icons and monasteries need not be inspired by a real interest in the past, but may merely be a casual contemporary fashion, other writers such as Shukshin, Baklanov and Granin have given a compassionate treatment of man's search for the meaning of existence,[41] while Soloukhin and Belov have emphasised the beauty and mystery of the old Russian way of life, with its closeness to nature and stable religious faith. Official alarm about the revival of interest in Russian religious philosophy was demonstrated in 1976 when the critic Kuznetsov repudiated the influence of *Landmarks* on Soviet writers as a slander or reactionary Western 'Sovietologists',[42] and again in 1982 when Anatoly Kim's novella *Lotus* (1981) was criticised for its allegedly oversympathetic presentation of Buddhist philosophy.[43]

The following survey of the treatment of the theme of science and religion in the works of writers favourable to idealist philosophy and religious values – mostly dissidents – will attempt to relate literature of the post-Stalin era to the Russian philosophical tradition. The aim is not to prove direct influences (although these can sometimes be inferred), but rather to demonstrate that certain major themes in classical Russian literature and philosophy have remained fundamental and constant preoccupations of Russian writers. Modern Russian writing, however, does not manifest a static attitude towards religious questions from the past, but a committed, creative search for a spiritual dimension to life, new values and ultimate meanings.

Scientific Progress and Spiritual Values

One major theme in the work of Russian dissident writers is a sceptical attitude towards the cult of science and technology in contemporary society. This is a development of the traditional Russian theme of the dichotomy between reason and wisdom which can be traced back to the writings of the mystic Grigory Skovoroda (1722–94). Skovoroda regarded spirit as the true reality; science, progress and history were insignificant and powerless to satisfy man's spiritual yearning: 'The sciences do not fill up the abyss of our souls.'[44] Subsequently this theme was taken up, among others, by Tolstoy and the religious philosopher Konstantin Leontyev (1831–91), who harboured a deep distrust of human reason and contemporary culture, and for whom a long black passenger train obstructing a peasant religious procession epitomised the destructive effect of technology on religion and human life.[45]

A protest against the harmful effects of modern science similar to that voiced by Russian religious philosophers first began to be echoed in Soviet underground poetry of the 1950s and 1960s. Natalya Gorbanevskaya, writing in the underground journal *Feniks*, presents an apocalyptic vision of the 'mushroom rain' or fall-out after a nuclear war which prevents her from seeing the face of God.[46] Sergei Morozov, a member of the dissident group SMOG, which disliked science and progress and wished to return to the spiritual values of an earlier age, declares:

I have believed in something better
In an age of ballistic rockets.[47]

The unpublished poet Stanislav Krasovitsky stresses the primacy of religious faith over the increasing mechanisation of life, expressing the hope in a poem of 1958:

> That the Spirit's presence might triumph
> Amid the minutiae of the computers.[48]

Perhaps the most explicit reiteration of the traditional Russian scepticism towards science can be discerned in Sinyavsky's *Thoughts Unaware* (1966), a collection of lyrical meditations which highlight the spiritual barrenness of modern man in a world dominated by science and technology, and express a deep personal religious faith. Sinyavsky contends that in the past men in their daily round had a much closer connection with the life and mystery of the universe than they have now. He paints a Tolstoyan picture of the old Russian peasant living simply, close to nature, observing the rites and festivals of a religion which has existed for thousands of years. By contrast, modern man, for all his advanced scientific knowledge, is devoid of moral and spiritual values because he has lost his roots and his link with the land. Sinyavsky attributes the decline of faith in God to the spread of urban comfort and the scientific and industrial advance of mankind. Surrounded by his own artefacts, man feels that he has created the universe; modern products overwhelm him and shut out the divine voice which has always been heard in the silence of nature.

Sinyavsky rejects the accumulation of knowledge and information as opposed to wisdom and understanding. In a passage which recalls Psalm 139 he suggests that no matter where we travel by advanced means of communication, we will still remain in the same place in relation to heaven. Reason, which has created the atom bomb, has developed to the point of self-destruction. Notwithstanding all his education, man ultimately stays just as naked and alone as he was in childhood, is in sleep, and will be when facing death. Man mistakenly attempts to replace the spiritual world with the material: 'We flush our dung down hygienic lavatories and think that we are saved.' For Sinyavsky the purpose of life is to develop the individual's soul; he turns from the spectacle of man's scientific progress to contemplation of God, declaring: 'It is necessary to believe for the simple reason that God *is*.'[49]

In many of his works Solzhenitsyn shows that science cannot answer the fundamental question: 'What is the meaning of life and how shall we live?' He himself has confirmed the interpretation of his work offered by the priest Alexander Schmemann: that it is based on 'the triune intuition of creation, fall and redemption'.[50] For Solzhenitsyn the world created by God was originally good, but now 'lies in evil' because man has fallen from a state of grace and freely *chosen* evil; the rediscovery of personal conscience will, however, offer man the possibility of rebirth and salvation, a concept far removed from an optimistic, humanist faith in reason and progress. In *Cancer Ward* Solzhenitsyn follows Tolstoy in emphasising the primacy of conscience over material values, and shows that it is not science, or even a belief in ethical socialism, but mystical or religious faith to which men turn when they are old or dying. As Solzhenitsyn comments ironically in relation to the dedicated scientist Vadim: 'In the final resort science can never destroy faith entirely.'

The central message of Solzhenitsyn's play *Candle in the Wind* is the view that eternal values such as art, nature, individual conscience, love and human kindness are more important than materialism and scientific progress. Through his autobiographical portrait of Alex, who has learned in prison and exile that human beings can live, enjoy nature and attain fulfilment without such benefits of modern technology as electricity, drainage and running water, Solzhenitsyn expresses the 'Skovorodian' idea that science is not an essential component, but only peripheral to human life. Alex's view that science epitomises the 'soullessness' of the twentieth century is graphically illustrated by the neuro-stabilisation experiment on his cousin Alda. Solzhenitsyn implies not only that science may do violence to human individuality, but also that it will produce a false transformation, enabling Alda to 'profit from life', but eliminating the precious spiritual dimension of her personality. Solzhenitsyn suggests that men have no right to transform human nature either by science or social engineering, as this may deprive the individual of his most precious possession – his immortal soul. The religious nature of this theme is emphasised by the appearance of Aunt Christina (whose name possesses religious significance) and her reading of St Luke's parable about the need to let a man's light – his soul – shine forth before all men.

A Slavophile mistrust of the pretensions of Western natural and social science is epitomised by Solzhenitsyn's Matryona, with her simple rural wisdom as opposed to modern man's worship of reason and progress. She is unimpressed by the advances of contemporary science: when she hears a radio broadcast about the invention of new machines she grumbles: 'Nothing but new-fangled things these days. People won't want to go on working with the old machines, so where will they put them all?', and she reacts to the news that rain has been induced by 'seeding' clouds from aeroplanes with a puzzled, indifferent comment: 'If they tamper with things much more, we won't know whether it's winter or summer.'[51] Solzhenitsyn implies that modern technology is a dehumanising influence, conducive to loss of individuality and loss of contact with nature. For Solzhenitsyn, as for Leontyev, trains symbolise the destructive power of science: the sensitive Alda in *Candle in the Wind* is startled by the noise of a passing train; Matryona fears death and eventually dies on the rails. The death of Matryona, who is portrayed as a long-suffering holy innocent, represents the death of the old spiritual values associated with the traditional way of life of rural Russia.

A similar romantic emphasis on the innocence and purity lingering in the Russian countryside can be discerned in Solzhenitsyn's *Prose Poems*, most of which were written in the 1950s and collected together in about 1962, and which immediately acquired enormous popularity in the USSR after he began circulating them in *samizdat* in 1964. Solzhenitsyn totally repudiates the secularism of modern life, but perceives two alternative sources of spiritual consolation for modern Soviet man: nature, and the aesthetic and religious values associated with ancient rural Russia.[52] Solzhenitsyn's appreciation of the spiritual values of old Russia has been echoed, without the sharp political and explicitly religious dimensions, in many published works of 'village prose', such as Belov's *Harmony* (1979–81).[53]

The Compatibility of Science and Religion

Another significant theme in Russian thought which runs contrary to the conventional Soviet view of the relationship between science and religion is the recognition that science and religion or idealist philosophy are not necessarily incompatible. Several major Russian religious philosophers such as Fyodorov and Solovyov have, in fact, manifested a deep interest in science and modern philosophy. In the twentieth century a number of well-known Russian scientists have also been religious philosophers: for example Father P. A. Florensky and the physicist O. D. Khvolson; other famous scientists who have held religious convictions include the physiologist I. P. Pavlov, the physician V. F. Voino-Yasenetsky, whose religious title was Archbishop Luke (1877–1961), and Vernadsky and Tsiolkovsky, both one-time disciples of Fyodorov.

An influential work which attempts to reconcile science and religion, Teilhard de Chardin's *Le Phénomène Humain* (1955), was published in Moscow in an abridged translation in 1965. Teilhard's work, which possesses some parallels with the thought of Vernadsky, excited interest among Soviet intellectuals in the 1960s; and in the 1970s there was much discussion of his ideas by Soviet theorists (although all reject the religious aspects of his thought), and by Orthodox theologians, who now show more concern about questions of science and technology.[54]

An anonymous questionnaire prepared by Mark Popovsky and distributed to 100 Soviet scientists in the 1970s elicited 41 replies; to the question 'Are religious faith and scientific work compatible in present-day conditions?', 5 answered with a definite no, 2 replied 'Probably', while 34 answered yes. The influence of literature was manifested in the answer of one Doctor of Philosophical Sciences who said: 'I agree with the Strugatsky brothers, who wrote in *The Inhabited Island* that "conscience determines the scientist's aim, while science, thought and reason provide him with the means of achieving it. Religion prevents the mind from choosing evil aims." '[55] Although Popovsky's sample was extremely small, in the absence of proper techniques of market research it can be inferred that many Soviet scientists see no incompatibility between science and religion.

Dissident works also provide a strong challenge to the conventional Soviet view of the irreconcilability of science and religion. Sinyavsky argues in his essay *What is Socialist Realism?* that science and religion belong to two different spheres. Science, like primitive animism, is an expression of man's natural need to investigate his environment, but it does not answer the question 'Why?', only the question 'How?', and consequently cannot be an aim in itself, only a means to an end.[56] Solzhenitsyn also contradicts the accepted Soviet view that 'scientific' Marxist materialism is the only possible philosophy for a scientist and engineer (or indeed any Soviet citizen) to hold. In *The First Circle*, with Professor Mordukhai-Boltovskoi, one of his teachers at Rostov University, in mind, Solzhenitsyn depicts the old mathematician Goryainov-Shakhovskoi, who frequently produces mathematical proofs of the existence of God and attacks Marxist materialism, arguing that Marx was wrong in calling Newton a materialist, for 'Newton believed in God, like every other great scientist'. Solzhenitsyn takes pleasure in refuting the crude Soviet propaganda which claims that scientists must necessarily be

materialists and atheists. His allusion to Newton is a deliberate
repudiation of the Soviet authorities' misrepresentation of the history of scientific thought – a life-size bust of Newton is displayed in
the Leningrad Museum of Atheism, without any mention of his
religious faith.

Many of the scientists whom Solzhenitsyn depicts in *The First
Circle* are searching for spiritual fulfilment. When Nerzhin's wife
asks him if he has begun to believe in God, he intimates that he has
by mentioning the names 'Pascal, Newton, Einstein', all of whom
were religious believers. Solzhenitsyn does, however, emphasise
that man's spiritual odyssey does not necessarily preclude an interest in science. Indeed, he sometimes suggests that mathematics is
a particularly attractive branch of science because it offers the
incontrovertible, absolute truth, a kind of Platonic ideal, as
opposed to other sciences which succumbed to persecution and
opportunism under Stalin. By emphasising the value of science
Solzhenitsyn is concerned to refute the new myth accepted by some
members of the Soviet intelligentsia: the view that the advance of
science and technology alone is to blame for the erosion of humane
values in modern society. In contrast with Sinyavsky, who allegedly
maintained that he would disown his son if he became an engineer,[57]
Solzhenitsyn stresses that science itself, which was once elevated
into a cult, should not now be turned into a scapegoat for every evil
in contemporary society, for it is man's use of science which may be
either good or evil.

Pasternak's *Doctor Zhivago* reflects both Fyodorov's theories
and neo-Kantian philosophy in its suggestion that there is no inevitable incompatibility between science and religious faith or philosophical idealism. In the course of his philosophical studies
Pasternak had been particularly impressed by the Marburg School's
use of the critical method, its interest in the 'fact of science' and its
use of primary sources, 'those genuine inventories of ideas which
human thought has accumulated in the history of science'.[58] The
philosophy of the Marburg School was a form of epistemological
idealism derived from modern scientific discoveries. The crisis in
physics during the last decades of the nineteenth century had encouraged Cohen to proclaim that 'theoretical idealism has begun to
shake the materialism of the scientists, and perhaps will soon overcome it', and that 'idealism permeates modern physics' – a view for
which he was attacked by Lenin.[59] Cohen's influence is reflected in
Zhivago's rejection of materialist ideology and his original views on

science and medicine. Zhivago's unorthodox ideas cause problems for the Soviet authorities; on the one hand, they praise his talent for diagnosis, a manifestation of the intuition they despise; whereas on the other hand, he is accused of 'idealism, mysticism, "neo-Schellingism" ', of harking back to 'Goethe's nature philosophy'. In contrast to the conventional Soviet view that science corroborates the dogmas of Soviet ideology, Zhivago uses science to confirm his own intensely individualistic view of the world, writing a pamphlet on 'personality as the biological basis of the organism'. Pasternak regards science not as a mass activity performed by materialists, but, following the Marburg philosophers, as a pursuit akin to art, a means whereby the individual affirms his liberty through the creation of absolute truth and beauty, bequeathing his personal vision of the world to posterity through the immortal 'collective unconscious'.

Science and the Supreme Value of Life

Another theme treated in literature can be traced to the writings of Vasily Rozanov (1856–1919), a religious existentialist who emphasised the absolute uniqueness and preciousness of ephemeral individual existence. Rozanov rejected Christianity's emphasis on suffering in favour of the 'joy of life' symbolised by a young girl admiring a freshly picked rose.[60] A *samizdat* essay on Rozanov by the young writer Venedikt Erofeev testifies to the intelligentsia's knowledge of his writings in the 1960s.[61] In post-revolutionary fiction, joyful gratitude for the gift of life is most clearly expressed in Pasternak's early collection of poetry *My Sister Life* (1917) and given a more explicit religious emphasis in *Doctor Zhivago* and his later poetry. Pasternak's views possessed a powerful attraction for Soviet intellectuals in the post-Stalin era, some of whom, disenchanted by Marxism's monistic emphasis on historical development and technological progress, turned towards worldly hedonism, while others embraced a deeper Christian existentialism.

A 'Rozanovian' or 'Pasternakian' emphasis can be discerned in some of the poems of Vladimir Soloukhin which exalt the wonders of nature above man's technological achievements. In his 1960 poem entitled *The Threads are Tied into a Knot* Soloukhin depicts the intricate construction of an elephant, a flower and a human being and stresses the inability of man to create the miracle of life itself:

Where are the rows of test-tubes, retorts and Bunsen burners?
Where are the instruments?
Where is the professor's pensive head?[62]

In another poem of 1960, *The Head*, the discovery of a bird's skull leads the poet to reflect on the extraordinary complexity of the brain which cannot be rivalled by 'three hundred thousand machines, crowded into a huge hall'.[63] He refers ironically to the research being carried out by the Institute for the Study of the Brain, arguing that science can disclose little of importance about the human mind. Soloukhin stresses the importance of the irrational side of man composed of dreams, memories and emotions which science is unable to investigate.

Although the religious nature of Soloukhin's theme was not made explicit in his early poetry, in his collection of meditations *Pebbles on my Palm* (1981) he goes much further, postulating a 'higher, reasonable element' which created the world, because he cannot imagine how a harmonious universe functioning according to precise scientific laws could have arisen purely by chance: 'The main question today is not, does a higher form of reason exist? but – does this higher reason know about me, and does it care about me at all?' This passage angered some readers of *Kommunist* who wrote to the editor complaining that Soloukhin was 'playing about with the idea of God' and advancing religious arguments unworthy of a Soviet writer. Soloukhin – a party member – was reprimanded at a meeting of the Party Bureau of the Moscow Poets' Group of the RSFSR Writers' Union and forced to assert publicly that he is in fact a convinced atheist.[64]

A more explicit sense of the miraculous, unrepeatable nature of God's universe permeates the literary work of Andrei Sinyavsky, who was influenced by his close study of Pasternak and symbolist poetry of the early twentieth century and has written a book on Rozanov. In *The Makepeace Experiment*, for example, he evokes the 'magical crystallography of every one of the snowflakes God sends fluttering down from the sky like miniature humming birds'. The religious dimension is also evident in Solzhenitsyn's prose poem *The Duckling*, which affirms that man, for all his scientific achievements, will never be able to produce in a test tube anything as wonderful as a living creature.

Pasternak's *Doctor Zhivago*, with its combination of pagan pantheism and Christian values, presents the fullest expression of the beauty of the moment and the supreme value of the individual's life in modern Russian prose. Zhivago attacks the official Soviet notion, especially prominent during the era of the First Five Year Plan, that science and technology can be used to change the world. He believes that man participates in history by living, not by preparing to live, and that the idea of working for some great future aim is absurd. Lara and Zhivago have a profound sense of the community of all creation, which is totally alien to 'such petty trifles as reshaping the world'. Zhivago expresses Pasternak's fundamental conviction that life is too mysterious and complex to be reshaped by political dogma, social decree or scientific progress. Pasternak's views have been echoed in published fiction of the 1970s, for example Rasputin's *Farewell to Matyora* and Astafyev's *Queen Fish*, which question man's pretensions to master nature and disrupt traditional rural life by technological and political change.

Science and Irrationality

Another current in Russian philosophy which exerted a deep influence on Soviet writers was the anti-rationalist trend associated primarily with the works of Dostoevsky. Dostoevsky's *Notes from Underground*, written as an artistic response to Chernyshevsky's *What is to be Done?* (1863) remains a powerful refutation of the Westernist cult of science and of all rationalist, utilitarian theories of man, including Marxism-Leninism. Similarly, the Christian existentialist Lev Shestov (1866–1938) argued that logic is not the only way to knowledge, and that ultimate truth can be attained only through faith and revelation.[65] Like Dostoevsky's Underground Man, Shestov attacks the fundamental presuppositions of positivistic science, especially the principle of regularity in the sequence of the phenomena of nature and the idea of causal necessity that is presumed to govern them. He believes that the universe is so constituted as to permit at any moment the most fantastic metamorphoses – one curved ray of light could transform nature. A view closely resembling that of Shestov is expressed in Sinyavsky's *Thoughts Unaware*:

> The laws of nature are a miracle extending in space and time. Thanks to them snowflakes, mammoths, sunsets and other chefs d'oeuvre of creation can exist, periodically arise and develop according to a definite tradition (the tradition of conservation of energy, or gravity etc.). A new miracle can break this tradition.

In the post-Stalin period some works published in the USSR attempted, indirectly, to attack the science and rationalism propagated by the Soviet authorities. Stories by Kazakov, Tendryakov and Nagibin began to depict eccentrics, misfits and failures, without supplying any didactic message;[66] such poets as Voznesensky, Yevtushenko and Akhmadulina started to explore their own individuality and to search for new spiritual values. Voznesensky evokes the terrors which may lurk in the world of science in a half-humorous, half-serious manner, as, for example, in the image of the motorcycle driving up a vertical wall. In *Antiworlds* he comically exploits Dirac's discovery of anti-matter – a concept regarded with suspicion by the Soviet authorities – in order to convey the sense of an absurd world which is not rationally explicable.[67] In literature of the 1970s a view similar to that of Shestov and Sinyavsky about the possibility of alternative universes was explored in science fiction and fantasy: for example in Zalygin's *Oska the Funny Boy*, the Integral imagines another world in which people are ten metres high, or molecules are three times larger or smaller than at present.

Sinyavsky is the modern Russian writer standing most directly in the tradition of the 'irrationalists' Dostoevsky, Shestov, Rozanov and Berdyaev who revolt against science on metaphysical grounds. Sinyavsky both rebels against the misuse of science and technology by a totalitarian state, and against a 'scientific' ideology based on historical determinism which runs counter to a spiritual view of man as divine in origin, with an immortal, unfathomable soul. In his *Fantastic Tales* he exalts the subjective and irrational, concentrating on elements of human self-will and illogicality – illicit, pathological sex, drunkenness and abnormal states of mind – in order to emphasise man's spiritual freedom and total divergence from the determinist blueprint of materialist philosophy.[68] In *The Icicle*, for example, the hero's clairvoyance and ability to read past and future incarnations recall Shestov's view that positivism is adequate as far as it goes, but that there may be a man or men who have existed more than once.

Irrationalist philosophy also has an important bearing on social questions. In Dostoevsky's view Utopian socialism, with its dream of universal prosperity and an earthly paradise, totally ignores the essentially immoral, wilful nature of man; and the Underground Man rejects the concept of a heaven on earth bought at the price of transforming mankind into tame domestic animals or mere cogs in a gigantic machine. Dostoevsky's prophetic novels *The Devils* and

The Brothers Karamazov and the writings of Berdyaev and Bulgakov are particularly implacable towards doctrines which elevate man into a god, failing to acknowledge that man is finite, limited, congenitally evil. They imply that socialism is an anti-Christian doctrine, a 'godless theology' based on Satanic pride and leading to a metaphysical void. The earthly paradise established by the elite at the expense of the freedom of the masses will be a uniform, philistine society where, in the words of Dostoevsky's intellectual revolutionary Shigalyov, 'All shall be equal and all shall be slaves.'

Sinyavsky's *Makepeace Experiment* follows this philosophical tradition in its satire of the Marxist dream of uninterrupted scientific progress towards the communist Utopia. The narrator imagines a consumer paradise of the future in which man has merely to press various buttons in order to satisfy his needs, but is soon bored and satiated. In a reference to Mayakovsky's play *The Bedbug* (1928–9), which expressed the poet's distaste for the notion of a sterile, inhuman Utopia of robots, Sinyavsky suggests that after experiencing the marvels of science man will sink into utter despair: 'Is this all there is? Is this what came of inventing the steam engine? I'd be better off crawling with lice and rotting away in my primitive state. I wish I were swinging by the tail from a eucalyptus branch! Give me darkness! Give me shadow!'[69] Like Mayakovsky, he identifies with fallible, mortal man in a world of growing inhumanity, implying that the man of the future will eventually take to drink, drugs and hooliganism and destroy the scientific devices created for his benefit.

Sinyavsky illustrates the conflict between 'scientific' ideology and a religious conception of man. By the use of religious imagery he highlights the Dostoevskian theme that socialist theories destroy human freedom: the one man who fails to submit to the spirit of Lyonya Tikhomirov's dictatorship and indulges in a drunken orgy to exercise 'his own stupid will' is later found dead, lying 'spread-eagled, like an image of Christ'. Sinyavsky further suggests that man's dream of scientific progress results in inevitable failure because it attempts to transform nature and man and oppose the will of God. As an ancient monastery is about to be destroyed, Lyonya hears the voice of his ancestor Samson Samsonovich asking why it is when inanimate objects are content merely to exist in the natural world designed by God, 'that man alone in his blindness dares to shatter the harmony of being with his irresponsible din?

How dare he change the course of mighty rivers or fell ancient trees nurtured for a higher purpose than his?' Tikhomirov finds, moreover, that reason is powerless to combat his own mother's religious faith. The voice of Samson warns him against trying to change nature, ancient beauty and the simple religious faith of the peasantry by scientific argument and radical social change: 'Mould and reshape your minds as much as you will, turn yourselves into cogs and wheels, the whole crazy mob of you, for all I care! But keep your hands off trees and stones and old women . . . keep them off your wretched mothers!' A pious old man affirms that Tikhomirov is a sorcerer, the Antichrist assisted by devils. His regime, based on the assumption that human beings can rely on science and intellect alone to change the world, has created a metaphysical void: man has ventured beyond the limit of his powers and is delivering the world to Satan. Eventually, when Tikhomirov can no longer control his thoughts, the town is plunged into chaos. His mother, who represents the permanent values in life – nature, kindness and religious faith – asks the priest to pray for the peace of the souls of her son and Samson Samsonovich. Although Sinyavsky uses irony to distance himself from this religious ritual, he nevertheless shows that religious faith is one constant feature in an unstable world.

The Ends and Means of Scientific and Social Progress

Another significant theme in Russian thought is the moral problem of ends and means. In *From the Other Shore* Herzen had provided a forcible repudiation of the socialist and utilitarian doctrine that vast suffering in the present must be undergone for the sake of ineffable felicity in the future, arguing that one generation must not be sacrificed in the name of the welfare of its remote descendants, which, in any case, is none too certain.[70] Such a view was also implicit in Dostoevsky's *Devils* and Struve's contribution to *Landmarks*.

By the post-Stalin era many Soviet intellectuals were aware that the prophecies uttered by Dostoevsky and the contributors to *Landmarks* had actually come to pass. The question of whether the end of achieving industrial progress and building communism was so desirable that it justified the means used by Stalin, implicit in the image of the forest in Leonov's *Russian Forest* and in the published works of a few liberal writers, for example Tendryakov and Voznesensky, is more explicitly presented in such dissident works as Sinyavsky's *The Trial Begins* and Pasternak's *Doctor Zhivago*.

Pasternak's hero, for example, directly states that he is not enthusiastic about the 'ideas of general self-perfection' prevalent since the Revolution, and that, in any case, they have already cost such 'a sea of blood' that he is not sure if 'the end justifies the means'.

In Solzhenitsyn's *First Circle* this subject constitutes the main bone of contention between Rubin and Sologdin: whereas Rubin believes that Stalin's great aim justifies his means, Sologdin expresses the author's view: 'Wicked means destroy the end.' Solzhenitsyn poses the fundamental question: why has a revolution which aimed at liberating man and developing science and technology in order to promote human happiness in fact produced a tyranny and untold human suffering? He suggests that such a revolution based on 'scientific' ideology ignores the true nature of man known to religious philosophers, failing to take into account either the depth of his innate depravity or the lofty nobility of his freedom and conscience. Any world-view founded on reason alone will inevitably lead to terror and end up by enslaving man – for this reason Nerzhin fails to support Gerasimovich's plan for a new coup by the scientific elite. Solzhenitsyn, like many other dissident writers, affirms that every individual embodies a supreme value in himself, and must neither sacrifice his present life for the happiness of future generations, nor abandon God and fall into the trap of deifying man.

Notes

1. *Kommunist*, 1962, no.14, pp. 50–8.
2. W. Kolarz, *Religion in the Soviet Union* (London, 1961), p. 21.
3. *Izvestiya*, 16 July 1961; Yu. Dashevsky, *LG*, 30 Oct. 1958.
4. V. Polonsky, *Ocherki literaturnogo dvizheniya revolyutsionnoi epokhi* (M, 1929), pp. 82–3.
5. T. Oleshchuk, 'Za konkretnost nauchno-ateisticheskoi propagandy', *Kommunist*, 1958, no. 5, pp. 111–18; *NR*, 1961, no. 9, p. 14.
6. *NR*, 1962, no. 3, p. 6; V. Grigoryev, 'Kto pomozhet Sergeyu?', *NR*, 1963, no. 6, pp. 74–6.
7. *Nedelya*, 19–25 Nov. 1961.
8. *Kommunist*, 1958, no. 17, pp. 91–8.
9. A. Zyazeva, *UG*, 17 Mar. 1960.
10. A. Polovnikov, N. Seliverstov, *LG*, 14 Oct. 1954.
11. *NR*, 1961, no. 3, pp. 3–4.
12. V. Kornilov, *Rovesniki, Den poezii 1956*, p. 103; N. Evdokimov, *Greshnitsa* (1960).
13. S. Bondarin, *Nikola-na-vodakh, NS*, 1961, no. 3.
14. P. Cherkashin, 'O sotsialnykh kornyakh religii', *VF*, 1958, no. 6, p. 40.
15. V. Shaposhnikova, *Na Lyunde, NS*, 1958, no. 1.

16. Kaverin, *Yunost, Sob.soch.*, vol. 4, p. 185; Yu.German, *Delo, kotoromu ty sluzhish* (L, 1959), pp. 350–3.

17. V. Tendryakov, *Chudotvornaya, Znamya,* 1958, no. 5.

18. See Wells, 'Theme of Science', pp. 597–8 for a select bibliography.

19. Evdokimov, *Greshnitsa, Znamya,* 1960, no. 12, p. 13; Yu.Polukhin, *Omut, MG,* 1960, no. 2, p. 113.

20. Tertz (Sinyavsky), *The Trial Begins,* 39–40; cf. Krupskaya, *Izvestiya,* 27 Apr. 1937.

21. Yu.Levada, 'Zloklyuchenie religioznogo modernizma', *NR,* 1961, no. 6, pp. 12–17; and the character of the Monk in Levada's play *Faust i smert* (1960).

22. S.Lvov, *Spasite nashi dushi, Yunost,* 1960, no. 2, pp. 4, 42, 46.

23. M. Sharonova, *UG,* 5 June 1958.

24. B. Grushin, V. Chikin, *Ispoved pokoleniya* (M, 1962), pp. 148–50.

25. Tendryakov, *LG,* 5 Mar. 1960.

26. Popovsky, *Science in Chains,* p. 226.

27. G. Kelt, *KP,* 15 Aug. 1965.

28. V. Tendryakov, *Apostolskaya komandirovka, NR,* 1969, nos 8–10.

29. Hosking, *Beyond Socialist Realism,* p. 97; F. Kuznetsov, 'Dukhovnye tsennosti: mify i deistvitelnost', *NM,* 1974, no. 1, pp. 211–31.

30. I. Kryvelev, *Izvestiya,* 27 June 1970.

31. Tendryakov, *Chrezvychainoe* (M, 1972); discussed in Kuznetsov, 'Dukhovnye tsennosti'.

32. Tendryakov, *Sob.soch.*, vol. 4 (M, 1980); Tendryakov, *Rasplata* (M, 1982).

33. Hosking, *Beyond Socialist Realism,* p. 97.

34. Tendryakov, *Zatmenie, DN,* 1977, no. 5.

35. Zinoviev, *V predverii raya,* pp. 351–62.

36. Zinoviev, *My i zapad* (Lausanne, 1981), pp. 34–5.

37. A. Voznesensky, *Akhillesovo serdtse* (M, 1966), pp. 5, 7; Yu. Kazakov, *Adam i Eva* (1962).

38. N. Berdyaev *et al., Vekhi: sbornik statyei o russkoi intelligentsii,* 2nd end (M, 1909).

39. D. Blagov, 'A. Solzhenitsyn i dukhovnaya missiya pisatelya', *Grani,* no. 64 (1967), pp. 116–49; no. 65 (1968), pp. 194–201.

40. A. Dobrovolsky, 'Vzaimootnoshenie znaniya i very', *Grani,* no. 64 (1967), pp. 194–201.

41. Yu. Trifonov, *Predvaritelnye itogi, NM,* 1970, no. 12; V. Shukshin, *Veruyu!, Zvezda,* 1971, no. 9; G. Baklanov, *Predel, Moskva,* 1974, nos 3–4; Granin, *Kartina, NM,* 1980, no. 2, pp. 90–1.

42. F. Kuznetsov, 'S vekom naravne', *NM,* 1975, no. 2, pp. 229–53.

43. A. Kim, *Lotos,* in *Nefritovyi poyas* (M, 1981); discussed in *LO,* 1982, no. 3, pp. 40–1.

44. G. Skovoroda, *A Conversation among Five Travellers Concerning Life's True Happiness,* in J. Edie, J. Scanlan *et al.* (eds.), *Russian Philosophy,* vol. 1 (Chicago, 1965), p. 41.

45. K. Leontyev, *Sochineniya* (M, 1912–14), vol. 8, p. 212; see also L. Tolstoy, *The Law of Violence and the Law of Love,* in Edie *et al., Russian Philosophy,* vol. 2, p. 216.

46. N. Gorbanevskaya, *Gribnoi dozhd, Grani,* no. 52 (1962), p. 166.

47. S. Morozov, untitled poem dated Jan. 1957, *Grani,* no. 61 (1966), p. 21.

48. G. Kline, 'Religious Themes in Soviet Literature', in R. Marshall, Jr. (ed.), *Aspects of Religion in the Soviet Union* (Chicago and London, 1971), p. 163.

49. A. Tertz (A. Sinyavsky), *Mysli vrasplokh* (M, 1966), pp. 84, 87, 95–6, 110.

50. J. Dunlop, R. Haugh, A. Klimoff (eds.), *Aleksandr Solzhenitsyn: Critical Essays and Documentary Materials* (Belmont, Mass., 1973), pp. 39, 44.

51. Solzhenitsyn, *Matryona's House*, in *Stories and Prose Poems*, trans. M. Glenny (Harmondsworth, 1973), p. 25.

52. Solzhenitsyn, *Freedom to Breathe, The Ashes of a Poet, A Journey Along the Oka*, in *Stories*, pp. 193, 195–6, 203–4.

53. V. Belov, *Lad, NS*, 1979, nos 10–12; 1981, nos 1, 6, 7.

54. I. Zabelin, *Fizicheskaya geografiya v sovremennom estestvoznanii* (M, 1978); I. Ivanov, V. Kharitonov, G. Chakov, 'Pravoslavie i teiyardizm', *FN*, 1977, no. 6.

55. Popovsky, *Science in Chains*, pp. 230–3.

56. Tertz, *Fantasticheskii mir*, p. 404.

57. Hayward and Labedz, *On Trial*, p. 338.

58. Pasternak, *Safe Conduct*, pp. 191–2.

59. H. Cohen, 'Preface' to F. Lange, *Geschichte des Materialismus*, 5th edn (1896), p. xvi; condemned in Lenin, *Materialism and Empirio-criticism* (M, 1947), pp. 291–3, 318.

60. V. Rozanov, *Izbrannoe*, ed. Yu. Ivask (NY, 1956), p. 377; *Solitaria*, trans. S. Koteliansky (London and NY, 1927), p. 98.

61. Yu. Maltsev, *Volnaya russkaya literatura, 1955–75* (Frankfurt, 1976), pp. 187–8.

62. V. Soloukhin, *Imeyushchie v rukakh tsvety* (M, 1962), pp. 17–18.

63. Ibid., p. 21.

64. Soloukhin, *Kameshki na ladoni, NS*, 1981, no. 3, p. 39; readers' letters and editorial comments in *Kommunist*, 1982, nos 2, 8.

65. L. Shestov, *Athen und Jerusalem* (Graz, 1938), pp. 34, 230; *In Job's Balances*, trans. C. Coventry, C. Macartney (London, 1932).

66. Tendryakov, *Troika, semyorka, tuz* (1960); Kazakov, *Otshepenets* (1959); Nagibin, *Devochka i ekho* (1965).

67. Voznesensky, *Antiworlds*, pp. 92–5.

68. A. Tertz (A. Sinyavsky), *The Icicle and Other Stories*, trans. M. Hayward, R. Hingley (London, 1963).

69. Tertz, *Makepeace Experiment*, p. 29; cf. V. Mayakovsky, *Klop, Polnoe sob.soch.*, vol. 11(1968), p. 263.

70. A. Herzen, *From the Other Shore*, trans. M. Budberg (London, 1956), pp. 36–7.

PART THREE

SCIENCE, LITERATURE AND PUBLIC POLICY

7

SCIENCE, LITERATURE AND
   PUBLIC POLICY

Although lack of precise information makes the true nature of the relationship between science, literature and public policy in the USSR difficult to determine, the internal evidence of the literature itself, press reports and the testimony of dissidents enable us to reach some tentative conclusions.

The Selection and Treatment of Scientific Themes

The burden of the evidence suggests that in the post-Stalin era Soviet writers were given no specific directives by the party leaders to write on the theme of science and technology, as appears to have been the case in the periods of severest regimentation, the years 1928–32 and 1946–53. Indeed, as early as 1954 Khrushchev, when approached directly by Bek and Ehrenburg, refused to dictate ideas to them.[1] Unfortunately, however, all too little is known about the private links which undoubtedly exist between highly-placed officials and the more privileged and influential writers. It seems likely, for instance, that Ehrenburg's *Thaw* was directly sanctioned by important political figures, perhaps by Malenkov himself, since it presents a schematic amalgam of new topics discussed in public by the party in 1954, including Malenkov's policy of promoting consumer goods. In general, however, speeches by the party leaders, *Pravda* editorials embodying the views of the Central Committee's Department of Agitation and Propaganda (after 1966 the Department of Propaganda) and the speeches of literary functionaries suggested guidelines but did not choose material for individual writers by official mandate. An exception to the usual absence of explicit party directives occurred in March 1963, when Khrushchev warned authors against producing any more works about prison camps, anti-Semitism or the 'fathers and sons' conflict. On the whole, however, the authorities rely upon the servility of writers, in conjunction with frequent exhortations to obey the principles of socialist realism, and the general suggestions and recommendations passed down from the party leaders through the editors.

Although in the post-Stalin period writers and critics constantly urged their fellows not to write to order on subjects which did not interest them,[2] most writers continued to choose scientific topics favoured by the party. As there is no report of any specific meeting in the Union of Writers at which a prominent scientific administrator outlined the party's current science policy (unlike the periodic briefings to writers on military policy), this can be ascribed to Soviet authors' persistent use of the press as a source of subject matter. It can be assumed that many writers read official statements and articles on scientific policy in newspapers and journals, and then decide on their own initiative to write on a theme suggested by these statements. According to Mark Popovsky, Soviet writers prefer topics which are much in evidence in the newspapers – particularly the practical application of scientific work and prestige projects such as space travel – because they know such subjects will ensure the publication of their works.[3] Authors are, moreover, aware that most editors establish a quota system for literary works on certain subjects, for example industry, agriculture and the war, and attempt, whenever possible, to satisfy a current demand.

Since many writers use such sources as the press and works of non-fiction which are subject to an even more rigid system of political tutelage than fiction, they select from scientific topics which have already been preselected by the party, and treat them according to the party line. Writers often use literature to explain and popularise new fields of scientific research and development which the party wishes to promote: for example, the development of polymer chemistry is encouraged in Lvova's *Elena*; and references to the gasification of coal and the diversion of Siberian rivers appeared in Ketlinskaya's *Otherwise There is No Point in Living* soon after these projects had been discussed in the press.[4] Some writers ensure the topicality of their works by depicting conflicts based on current press reports: thus the plot of Elena Katerli's *Distant Road* (1956) mirrors the real case of a mining engineer whose invention of a coal excavator had allegedly been obstructed by bureaucratic officials.[5] The close reflection of articles from the central press is particularly common in works dealing with industrial technology or agricultural science, since these subjects stand in a close relation to party policy; fiction treating more abstract disciplines is frequently based on articles in academic journals: for example, Lvova's *Elena*, which deals with physics and the philosophy of science, draws heavily on the journal *Voprosy Filosofii*.

However, while opportunists, dogmatists and party members continued the practice of journalistic writing on topical themes in the post-Stalin period, liberal authors and those with a deeper knowledge of science simply chose themes which interested them. Kaverin's very first unpublished story, *The Eleventh Axiom* (1920), had a scientific theme; and he relates that he chose the subject of microbiology for his trilogy *The Open Book* after a student had suggested to him in the 1930s that it was an important contemporary topic deserving a fictional treatment.[6] Although Kaverin did not mention this in public, the fate of his own brother, the microbiologist L. A. Zilber, must also have exerted a powerful influence on him. Leonov's *Russian Forest* displays evidence of the author's painstaking research into the history and concepts of Russian forestry, testifying to a long-standing interest first shown in his earlier novel *Soviet River*. Many Soviet writers choose scientific and technological themes linked directly with their own personal experience: thus Aksyonov wrote about doctors; Granin about electrical engineering; Mishnev about biology; Troepolsky about agricultural science; and Grekova about military research. Other writers obtained grants from the Literary Fund of the Writers' Union in order to conduct research into the scientific world: for example, the notes for Nikolaeva's unfinished novel, 'Powerful Interaction', show that she had visited a physics institute to gather material for her work.[7]

There are striking differences between the levels of scientific competence of various Soviet writers. The authentic treatment of scientific themes in the novels of Kaverin, Leonov, Granin and Gor leads us to conclude that they must have obtained up-to-date information about the preoccupations of Soviet scientists from scientists themselves, while such writers of scientific documentaries as D. Danin and M. Popovsky evidently took pains to engage in thorough research in their subjects. Others, such as Lvova and Golovanov, write very superficially, while such dogmatists as Shevtsov and Rybak betray their complete ignorance of science.

All Soviet writers have to operate within the range of themes considered fit for fictional treatment, and to take account of a series of taboos. Party ideologists and censors eliminate certain vital subjects such as a realistic depiction of the purges, labour camps and special prisons, and a frank discussion of the effect of secrecy, bureaucracy and anti-Semitism on Soviet science. Then, having selected 'safe' themes, they establish a certain hierarchy of importance: in Khrushchev's time, for example, the recognition of Stalin's harmful impact on science and technology, accompanied by fulsome praise of the party's beneficent influence, was almost mandatory. Other topics, such as the contrast between the peaceful Soviet use of atomic energy and the war-mongering intentions of the capitalist countries, were considered desirable; while a third category, including references to secret research institutes, accidents incurred in the course of scientific work and the backwardness of certain branches of science due to the persecution endured in the past, were now permissible (in moderation).

The stock of taboos in literature on scientific themes did not remain constant throughout the post-Stalin period, and the taboos themselves were not all equally sensitive. The liberalisation of the post-Stalin period expressed itself in the lifting of certain taboos, first in the press and then in fiction. The party's Propaganda Department would instruct a newspaper editor to open up a new topic, hitherto banned, such as the information about Soviet achievements in atomic research permitted in 1954, and the general allusions to secret research establishments allowed in the early 1960s. The conformist Soviet writer did not have anything directly to do with this process of lifting taboos; he would take up new topics either after reading the papers, or as a result of information obtained from editors or party members in the Union of Writers.

Certain themes remained permanently banned in the post-Stalin era. It was forbidden to discuss the relationship between science and government (except, perhaps, obliquely in science fiction),[8] the effect of the fall-out produced by Soviet nuclear tests, the indifference of scientists to Soviet ideology or their desire to acquire greater political power. Writers were not permitted to question explicitly the actual goals of Soviet scientific policy; they continued to stress the humanitarian aims of scientific research, and made no mention of the enormous resources devoted to the development of Soviet military technology.

There is insufficient evidence to infer whether, when a writer himself had, on whatever grounds, chosen a specific scientific theme, he discussed its treatment with party members or other colleagues in the party or the Writers' Union. It seems possible that members of the party fraction in the union debated such subjects among themselves or with high-level party functionaries, as scientific journalists did in their editorial offices. It is, however, highly unlikely that the treatment of scientific themes was discussed in general meetings of the Writers' Union. The most talented Soviet writers had always ignored the union as far as possible; and throughout the 1950s writers became increasingly indifferent to union meetings at which the Board and Presidium merely confirmed decisions already taken by a few members of the Secretariat. After the persecution of Pasternak in 1958 most honest writers had, failing efforts to disband it, largely ignored the union's work and meetings.

It might have been expected that individual writers' treatment of the theme of science and technology, either in manuscript or finished form, would have been discussed in the creative sections of the Union of Writers, which were intended to be centres of literary activity. It seems, however, that these institutions – the Prose Section, Poetry Section and others – were becoming increasingly less valuable as a result of the centralised control of the Union. Only rarely did authors read work in progress and engage in a genuine exchange of opinions; on the whole the sections only discussed published works and unpublished manuscripts by young writers who aspired to membership of the union. Thus, while young and inexperienced writers may well have consulted some of the senior authors in the appropriate section of the union before submitting their manuscripts for publication, and literary hacks may have sought the advice of members of the party fraction in the union, the apathy and even resentment towards the union implied by proposals that the creative sections should be abolished altogether[9] suggest that it was highly unlikely that established writers debated their treatment of scientific themes in formal union meetings.

That is not to say, however, that writers did not hold informal discussions with literary colleagues: Kuznetsov admitted that he was given advice by older writers, and Etkind regards such contacts as 'the best thing there is in the Union of Writers'.[10] Authors sometimes read unpublished manuscripts recommended by the Prose Section to their fellows, but this only attracted interest in rare cases, such as Aksyonov's reading of his experimental story *The Steel Bird* in 1966.[11] It would seem that the more talented writers usually worked alone and kept their unpublished manuscripts to themselves.

Literary Controls

It has been demonstrated that, notwithstanding the party's more relaxed cultural policy after Stalin's death, the majority of fictional works on scientific themes remained firmly harnessed to the didactic purposes of the party; only a handful of liberals attempted to break through entrenched taboos. Some studies of post-Stalin literature, for example those of George Gibian, Deming Brown and Geoffrey Hosking, deliberately exclude most official socialist realist literature in order to concentrate on more interesting works. While justified on aesthetic grounds, this gives a false impression of the literary output of the period as a whole. The labels 'liberal' and 'dogmatist' are a convenient shorthand for the Western commentator, but in actual fact, as Martin Dewhirst points out, only a small percentage of the members of the Writers' Union can be identified clearly with one or the other group. The overwhelming majority of Soviet writers are conformist, since they have a vested interest in the security provided by the *status quo*.[12] There are two major reasons for writers' continuing adaptation to the party line: the psychology of writers themselves and the persistence of literary controls.

The main difference between the Stalin and post-Stalin periods is that it was no longer all writers who adhered rigidly to the party line on science, but primarily writers of the older generation, members of the party and those associated with the camp of literary dogmatists – such men as Kochetov, the editor of *Literaturnaya Gazeta* until 1959 and of *Oktyabr* after 1961, and V. Kozhevnikov, the editor of *Znamya*. Such leading literary functionaries, having rejected exclusively literary careers and obtained advancement in the administrative hierarchies of the Writers' Union and the party, used their influence to support official policies and maintain their positions unchanged. It is difficult to determine whether such men were true conformists – that is, people who had really persuaded themselves that submission was right and necessary – or cynics only concerned with safeguarding their power and privileges. Other conformists were older writers for whom the habit of compliance had become ingrained, or party members obliged to submit to the principle of 'democratic centralism': that is, the defence of decisions taken by the majority. Few communist writers, whether members of the Central Committee like Tvardovsky and Simonov, or such rank and file members as Granin and Ketlinskaya, repudiated the party line, for, as Etkind asks, 'The party is an all-powerful church: were heretics ever very common?'[13] On a more practical level, to leave the party means social suicide, or an equivalent to the statement of a wish to leave the country.

Non-party men also adapt to the party line through expediency if they wish to pursue a literary career. Self-censorship is the fundamental and most effective kind of literary control; the writer, eager to see his work in print, is unlikely to conceive of it, at any stage, in a form that would render it unsuitable for publication – or, at the very least, to submit to an editor anything which would stand no chance of being accepted. The documentary writer Alexander Popovsky, for example, admitted that every time he attempted to write a controversial line his 'hand fell'.[14] The harsh experience of the Stalin era had taught writers many different kinds of insincerity: the portrayal of stereotyped characters, the embellishment of reality, cunning devices of omission or the avoidance of the controversial. If even Solzhenitsyn altered his manuscripts before sending them to Tvardovsky, it can safely be assumed that most works published in the Soviet Union contain a measure of self-censorship.

There are a variety of psychological pressures leading to conformism. First, the Soviet educational system and the numerous techniques of ideological indoctrination must have some effect, however incalculable, on writers. Secondly, during the immediate post-Stalin period writers were conditioned by the fear inculcated by Stalinism which deprived them of true inner freedom, and after 1966, by the memory of the Sinyavsky-Daniel trial. Some had lost confidence in their own ideas and actually wanted directives to be handed down from above; others were conscious of the many KGB agents, active and retired, who permeated the Union of Writers.[15] Very few writers had sufficient daring to go over to outright opposition: most regarded individual protest as futile or lacked the courage to assume the nightmarish status of an underground writer, which from the state's point of view was 'a life of crime, for which strict penalties and deterrents are laid down'.[16] No one who has not experienced the pressures on a writer in a totalitarian state has the right to pass judgement on Soviet writers, but, as Amalrik has pointed out, 'No form of coercion can be effective without those who are prepared to submit to it.'[17]

A third important reason for submission was the writer's own desire for publication. Kuznetsov admits that he sometimes gave himself the luxury of writing completely freely, then put his manuscripts in jars and buried them in the ground.[18] Most writers, however, have a perfectly natural desire to communicate at least something to their contemporaries. The party relies heavily on this psychological need: as *Izvestiya* commented cynically: 'Naturally, everyone is entitled to write what he likes and how he likes. But must everything that is written be published in a journal?'[19]

Fyodor Panfyorov is one writer who manifested great assiduity in securing the publication of a series of novels by endorsing the changing industrial policies of the victorious faction in the party leadership during the power struggles after Stalin's death. In *Volga — Mother River* (1953), Panfyorov praised Muratov, a Secretary of the Central Committee – a character obviously modelled on Malenkov, the Chairman of the Council of Ministers – for his advocacy of increased production of consumer goods.[20] Subsequently Khrushchev's rivalry with Malenkov made him take an opposing view in public, and throughout 1954 he strengthened his position at Malenkov's expense by emphasising the likelihood of war and the need to strengthen Soviet defence and heavy industry. Malenkov was forced to resign the premiership in February 1955 and was dismissed from the Presidium in June 1957 as a member of the 'Anti-Party Group'. Accordingly, Panfyorov opportunistically adapted to this new situation in his sequel *Meditation* (1957), altering his analysis of Muratov's character to suit the needs of the moment. Muratov, once accorded such high praise, is now accused of the political error of preferring consumer goods to the development of heavy industry.[21] In his later novel, *In the Name of the Young* (1960), published after Khrushchev had established dominance over the party, Panfyorov launches a sharp attack on Ilya, a former minister, for his 'criminal' opposition to Khrushchev's policy of establishing regional economic councils (*sovnarkhozy*). Connecting Ilya and his associates with the 'Anti-Party Group', he claims that Ilya's protest against Khrushchev's beneficial policy was motivated solely by personal resentment at his enforced retirement.

The party offers many incentives to conformity and disincentives to rebellion. The money, perquisites and rewards available to Soviet writers render more submissive to the party's demands a group which could, potentially, include a large proportion of unconventional individualists. Financial inducements are manipulated in order to produce the kind of 'science novel' required by the regime. The scales of payment are structured to reward writers for the public utilisation of their works, measured by the size and number of editions. Since writers are paid according to quality, meaning not only the level of literary craftsmanship, but also the 'timeliness and importance' of the topic and the 'ideological purposefulness' of the work,[22] a party-line novel on the contemporary state of science and technology could reap great financial benefits. Such hack works as Kozhevnikov's *Introduce Yourself, Baluev!* and Kolesnikov's 'Altunin' series are published in multiple editions and frequently reprinted, regardless of whether they sell or are left lying in warehouses and bookshops for years. A Soviet editor may exploit an advance of money to persuade a writer to cut his work before publication, as in the case of Kuznetsov's *Continuation of a Legend*. Material incentives can also be used to encourage writers to rewrite their works, correcting former 'mistakes' and incorporating changes in party policy.

Writers are also influenced by the penalties which may face them if they publish 'incorrect' works. One danger is a hostile review. In the new version of *The First Circle* Solzhenitsyn explicitly states that in Stalin's time authors were affected by the threat of censure by Vladimir Ermilov, the influential editor of *Literaturnaya Gazeta*, which might lead to public obloquy or arrest. In the post-Stalin era the situation became more complex, since critics, like writers, were divided into two camps. The dogmatists, including such men as Elsberg and Ermilov, who had built their careers on sycophancy and denunciation, could be relied upon to denounce liberal literary works on scientific themes, as any attack on the Stalinist past was also an attack on their own records, writings and revenues. On the other hand, such liberal critics as Mark Shcheglov, Vladimir Lakshin and Andrei Sinyavsky issued effective, caustic reviews of neo-Stalinist works. In the post-Stalin era criticism still exerted an important influence on Soviet writers, but censure by dogmatist critics was only ominous for progressive writers on scientific themes if the party's cultural policy had changed in the critics' favour, as, for example, in 1957, when Dudintsev was castigated for his alleged denunciation of the party's role in helping inventors, and Elsberg accused Granin and Gorbunov of failing to convey the 'poetry of science'.

Soviet writers still had to pay particular attention to the views of the party press. If *Pravda* and *Izvestiya* commented on literature, all other papers hastened to agree, as they did after the criticism of the writers associated with *Literaturnaya Moskva*. *Pravda* articles were particularly important, as they represented the views of the top party leadership, and novelists had to make the recommended changes before their work could be published again: thus Nikolaeva rewrote her novel *Battle on the Way* after criticism of the first version; and Kaverin changed *Searches and Hopes* for his *Collected Works* published in 1966. It may be because Dudintsev refused to alter *Not by Bread Alone* that it was not reissued until 1979.

The Union of Writers had the power to punish lack of political responsibility by a graded hierarchy of rebukes, warnings, reprimands and severe reprimands culminating in the supreme sanction – expulsion from membership of the union. The psychological warfare involved in such procedures can be an extremely painful experience. The *prorabotka* or disciplining of writers entails verbal assault against individuals at specially convened meetings carefully prepared in advance by the party. In the period 1953–64 there were relatively few instances of expulsion from the union reported in the press, but it seems that more exclusions took place than were admitted in public.[23] Many of the best Soviet writers have been expelled from the union: for example Pasternak (1958), Solzhenitsyn (1969) and Voinovich (1974); while in more recent years such writers as Vladimov and Aksyonov have taken the unprecedented step of protesting against their treatment by resigning from the union.

A non-conformist writer could also be deprived of his livelihood by a ban on the publication of his works. In 1964, for example, Dudintsev was reportedly being punished by poverty and forced to make his living by translation.[24] Most writers faced with such a situation were obliged to compromise and write recantations in order to be readmitted to Soviet literary life; this was the reaction of most of the writers criticised in 1957, 1963 and 1968. In some cases more extreme sanctions were employed against erring writers. Surveillance by the KGB, phone-tapping, the planting of microphones, house searches and the confiscation of manuscripts, common occurrences in Stalin's time, also affected such writers as Kuznetsov, Grossman and Solzhenitsyn in the Khrushchev period. Harsh administrative measures such as incarceration in mental hospitals were, however, only employed against writers in rare instances before the fall of Khrushchev; in general officials limited themselves to giving reprimands to non-conformist writers.

Because of the international scandal caused by the Sinyavsky-Daniel trial, after 1966 the Soviet authorities displayed greater sophistication in their treatment of errant writers. They increasingly used the method of deportation (as in the case of Solzhenitsyn) or severe harassment designed to force dissident writers to emigrate. After Voinovich had signed the letter protesting against the Galanskov-Ginzburg trial of 1968 there was a ban on the publication of his work for several years; and his *Ivankiad* graphically describes how in the 1970s the authorities cut off his phone and tried to force him to give up his flat to General Ivanko, a KGB official in the Union of Writers; in May 1975 he was even given a poisoned cigarette by KGB men in the Metropol hotel. Eventually he decided to emigrate for the sake of his own health and that of his family.[25] Similarly, Georgy Vladimov, who emigrated in 1983, claimed that he had been subjected to a campaign of 'critical execution . . . and material repression' for years following the official publication in *Novy Mir* of his novel *Three Minutes' Silence* (1969).[26]

All these factors – psychological considerations, incentives and penalties – influence the activity of the writer sitting at his desk. But if he does actually write something controversial, there is a whole series of literary controls designed to emasculate his work before it appears in print. The Soviet authorities attempt to control what Sinyavsky terms the 'literary process' through such agencies as the official censorship *Glavlit*, the State Committee for Publishing, Polygraphy and the Book Trade (until October 1973 the State Committee for the Press), local party organisations, the Departments of Culture and Propaganda of the Party Central Committee, the Ministry of Culture and the KGB.

Such observers as Arkady Belinkov and Nadezhda Mandelstam, however, consider that all these organisations together are less responsible for the state of Soviet literature than are writers themselves, or rather, the Union of Soviet Writers.[27] During the post-Stalin era real power has resided in the hands of an inner circle of four or five influential bureaucrats who form a Bureau of the Secretariat of the Union (an unofficial arrangement formalised in 1971) – such literary functionaries as Surkov, Sobolev and Fedin in the 1950s, and Markov, Chakovsky and Kozhevnikov in the 1980s. They administer the rewards and punishments meted out to writers and control a substantial literary and publishing network. Commissions of the Writers' Union sometimes debate the work of individual writers before publication, usually when there is some difference of opinion between an author and publisher, as in the case of Solzhenitsyn's *Cancer Ward*. Party officials would often consult with cultural luminaries before taking action against erring writers, as, for example, in the Pasternak affair, when Surkov advised Polikarpov, the head of the Propaganda and Agitation Department, to take a hard line.[28] Since the mid-1960s publishing houses have no longer been obliged to consult the Writers' Union before approving works of fiction for publication, but the union still wields considerable power. The party leaders are generally content to leave the control of literature in the hands of literary and party officials, and only intervene in exceptional circumstances. Khrushchev, for example, made speeches on literature in 1957 and 1963, and personally authorised the publication of Solzhenitsyn's *Ivan Denisovich* in 1962. He later claimed that he had been misled over the Pasternak affair and would have published *Doctor Zhivago* if he had realised that Pasternak was a great writer and that the novel's suppression would have caused an international scandal.[29] Brezhnev was alleged to 'read nothing', but a rare case of his personal intervention seems to have been his order that Shukshin's film *Snowball Berry Red* (1974) be passed by the censorship.[30]

Probably the most important level of literary control and censorship is the work done in the editorial offices of literary journals and publishing houses. The vital function of the editors is another facet of the totalitarian regime's reliance on the writers themselves to administer literary controls. Editors were influential literary figures, usually members of the party, who were more familiar with current publishing policy than most authors. Anxious to avoid unnecessary trouble at a later stage, and eager to safeguard their journals and their own positions, editors demanded substantial cuts and revisions long before manuscripts could be submitted to *Glavlit*. Many editors were not obscurantists like Kochetov, but men who had been broken and defeated by the trials of the past, and were too timid to take advantage of the new, legitimate opportunities for freer artistic expression.

The relationship between writers and editors is far from easy. A writer's manuscript can be altered or vetoed by many people in a publishing house: the junior, senior and chief editor; any number of publisher's readers; and the director of the publishing house. Many writers are slavishly dependent on the caprices and vested interests of editors and reviewers for the fate of many years' work. Editors too are under considerable pressure, since they can be reprimanded or dismissed for permitting the publication of works containing political 'errors'. Such incidents as the dismissal of Tvardovsky in 1954 and the final disbandment of *Novy Mir*'s editorial board in

1970 led to excessive caution on the part of editors and reviewers who felt the need to anticipate future twists and turns in party policy. The many-layered censorship in editorial offices inevitably tends to produce dull, uniform, but ideologically orthodox works. In the 1950s there was a spate of complaints from writers about revisions, sometimes made without an author's knowledge or consent, which rendered all works indistinguishable from each other.[31] In 1967 editors were instructed not to alter manuscripts without the author's consent, but consent was usually given if writers wished their works to be published.

These factors are an unfortunate source of frustration for the commentator on Soviet literature. We are forced to admit that we do not really know Soviet fiction on the theme of science and technology (or on any other theme), since we have only the published, as opposed to the written, word to go by. Yet, as Kuznetsov and Solzhenitsyn have shown, the manuscript of a Soviet writer may exist in at least three versions: the genuine original; a text cut or emended before or after submission to the editors; and the published version, stereotyped, censored and emasculated, which eventually reaches the reader and becomes part of 'Soviet literature'. The experience of such writers as Voinovich, Nekrasov, Gladilin, Kuznetsov and Solzhenitsyn with *Novy Mir* and *Yunost* in the early 1960s suggests that many of the more interesting works on the theme of science and technology which appear in print have been revised and censored by editors to some extent. Moreover, if such respected literary figures and party stalwarts as Fadeev and Sholokhov were obliged to revise their books, this must also have happened to many less talented writers. The literary bureaucrats who control most journals and publishing houses are a major source of resistance to pressures for liberalisation.

Certain vivid personal stories highlight the persistent problems facing many Soviet writers. Mark Popovsky, for example, experienced great trouble in securing the publication of his work *On the Traces of the Retreating* (1963), which deals with the difficulties of doctors and epidemiologists in Stalin's time. His editor at the Molodaya Gvardiya Publishing House, a woman eager not to jeopardise the acquisition of a flat recently promised to her, sent Popovsky's manuscript on her own initiative to the KGB, whereupon General Belokonev, the main KGB official in charge of literature, cut out substantial parts of it. Although Popovsky himself was summoned to the KGB, he refused to agree to the cuts, knowing that the chief editor wanted to fulfil the annual plan of the publishing house, which included his book. It was not until the editor burst into tears, complaining that she could not get married until she obtained a flat, which depended on the publication of his work with the KGB's corrections, that Popovsky angrily told her to cut what she liked; later he regarded his published book with disgust.[32] This experience is clearly not an isolated incident: a similar fictional episode is related in Kron's novel *Insomnia*.

It thus seems highly likely that there was a discrepancy in many cases between what a writer thought, what he wrote in manuscript and what was eventually published. Unfortunately, however, with the rare exception of such works as Kuznetsov's *Babii Yar*, Bulgakov's *The Master and Margarita* and Iskander's *Sandro from Chegem*, which have been published in a censored version in the USSR and have appeared in full in the West, we have no idea how much was omitted from the original manuscripts of most Soviet writers. It is also impossible to measure the precise contribution made by the author's self-censorship, editorial revisions and official censorship in the process of preparing a manuscript for publication. Probably most works were a product of the collaboration between an author and his editor, as in the case of Aksyonov's *Colleagues*;[33] one also suspects the presence of a combination of self-censorship and editorial censorship when such authors as Granin, Kaverin and Bek wrote 'safe' works at one time, then tested the limits of the permissible at other times. Sometimes a particularly crude piece of writing suggests editorial interference, as in the passages on the atomic bomb at the end of Granin's *The Seekers* and *Into the Storm*. *Glavlit* and the special atomic and space censorship agencies were largely concerned with excluding factual information not supposed to be mentioned in literature, leaving ideological matters to editors and party officials. A member of the editorial board of *Novy Mir*, David Dar, has claimed that the District Party Committee was more influential in permitting or banning literary works than the official censorship *Glavlit*.[34] It was in order to circumvent the district party authorities and Central Committee that Tvardovsky took Solzhenitsyn's *Ivan Denisovich* directly to V. S. Lebedev, Khrushchev's personal aide.

Sometimes, however, *Glavlit* exercised its power to hold up or ban a book already accepted for publication, as in the case of G. Svirsky's manuscript about cyberneticists, 'State Examination' (1954), which received the imprimatur of the Sovetskii Pisatel Publishing House, but was withheld by the censorship.[35] *Glavlit* could also make suggestions to the party authorities: for example, a report from *Glavlit* claiming that the journal *Znanie-sila* was publishing science fiction stories containing political allusions resulted in a reprimand to the journal from the Department of Propaganda.[36] One indisputable fact is that censorship, whether exercised by editors or *Glavlit* employees, affects a large number of writers. As Kaverin states: 'It would be difficult to find even one serious writer who does not have in his drawer a manuscript which he has conceived and produced and which has been prohibited for inexplicable reasons, quite beyond the limits of good sense.'[37] One recent case is Tendryakov's story *Sixty Candles*, which was reportedly the subject of editorial consultations for ten years before its eventual publication in 1980.[38]

Our examination of Soviet fiction on scientific themes in the post-Stalin era suggests that the practice of rewriting fiction for political reasons was still the rule rather than the exception. The frequent oscillations in the party line meant that works once useful to the regime became harmful in the light of later developments: for example, works praising Lysenko's agrobiology or Khrushchev's chemical campaign became obsolete after 1964. Some works, such as Dudintsev's *Not by Bread Alone*, were suppressed for a long time; others, such as Nikolaeva's *Battle on the Way*, needed only minor ideological corrections. One of the techniques employed was substitution: the replacement of undesirable passages with revisions reflecting the current party line. One particularly blatant case of rewriting was Pogodin's play *When Lances are Broken*.[39] The hero of the original version of the play, published in 1953, was the microbiologist Chebakov, whose theory that viruses can turn into microbes was reminiscent of that of the pseudo-scientist G. M. Boshyan, whose work was officially repudiated in 1954. As a correspondent to the journal *Nash Sovremennik* commented ironically, Pogodin's ' "biological" play saw the footlights after the conceptions of the adventurer in microbiology had been proved completely false'.[40] The revised version of the play, published in 1960–1, testifies to Pogodin's need to adapt to the changed situation: the ending has been completely altered, and Chebakov is portrayed as a charlatan.[41]

Another method of revision was the addition of long moralising passages, such as the new chapters about philosophy of science added in the second version of Lvova's *Elena*. The most commonly used technique was deletion: undesirable passages were simply removed from the new editions of the work, as, for example, in Ehrenburg's *Thaw*, Kaverin's *Searches and Hopes* and Tendryakov's *On Apostolic Business*. Usually these editorial tamperings were not made public; the obvious aim was to convey the impression that the new edition was only a reprint.

Liberal and Dissident Literature

Although the manifold pre- and post-publication controls ensure that Soviet fiction closely adheres to the fluctuating policies of the party leaders, some writers managed, in the post-Stalin period, to diverge from the party line and express unorthodox views. The main reasons for this were the party's changing cultural policy, the relative autonomy of editors, the proliferation of journals and publishing houses, the attitudes of writers themselves and, perhaps, the general chaos in Soviet publishing policy.

Up to 1970 the rapid alternation of ideological 'thaws' with 'freezes' meant that there was a marked difference between what could be published from one year to the next. Both communist and non-party writers were eager to take advantage of the cultural 'thaws' of 1954, 1956 and 1962, the confused interval of 1965 and the renewed hope aroused by the failure to rehabilitate Stalin in 1966, in order to publish interesting works, some of which may have been written several years earlier. The appearance of frank works is also due to the erratic, unpredictable nature of the censorship; before 1964 there were times when it seemed that Khrushchev himself even favoured the suggestion that censorship should be abolished altogether.[42]

In the post-Stalin period Soviet editors have possessed a fair amount of independence. Although the party leaders had the power to permit or ban works, for the most part the policy of a chief editor of a journal or publishing house determined what would appear in print, and in what form. This led to certain inconsistencies in editorial censorship: cautious or reactionary editors would insist on substantial cuts, while a more courageous, liberal editor such as, notably, Alexander Tvardovsky, the editor of *Novy Mir*, would cut the minimum amount necessary for works to pass the censorship, and would strive to publish works which he considered worthwhile, often at grave personal risk. Another possible reason for *Novy*

Mir's relatively independent line has been suggested by Sinyavsky, who contends that there may have been 'some sort of tacit agreement' between Tvardovsky and the Central Committee's Department of Propaganda that *'Novy Mir* was allowed to go further than other journals'.[43] Certain editors held progressive views on specific topics: for example S. A. Voronin, the editor of the Leningrad journal *Neva*, was sympathetic to the classical geneticists. In 1963 he decided on his own initiative to publish an article by Zhores Medvedev and a colleague, V. Kirpichnikov, explaining new genetic theories, after a conversation with Kirpichnikov, whom he knew personally. Voronin was subsequently reprimanded by the Leningrad Party Committee and dismissed from his post.[44] Tvardovsky's decision to publish outspoken works on agricultural science can perhaps be attributed to his close interest in agricultural questions due to the personal tragedy of his father's 'dekulakisation' and his own fortuitous survival.

The increased responsibility of editors led to a fairly pronounced political differentiation of Soviet journals and publishing houses which can roughly be divided into 'liberal' ('revisionist') and 'conservative' or 'dogmatist' ('neo-Stalinist'). In general *Novy Mir* and *Teatr* are considered 'liberal', while *Oktyabr, Ogonyok* and *Zvezda* are regarded as 'conservative'.[45] However, 'liberalisation' sometimes spread from *Novy Mir* to other more 'conservative' journals like *Znamya, Neva* and *Moskva*. One reason for this was the need to compete commercially; editors were prepared to take political risks in order to boost their circulation. Some writers have admitted that they 'played off' one publisher against another, taking advantage of the antagonism and competition between *Novy Mir* and *Oktyabr, Yunost* and *Molodaya Gvardiya* in the 1960s.[46] Although there has been no substitute for Tvardovsky's *Novy Mir*, since 1970 the most interesting literary journal has been *Nash Sovremennik (Our Contemporary)*, a journal of relatively small circulation (230,000 in 1984) which has published many of the 'village prose' writers. There is a perceptible difference between the Russian nationalist views expressed in *Molodaya Gvardiya* in the 1960s and *Nash Sovremennik* in the 1970s and 1980s, and the 'Soviet patriotism' of *Druzhba Narodov (Friendship of the Peoples)*, suggesting that these two viewpoints represent different tendencies within the party leadership.[47] Another interesting development has been the liberal editorial policy of certain Russian-language literary journals in the non-Russian republics, for example *Prostor* in Kazakhstan, which gave 'literary asylum' in 1966 to an article by Mark Popovsky on Academician Vavilov[48] and Kaverin's novel *Dual Portrait*; and the Siberian journals *Baikal* (Ulan-Ude) and *Angara* (Irkutsk) which published controversial works by the Strugatsky brothers. Similarly, small provincial publishing houses would sometimes publish unorthodox prose and verse: it is possible, for example, that Mishnev's novel *The Academic Degree*, containing outspoken criticism of Lysenko, could only have appeared in Minsk; and the Strugatskys' *Snail on the Slope* has only been published in full in Estonian.

Another important reason for the appearance of frank works in the post-Stalin era was the pressure for change emanating from the writers themselves. One new characteristic of the period was the fact that authors could no longer be penalised for something already edited and passed by the censorship. This change was extremely significant, because it encouraged writers to search for means of outwitting the censorship. Some of the more talented authors concerned with scientific themes managed to express a measure of individuality through the use of various Aesopian devices. Such writers as Leonov and Granin raise complex topical problems in the main body of their work, while balancing these critical elements with orthodox ideological explanations or insuring themselves against criticism by adding artificial happy endings. Some works, for example Dudintsev's *Not by Bread Alone* and Trifonov's *House on the Embankment*, speak of the present in the guise of describing the past. Significant ideas or criticisms of party policy may be put into the mouth of a villain or apparent fool; or, alternatively, people with ideologically 'correct' views are shown to be simpletons or rogues. Obscure allusions comprehensible only to a scientific audience may imply disapproval of certain policies and people: for example, the reference in Gor's *University Embankment* to the theories of the Austrian biologist Paul Kammerer, who committed suicide in 1926 when confronted with evidence of fraud in a famous 'Lamarckist' experiment to prove the inheritance of nuptial pads in the midwife toad, suggested Lysenko's fraudulent experiments to demonstrate the inheritance of acquired characteristics.[49] Other devices are the use of imagery and symbolism, as in Leonov's *Russian Forest*; the 'opposition' of Lenin and the 1920s to the Stalin era; the presentation in the narrative of the discrepancy between propaganda and reality; and the use of the genres of science fiction and fantasy.

It would seem that, in the post-Stalin period, there was almost nothing which could not be said between the lines; Soviet writers even seemed to prefer this allusive manner which offered a challenge to their ingenuity. It is highly unlikely that editors and censors were deceived by the frequently transparent Aesopian devices used to express unorthodox ideas. One supects that some editors help writers to devise indirect methods of expression, and that some censors are by no means unsympathetic to the censored; it is sufficient that an author should make some attempt to disguise his real intention so that the censor can also 'cover' himself if called to account. The Soviet public is politically aware, inoculated against ideological clichés and accustomed to deciphering such Aesopian language.

It would seem that, within strictly defined limits, there was a surprisingly broad spectrum of opinion available to the Soviet reader in the post-Stalin period, reflecting the general antagonism between liberals and dogmatists in both science and art. In the 1950s the 'Old Guard' in science and literature recognised their mutual interest, and joined together to defend their power, positions and even their lives against their opponents. This alliance was particularly evident in literature on the genetics dispute: literary conservatives like Kochetov and Fish made common cause with the Lysenkoites in science. At the same time a new alliance was emerging between progressive writers and honest scientists of any age – famous academicians and young research workers. Progressive writers began to express views gaining currency among the scientific intelligentsia, rather than slavishly following the party's dictates. Some authors, including Kaverin, Mishnev and Gor, gave a sympathetic treatment of the work and ideas of the classical geneticists. Other liberal writers chose to expound a view associated with a certain eminent scientist which had not necessarily been given the blessing of the party. The physicist D. Danin, for example, in his scientific documentary *The Inevitability of a Strange World* (1960), a lyrical explanation of quantum mechanics for the layman, endorsed the position of Academician Fock on the philosophical implications of quantum mechanics;[50] while Granin in *Into the Storm* expressed a desire for fundamental theoretical research untrammelled by utilitarian considerations, a view advocated by Academician N. Semyonov and others in a controversial debate of 1959.[51]

Liberals and dissidents treating scientific themes are by no means monolithic groups of like-minded people, but collections of diverse individuals with divergent points of view. The liberal camp can be divided into several distinctive groups. First, the party's de-Stalinisation campaign created a new type of bogus liberal or opportunist: for example Nikolaeva, who in *Battle on the Way* skilfully blended critical and conformist elements to attack just as much as and no more than the party allowed. Secondly, there were a small number of 'licensed liberals',[52] most notably Ehrenburg and Yevtushenko, who enjoyed close relationships with the party leaders and were allowed to publish apparently bold works such as *The Thaw* and *The Bratsk Hydro-electric Station* in order to create the misleading impression that the Soviet Union was in the process of a general liberalisation. A certain amount of licence was also given to Dorosh and Troepolsky in their handling of agricultural themes, and to Tendryakov in his treatment of science and religion, because they were useful to the party.

Thirdly, some writers who belonged to the Communist Party found themselves increasingly in conflict with the cultural bureaucracy in the post-Stalin period. Although rank and file party members such as Granin and Ketlinskaya generally followed the party line, they chose to publish works condemning the 'personality cult' in science at times when the party's cultural policy had become more relaxed. Moreover, party members sometimes infringed the requirements of socialist realism by politically neutral writing on themes connected with science and technology: this is illustrated by Granin's *Personal Opinion* and the deviation from official attitudes towards science shown in the stories of Tendryakov and Soloukhin. Tvardovsky, a progressive writer, a party member and an outstanding literary functionary, was, naturally, obliged to conform to party dictates up to a certain point, but nevertheless managed to publish works critical of certain aspects of the party's scientific and economic policy.

A difference of attitude also existed between the older and younger generation of liberals. Writers who had been 'fellow travellers' in the 1920s, such as Kaverin, Leonov and Pasternak, had preserved close links with the traditions of the West and classical Russian literature, and had always regarded with varying degrees of scepticism the party's claim to possess a monopoly of the truth. They looked on 1956 as an opportunity of giving expression to a limited amount of this long-standing doubt, and to criticise aspects of Soviet life about which they had formerly been obliged to keep silent. For the younger generation, some of whom had been sincere and devoted communists, 1956 brought the painful realisation that Stalin was not infallible, and that they themselves had been guilty of blindness, cowardice and complicity in half-truths. Some, like Sinyavsky, found the dethronement of Stalin so traumatic that they became outright dissidents.[53]

Most dissident writers were not anxious to overthrow the Soviet system, but merely sought greater freedom of artistic expression and the right to discuss important social issues in literature. They were certainly not an organised group, but a collection of solitary individuals who came from the two camps of liberals: older writers like Pasternak, and disillusioned younger ones like Solzhenitsyn, Sinyavsky and Daniel. There were different types of *samizdat* works of varying degrees of boldness. By no means all were deliberately circulated in manuscript by their authors; but by the 1960s the very act of submitting a work for publication meant that it would be reproduced for the benefit of editors and reviewers, and if it were not published, would be distributed to friends, copied again and eventually might be published abroad. This seems to have occurred in the case of one chapter of Solzhenitsyn's *Cancer Ward*, the first part of Voinovich's *The Life and Extraordinary Adventures of Private Ivan Chonkin*, Akhmatova's *Requiem*, the Strugatskys' *Ugly Swans* and Tvardovsky's *By Right of Memory*. Sometimes, however, writers chose to resort to *samizdat* themselves because they were denied legitimate publication: this is illustrated by Solzhenitsyn's *Prose Poems* and Medvedev's manuscript on Lysenko. The choice of *tamizdat* (publication in the West) could also be motivated by different considerations. The cautious Alexander Bek, after repeated attempts to publish his novel *The New Appointment* in the USSR, was eventually driven to send the manuscript abroad; while bolder writers such as Tarsis, Sinyavsky and Daniel knew that their works were totally unacceptable to Soviet publishers and sent them directly to the West for publication.

Although in the Khrushchev years there was often no clear distinction between what might or might not be published in the Soviet Union, by the late 1960s and 1970s, when there were no signs of cultural relaxation, writers increasingly resorted to *samizdat* or publication abroad. Even in the 1970s, however, some interesting literary works on scientific and other themes continued to be published in the USSR. This was due to a combination of factors. In the first place, it is undeniable that writers whose political loyalty is beyond doubt are permitted more than those who question the whole basis of the Soviet state. Aitmatov, for example, is alleged to be allowed to publish some apolitical or controversial works because, in his journalistic writings and public appearances, he supports Soviet policy, especially on national minorities.[54] Similarly, Trifonov was said to be able to publish some relatively honest prose because he was a Stalin Prize winner.[55] Although such instances suggest that certain writers may have special relationships with the literary and political authorities, it is going too far to postulate a general 'deal' between the Soviet regime and the liberal literary intelligentsia.[56]

The personal preferences of the party leaders may also exert some influence on what is permitted in fiction. In 1980 Sinyavsky convincingly argued that some leeway had been allowed to 'village prose' writers, because many of the Soviet leaders came from a peasant background themselves and felt a secret nostalgia for the Russian village before collectivisation and, perhaps, a 'certain sense of guilt towards the peasantry'.[57] Similarly, the expression of moderate Russian nationalist sentiments was allowed in literature and criticism because Brezhnev and Suslov had some sympathy for such views. Katerina Clark has pointed to certain parallels between 'village prose' of the Brezhnev era and Zhdanovite fiction of the late Stalin period: its emphasis on idealised heroes, traditional family values and closeness to the soil (and hence to agricultural production, which the leadership wishes to encourage).[58] The *émigré* critic Yury Maltsev has argued, more cynically, that Russian nationalist sentiments were permitted in 'village prose' because they represent the only point of contact between the Soviet leadership and the population.[59]

Another interpretation of the appearance of interesting literary works in the 1970s is offered by Sinyavsky, who suggests that the existence of *samizdat* and *émigré* literature had a significant influence both on Soviet writers and on officials in charge of literature. In his opinion, the very fact that certain problems can be discussed more frankly in *samizdat* 'has forced official writers into more critical positions, if only for the sake of their own self-respect'. At the same time, *samizdat* and the activities of dissidents have obliged the censorship to deal more leniently with certain official writers, who are permitted to treat quite boldly 'subjects which, although not the most burning in social or political terms, are nonetheless of considerable peripheral interest, like the subject of the Soviet past and individual destinies'. The Soviet authorities are obliged to tolerate liberal writers, because if they banned them completely they would resort to *samizdat* and emigrate to the West.[60]

The information which we do possess about Soviet literature since Stalin, albeit frustratingly incomplete, provides less evidence for the picture of a monolithic totalitarian regime imposing a consistent policy on Soviet writers than for the view that, within certain limits set by the political authorities at any given time, haphazard chaos reigns.[61] Chance plays a large part in determining Soviet literary policy: much depends on the ambitions, tact and good fortune of the authors themselves, the competence and caprices of individual editors, censors and political leaders, and changing political circumstances. Often there seems no good reason why one work is published and another is not; as Gladilin has said, 'The magazine employees themselves didn't know what they were doing.' Since Stalin's time Soviet publishing houses and censorship agencies have largely been managed by incompetent, philistine officials who have made their careers in party and ideological work. Gladilin states frankly:

> In the last forty years it has become a tradition in our country for executive positions in the field of literature to be sinecures for failures, for failures, naturally, from the ranks of party functionaries. This one couldn't cope with the chemical industry, that one mucked up agriculture, a third disgraced himself in the United Nations . . . Where do you stick such people? Still, they've got *nomenklatura*. Ah, let them go manage literature and art!

The low priority which the Soviet leadership accords to literature is illustrated by the allegation that Molotov once threatened Malenkov: 'I'll appoint you People's Commissar of Culture . . . that'll teach you!'

Another possible explanation for such periodic 'cultural "miracles" ' as the publication of Trifonov's *House on the Embankment* is economic dependence on the West. This opinion was expressed in 1979 by Gladilin, who claimed that 'a few well-known disobedient writers', especially Jews, would be useful as potential scapegoats if *détente,* American grain and high technology were no longer available.[62] The corollary of this view – that the end of *détente* might lead to renewed cultural repression – seems to have been proved correct in the 1980s.

The Reception and Impact of Literature about Science

Because of extremely limited evidence, it is difficult to determine precisely the reception of literature on scientific themes in the Soviet Union. Nevertheless, whatever the exact distribution of favourable and unfavourable reactions among the population, there is no doubt that conformist literature on scientific themes falls below the level of effectiveness that the Soviet leaders would like. The strident, repetitive, cliché-ridden tone of socialist realist fiction is not the tone of writers who are sure of their audience and feel that they are speaking to a convinced, loyal population, but rather reflects the insecurity of political leaders who possess little faith in the extent to which people can be expected to believe the maxims put to them without constant restatement. The incomplete success achieved by the party in enlisting literature as propaganda is also demonstrated by the periodic need to tighten controls and criticise writers for their inadequate performance. The ineffectiveness of propaganda in favour of the 'NTR' is most clearly shown by the growth of a spirit of opposition among the scientific community and the emergence of apolitical and *samizdat* fiction expressing scepticism about the value of science.

The difficulty of moulding propaganda and reality into a coherent work of art renders it improbable that any of the run-of-the-mill works on science and technology published in the post-Stalin period, for example Kozhevnikov's *Introduce Yourself, Baluev!* and Ketlinskaya's *Otherwise There is No Point in Living*, were popular with the public. It is likely that the decline of the long 'production novel' from the mid-1950s owed something to the Soviet reader's tendency to leave them lying on the shelves. The treatment of scientific themes in such works as Lvova's *Elena* was particularly ineffective, as it was nothing more than uninformed propaganda at two removes – the original distortions in the press expressed in a simplified form for the general reader.

In the 1950s and 1960s the Soviet public expressed what choice it had in a preference for translations of world literature, nineteenth-century Russian classics and, later, for *samizdat* works. However, some novels and stories on scientific subjects were widely read and discussed in the post-Stalin period. It would seem that, in the absence of many works of literary merit, the Soviet public had a political interest in reading, gaining a sort of substitute pleasure from observing the way in which various authors handled delicate situations. Such novels as Ehrenburg's *Thaw* and Dudintsev's *Not by Bread Alone* acquired a large readership because of their political importance. Yury German's adventure stories won some popularity among Soviet workers, while controversial neo-Stalinist works by writers like Kochetov and Shevtsov caused a stir. It is also probable that the works of Granin, Kaverin and Gor, which showed a genuine knowledge of, and interest in, scientists and their problems, evoked a ready response among the scientific and technical intelligentsia. In the 1970s and 1980s, with the exception of science fiction and the 'production plays' of Bochkaryov, Dvoretsky and Gelman, works dealing with scientific and technical themes have not enjoyed much popularity; the Soviet public prefers 'village prose', 'everyday prose', the detective stories of the brothers Vainer, the spy thrillers of Yulian Semyonov, historical romances and family chronicles.

The Soviet leaders use fiction as a means of understanding their major domestic problems. Since the general public has no means of voicing open criticism of the regime, novels and stories offer a substitute. Debates about topical novels on the theme of science and technology in gatherings of party officials, cultural bureaucrats, collective farmers, scientists, factory workers and students enable the authorities to justify their own policies and at the same time to find out the issues of current concern to people. Because the author, the critic and the regime itself treat literature as life and the Soviet public reads in a socially relevant way, debates about such works as *The Russian Forest, The Thaw* and *Not by Bread Alone* in the 1950s and about 'production literature' and 'village prose' in the 1970s afford fascinating insights into Soviet society.

It is difficult to determine exactly how far the regime makes conscious use of this means of eliciting information about the mood of the Soviet population. Discussions of literature can certainly provide a safety-valve for social tensions, and may indicate to the regime the need for reform. The debate about Dudintsev's novel, for example, demonstrated the seriousness of the problem of bureaucracy and the depth of feeling among liberal writers and students, leading Khrushchev simultaneously to take measures curbing the tide of liberalism and introducing economic decentralisation.

The precise influence which literature exerted upon scientists and policy-makers is a matter of speculation. It would seem, however, that the de-Stalinisation campaign enabled literature to create a new phenomenon in the Soviet Union: public opinion. Attacks on liberals by dogmatists during the years 1957–8 suggest that the Twentieth Congress had led to the emergence of a literary intelligentsia unamenable to party control and consequently exercising considerable moral authority: thus Lev Nikulin, a figure notorious for his denunciations of honest writers, including Babel, spoke disparagingly of 'small groups which try to make a "literary climate", impart their taste to youth and create a certain sham "public opinion" '.[63] Liberals associated with the journal *Novy Mir* were also committed to the belief that their journal was helping to create a changed climate of opinion to which the party would respond. Speaking of Dorosh's agricultural sketches, the critic Lakshin said that he was one of those writers 'whose articles and sketches helped to strengthen public opinion which is called upon to assist the party to improve the position of the countryside'.[64]

The alliance between the literary and scientific intelligentsia became increasingly effective from the early 1960s and was occasionally able to influence party policy. The growth of public opinion may, for example, have helped to stimulate the party to rectify the faults in Soviet medicine. The persistent shortage of medicines was a particularly controversial topic during the post-Stalin period, especially as the country continued to export medicines. Because of this taboo Mark Popovsky was unable, for a long time, to conclude an agreement with a publisher for a book on pharmacologists. However, mild references to Soviet backwardness in the production of antibiotics were allowed to appear in such works as Kaverin's *Searches and Hopes* and Gor's *University Embankment* before the deficiency had been officially acknowledged by the party. The backwardness of the Soviet medical industry was publicly recognised by a decree of 20 January 1960 which sought to increase the output of all kinds of items, from thermometers to penicillin.

During the years 1962–3, published and *samizdat* works by writers and scientists combined to create a climate of opinion hostile to Lysenkoism. The reading public sympathetic to the classical geneticists — scientists of all disciplines, journalists and writers — in their turn influenced public figures and directors of the national economy. Undoubtedly, the growth of public opinion was a contributory factor in the party's eventual change of policy towards Lysenko, although, as Mark Popovsky argues, a changed intellectual climate alone could not have achieved anything without the fall of Khrushchev.[65] Unfortunately, in the long run this proved to be only a partial victory: it benefited the scientists, but was of little lasting value to writers. For the liberal writers, however, one positive and enduring result of their participation in the genetics dispute was their relationship with the scientific community which continued after 1964. The growth of *samizdat* and the increasing cohesiveness of the Soviet intelligentsia meant that public opinion in the Soviet Union could never again be completely suppressed.

In the post-Khrushchev period both mainstream literature, science fiction and discussions in the press about the 'scientific and technological revolution' helped to keep the issue of the limitations and potential dangers of science before the Soviet public. Writers, scientists and industrial managers continued to participate in debates about conservation, agriculture and industrial management which alerted people's attention to important social questions. At the Twenty-Sixth Congress of 1981 Brezhnev stated: 'It's gratifying that in recent years literature, the cinema and the theatre have been raising serious problems over which it really wouldn't hurt the state planning committee to do some "sweating". And it's not the only one.' Nevertheless, the evidence suggests that policy changes only occurred when the literary and scientific intelligentsia had won the support of the party leaders.

Notes

1. Dewhirst and Farrell, *Soviet Censorship*, p. 5.
2. Pomerantsev, 'Ob iskrennosti'; Kaverin, *LG*, 22 Dec. 1954.
3. M. Popovsky, letter.
4. Lvova, *Elena* (1955), cf. M. Dubinin, *Pravda*, 11 Nov. 1955; Ketlinskaya, *Inache zhit ne stoit*, cf. F. Kleimenov, *Pravda*, 21 Sept. 1956.
5. E. Katerli, *Dalnyaya doroga* (L, 1956); cf. I. Sopov, *Izvestiya*, 5 Oct. 1956.
6. *Kultura i Zhizn*, 1957, no. 1, pp. 11–13.
7. *LG*, 9 Jan. 1964.
8. W. Smirniw, 'Satirical Trends in Recent Soviet Science Fiction', in E. Bristol (ed.), *Russian Literature and Criticism* (Berkeley, 1982), pp. 193–206.
9. V. Kaverin, E. Kazakevich *et al.*, *LG*, 26 Oct. 1954; B. Kerbabaev, *LG*, 11 Sept. 1958.
10. A. Kuznetsov, *Daily Telegraph*, 7 Aug. 1969; Etkind, letter.
11. A. Gladilin, 'Stalnaya ptitsa', *Kontinent*, no. 14 (1977), pp. 356–9.
12. M. Dewhirst, 'Soviet Russian Literature and Literary Policy', in A. Brown, M. Kaser (eds.), *The Soviet Union since the Fall of Khrushchev* (London and Basingstoke, 1975), p. 195 n. 28.
13. Etkind, *Notes*, p. 7.
14. M. Popovsky, letter.
15. A. Kuznetsov, *Sunday Telegraph*, 10 Aug. 1969; V. Voinovich, *The Ivankiad*, trans. D. Lapeza (London, 1978), pp. 53–6.
16. A. Sinyavsky, 'Literaturnyi protsess v Rossii', *Kontinent*, no. 1 (1974), pp.

143–4.
17. A. Amalrik, 'An Open Letter to Kuznetsov', *Survey*, nos 74–5 (Winter-Spring, 1970), p. 97.
18. Kuznetsov, *Daily Telegraph*, 7 Aug. 1969.
19. V. Zhuravlyov, *Izvestiya*, 3 Sept. 1957.
20. F. Panfyorov, *Volga – matushka reka* (M, 1954), p. 30. (first published, N M, 1953, nos 11, 12).
21. F. Panfyorov, *Razdumye*, *Znamya*, 1958, no. 7, p. 101.
22. V. Serebrovsky, *Voprosy sovetskogo avtorskogo prava* (M, 1956), p. 139.
23. E. Swayze, *Political Control of Literature in the USSR, 1946–1959* (Cambridge, Mass., 1962), p. 290.
24. Mihajlov, *Moscow Summer*, p. 44.
25. Voinovich, *Ivankiad*; 'Proisshestvie v Metropole', *Kontinent*, 1975, no. 5, pp. 51–96; Matich, *Third Wave*, pp. 139–46.
26. G. Vladimov, *RM*, 3 Mar. 1983.
27. Dewhirst and Farrell, *Soviet Censorship*, pp. 12–13; N. Mandelstam, *Hope Abandoned*, p. 410.
28. Dewhirst and Farrell, *Soviet Censorship*, p. 13.
29. N. Khrushchev, *Khrushchev Remembers: The Last Testament*, trans. and ed. S. Talbott (NY and London, 1971), pp. 76–7.
30. H. Smith, *The Russians* (London, 1976), p. 464.
31. *LG*, 24 July 1956.
32. Popovsky, letter; *Po sledam otstupayushchikh* (M, 1963).
33. Gladilin, *Making and Unmaking*, p. 53.
34. Frankel, *Novy Mir*, pp. 185–6, n. 26.
35. Brumberg, *In Quest of Justice*, pp. 283–9.
36. Dewhirst and Farrell, *Soviet Censorship*, p. 53.
37. Labedz, *Solzhenitsyn*. p. 172.
38. G. Hosking, conference paper, Oxford, 1982.
39. N. Pogodin, *Kogda lomayutsya kopya* (M, 1953).
40. G. Ivanenko, *NS*, 1957, no. 1. p. 331.
41. N. Pogodin, *Sobranie dramaticheskikh proizvedenii*, vol. 4 (M, 1960–1).
42. Solzhenitsyn, *Oak and Calf*, p. 42.
43. Sinyavsky, 'Samizdat', p. 8.
44. Zh. Medvedev, interview.
45. Etkind, *Notes*, p. 175; Finkelstein, letter.
46. Solzhenitsyn, *Oak and Calf*, pp. 120–7; Gladilin, *Making and Unmaking*, p. 424.
47. G. Hosking, 'The Politics of Literature', in J. Cracraft (ed.), *The Soviet Union Today* (Chicago, 1983), pp 273–5.
48. M. Popovsky, 'Tysyacha dnei akademika Nikolaya Vavilova', *Prostor*, 1966, nos 7, 8.
49. Gor, *Universitetskaya naberezhnaya*, *Neva*, 1959, no. 11, p. 18. On Kammerer, see A. Koestler, *The Case of the Midwife Toad* (London, 1971).
50. D. Danin, *Neizbezhnost strannogo mira* (M, 1960); on Fock, see Graham, *Science and Philosophy*, pp. 93–101.
51. N. Semyonov, *Izvestiya*, 9 Aug. 1959.
52. R. Hingley, *Russian Writers and Soviet Society* (London, 1979), p. 233.
53. Tertz, *Fantasticheskii mir*, pp. 444–5.
54. N. Shneidman, 'Interview with Chingiz Aitmatov', *RLT*, 1979, no. 16, pp. 261–2.
55. C. Proffer, 'Writing in the Shadow of the Monolith', *New York Review*, 19 Feb. 1976, p. 9.
56. Discussed in N. Cornwell, 'Through the Clouds of Soviet Literature', *The Crane Bag*, (1983) vol. 7, no. 1, pp. 25–6.

57. Sinyavsky, 'Samizdat', p. 11.
58. K. Clark, 'Zhdanovist Fiction and Village Prose', in Bristol, *Russian Literature*, pp. 36–48.
59. Yu. Maltsev, 'Promezhutochnaya literatura i kriterii podlinnosti', *Kontinent*, 1980, no. 25, p. 316.
60. Sinyavsky, 'Samizdat', pp. 13, 9–10.
61. Cornwell, 'Through the Clouds', p. 25.
62. Gladilin, *Making and Unmaking*, pp. 44, 146, 151.
63. L. Nikulin, *LG*, 20 Nov. 1958.
64. V. Lakshin, 'Tri mery vremeni', *NM*, 1966, no. 3, p. 227.
65. M. Popovsky, letter.

CONCLUSION

The Choice of Scientific Themes

Khrushchev's de-Stalinisation campaign considerably widened the extremely narrow choice of scientific themes permitted to writers in Stalin's time. One major new theme was the general effect of Stalinism on science and technology, its particular impact on specific sciences, and the changes in the scientific world after Stalin's death. Writers were also able to investigate problems affecting Soviet science in the contemporary post-Stalin era: conflicts between plan-fulfilment and technological innovation, pure and applied science and individual and collective work; the question of ideological interference with scientific research and the scientist's relationship with the political authorities.

The post-Stalin era was the first period since the 1920s when writers chose scientific themes more or less freely, and not through indoctrination or intimidation. There seem, nevertheless, to have been two distinct types of 'science novel' published in the USSR since Stalin's death. The first kind was written by a literary hack, a conformist writer of the older generation or a party member, who usually chose a safe, topical theme, basing his work on the official press and the latest pronouncements of the party leaders. Such writers frequently had no scientific training, had evinced no interest in science in their earlier works, and regarded a scientific topic as an extension of the Stalinist 'production novel'. The second, more interesting kind of 'science novel' was written by a liberal writer with a genuine interest in the problems of scientists, either because of his own educational background or his close contact with the scientific world. The selection of specific themes depended to a large extent on the personality of the individual writer. While the conformist writer still operated within a circumscribed area drawn both by the official censorship and his own self-censorship, the liberal writer was eager to treat subjects which had formerly been taboo, as soon as the party's cultural policy became more tolerant and the censorship more relaxed.

The Treatment of Scientific Themes

In their treatment of scientific themes the majority of Soviet writers, assisted by their editors, still adhered very closely to the changing scientific and political policies favoured by the party leaders. The treatment of the impact of Stalinism on science provides the most striking example of writers' adaptation to the vagaries in party policy. Khrushchev, having denounced Stalin, had little reason to maintain the Stalinist version of events, and therefore allowed writers access to some previously forbidden areas of investigation. However, since the truth about Soviet science under Stalin was an issue too sensitive for unbiased enquiry, Khrushchev imposed his own variety of myth on writers. Although abusive references to Stalin's influence on science became almost as obligatory in the post-Stalin period as laudatory references had been in the past, the party's conduct was uniformly presented as impeccable. A truthful depiction of Stalin's special prisons, the human cost at which industrialisation had been achieved, or the full effect of the purges on the scientific world would have raised certain politically awkward questions and suggested almost universal corruption through fear on the part of communist officials. It was possible to present certain discredited members of the party leadership as corrupt, but if the majority of the party had been shown as having seen through Stalin and thus having connived at his crimes, the party would have lost all claim to moral authority. For this reason writers blamed most errors on Beria or Stalin himself, or explained them away by the euphemistic term 'the cult of personality'. While conceding that some lingering after-effects of Stalinism still persisted, they claimed that the severest problems were being successfully eliminated by the party. Scientists and engineers were being released from the camps, secrecy and chauvinism were fast disappearing, bureaucracy and corruption were faults appertaining only to a few isolated individuals, and the party was tackling the problem of technological innovation. The majority of post-Stalin fiction confirms the truth of Sinyavsky's assertion that the de-Stalinisation campaign caused uncertainty and confusion to Soviet writers; the most successful were those who were able 'to present our achievements as plausibly as possible and our shortcomings as mildly, delicately and implausibly as possible'.[1]

Although literature generally emphasised and welcomed the relaxation in many branches of science, Soviet writers were still severely restricted in their treatment of certain topics. Since Khrushchev still supported Lysenko, published fiction was unable, before 1964, to deal frankly with Lysenko's harmful influence on genetics and agricultural science; and the superiority of a materialist approach to quantum mechanics, chemistry and psychology continued to be stressed. A particularly stringent censorship still applied to the discussion of any subject which impinged on sensitive areas of current party policy, such as agriculture, nuclear policy, space technology and chemistry. Accordingly, writers treated agricultural science with greater caution than the more abstract subject of genetics; extolled the peaceful exploitation of atomic energy; failed to mention Soviet backwardness in chemistry and cybernetics; and did not challenge the enforced anonymity of the designers of the space programme.

Within this general conformity there were, however, certain differences of approach at different times. When Khrushchev was seeking to introduce far-reaching reforms, authors were able to be most outspoken in their exposure of the problems of Soviet science; but when he was attempting to stem the tide of liberalisation, they were obliged to paint a less black picture of the scientific world. While both the 'liberal' journal *Novy Mir* and the 'conservative' *Oktyabr* made only limited revelations about the Stalin era, 'dogmatists' had a greater tendency to imply that the sufferings of the past had been ultimately justified by the achievements of the present.

After the Brezhnev regime had established a centrist line on the Stalin question in the 1960s, the Stalin era once again became a very delicate subject for Soviet writers to handle, especially as many aspects of the system which Stalin had created remained intact. The labour camp theme, a 'miracle' which had only been allowed, in Sinyavsky's words, because of 'the political exigencies of Khrushchev's power struggle',[2] was once again prohibited. Among the few references to Stalinism which occasionally surfaced in fiction of the 1970s were the suppression of Soviet genetics and allied sciences (a theme permitted because Lysenko had been toppled by the Brezhnev-Kosygin regime) and a general criticism of the corruption and opportunism among scientists in the Stalin era (a less controversial suggestion than any implication that such vices could be engendered by contemporary Soviet society).

In the post-Stalin era, the majority of writers still fulfilled the function of propagating the dominant myths sponsored by the party leaders: this is particularly evident in fiction euologising the space programme and the construction of BAM. When they criticise aspects of Soviet science and society, writers generally conform to the same standards as those which determine the content of the 'self-criticism' columns of newspapers, failing to challenge the party and its policies directly, and giving no indications of the presumed cause of any failure beyond the simple assertion that particular individuals or organisations have failed to perform their duty. Most probably the Soviet authorities hope that conformist fiction will serve to divert hostility from the party leaders who formulate policies against the officials who execute them. The conformity of most fiction on scientific themes can be ascribed to writers' persistent use of the press as a source of subject matter; the psychology of writers themselves, particularly their desire to safeguard their positions and privileges and their willingness to resort to self-censorship in order to secure the publication of their work; and the strict system of literary controls, of which perhaps the most important is the censorship conducted in editorial offices.

The persistence of propaganda in Soviet literature of the post-Stalin era has certain implications for the structure of society. Vera Dunham has argued convincingly that in the years 1945–53 the Soviet leadership formed a tacit alliance with the rapidly growing managerial and professional 'middle class' in order to enable the regime to survive.[3] The term 'middle class' cuts across differences of position, occupation and income, implying an attachment to a specific 'bourgeois' set of manners, values and attitudes. Many writers belonged to this class, and it was therefore in their interests to support party policy and maintain their positions and privileges. After Stalin's death these considerations still prevailed; and writers continued to assist the party leaders in their goals of modernisation and technological progress, expressing values designed to appeal to entrenched 'middle-class' scientists, engineers and technicians who constituted an important part of their readership. The continuing alliance between 'middle-class' scientists, writers and the party leaders helps to explain the conformity of much literature on the theme of science after the era of mass terror had ended.

It has, however, been the central argument of this book that Soviet fiction of the post-Stalin era paints a much less favourable picture of the development of Soviet science in the Stalin and post-Stalin periods than is admitted in official propaganda. While the majority of authors used the margin of freedom permitted to them after 1953 to demonstrate their obedience to the dictates of the party, a minority of progressive writers took advantage of the party's fluctuating cultural policy and the independent views of certain editors in order to publish works which diverged from the party line. In 1956 such writers as Dudintsev, Granin and Kaverin began to probe the limits of their new freedom, suggesting that corruption in science had been extremely widespread in Stalin's time, and that the situation had not significantly changed since Stalin's death. Moreover, progressive writers used the portrayal of bureaucracy in the scientific world as a powerful means of exposing the vices of literary functionaries, and even, implicitly, of the Soviet leadership itself. After the Hungarian Revolt these outspoken works were subjected to severe criticism from literary dogmatists and party officials. Their authors had infringed the unwritten rule by which writers were allowed to condemn individual bureaucrats and careerists as a form of 'self-criticism' in order to demonstrate their support for the party's economic reforms or Khrushchev's denunciation of his political rivals, but were forbidden to suggest that people felt a fundamental distrust and alienation from the top echelons of the *apparat*. Explicit criticism of the whole bureaucratic establishment was still blocked by the regime, as this could have led to widespread disillusionment with the party and its leaders. In the Khrushchev period, vices of bureaucracy and careerism were generally attributed to the legacy of the Stalin era, but by the late 1960s and 1970s it became increasingly less easy, as Soviet society grew older, to represent negative characters and traits as mere survivals of capitalism, or even as features generated exclusively by the Stalin regime. Writers could not fail to imply both that the Soviet organisation of science tended to breed its own brand of vice and virtue, and that it was impossible for any society, however advanced, to succeed entirely in eradicating human frailty.

Some writers diverged from the party line in their treatment of certain specific topics. A few managed to imply, while Lysenko still enjoyed the protection of Khrushchev, that the persecution of geneticists had caused considerable damage to Soviet agriculture. Whereas official sources unanimously praised the achievements of the party-sponsored 'scientific and technological revolution', some literary works continued to depict major defects in Soviet science, demonstrating that they were by no means all being successfully eliminated by the party. They showed that certain social and psychological problems caused by the Stalin era — fear, mediocrity, the pernicious influence of 'Stalin's heirs', the tension between 'fathers and sons' — still hindered the development of Soviet science in the immediate post-Stalin period. When dealing with the perennial problems inherent in the whole structure of Soviet science, literature suggests that there were several areas of conflict between the scientific intelligentsia and the party and government bureaucracy. Scientists were opposed to the imposition of a rigid plan and the principle of strict utilitarianism on their work. Many wished for a more individualist approach to research, with greater emphasis on initiative and personal fulfilment. Some were attempting to shed political and ideological control over their research, to use scientific methods of analysing the Soviet economy and society as a whole, and even, in some cases, to dream of replacing the party bureaucracy with a technocratic elite capable of creating a more rational society.

Soviet fiction of the post-Stalin period reflects the fundamental contradiction in the Soviet attitude towards science. It is undeniable that the Soviet authorities spend immense sums of money on subsidising scientific research and technological application which have made the USSR one of the most advanced countries in the world; this generosity, however, is extended only towards officially approved aspects of science and technology. As some Soviet writers admit, the other side of the coin is an intolerance of all scientific ideas appearing to threaten the doctrine of dialectical materialism, a distrust of theoretical research which does not promise immediate practical results and a hostility towards technological innovation conceived by individuals outside the party's plan.

Once the threat of Stalin's terror had been removed, the individualist, non-conformist outlook of progressive Soviet writers led them to reject the official optimism demanded of them, and they began to produce a new kind of semi-truthful literature which co-existed with, but bore little relation to, the literature of socialist realism. The character of the scientist or inventor was increasingly used as a vehicle for the exploration of general social and moral problems, for example the question of the gifted individual's place in the community and the conflict between idealists and careerists. Soviet writers suggest that science — and, by implication, any creative activity — may either be undertaken for the general good or misused for power and personal gain. Such figures as the persecuted idealist Lopatkin in Dudintsev's *Not by Bread Alone* and the opportunist Minaev in Granin's *Personal Opinion* evoke the tragic fate of the Soviet artist, and of the intelligentsia as a whole, in the Stalin and post-Stalin eras. The character of the bureaucrat or careerist is used not only to draw attention to the harmful atmosphere of the Stalin era, but also to demonstrate that evil is inherent in human nature, and that the notion of the 'new socialist man' is a myth.

Soviet fiction of the post-Stalin period reflects the growing alliance between writers and scientists. They shared a common interest and purpose, for science, like art, was subject to the totalitarian state and its dominant ideology. In Stalin's time science and scientists had suffered a similar fate to that of art and artists. Both the scientific and artistic community had split in two under the impact of Stalin's terror: those who co-operated with the regime were rewarded with power, prestige and material goods, whereas those who resisted were dismissed from their jobs, exiled or imprisoned. In 1956 the de-Stalinisation campaign encouraged progressive artists and scientists to struggle against 'Stalin's heirs' in institutes, literary organisations, the party and the government. The co-operation between the scientific and artistic intelligentsia, which began in the 1950s as a campaign for greater intellectual freedom later developed into a full-scale 'human rights movement' concerned with legal and political reform.

Soviet Fiction as a Mirror of Science and Society

Naturally, a study of Soviet fiction cannot replace political and social analysis, because, as Basile Kerblay suggests, literature tends to 'present problems in psychological terms, as the result of conflicts of temperament at the factory, building site or laboratory, in particular between conservatives and innovators',[4] rather than to suggest objective causes of tension. Nevertheless, fiction dealing with science and technology is of value to the historian and political scientist because, first, it bears so close a relation to current events that it enables us to monitor subtle shifts in party policy and the content of scientific debate; and secondly, because it affords insights into the reality of Soviet science.

Although Soviet literature is primarily useful for the confirmation of facts known through other sources, some works, such as Gallai's *Tested in the Sky* and Pobozhy's *Dead Way*, contain previously unknown information which could not be obtained through any other medium. Apart from such unusual works which managed to evade the censor during Khrushchev's de-Stalinisation campaign or the confused interval after Khrushchev's fall, it is only *samizdat* works that present genuinely new information. Solzhenitsyn, in particular, often reveals new facts about the Stalin period in his literary work before amplifying them in his political writings: his novel *The First Circle* was the first work to reveal the existence and organisation of Stalin's 'special prisons' for scientists. Bek's *New Appointment* depicts the harmful effect of Stalin's sponsorship of a project for introducing electrically-powered turbines and suggests reasons for the death of Stalin's Minister of Ferrous Metallurgy, Tevosyan.

Soviet literature possesses historical value as the first medium to raise significant issues in public in the Soviet Union. Through fiction, certain important kinds of knowledge were made available for the first time to those sections of the reading public who were not already privy to the information through their professional activities. In the first place, the literary material is interesting because it sheds light on the fate of individual scientists in the Stalin and post-Stalin periods. While only *samizdat* works refer to real tragedies such as the death of Nikolai Vavilov and the suicide of Ordzhonikidze, fictional characters in novels and stories were sometimes modelled on real prototypes. Such references were undoubtedly transparent to a section of the scientific intelligentsia at the time of publication; and such cautious disclosures may have led other sections of the Soviet reading public, even if they were unfamiliar with the actual prototypes of these characters, to draw far-reaching conclusions about the persecution of eminent scientists in the Stalin and post-Stalin eras. It is also probable that the recurring fictional portraits of influential pseudo-scientists would have pointed readers in the direction of the notorious Lysenko and his disciples. Although by itself the 'revelation' about the arrest of an individual scientist or engineer in one work of fiction published in the Soviet Union is hardly startling, the aggregate weight of evidence in post-Stalin literature, which depicts arrests in many branches of science and technology, is impressive. When combined with the genuine disclosures of *samizdat* works, it is overwhelming. Only in fiction of this period could the Soviet public obtain any indication of the scale on which the persecution, arrest and imprisonment of scientists was carried out in Stalin's time.

The discerning reader would also have noticed that, although the

majority of Soviet writers treated scientific topics after they had
been discussed in the press, some liberal writers entered scientific
discussions before they had been concluded with a party pronouncement or directive. In *The Russian Forest* Leonov discussed
important problems of Soviet forestry before they had been brought
into the open; Mishnev condemned Lysenko's theory of the lack of
intra-species competition before it had been denounced by the
party; Dorosh indicated the harmful effect of certain agricultural
campaigns still supported by Lysenko and Khrushchev; and Granin
stressed the importance of theoretical research before the party line
on this subject had become clear.

By concentrating on the fabric of everyday life in scientific institutes, literature is able to portray the world of Soviet science in
greater detail than a scholarly investigation by a social scientist.
Works of fiction shed light on many corrupt practices employed by
Soviet scientists: plagiarism, the deliberate falsification of scientific
data, the rejection or enforced rewriting of dissertations, rumour-
mongering and denunciation, collaboration with government officials and the propagation of impractical schemes based on the
deceptive promise of rapid economic benefits. Literature also
informs us about the day-to-day problems faced by Soviet scientists
and engineers — questions of planning and organisation, the difficulty of getting inventions accepted, the need to justify theoretical
research, to cope with secrecy and anti-Semitism, to adapt to constant oscillations in party policy. Although post-Khrushchev literature has been generally less revealing about the reality of Soviet
science, it nevertheless suggests that certain problems have
remained constant since Stalin's time.

Above all, fiction, whether published in the USSR, circulated in
samizdat or published abroad, is an effective means of conveying
the effects of public policy on individual human beings, exploring
relationships between people and highlighting changing social attitudes. Literature evokes the psychological impact of the Stalin
period on individual Soviet scientists: enforced silence or duplicity
on the part of men of only ordinary courage; the cynicism and
careerism of men who had risen to prominent positions under
Stalin; the difficulty of readjustment experienced by scientists
released from the camps; the general timidity and lack of initiative
among research workers even after de-Stalinisation. In the absence
of proper market research, and in view of the rigid censorship
fettering the political and scientific press, works of fiction can

provide interesting insights into the likes and dislikes of scientists and their professional relationships: the tension between superiors and subordinates, scientists and engineers, workers and intellectuals and scientists of different generations. Soviet literature also contains clues about the social and political ideas held by Soviet scientists. Liberal works of 1956 and 1962–3 show that scientists were struggling for greater freedom from party and government interference, and were emerging as an important pressure group, conscious of their power and prestige in Soviet society. Even conformist and conservative literature provides valuable evidence by extrapolation: the vehemence with which such ideas as 'revisionism', 'philosophical neutralism' and rule by technocrats are attacked reflects their growing influence in Soviet society.

Although post-Khrushchev fiction has become less politically explicit, it comes closer to the reality of Soviet life than works of social science because it reminds us of the significance of the moral choices made by individuals, whatever the social constraints within which they operate. Literary portraits tend to corroborate the classification of the different types of Soviet scientist proposed by David Joravsky.[5] The first type is the 'learned opportunist': a man who knows the moral requirements of his discipline, but shows no *moral* commitment to uphold them against political condemnation. Such characters as Glebov in Trifonov's *House on the Embankment* and Uspensky in Kron's *Insomnia* would fit into this category. Another type is the 'pliable man of principle' who, in times of conflict, tries to be true to his discipline, while placating the political authorities by verbal play, avoiding sensitive topics or by other more or less minor concessions — like such figures as Komissarov's Starik or Bondarenko's Dubrovin. A third type is the 'intransigent specialist', who within his discipline will concede nothing to political authority except silence, if that is the only way he can avoid saying things his discipline tells him are untrue — prominent literary examples are Kaverin's Konshin and Gerasimovich's Ukladnikov. Another type who figures very prominently in Soviet fiction is the 'ignorant opportunist' who knows little about science, but defers to whatever authority is dominant, scientific or political. Many of the administrators depicted in Soviet fiction correspond to this description.

One small group mentioned by Joravsky, but not portrayed in fiction published in the USSR, for obvious reasons, is the 'Varangian': a scientist who shows even greater resistance to political authority, and not only defends truth within his discipline, but ranges far wider, defending autonomous thought against political authority in other fields. Examples of this type in real life are Sakharov, Zhores Medvedev and Shafarevich, and in the humanities, Zinoviev and Etkind. In dissident literature such characters as Nerzhin, Gerasimovich and Sologdin in Solzhenitsyn's *First Circle*, and Schizophrenic, Slanderer and Bawler in Zinoviev's *Yawning Heights* would fit into this category.

Some published fiction depicting the conflict between scientists and administrators, coupled with franker works by Gladilin and Zinoviev, lends support to the view of Western scholars that there may be an intrinsic incompatibility between the Soviet regime's aim of improving scientific performance with a view to obtaining greater economic return from their investment, and their attempt to enhance the role of the party in science. Literature provides anecdotal evidence to corroborate the impassioned, pessimistic view of the problems of Soviet science expressed in Mark Popovsky's *Science in Chains*. At first sight this account appears irreconcilable with our knowledge of the USSR as creator of the Salyut space station and nuclear superpower. It is, however, perfectly conceivable that the great successes achieved by the Soviet state in certain politically important areas upon which enormous resources have been lavished can co-exist with the inefficiency, bureaucracy and loss of individual freedom endemic in the Soviet organisation of science as a whole. As a corrective to such a bleak view, however, it is necessary to emphasise the improvements which have occurred since Stalin's death, and to compare the state of Soviet science with the contemporary problems affecting scientists elsewhere in the world.

General Attitudes to Science in Soviet Fiction

Since 1964, with the exception of science fiction, scientists and engineers have been portrayed less frequently in the works of the more interesting and popular Soviet writers, although Klaus Mehnert overstates the case when he suggests that the NTR barely features at all in Soviet fiction.[6] One possible explanation for the paucity of scientist heroes in recent fiction is that a growing ambivalence towards science and technology in Soviet society has made it difficult even for conformist writers to present the scientist in simple terms as a heroic figure, as authors did in the 1950s. More-over, the scientist has become a less attractive figure for liberal writers, perhaps because the dethronement of Lysenko has made the persecuted scientist less plausible as an image of the honest artist. The NTR, however, has continued to feature prominently in Soviet fiction, albeit in a more oblique fashion. In their different ways, both 'village prose' and 'war prose' testify to an awareness of the possible negative consequences of scientific progress unchecked by moral values.

This changed emphasis is one aspect of Soviet writers' increasing use of fiction as a medium for the discussion of more general socio-political, moral and philosophical issues raised by the development of science and technology. The widely divergent atti-tudes expressed in post-Stalin literature — worship of science and mistrust of science — reflect the fundamental dichotomy between the exaltation of science in Soviet society and the misuse of science by a totalitarian regime. Conformist fiction of the post-Stalin era still endeavoured to inculcate enthusiasm for science and tech-nology, to demonstrate a close connection between science and Soviet ideology and to use science as anti-religious propaganda. On the other hand, it was literature which, in the early 1960s, provided the first medium for the expression of a certain ambivalence or doubt about the implications of scientific and technological development. Some published works began, cautiously, to question the goals of Soviet scientific policy and to attack the excessive emphasis laid upon science in Soviet society. Dissident writers ventured much further, indicating that science and ideology may frequently come into conflict, providing a more complex explora-tion of the relationship between science and religion, and even propounding the heretical view that Marxism itself bears more relation to a religious dogma than to a 'scientific' explanation of the world.

The coexistence of such divergent trends in post-Stalin fiction is a manifestation of the new division between 'Westernists' and 'Russophiles' in Soviet society. The 'Westernists', influenced by the Russian radical tradition, orthodox Marxism-Leninism and the ideas of the 'God-builders', still pin their faith on science and technology as a means of achieving a prosperous and happy future. Other writers, who derive inspiration from the alternative, Slavo-phile current of thought, indicate the limitations of science, em-phasise the superiority of moral over purely scientific values, and advocate the moral and spiritual values associated with ancient rural Russia.

Fiction of the Khrushchev period, far from merely propagating official Marxism-Leninism, reflected in embryo most of the main currents of thought among the Soviet intelligentsia which became more marked in the later 1960s and 1970s. One significant trend was worship of science, a viewpoint especially prevalent among scientists and technologists. Literature suggests that there was still a genuine enthusiasm for scientific progress in the post-Stalin period, and that science and technology were largely replacing Soviet ideology as an object of faith. The romantic, Utopian view of science expressed in literature of the Khrushchev era later received amplified expression in works by such Soviet scholars as the philosophers E. T. Faddeev and A. D. Ursul, the astrophysicist I. S. Shklovsky and the geographer I. M. Zabelin, who manifest a new concern for humanity as a whole and an interest in the 'cosmic' dimension of human existence.[7] One of the most notable features of such discussions has been the revival of interest in the ideas of a number of great Russian thinkers of the past, particularly the theories of Tsiolkovsky, Vernadsky and even Fyodorov (divested of their religious connotations). The heritage of such progressive, humanist thinkers has been used by certain scientists and writers, for example Yevtushenko in his novel *Wild Berries*, to legitimise ideas reminiscent of those of the 'God-builders' which cannot easily be reconciled with official Marxism-Leninism.

Nevertheless, although the traditional Soviet belief in science and humanist rationalism is still an influential trend of thought in the USSR, some of the fears about scientific development tentatively expressed in published fiction in the years 1953–64 and more forcibly voiced by dissident writers have in the post-Khrushchev period been developed by Soviet scientists and even by official theorists of the 'scientific and technological revolution'. There has been a perceptible shift of emphasis from unconfined optimism with regard to the prospects of science and technology towards a more subdued, realistic assessment, coupled with greater concern for the human and social implications of scientific progress[8] and a heightened awareness of the dangers of resource depletion, environmental pollution and the development of nuclear power.[9] Significantly, some of the anxieties expressed by Solzhenitsyn in *Letter to Soviet Leaders* about the implications of unlimited economic growth were discussed in official journals in the late 1970s, even by men close to the party leadership, for example I. T. Frolov, Chairman of the Council for the Philosophical and Social Problems of Science and Technology, demonstrating the narrowing gap between official and dissident thought.[10]

A sceptical attitude towards science and technology has proved an enduring theme in Soviet fiction, especially in the works of the 'village prose' writers who depict the poverty of the collective and state farms, implying criticism of the dichotomy between propaganda for Soviet scientific achievements and the failure to fulfil ordinary people's needs. At the same time such writers as Rasputin and Soloukhin lament the deterioration of the countryside and the disappearance of the traditional Russian way of life and its values. Deeper moral and philosophical questions such as the desirability and limitations of scientific progress, which had previously only been raised by dissident writers, were discussed in the late 1960s and 1970s by such writers as Rasputin, Tendryakov and the Strugatsky brothers.

Some works of post-Stalin fiction suggest that enthusiasm for scientific progress could sometimes be accompanied by a belief in a genuinely scientific, more democratic form of Marxism. Another emerging current of thought was an emphasis on humane values common to the Western liberal tradition. Sometimes disillusionment with both Marxism-Leninism and technological Prometheanism led to a rediscovery of spiritual and, in particular, of religious values. In *Doctor Zhivago*, for example, Pasternak inverts the conventional figure of the scientist-hero in order to uphold moral values, individual creativity and spiritual freedom. Religious themes, only implicit in published literature, were more prominent in the works of dissident writers such as Sinyavsky and Solzhenitsyn, who developed many of the traditional themes of Russian religious literature and philosophy which still possessed relevance for the modern world: the spiritual barrenness of man in the technological age; the compatibility of science and religion; the supreme value of the individual's ephemeral life; the importance of the irrational side of man's personality; the impossibility of substituting Utopian socialism for faith in God.

The Significance of Literature on Scientific Themes

There are two possible interpretations of the value of fiction on scientific themes, and indeed of Soviet literature in general in the post-Stalin era — one optimistic, the other pessimistic. The pessimists would argue that Soviet literature closely reflects the fluctuating policies of the party, and that even in the relatively relaxed Khrushchev period most writers, except for a handful of liberals and dissidents, did not essentially diverge from the party line. Solzhenitsyn and the *émigré* critic Yury Maltsev, for example, contend that only *samizdat* works are worth consideration, as published literature is subject to so many restrictions that even in the 'thaw' years of 1956 and 1962 only half-truths could be cautiously disclosed; there was no meaningful distinction between various Soviet journals when in the early 1960s, at the height of de-Stalinisation, even Tvardovsky compelled writers to cut and revise their works. Even if some reality percolated through in the description of problems facing a scientist or engineer, it was difficult for writers to suggest any practical improvements to Soviet society; with the exception of a few writers on agricultural themes, most authors could only propose attractive but completely Utopian solutions.

On the other hand, the optimists, following Lakshin and Svirsky, would point more charitably to the fairly wide variety of opinions available to the Soviet reader, and to the attempt of such journals as *Novy Mir, Neva* and *Yunost* to tell some of the truth about the problems of Soviet science in the 1960s, and of *Nash Sovremennik* to publish interesting works of 'village prose' in the 1970s. They would regard Solzhenitsyn's view that there can be no literature without absolute truth as an extremist position. These diametrically opposed viewpoints demonstrate that the existence of editorial control and official censorship inevitably turns the freedom of individual writers into a purely relative question.

An analysis of literature on scientific themes thus raises the wider question of whether the progressive Soviet writer should be praised for his outspokenness or blamed for his timidity. It is certainly true that the only works of fiction able to discuss the effect of Stalinism on science completely honestly were works not published in the Soviet Union. Published works all contain a strong element of political calculation, and their feeble, guarded treatment of Stalin's terror tends to corroborate Amalrik's description of the Soviet 'creative intelligentsia' as 'people accustomed to thinking one thing, saying another and doing a third'.[11]

The pejorative term 'intermediate literature' has been coined by Maltsev to denote the works of such liberal writers as Abramov,

Belov, Rasputin, Shukshin, Tendryakov and Trifonov which have been published in the USSR. Maltsev berates 'village prose' writers for their failure to handle the theme of collectivisation; Trifonov for his superficial evocation of the Stalin era in *The House on the Embankment*; and Tendryakov for failing to refer frankly to the Russian religious renaissance or the persecution of religious dissidents. In Maltsev's opinion there are two Russian literatures: truthful *samizdat* and *émigré* literature and false literature published in the USSR. His conception of 'two literatures' is, however, a dogmatic view which has been rejected by other *émigré* writers,[12] and fails either to admit that political explicitness does not always make for good literature (as is demonstrated by some *émigré* fiction) or that such writers as Rasputin and Tendryakov may have other purposes than those which the critic would like them to have. Yet there is some truth in Maltsev's view that works by Rasputin, Belov, Trifonov and others have been published because they are useful to the party, helping to improve the image of the USSR at home and abroad. As he states, 'Permitted truth is suspicious by virtue of the very fact of its having been permitted.'[13]

Nevertheless, the balance of the evidence favours a less extreme view of published Soviet literature. Post-Stalin fiction is significant, because it sheds light on the thinking of the Soviet intelligentsia after half a century of Soviet economic and cultural policy, at a time when it had been violently wrenched out of the mainstream of European development and all but physically destroyed by Stalinism. After Stalin's death most published fiction on the theme of science and technology maintained its propaganda role, but the content and treatment of the socio-political 'message' increasingly became a matter of debate between the party and opposed factions of writers. Liberal writers began to reflect the views of the scientific intelligentsia, rather than those of the party leaders; and because of the party's vacillation at crucial moments, the tenacity and skill of the liberals, the demoralisation and unpopularity of the dogmatists, literature was not only a vehicle for the propagation of official views on science, but also a powerful ally of the scientific intelligentsia in its struggle to emancipate itself from them.

In the post-Stalin era literature demonstrated the possibility of pluralism in Soviet society; it became a public forum in which a variety of views differing both from one another and from the pronouncements of the party leaders could be debated. The differences in the treatment of themes have been shown to be more a reflection of each individual author's personality than of varying political trends, suggesting that the party could not entirely control Soviet writers. Despite its lack of genuine independence, Tvardovsky's *Novy Mir* attracted many good writers and critics and preserved readers' faith in literature, showing that it could discuss new ideas and tell at least part of the truth. The journal advocated a modest 'socialism with a human face', and its very existence up to 1970 seemed to many the pledge of a possible healthy future development of society. Although there is a great difference between a controlled and a free literature, the efforts of writers to liberate themselves from concepts imposed from above are significant, despite their limited nature. Soviet authors had been encouraged to pose fundamental questions about Soviet life, and they continued to do so, even if they were increasingly forced to resort to *samizdat* or publication abroad.

Etkind has spoken of 'the golden days of Khrushchev';[14] and indeed, the attempts of some writers to express views which differed from the public pronouncements of the party leaders in 1956 and 1962–3 appear even more impressive in view of the repressive policies reimposed on them in the mid-1960s. Yet although the distinction between 'liberals' and 'dogmatists' became less explicit, it did not disappear with the fall of Khrushchev and the spread of *samizdat*, as Ronald Hingley implies; nor, in Shneidman's phrase, was complete 'ideological conformity' achieved in literature of the 1970s.[15] There is still a great difference of talent and emphasis between such 'conservatives' or 'reactionaries' as Kozhevnikov, Chakovsky and Markov, and such 'legal liberals' as Voznesensky, Rasputin, Iskander, Aitmatov and Yevtushenko. The labels 'liberal' and 'dogmatist', however, convey the misleading impression that writers can be consistently classified in one particular category, that such groups are homogeneous and that their members possess a coherent set of convictions. A more satisfactory choice of terms might point to Etkind's moral distinction between 'honest writers' and 'reliable littérateurs' (or to Svirsky's sharper dichotomy between 'people of conscience and mercenaries — those who had their price').[16]

An analysis of literature of the 1970s and 1980s would tend to corroborate Sinyavsky's view that 'with all its historical breaks and discontinuities, there is one Russian literature', but also the opinion of the *émigré* writer and journalist Sergei Dovlatov that the contemporary literary process is extremely diverse. In Dovlatov's view there are not two tendencies in Russian literature, but three: within the Soviet Union there are the 'official, loyalist tendency' and the 'liberal-democratic trend'; and the third branch is *émigré* literature plus *samizdat*, which 'gravitates towards literature in exile'. On purely aesthetic grounds it is difficult to disagree with Gladilin's statement that 'there are two literatures: good literature and bad literature, party criticism and objective criticism',[17] but even 'bad literature' and 'party criticism' may possess considerable socio-logical interest for the analyst of Soviet society.

The accession of Gorbachov opens a new era in Soviet politics, and our examination of the 'literary process' since Stalin enables us to look forward to the future with cautious optimism. Although subsequent events shattered the hopes raised by the 'thaw' of the 1950s and early 1960s, the experience of the Khrushchev years remained very significant, since it had proved to writers that a certain liberalisation was possible from within the system, and, given changed circumstances, could be so again.

Notes

1. Tertz, *Fantasticheskii mir*, p. 445.
2. Sinyavsky, 'Samizdat', p. 9.
3. Dunham, *In Stalin's Time*.
4. B. Kerblay, *Modern Soviet Society*, trans. R. Swyer (London, 1983), p. 226.
5. D. Joravsky, 'Political Authorities and the Learned Estate', *Survey*, vol. 23 (Winter 1977–8), no. 1 (102), pp. 36–41.
6. Mehnert, *The Russians*, pp. 216, 254–5.
7. E. Faddeev, *FN*, 1973, no. 5, pp. 96–100; A. Ursul, *Chelovechestvo, zemlya, vselennaya* (M, 1977); I. Shklovsky, *Vselennaya, zhizn, razum* (M, 1980); I. Zabelin, *Fizicheskaya geografiya v sovremennom estestvoznanii* (M, 1978).
8. See editorials in *VF*, 1968, no. 7; 1971, no. 12; 1974, no. 2.
9. Shklovsky, *Vselennaya*; V. Marakhov, *FN*, 1973, no. 5, pp. 87–92; *VF*, 1981, no. 1, pp. 165–8.
10. I. Frolov, *Perspektivy cheloveka* (M, 1979).
11. Amalrik, 'Open Letter', p. 97.
12. Matich, *Third Wave*, pp. 23–50; *Odna ili dve russkikh literatury?* (Lausanne, 1981).
13. Yu. Maltsev, 'Promezhutochnaya literatura', p. 320.
14. Etkind, *Notes*, p. 52.
15. Hingley, *Russian Writers*, p. 50; N. Shneidman, *Soviet Literature in the 1970s* (Toronto, 1979) is subtitled 'Artistic Diversity and Ideological Conformity'.
16. Etkind, letter; Svirsky, *Soviet Writing*, p. 143.
17. Matich, *Third Wave*, pp. 23, 37–8, 40.

SELECT BIBLIOGRAPHY

All the works consulted in the preparation of this study are too numerous to list. The following short bibliography consists of recent general books in English on post-Stalin literature, science and society.

Literature

Brown, D., *Soviet Russian Literature since Stalin* (CUP, Cambridge, 1978)

Brown, E. J., *Russian Literature Since the Revolution,* revised and enlarged edn (Harvard University Press, Cambridge, Mass. and London, 1982)

Clark, K., *The Soviet Novel: History as Ritual* (University of Chicago Press, Chicago and London, 1981)

Crouch, M. and Porter, R. (eds.), *Understanding Soviet Politics through Literature: A Book of Readings* (George Allen & Unwin, London, 1984)

Dewhirst, M. and Farrell, R. (eds.), *The Soviet Censorship* (Scarecrow Press, Metuchen, NJ, 1973)

Dunham, V., *In Stalin's Time: Middle-class Values in Soviet Fiction* (CUP, Cambridge, 1976)

Etkind, E., *Notes of a Non-Conspirator,* trans. P. France (OUP, Oxford, 1978)

Frankel, E. R., *Novy Mir: A Case Study in the Politics of Literature, 1952–1958* (CUP, Cambridge, 1981)

Gibian, G., *Interval of Freedom: Soviet Literature during the Thaw, 1954–1957* (University of Minnesota Press, Minneapolis, 1960)

Gladilin, A., *The Making and Unmaking of a Soviet Writer: My Story of the 'Young Prose' of the Sixties and After,* trans. D. Lapeza (Ardis, Ann Arbor, 1979)

Hayward, M., *Writers in Russia: 1917–1978,* ed. P. Blake (Harvill Press, London, 1983)

— and Crowley, E. (eds.), *Soviet Literature in the Sixties* (Praeger, NY, 1964)

Hingley, R., *Russian Writers and Soviet Society 1917–1978*

(Weidenfeld & Nicolson, London, 1979)

Hosking, G., *Beyond Socialist Realism: Soviet Fiction since Ivan Denisovich* (Elek/Granada, London, 1980)

Johnson, P., *Khrushchev and the Arts: The Politics of Soviet Culture, 1962–1964* (MIT Press, Cambridge, Mass., 1965)

Lakshin, V., *Solzhenitsyn, Tvardovsky and 'Novy Mir'*, trans. and ed. M. Glenny (MIT Press, Cambridge, Mass., 1980)

Mehnert, K., *The Russians and Their Favorite Books* (Hoover Institution Press, Stanford, 1983)

Shneidman, N. N., *Soviet Literature in the 1970s: Artistic Diversity and Ideological Conformity* (University of Toronto Press, Toronto, 1979)

Solzhenitsyn, A., *The Oak and the Calf: Sketches of Literary Life in the Soviet Union*, trans. H. Willetts (Collins & Harvill Press, London, 1980)

Spechler, D., *Permitted Dissent in the USSR: Novy Mir and the Soviet Regime* (Praeger, NY, 1982)

Svirski, G., *A History of Post-war Soviet Writing: The Literature of Moral Opposition*, trans. and ed. R. Dessaix, M. Ulman (Ardis, Ann Arbor, 1981)

Walker, G., *Soviet Book Publishing Policy* (CUP, Cambridge, 1978)

Soviet Science, Politics and Society

Brown, A. and Kaser, M. (eds.), *The Soviet Union since the Fall of Khrushchev* (Macmillan, London, 1980)

—, *Soviet Policy for the 1980s* (Macmillan, London, 1982)

Byrnes, R., *After Brezhnev: Sources of Soviet Conduct in the 1980s* (F. Pinter, London, 1983)

Cohen, S., Rabinowitch, A. and Sharlet, R. (eds.), *The Soviet Union since Stalin* (Macmillan, London, 1980)

Graham, L., *Science and Philosophy in the Soviet Union* (Allen Lane, London, 1971)

Joravsky, D., *The Lysenko Affair* (Harvard University Press, Cambridge, Mass., 1970)

Kelley, D. (ed.), *Soviet Politics in the Brezhnev Era* (Praeger, NY, 1980)

Kerblay, B., *Modern Soviet Society,* trans. R. Swyer (Methuen, London, 1983)

Kneen, P., *Soviet Scientists and the State: an Examination of the Social and Political Aspects of Science in the USSR* (Macmillan, London, 1984)

Medvedev, R., *Let History Judge: The Origins and Consequences of Stalinism*, ed. D. Joravsky (Macmillan, London, 1971)

—— and Medvedev, Zh., *Khrushchev: The Years in Power*, trans. A. Durkin (OUP, Oxford, 1977)

Medvedev, Zh., *The Rise and Fall of T. D. Lysenko*, trans. I. M. Lerner (Columbia University Press, NY, 1969)

——, *The Medvedev Papers: The Plight of Soviet Science Today*, trans. V. Rich (Macmillan, London, 1971)

——, *Soviet Science* (OUP, Oxford, 1979)

——*Andropov: his Life and Death* (Blackwell, Oxford, 1983)

Popovsky, M., *Science in Chains: The Crisis of Science and Scientists in the Soviet Union Today*, trans. P. Falla (Collins & Harvill Press, London, 1980)

Sakharov, A., *Sakharov Speaks*, ed. H. Salisbury (Collins & Harvill Press, London, 1974)

The State of Soviet Science, ed. by the editors of *Survey* (MIT Press Cambridge, Mass., 1965)

Vucinich, A., *Empire of Knowledge: the Academy of Sciences of the USSR, 1917–1970* (University of California Press, Stanford, 1984)

English Translations of Post-Stalin Literature

Abramov, F., *The Dodgers*, trans. D. Floyd (Flegon Press, London, 1963)

——, *The House*, extract in Crouch and Porter, *Understanding Soviet Politics*, pp. 119–25

Aitmatov, Ch., *The Day Lasts Longer than a Hundred Years*, trans. J. French (Macdonald & Co., London and Sydney, 1983)

—— and Mukhamedzhanov, K., *The Ascent of Mount Fuji*, trans. N. Bethell (Noonday, NY, 1975)

Aksyonov, V., *Colleagues* (FLPH, M, no date)

——, *A Starry Ticket*, trans. A. Brown (Putnam, London, 1962)

——, *The Steel Bird and Other Stories* (Ardis, Ann Arbor, 1979)

Arzhak, N. (Yu. Daniel), *This is Moscow Speaking*, in P. Blake and M. Hayward (eds.), *Dissonant Voices in Soviet Literature* (Pantheon Books, NY, 1962)

Astafiev, V., *Queen Fish*, trans. K. Cook *et al.* (Progress, Moscow,

1982)

Avdeenko, A., *The Sweat of One's Brow*, extract in Crouch and Porter, *Understanding Soviet Politics*, pp. 109–19

Belov, V., *That's How It Is, Soviet Literature*, 1969, no. 1

——, *Carpenter Stories* (excerpts) in C. and E. Proffer (eds.), *The Ardis Anthology of Recent Russian Literature* (Ardis, Ann Arbor, 1975)

Bondarev, Y., *The Shore*, trans. K. Hammond (Raduga, M. 1984)

Bulgakov, M., *The Master and Margarita*, trans. M. Glenny (Fontana, London, 1969)

Dudintsev, V., *Not by Bread Alone*, trans. E. Bone (Hutchinson, London, 1957)

——, *A New Year's Tale*, trans. M. Hayward (Hutchinson, London, 1960)

Efremov, I., *Andromeda. A Space-age Tale*, trans. G. Hanna (FLPH, M, 1960)

Ehrenburg, I., *The Thaw*, trans. M. Harari (Mayflower Books, London, 1966)

——, *The Spring*, trans. H. Higgins (Mayflower Books, London, 1966)

——, *People, Years and Life. Selections,* ed. C. Moody (Pergamon, London) ∣

Emtsev, M. and Parnov, E., *World Soul*, trans. A. Bouis (Macmillan, NY, 1978)

Granin, D., *Those Who Seek* (FLPH, M, no date)

——, *A Personal Opinion*, in E. Stillman (ed.), *Bitter Harvest* (Praeger, NY, 1959)

——, *Into the Storm* (Progress, M, 1965)

——, *The Picture*, extract in Crouch and Porter, *Understanding Soviet Politics*, pp. 89–98

Grekova, I., *The Department,* extract in Crouch and Porter, *Understanding Soviet Politics*, pp. 197–207

Grossman, V., *Forever Flowing*, trans. T. Whitney (André Deutsch, London, 1973)

Iskander, F., *The Coat-ibex Constellation*, trans. H. Burlingame (Ardis, Ann Arbor, 1975)

——, *Sandro of Chegem*, trans. S. Brownsberger (Cape, London, 1983)

Kaverin, V., *The Open Book*, trans. B. Pearce (Lawrence & Wishart, London, 1955)

Kazakov, Yu., *The Smell of Bread and Other Stories*, trans. M.

Harari (A. Thomson, London, 1965)

Kochetov, V., *The Zhurbins*, trans. R. Daglish (Progress, M, 1953, 1980)

——, *What Is It You Want, Then?*, trans. and ed. M. Glenny, in *Selected Readings in Soviet Literature* (Milton Keynes, 1976)

Kolesnikov, M., *School for Ministers: a Trilogy*, trans. L. Tudge (Progress, M, 1980)

Kron, A., *Insomnia*, excerpt in Crouch and Porter, *Understanding Soviet Politics*, pp. 55–63

Kuznetsov, A., *Babi Yar*, trans. D. Floyd (Penguin, Harmondsworth, 1982)

Leonov, L., *The Russian Forest*, trans. B. Isaacs, 2 vols (Progress, M, 1966)

Mandelstam, N., *Hope Against Hope*, trans. M. Hayward (Harvill, London, 1970; Penguin, Harmondsworth, 1975)

——, *Hope Abandoned*, trans. M. Hayward (Harvill, London, 1974; Penguin, Harmondsworth, 1977)

Markov, G., *Siberia*, trans. K. Cook (Progress, Moscow, 1975)

Metropol: A Literary Almanac, ed. V. Aksyonov *et al.* (Norton, NY, 1983)

Nilin, P., *Married for the First Time*, extract in Crouch and Porter, *Understanding Soviet Politics*, pp. 140–52

Okudzhava, B., *Good-bye, Schoolboy!*, trans. R. Szulkin, in K. Pomorska (ed.), *Fifty Years of Russian Prose: from Pasternak to Solzhenitsyn*, vol. 2 (MIT Press, Cambridge, Mass., 1971)

Pasternak, B., *Doctor Zhivago*, trans. M. Hayward and M. Harari (Collins & Harvill, London, 1958; Fontana, London, 1961)

——, *Safe Conduct and Other Works*, trans. A. Brown (Elek, London, 1959)

——, *An Essay in Autobiography*, trans. M. Harari (Collins & Harvill, London, 1959)

Pavlenko, P., *Maria*, excerpt in Crouch and Porter, *Understanding Soviet Politics*, pp. 66–73

Rasputin, V., *Farewell to Matyora*, trans. A. Bouis (Macmillan, NY, 1980)

Shalamov, V., *Kolyma Tales*, trans. J. Glad (Norton, NY, 1980)

Shukshin, V., *I Believe!*, trans. G. Hosking, in Shukshin, V., *Snowball Berry Red and Other Stories*, ed. D. Fiene (Ardis, Ann Arbor, 1979)

Soloukhin, V., *A Walk in Rural Russia*, trans. S. Miskin (Hodder & Stoughton, London, 1967)

Solzhenitsyn, A., *One Day in the Life of Ivan Denisovich*, trans. R.

Parker (Gollancz, London, 1963; Penguin, Harmondsworth, 1970)

——, *For the Good of the Cause*, trans. D. Floyd and M. Hayward (Praeger, NY, 1964; Sphere Books, London, 1964)

——, *The First Circle*, trans. M. Guybon (Collins & Harvill, London, 1968; Fontana, London, 1970)

——, *Cancer Ward*, trans. N. Bethell and D. Burg (Bodley Head, London, 1968; Penguin, Harmondsworth, 1971)

——, *Stories and Prose Poems*, trans. M. Glenny (Bodley Head, London, 1970; Penguin, Harmondsworth, 1973)

——, *Candle in the Wind*, trans. K. Armes and A. Hudgins (Bodley Head, London, 1973; Penguin, Harmondsworth, 1976)

Strugatsky, A. and Strugatsky, B., *Far Rainbow*. trans A. Myers (Mir, M, 1967)

——, *The Second Martian Invasion*, in C. Bearne (ed.), *Vortex* (MacGibbon & Kee, London, 1970)

——, *Hard to Be a God* (Seabury, NY, 1973)

——, *Monday Begins on Saturday*, trans. W. Ackerman (Eyre Methuen, London, 1975)

——, *The Final Circle of Paradise*, trans. L. Renan (Daw Books, NY, 1976)

——, *Prisoners of Power*, trans. H. Jacobson (Macmillan, NY, 1977; Penguin, Harmondsworth, 1983)

——, *Tale of the Troika*, in *Roadside Picnic and Tale of the Troika*, trans. A. Bouis (Macmillan, NY, 1977)

——, *Definitely Maybe*, trans. A. Bouis (Macmillan, NY, 1978)

——, *Roadside Picnic*, trans. A. Bouis (Penguin, Harmondsworth, 1979)

——, *The Ugly Swans*, trans. A. S. Nakhimovsky and A. Nakhimovsky (Macmillan, NY, 1979)

——, *Snail on the Slope*, trans. A. Myers (Gollancz, London, 1980)

——, *The Beetle in the Anthill*, trans. A. Bouis (Macmillan, NY, 1980)

Tarsis, V., *Ward 7*, trans. K. Brown (Dutton, NY, 1965)

Tendryakov, V., *Potholes*, in C. P. Snow and P. H. Johnson (eds.), *Stories from Modern Russia: Winter's Tales 7* (St Martin's Press, NY, 1962)

——, *Short Circuit*, in T. P. Whitney (ed.), *The New Writing in Russia* (University of Michigan Press, Ann Arbor, 1964)

——, *Three, Seven, Ace and Other Stories*, trans. D. Alger *et al.* (Harvill, London, 1973)

326   *Select Bibliography*

———, *A Topsy-Turvy Spring: Stories,* trans. A. Miller and A. Pyman (Progress, M, 1978)

———, *On Apostolic Business,* excerpt in Crouch and Porter, *Understanding Soviet Politics,* pp. 176–86

Tertz, A. (A. Sinyavsky), *The Icicle and Other Stories,* trans. M. Hayward and R. Hingley (Collins & Harvill, London, 1963)

———, *The Trial Begins,* trans. M. Hayward (Collins & Harvill, London, 1960; Fontana, London, 1977)

———, *The Makepeace Experiment,* trans. M. Harari (Collins & Harvill, London, 1965; Fontana, London, 1977)

———, *Unguarded Thoughts,* trans. M. Harari (Collins & Harvill, London, 1972)

Trifonov, Yu., *The Students,* trans. I. Litvinova and M. Wettlin (FLPH, M, 1953)

———, *Another Life and The House on the Embankment,* trans. M. Glenny (S & S Press, Austin, Texas, 1983)

———, *The Long Goodbye: Three Novellas,* trans. H. Burlingame and E. Proffer (Ardis, Ann Arbor, 1978)

Voinovich, V. *The Life and Extraordinary Adventures of Private Ivan Chonkin,* trans. R. Lourie (Cape, London, 1977; and Penguin, Harmondsworth, 1979)

———, *The Ivankiad (or the Tale of the Writer Voinovich's Installation in his New Apartment),* trans. D. Lapeza (Cape, London, 1978; Penguin, Harmondsworth, 1979)

———, *In Plain Russian: Stories,* trans. R. Lourie (Cape, London, 1980)

Voznesensky, A., *Antiworlds and The Fifth Ace,* ed. P. Blake and M. Hayward (OUP, London, 1968)

Yashin, A., *Levers,* trans. D. Lapeza, in C. and E. Proffer, *Ardis Anthology*

Yevtushenko, E., *A Precocious Autobiography,* trans. A. MacAndrew (Collins & Harvill, London, 1963)

———, *Bratsk Station and Other New Poems* (Praeger, NY, 1967)

———, *Wild Berries,* trans. A. Bouis (Macmillan, London, 1984)

Zalygin, S., *South American Variant,* trans. K. Windle (University of Queensland Press, St Lucia, Queensland, 1979)

Zinoviev, A., *The Yawning Heights,* trans. G. Clough (Bodley Head, London, 1979; Penguin, Harmondsworth, 1981)

———, *The Radiant Future,* trans. G. Clough (Bodley Head, London, 1981)

INDEX

78, 306
Huxley, A.
Science, Liberty and Peace 165
ideology
and science 86–90, 137, 146–7,
157–60, 220
see also Communist Party;
Marxism; politics
Ilyichov, L. 13–14
immortality
in Russian thought 135–6, 145–6,
220
individualism
as a supreme value 149–55, 157,
261–3
individual and collective work 83–6,
103–4, 105–6, 113–15
industry 118–26, 176–9
malpractices in 124–6
management of 120–4
under Stalin 44–7
see also alienation, automation
Inyushin, V. 207–8
Iskander, F. 19, 21, 318
Sandro from Chegem 286
The Goat-Ibex Constellation 219,
242
Ivanko, I. 283
Ivanov, L.
In Native Places 171
The Fate of the Harvest 171
Ivanov spy case 206
Izvestiya 11, 248, 281

Johnson, P. 13
Joravsky, D. 311
Joyce, J. 16

Kabo, L.
The Difficult March 50
Kafka, F. 16
Kammerer, P. 290
Kamyanov, V. 191
Kantorovich, V.
The Story of Engineer Ganshin 88,
91–2
Kapitsa, P. 42, 80, 85, 86, 95, 96, 216
Karanov, Y. 173
Kashtanov, A.
The Pedlars 125–6
Kataev, V. 74, 176
Time, Forward! 7
Katerli, E.

The Distant Road 274
Kaverin, V. 7, 92, 93, 100, 107, 148,
155, 275, 286–92 *passim*, 297, 298,
306
A Piece of Glass 73, 80, 214
A Two-hour Stroll 106, 108–9, 311
Dual Portrait 43, 71
Searches and Hopes 38–40, 41, 76–7,
110, 140, 282
The Eleventh Axiom 275
The Open Book 50–1, 275
Kazakevich, E.
The Star 10
Kazakov, Y. 21, 253, 264
Keldysh, M. 65
Kerblay, B. 308
Ketlinskaya, V. 278, 292
*Otherwise There is no Point in
Living* 33, 42, 142, 274, 296
KGB (Committee of State Security)
and science 114–15, 209–10
and writers 14–15, 19–20, 106, 222,
279, 282–3, 285–6
Khikmet, N.
Did Ivan Ivanovich Exist? 32
Khrushchev, N.
agricultural policy 170–1, 172
and Lysenko 42–3, 304, 306
attitude to science 65–6, 133, 137,
147, 158, 216
chemical campaign 142, 287
cultural policy 10–14, 42, 74, 273,
276, 284, 288
de-Stalinisation policy 71, 156, 163
industrial policy 176–7, 178
nuclear policy 195, 196, 197
religious policy 238
'Secret Speech' 2, 12, 33, 73
Khvolson, O. 258
Kim, A. 22
Lotus 254
Kirpichnikov, V. 289
Kirsanov, S.
Seven days of the Week 151
Kochetov, V. 210, 278, 291, 297
The Ershov Brothers 50, 67, 93, 94–5
*The Secretary of the District Party
Committee* 78, 147, 177, 197
What Do You Want, Then? 198
Youth is With Us 37, 145
Kolakowski, L.
I'll Tell You What Socialism Is . . .
165
Kolesnikov, M.